Taking Heaven by Storm

Taking Heaven by Storm

Methodism and the Rise of Popular Christianity in America

John H. Wigger

New York   Oxford
Oxford University Press
1998

Oxford University Press

Oxford   New York
Athens   Auckland   Bangkok   Bogota   Bombay   Buenos Aires
Calcutta   Cape Town   Dar es Salaam   Delhi   Florence   Hong Kong
Istanbul   Karachi   Kuala Lumpur   Madras   Madrid   Melbourne
Mexico City   Nairobi   Paris   Singapore   Taipei   Tokyo   Toronto   Warsaw

and associated companies in
Berlin   Ibadan

Published by Oxford University Press, Inc.
198 Madison Avenue, New York, New York 10016

Oxford is a registered trademark of Oxford University Press

Library of Congress Cataloging-in-Publication Data
Wigger, John H., 1959–
Taking heaven by storm : Methodism and the rise
of popular Christianity in America
/ John H. Wigger.
    p. cm.—(Religion in America series)
Includes bibliographical references and index.
ISBN 0-19-510452-8
1. Methodist Church—United States—History—18th century.
2. United States—Church history—18th century.   3. Methodism—
History—18th century.   4. Methodist Church—United States—
History—19th century.   5. United States—Church history—19th
century.   6. Methodism—History—19th century.   I. Title.
II. Series: Religion in America series (Oxford University Press)
BX8236.W44 1998
287'.0973'09033—dc21   97-9359

1 2 3 4 5 6 7 8 9

Printed in the United States of America
on acid-free paper

For
Melodie,
Hannah, Allison, and Natalie
Edna A. Wigger
and in memory of
John W. Wigger

Preface and Acknowledgments

*T*his study is about the dynamics of early Methodist growth in America. Methodism was the largest popular religious movement between the Revolution and the Civil War, expanding on a scale that had never been seen before. It had a profound effect on the development of American culture and society, such that its impact can still be felt today. The bulk of my research focuses on recovering and interpreting the lives of early Methodists, particularly the itinerant preachers. Through their journals, memoirs, and records, I have tried to piece together the details of their lives, their shifting hopes and fears, their larger influence on the world around them, and it on them.

As with all projects of this nature, a great many people have given generously of their time and energy to help bring this study to where it now stands. I owe my primary intellectual debt in connection with this book to Nathan O. Hatch, whose brilliant book *The Democratization of American Christianity* provided the initial conceptual framework for this study. As my dissertation director, Nathan offered encouragement and unerringly good advice at each juncture at which I was uncertain as to how to proceed. I could not have asked for a wiser or more patient director. I benefited greatly from courses taken early in my graduate school career at the University of Notre Dame with Philip Gleason and Jay Dolan, both of whom are gracious teachers of the art of historical scholarship. George Marsden joined the Notre Dame faculty about halfway through the dissertation phase of this project, and has since taken a welcome interest in it, carefully reading chapter drafts and offering trenchant criticism and advice. As Chair of the Department of History during my final years at Notre Dame, Wilson Miscamble, C.S.C., went far beyond the requirements of his position on many occasions to help keep me employed and working on this book. I am quite sure that there is no university in America where I could have studied with a better or more collegial faculty.

A dissertation fellowship from the Louisville Institute for the Study of Protestantism and American Culture, a program of the Lilly Endowment, allowed me to devote the 1992–93 academic year to writing. A 1993–94 graduate teaching fellowship sponsored by the College of Arts and Letters and the Graduate School at the University of Notre Dame provided the opportunity to finish writing, while at the same time gaining valuable teaching experience. Kenneth E. Rowe and the other staff members at the Drew University Library and Methodist Center made a week I spent there in the summer of 1990 both enjoyable and profitable. A 1991 University of Notre Dame Zahm Research Travel Grant made it possible for me to visit the United Methodist Archives housed at Ohio Wesleyan University's Beeghly Library. There, Curator Susan J. Cohen offered generous assistance during a week-long foray into the records of Ohio Methodism. I would be extremely remiss if I did not thank Linda Gregory and the other staff members of the Interlibrary Loan Department of Notre Dame's Theodore M. Hesburgh Library for their professional service and patience with my many interlibrary-loan binges. Thanks also to my brother, Bill Wigger, who gave me the computer on which I am now typing. I also owe a special debt of gratitude to the Department of History at St. Olaf College, Minnesota, and in particular to Robert Entenmann, department chair during 1994–95 when I taught there. The year my family and I spent at St. Olaf was enjoyable and professionally rewarding. My new colleagues in the Department of History at the University of Missouri-Columbia have also given much needed encouragement and support since I arrived here in August 1996. A grant from the Research Council of the University of Missouri-Columbia helped to defray the cost of including illustrations in this volume.

During the early stages of this project John Haas, Michael Hamilton, and Bill Svelmoe read various chapter drafts, offering perceptive advice and criticism. More recently, others have generously read and critiqued individual chapters. Michael Fitzgerald of St. Olaf College and Robert E. Weems Jr. of the University of Missouri-Columbia offered helpful comments on chapter 6. Gail Bederman, Catherine Brekus, Mark Chaves, and Tom Luongo gave invaluable advice on chapter 7. Lester Ruth read and commented on chapters 2 and 4. Lester's own dissertation, " 'A Little Heaven Below': Quarterly Meetings as Seasons of Grace in Early American Methodism," is a superb study of one of early American Methodism's most important institutions, offering a more richly textured description of these gatherings than I do here. I also benefited greatly from the comments of an anonymous reader after the manuscript was in the hands of Oxford University Press.

Portions of chapter 5 first appeared as "Taking Heaven by Storm: Enthusiasm and Early American Methodism, 1770–1820" in the *Journal of the Early*

Republic 14 (Summer 1994), pages 167–194, and are reprinted by permission. Other elements of this study first appeared as "Holy, 'Knock-'Em-Down' Preachers" in *Christian History* 14:1 (1995), pages 22–25.

Finally, a word of gratitude for my family. My parents instilled in all their children an appreciation for the importance of family. They moved to South Bend in 1990, and it was a privilege to have them share our Notre Dame years, helping to raise their grandchildren. My father passed away unexpectedly in December 1995. I regret that he never had a chance to hold a copy of this book, but not nearly as much as I regret that our children will no longer have the benefit of his wisdom. I save my final word of thanks for my wife. To say that she has read every chapter several times over does not begin to describe the many ways that she has helped to make this work possible. That she married me even after I quit a secure engineering career one month before our wedding to enter graduate school perhaps gets closer to the truth. It is to our daughters, to my mother, to the memory of my father, and to Melodie—truest of friends—that I dedicate this volume.

Contents

List of Illustrations

Taking Heaven by Storm

I   *The Emergence of American Methodism*

Such, then, is the state of our nation; more deplorably destitute of religious instruction than any other Christian nation under heaven.

—Lyman Beecher, 1816

How oft we sigh
When histories charm to think that histories lie!

—Thomas Moore

*B*etween 1770 and 1820 American Methodists achieved a virtual miracle of growth, rising from fewer than 1,000 members to more than 250,000. In 1775 fewer than one out of every 800 Americans was a Methodist; by 1812 Methodists numbered one out of every 36 Americans. By 1830 membership stood at nearly half a million. While other denominations expanded in absolute numbers, the Methodists gained an ever larger share of the religious market. In 1775 Methodists constituted only 2 percent of the total church membership in America. By 1850 their share had increased to more than 34 percent. This growth stunned the older denominations. At mid-century, American Methodism was nearly half again as large as any other Protestant body, and almost ten times the size of the Congregationalists, America's largest denomination in 1776.[1]

These figures are even more impressive when one considers the movement's wider influence. In the late eighteenth and early nineteenth centuries, membership requirements were relatively strict, and discipline, for the most part, was firmly adhered to. Methodists carefully watched over one anothers public and private lives, and all members were required to attend a weekly small-group gathering, called a class meeting. Here their spiritual lives and temporal dealings were open to examination by the class leader, and they might also be asked to pray in public. This, no doubt, was a threatening proposition for many. So it is not surprising that many who had Methodist sympathies declined to enter into full "connection" with the church. The Methodist preacher William Capers noted that in Charleston, South Carolina, in 1811, Methodist "preaching might be attended with great propriety, for almost everyone did so, but who might join them? No, it was vastly more respectable to join some other Church, and still attend the preaching of the Methodists, which was thought to answer all purposes."[2] In 1805 Francis Asbury estimated that membership stood at 100,000, but that up to 1 million people "regularly attend our ministry."[3] Using a more conservative ratio of six adherents for every one member, it is still reasonable to assume that by 1790 Methodist adherents and supporters accounted for almost 9 percent of the aggregate American population, and by 1810 nearly 14 percent (see figure 1.1).[4]

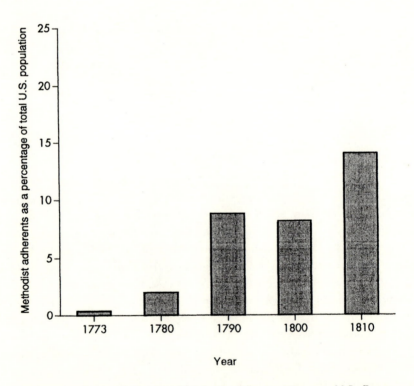

Figure 1.1. Estimated Density of Methodist Adherents. Sources: *U.S. Bureau of the Census,* Historical Statistics, A172–205; *and* Minutes of the Annual Conferences, *vol. 1.*

Early Methodism's spectacular success was due to a host of factors, some unique to Methodism and some endemic to American society as a whole. The replacement of state-sponsored churches with a religious free market, the pervasive impact of republican ideology, and the rising strength of America's geographic and cultural peripheries all worked to spur Methodism's advance. Methodists capitalized on these trends by identifying with middling people on the make—skilled artisans, shopkeepers, petty merchants, and ambitious small planters—making use of an efficient system of itinerant and local preachers, class meetings, love feasts, quarterly meetings, and camp meetings; embracing popular religious enthusiasm; creating a variety of new roles for women within the movement; and making Christianity accessible to African Americans, particularly in the upper South.[5] The early Methodist movement had the ability to shape culture and society as well as reflect it, but its influence was not without limitations. Methodism was both driven and constrained primarily by the needs, hopes, and fears of ordinary people, and almost entirely conducted by those from the middling and lower orders of society. Within this context the movement's style, tone, and agenda worked their way deep into the fabric of American life, influencing nearly all other mass religious movements that would follow as well as many facets of life not directly connected to the church.

In its early phase, the Methodist Episcopal Church was largely a southern phenomenon.[6] In 1790, 87 percent of the church's more than 57,000 members lived south of the Mason-Dixon line. There Methodists and Baptists came to dominate religious life to such an extent as to make the other sects an "almost invisible minority."[7] In 1810 full-fledged Methodist members represented over 8 percent of the total population of Delaware, more than 7 percent of the total population of Maryland, and perhaps about 15 percent of the adult population in each state.

But Methodism did not remain an overwhelmingly southern movement for long. By 1800 the proportion of Methodists living in the South had declined to just over 70 percent, while total membership had increased to over 63,000. Membership in New England and New York rose appreciably during this decade, climbing from fewer than 3,600 in 1790 to more than 12,200 by 1800. Conversely, membership declined considerably in Delaware, Maryland, Virginia, and Georgia during the 1790s, owing in part to the O'Kelly schism (see chapter 2) and to unrest over the church's antislavery rules.[8] By 1810, of the more than 170,000 members of the Methodist Episcopal Church in the United States, approximately 36 percent lived north of the Mason-Dixon line (see figure 1.2). In Pennsylvania, the number of Methodists increased more than 570 percent between 1790 and 1810, while the overall state population less than doubled during the same interval. In New York, membership increased from fewer than 3,400 in 1790 to more than 20,000 in 1810. By 1810 Methodism was growing at a faster rate than the aggregate population in every state and major territory in the Union (see the Ap-

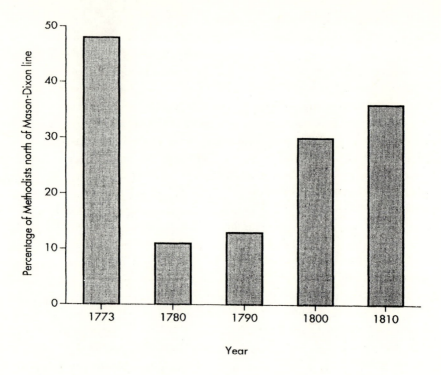

Figure 1.2. Methodists North of the Mason-Dixon Line. Source: Appendix.

pendix). American Methodism was a truly national phenomenon, unmatched in the breadth of its appeal by any other religious movement of the time. Methodists drew their converts not only from the unchurched of the western frontiers but also from the ranks of lapsed New England Congregationalists and nominal southern Episcopalians. Put simply, American Methodism was the largest, most geographically diverse movement of middling and artisan men and women in the early republic.

Nonetheless, precisely what influence this mammoth movement of middling folk exerted in the formative years of the early republic is a question few historians have paused to ask, as Nathan Hatch has recently noted.[9] In recent years, historians of American religion have increasingly turned their attention to those traditionally ignored by earlier scholars, including Pentecostals, Fundamentalists, Mormons, ethnic Catholics, and Jews; Shakers, utopian visionaries, and doomsday prophets; women, African Americans, and Native Americans. But even within this framework Methodism has largely been ignored.[10]

The lack of attention given to American Methodism is perhaps most striking when compared to the literature on its British counterpart. There, Methodism has received prolonged attention from scholars ranging from Elie Halevy, E. P. Thompson, Eric Hobsbawm, and Bernard Semmel to James Obelkevich, Robert Colls, John Rule, Gail Malmgreen, Deborah Valenze, David Hempton, and Alan Gilbert.[11] In many respects the study of British Methodism parallels that of American Puritanism, both in the number of studies to date and their sophistication. But the same cannot be said for American Methodism. In most American history textbooks Methodism disappears amid such diverse events of the so-called Second Great Awakening as Charles Finney's eastern crusades and the early nineteenth-century frontier camp meetings, most often exemplified by Cane Ridge.[12]

This need not be the case. Far from being bland and predictable, early American Methodism was a volatile and often raucous affair, existing almost completely outside the control of the new nation's cultural, political, and religious elite. Much of the character of evangelical Christianity in America stems, not from the established denominations of the colonial era, but from the upstart sects of the early republic, particularly the Methodists and Baptists.[13] This upwelling of religious fervor did not represent merely an extension of older institutions and ideas into new settings, but rather a fundamental reformulation of Christianity in America. At the popular level, the holiness ethos fostered by Methodism was more powerful than any abstract theological innovation of the time. Under Methodism's aegis, American evangelicalism became far more enthusiastic, individualistic, egalitarian, entrepreneurial, and lay oriented—characteristics that continue to shape and define American popular religion today.

It is no accident that American Methodism flourished after, and not before, the American Revolution. The revolutionary era marks a divide between two worlds—between, as Gordon Wood, Alan Taylor, and others have argued, an earlier world ordered through deference, hierarchy, and patronage and a later period in which ordinary people grew increasingly unwilling to consider themselves inherently inferior to anyone else.[14] Destined to fade away in postrevolutionary America was the traditional English world that George Eliot wrote of in *Adam Bede*, where "the keenest of bucolic minds felt a whispering awe at the sight of the gentry, such as of old men felt when they stood on tiptoe to watch the gods passing by in tall human shape."[15] The generation after the Revolution witnessed one of the most turbulent and dynamic periods in American history. It was this generation that began the process of working out the implications of the Revolution, particularly the rise of a free-market economy. There was a pervasive rootlessness to the period as many pulled up stakes to move west, or at least psychologically traded traditional concepts of deference for new ideas about democracy and equality. The years from 1780 to 1820 were, for some, a time of unparalleled opportunity and optimism; for others, they were a time of intense uncertainty and struggle; for nearly everyone, they were a period of unprecedented change. As one noted historian has observed, only rarely are large numbers of people open to large-scale change. The era immediately following the Revolution was just such a time.[16]

In 1770 the American colonies numbered just over 2 million people settled along the Atlantic seaboard, hemmed in by physical barriers, political limitations, and Native American resistance to their encroachment. By 1810 the population of the United States had swelled to over 7 million, with a flood of settlers pushing well beyond the Appalachian Mountains, creating wholly new demographic patterns and social structures. In 1770 the territories that would eventually become the states of Georgia, Kentucky, Ohio, and Tennessee contained only about 40,000 people of European or African descent. By 1810 the combined population of these same regions was over 1,150,000.[17]

More important, the disintegration of traditional eighteenth-century monarchical society brought an end to many patterns of paternal and dependent relationships. Equality became the rallying cry of the republican revolution, but once set in motion this rhetoric was carried far beyond the original vision of the revolutionary gentry by new, popular leaders. Laboring at a trade or profession was glorified, and the ancient tradition of aristocratic leisure was overturned. Methodists thoroughly embraced and helped to create this new ethic. "Be diligent. Never be unemployed. Never be triflingly employed," urged the church's book of *Discipline*. "No idleness is consistent with a growth in grace."[18]

One effect of all this leveling rhetoric about equality, the virtue of labor, and the improvement of the common man was to energize hundreds of thousands of Americans toward the pursuit of money. America became a land of people on the make, a society seemingly dominated by the "middling sort," or at least those who aspired to that estate. Speculative land fever infected all levels of society. In many places mobility and profit-mindedness destroyed any recognizable sense of community. Journeymen became less likely to live with their masters and more likely to be paid in cash. Masters, in turn, exchanged their roles as patriarchs and mentors to become managers and retail merchants. As a result, the moral authority of master artisans was eroded, and the craft apprenticeship system crumbled. From everywhere came reports of young apprentices becoming more "insolent and saucy."[19] Typical of many, Alfred Brunson abandoned his apprenticeship to a Connecticut shoemaker in 1808 at the age of 15, determining to "go to Ohio, study law, and rise, if possible, with the young State to whatever distinction merit might entitle me to." Converted along the way, Brunson eventually made his way to Ohio not to study law, but to spread the gospel as a Methodist preacher.[20]

For white Americans in general, an unprecedented sense of entrepreneurial energy pervaded the early national period. Rural farmers and urban merchants alike borrowed more money, married earlier, moved farther and more often, and had more children because they believed the future held bright promise.[21] Yet the period was not without its darker underside. Unparalleled borrowing led to unparalleled debt. Slavery increasingly stood out as a contradiction to the most basic principles of the Revolution. Though the Revolution raised new questions about the political and economic identities of women, real change was slow and uneven. Crime, violence, and the consumption of alcohol increased dramatically. Between 1800 and 1830 Americans drank an average of five gallons of hard liquor per year per capita—nearly triple today's rate of consumption and more than at any time before or since. It was a time in which "everything seemed to be coming apart."[22]

Amid so much change and uncertainty, it is hardly surprising to find that this was a period in which American religion was also transformed in deep and enduring ways. In fact, as both Nathan O. Hatch and Jon Butler have recently demonstrated, the post-revolutionary years were a pivotal era in Christianizing the American people, both women and men, African Americans, and those of European descent.[23] Older denominations rooted to traditional patterns of hierarchy steadily lost favor throughout the era. While the Presbyterians and, to a lesser extent, the Congregationalists and Episcopalians posted modest gains in absolute numbers, their rate of growth lagged far behind that of the Methodists and Baptists. This was true not only on the frontier but also throughout the United States. In the south Atlantic region, where the Methodists were prominent, the Episcopalians' share of church adherents dropped from 27 percent to 4 percent between 1776 and 1850.[24] In cities such as New York and Baltimore, the one religious sentiment that working-class men and women in general seem to have agreed upon was a strong dislike for established, European-style clericalism.[25] The early Methodist circuit rider James Quinn clearly understood the uniqueness of the American situation. Following the Revolution, wrote Quinn, "the anti-Christian union between the Church and state had been broken up, tithes and glebes could no longer be relied upon for Church revenue, and the religious orders of America were left free to choose their own course, and worship God, with or without name, in temple, synagogue, church, or meeting-house, standing, sitting, or kneeling, in silence or with a loud voice, with or without book."[26]

In many regions, and among the lower classes in particular, the clergy from some of America's oldest denominations stood in a precarious position on the eve of the Revolution. Tied to a vanishing hierarchy on the one hand, many were as yet unwilling to give up the hope of reaching the broader masses on the other. Perhaps no one personified this dilemma more acutely than Charles Woodmason. An English-born gentleman, Woodmason described himself as a "Planter and Merchant" before becoming an ordained Anglican missionary to the Carolina hinterland in 1766. Though ardently dedicated to his work,

Woodmason was appalled at the low condition of the backcountry settlers. At one stop he described his listeners as "of abandon'd Morals and profilge Principles—Rude—Ignorant—Void of Manners, Education or Good Breeding—No genteel or Polite Person among them."[27] He estimated that 94 percent of the young women he married were already pregnant, and that 90 percent of backcountry inhabitants suffered from venereal disease. "For thro' want of Ministers to marry and thro' the licentiousness of the People," wrote Woodmason, "many hundreds live in Concubinage—swopping their Wives as Cattel, and living in a State of Nature, more irregularly and unchastely than the Indians."[28] Worst of all, he was convinced that these deplorable conditions were largely "owing to the Inattention and Indolence of the Clergy."[29]

Yet for all his missionary zeal, Woodmason refused to shed his gentlemanly persona. The ever-widening divide that separated him from his listeners remained a mystery to him. Even in the stifling Carolina summer heat he continued to wear his wig and gown. Such displays made him a "Great Curiosity" to the backcountry settlers, while they remained "great Oddities" to him. "How dismal the Case—How hard the Lot of any Gentleman in this Part of the World!" lamented Woodmason.[30] Nor could he understand the appeal of two local preachers, one a Methodist and the other a Baptist: "Both of them exceeding low and ignorant persons—Yet the lower Class chuse to resort to them rather than to hear a Well connected Discourse."[31] The social distance between Woodmason and his audiences inevitably led to conflict. At one place he was told that "they wanted no D_____d Black Gown Sons of Bitches among them."[32] At another stop a group of Presbyterians "hir'd a Band of rude fellows to come to Service who brought with them 57 Dogs (for I counted them) which in Time of Service they set fighting . . . and I was oblig'd to desist and dismiss the People." But in this case, at any rate, Woodmason had a rare last laugh. After the service one of the dogs followed him home, "which I carried to the House of one of the principals—and told Him that I had 57 Presbyterians came that Day to Service, and that I had converted one of them, and brought him home. . . . This joke has made them so extremely angry that they could cut my Throat."[33]

Charles Woodmason was not alone in failing to understand the widening gulf between the established clergy and the common people, as the career of Devereux Jarratt (1733–1801) of Virginia demonstrates. The son of a middling carpenter and an early supporter of the Methodists, Jarratt early in life "contracted a prejudice against the *Church of England* . . . on account of the loose lives of the Clergy, and their cold and unedifying manner of preaching."[34] When Jarratt subsequently became an Anglican priest, he was determined to do better. Yet, notwithstanding this sentiment and his own ministry as a fervent advocate of experiential, heart-felt religion, by the end of his career Jarratt came to believe that "in our high *republican times*, there is more *levelling* than ought to be."[35] In particular, he felt betrayed by the Methodists, whom he believed had fallen under the control of "tinkers and taylors, weavers, shoe-makers and country mechanics of all kinds," prone to "jargon," "wild notions," and "furious gestures" in their preaching.[36]

The experiences of Woodmason and Jarratt were not universal, even in the South, but they were representative of the vulnerable position of estab-lished clergy and churches throughout much of America during the second half of the eighteenth century.[37] In the South in particular, the older religious establishment utterly failed to keep pace with the growth of the aggregate population. While traveling through North Carolina in 1772, where the Meth-odists would soon attract a large following, the itinerant Joseph Pilmore de-scribed the people as "sheep having no Shepherd." The region "is two hundred miles wide," wrote Pilmore, "and is settled near four hundred miles in length from the sea, and the Church established as in England; yet in all Country there are but eleven Ministers!"[38] Left strictly to the older denominations, Christianity in America might well have gone the way of the church in much of Europe, where throughout the nineteenth century religion steadily lost its influence over the populace. Instead, in the half-century following the Revolu-tion, Christianity in America was popularized in a way that it had never been before in Europe or in the colonies. From the Revolution on, no American church would become a large-scale movement without answering first and fore-most to the desires of ordinary folk.

Of course, popular beliefs and practices—those supported by the laity and advanced by their chosen leaders—had always found a place in American Christianity.[39] But prior to the Revolution much of what might be considered popular religion existed only on the margins of official Christendom. In the post-revolutionary years, American religion came so firmly under the sway of the laity that popular beliefs and customs became the very frameworks around which new churches were built. "We knew, and our people knew, that we were wholly dependent on them for our support," wrote Thomas Ware, an early Methodist circuit rider, "and that they could wield this check over us at any time they might deem it necessary."[40] This phenomenon paralleled develop-ments in other areas of American political and social life. Unlike its counter-part in Europe, organized Christianity in America wrenched itself free from state control. By allowing the people to become the final arbiters of religious taste, evangelical Christianity not only successfully survived the transition from colonial to post-revolutionary society, but even enhanced its image and appeal.

In many new and growing communities Methodism became the corner-stone of middling life. Early American Methodism appealed most broadly, not to the defeated and hopeless, but to those who had a realistic expectation of improvement. In Dayton, Ohio, in the mid-1810s the Methodist Church became a rallying point for opposition to a town government dominated by a close-knit group of merchants, professionals, and artisans, most of whom were Federalists and Presbyterians.[41] Whereas in older areas such impulses might have been held in check, in places like Dayton, society rested on too frail a foundation to prevent either Methodism or the secular forces with which it was so closely allied from building a large constituency. This also seems to have been the case in Baltimore, where by 1815 one out of every fourteen Baltimoreans was a Methodist. There, typical white male Methodists included master shoemakers who operated their own shops and employed a few apprentices and journeymen, shipwrights who worked at the local yards, and grocers who owned small businesses in town. By and large, Baltimore Methodism did not attract the more well-to-do merchants and professionals, nor did it appeal to the least privileged common laborers. Much the same was true in Philadelphia, New York, and numerous smaller towns across the nation.[42] The thirteen original members of the Methodist society in Providence, Rhode Island, for whom occupational data are available included two laborers, two cabinetmakers, a machine maker, a carpenter, a mason, a shoemaker, a rope maker, a tailor, a silversmith, a blacksmith, and an oysterman.[43]

Throughout the early national period, Methodism appealed to men and women of ambition—to those who were beginning on society's margins, but who were determined to do better for themselves and their families. While their opportunities varied from one region to the next, the desires that animated them largely did not. In some respects, Methodism's success undoubtedly fed on itself, with Methodists banding together to offer one another employment, housing, loans, credit, and much sought after political appointments. But in most cases, the root of Methodist success was more basic and more obvious. Methodism simply appealed to and nurtured the kinds of people most likely to do well in the fluid social environment of the time. It did so by encouraging individual initiative, self-government, optimism, and even geographic mobility—all of which gave American Methodism a decidedly modern cast. Both ideologically and through its organizational structure, Methodism taught people not to fear innovation and ingenuity. In short, Methodists accepted and encouraged the new values necessary for "improvement" in a market-driven society. It was these characteristics that meshed so well with life in the early republic and that helped propel both the Methodist Church and the Methodist people forward.

This ready willingness and ability to thoroughly assimilate into certain aspects of the culture of the early republic is also perhaps what most clearly distinguished the Methodists from other sectarian groups, including to some extent the Baptists. No other sectarian group of the early republic matched the Methodists' national focus or their overriding commitment to expansion. While the Baptists were often mission oriented and worked fervently to make new converts, they were also more often inclined to form tight, closed communities. The Methodist circuit system was far better suited to handle the rapid geographic expansion of the early republic when compared to Baptist congregationalism, but once a given region became more demographically stable, the circuit system lost much of its advantage. This partly explains why Methodist growth exceeded that of the Baptists in the post-revolutionary years and why the Baptists had closed the gap by mid-century.[44]

Like the American church that it inspired, British Methodism also grew rapidly in the late eighteenth and early nineteenth centuries, exerting a powerful influence on the societies and cultures in which it flourished. The spiritual journey of Methodism's founder, John Wesley (1703–1791), began early in life and took him through several stages. While a fellow at Oxford, Wesley was a leader of a group known by a variety of names, including the "Holy Club" and the "Methodists," which included his brother Charles and eventually George Whitefield. After a disappointing mission to Georgia, Wesley returned to England where he attended a meeting in Aldersgate Street on May 24, 1738. There, he later recounted, "I felt my heart strangely warmed. I felt that I did trust in Christ, Christ alone for salvation, and an assurance was given me, that he had taken away my sins, even *mine*, and saved *me* from the law of sin and death." Though the significance of this event for Wesley has been the subject of much debate, it clearly served as a paradigm for many early Methodists. Following Aldersgate, Wesley soon adopted open-air preaching and began building chapels and appointing lay preachers. By 1767 the Methodist movement included more than 25,000 members.[45]

As in America, Methodism in England grew fastest on the peripheries of society, gaining the most of any denomination from the expansion of the English population and economy between 1750 and 1850. As David Hempton notes, English Methodism was most successful wherever there was a migratory labor force and in areas where the traditional influence of squire and parson was fading. English Methodism grew rapidly in mining communities, seaports and fishing villages, market towns, factory villages, canal settlements, and the rural "highland" areas of northern and western England. Wesley, as John Walsh observes, "had a sharp strategic eye for the new industrial settlements out of the sound of church bells and away from the old community life of the village."[46]

Conversely, Anglicanism remained strongest in the arable lowland regions of southern and eastern England where traditional village life long predominated. Throughout the late eighteenth and early nineteenth centuries, Methodism was underrepresented among occupational groups connected with landed

interests—rural laborers and tenant farmers. With a keen perception of historical realities, George Eliot's classic novel *Adam Bede* describes the reception of
Methodism in a small rural village named Hayslope. Not surprisingly, those
most sympathetic toward Methodism in Eliot's tale come from artisan backgrounds. Adam and Seth Bede are carpenters, the captivating Methodist
preacher Dinah Morris is a cotton mill worker, and Hayslope's leading Methodist agitator is Will Maskery, the wheelwright. When a visitor to Hayslope is
told that Dinah is to preach on the village green, he exclaims, "In this agricultural spot? I should have thought there would hardly be such a thing as a
Methodist to be found about here. You're all farmers, aren't you? The Methodists can seldom lay much hold on *them*."[47] Though the visitor is mistaken
about the absence of artisans and mechanics in the area, he is correct about
Methodism's reception among the local farmers. "I'n no opinion o' the Methodists," exclaims Martin Poyser, a leading tenant farmer, "It's on'y tradesfolks
as turn Methodists; you niver knew a farmer bitten wi' them maggots." The
loquacious Mrs. Poyser, Dinah Morris's aunt, presents Eliot's clearest portrayal
of the dependency underlying this loyalty to the Church of England. The day
following Dinah's preaching, Mrs. Poyser fears the worst when she sees the
Reverend Irwine and the young heir Captain Donnithorne ride through her
gate. "I'll lay my life they're come to speak about your preaching on the Green,
Dinah; it's you must answer 'em, for I'm dumb. I've said enough a'ready about
your bringing such disgrace upo' your uncle's family . . . to think a niece o'
mine being cause o' my husband's being turned out of his farm."[48]

As in America, English Methodism's influence extended far beyond its
official membership roles. Though Methodists never accounted for more than
5 percent of the English adult population in the early nineteenth century, Alan
Gilbert estimates that chapel communities represented "something ap-
proaching 20 per cent of the most politicized section of the adult 'lower orders.'"[49] English Methodists, like those in America, tended to come from the
middle stratum of society. Artisans accounted for only about 23 percent of
those with occupations in the broader English population, compared with approximately 63 percent of all Wesleyans and 48 percent of all Primitive Methodists. The percentage of Wesleyans designated as merchants, manufacturers,
and shopkeepers was about the same as the aggregate population, while Primitive Methodists were overrepresented among colliers. As in America, English
Methodism made little impact on unskilled workers. Even Primitive Methodists and Bible Christians were more likely to be semiskilled than unskilled. In
short, English Methodism, like its American counterpart, attracted adherents
primarily from social groups in transition. Thomas Taylor, a Methodist
preacher in Yorkshire in the 1780s, perceived this connection when he wrote,
"There is but little trade in any part of the circuit; and where there is little
trade, there is seldom much interest in religion."[50] While relatively few En-

glish tenant farmers such as Eliot's Poysers joined the Methodists, in America agrarians constituted a major part of the Methodist constituency, owing largely to the high percentage of land ownership in America and the restless nature of the early republic's farming frontiers.

In England, as in America, Methodism allowed ordinary people to integrate their faith into the other perceived realities of their lives. Among the many richly textured local studies of the growth of early English Methodism is James Obelkevich's pathbreaking study of south Lindsey. As Obelkevich demonstrates, by the second quarter of the nineteenth century, Methodism dominated the religious life of south Lindsey. To be "religious" in the local argot meant to be a Methodist. Methodism was, as one Anglican contemporary noted, "the religion, such as it is, of the great mass of the Lincolnshire poor."[51] Among Obelkevich's Wesleyan Methodists, merchants, craftsmen, and to a lesser extent farmers played prominent roles as society stewards, local preachers, leading supporters, and employers of Methodist laborers. A step down the social ladder, the Primitive Methodists created a minority religious counterculture that challenged not only the older village culture and the Anglican Church but also the new social order. Primitive Methodism responded to the advent of capitalism with an ethic of self-discipline, providing adherents with a "deeper and more intense religious commitment than the rural poor had ever known."[52]

In a similar vein, John Rule's study of village culture in Cornwall and Robert Coll's work on the colliers of the northern coalfields demonstrate that Methodism, particularly Primitive Methodism, made a dramatic impact on working-class culture in these areas.[53] As in America, it was not the "defeated" and "hopeless" elements of English society who turned most enthusiastically to this new model of faith. Rather, Methodism, in Alan Gilbert's words, "echoed the *aspirations* rather than the *despair* of the working classes."[54] The primary difference between English and American Methodism was that Methodism in England was hemmed in by the more firmly hierarchical structure of English society, whereas in America it was freer to explore the limits of the separation of church and state.

In both England and America, Methodist theology and doctrine added impetus to the movement's social and cultural appeal. As Methodism's chief architect, John Wesley's thought was central for both English and American Methodism.[55] Wesley's theology was a blend of Anglican, Reformed, and Eastern Orthodox themes. He believed firmly in the primacy of scripture, but also held that experience (along with reason and tradition) could be a legitimate source of doctrinal judgment. In particular, in regard to sin and salvation, Wesley sought to blend the traditional Western juridical emphasis on justification and pardon from the penalty of sin with a more Eastern focus on the therapeutic nurturing of holiness. His faith was Arminian in the sense that he rejected both predestination (that God ordained some for eternal life, and others for eternal damnation) and the idea of a limited atonement (that Christ died only for the elect). At the same time, Wesley retained the Reformed doctrine of total depravity (the belief that sin corrupts every facet of a person's nature), believing that humans are incapable of reaching out to God on their own apart from God's enabling or prevenient grace.[56] Though not an innate human quality, the gift of prevenient grace is given to each person, empowering that individual to choose between eternal life and eternal damnation. Salvation thus becomes a cooperative effort with God. "By this theological device," notes Henry Rack, "Wesley was able to avoid the extremes of 'Pelagianism' (human beings saving themselves by their own unaided efforts) and Calvinism's denial of freewill and fixing of the elect and damned."[57]

Following Wesley, American Methodists clearly maintained that God's grace is resistible. Though God first reaches out to us, we are free to accept or reject eternal salvation. From the Methodist point of view, no choice could be more important. Moreover, conversion was a vocation, not a one-time event; it was possible for believers to turn from God and lose their salvation. This is why ordinary Methodists were so concerned with charting the course of their own religious experience, why Methodist sermons were often so passionate and direct. When Joseph Crawford preached Nabby Frothingham's funeral sermon in 1809, his text was 1 Corinthians 15: 55–57—"O death! Where is thy sting? O grave! Where is thy victory? The sting of death is sin; and the strength of sin is the law: but thanks be to God, which giveth us the victory, through our Lord Jesus Christ"—and his three points were:

I.   Sin, that brought Death into the world, and is in our text declared to be the *sting* of Death!
II. The several kinds of Death produced by sin.
III. The victorious exclamation, Through Jesus Christ our Lord.

After expounding on these points and using Frothingham's life as an illustration, Crawford declared to his audience in typical Methodist fashion, "your time may be very short; you know not who next may be swept away." "Let all ask the question, My merciful God, am I prepared should I be next; all stand in the gap—all are exposed—let all take the alarm."[58] The point of this and countless other Methodist sermons was clear: each person must daily choose his or her own eternal destiny.

Wesley's Arminianism was a progressive, demanding faith. Convinced that God was not lazy, he could see no reason why any of his followers should be, either. He was never motivated by abstract theological problems, but as he put it, by "experimental and practical divinity."[59] Mere orthodoxy was never enough; religion that was not directly experienced was essentially worthless. "The points we chiefly insisted on were: First, that orthodoxy, or right opinions, is, at best, a very slender part of religion, if it can be allowed to be a part of it at all," wrote Wesley in an early sketch of the rise of Methodism.[60] It was this emphasis on the necessity of direct personal experience that defined the Wesleyan way of salvation.

The dynamism of Wesley's doctrines, along with his stress on individual responsibility and opportunity, found a ready reception throughout post-revolutionary America. Methodism offered ordinary Americans the opportunity to seize control of their own spiritual destiny in much the same way that many were striving to determine their social and economic destinies.[61] Like Wesley, what American Methodists objected to most about Calvinism was what they perceived to be its passivity, not only in regard to ultimate salvation but throughout the course of daily life. Like Wesley, American Methodists were more interested in the affect of experience than in what they considered theological abstractions. Hence, they would often baptize converts in any way the candidate preferred—from sprinkling to total immersion.[62]

Of course, Wesley did not shape his message in response to American democracy, the frontier, or even Calvinism as it was understood by most Americans at the time, but in reaction to what he perceived to be the failings of the eighteenth-century Anglican Church. His message found a ready audience in America, but this is not to say, as Sydney Ahlstrom notes, "that the Methodist message was a 'democratic theology' or a 'frontier faith.'" Wesley's theology was fundamentally rooted in his own experience as an eighteenth-century Anglican. With its acknowledgment of human depravity and its demand for repentance and a life of strict piety, his Arminianism stems more from "the heart of the Puritan movement" than from the American experience.[63]

At the same time, it is important to note that the appeal of the Methodist message rested on more than a merely intellectual foundation. In the half-century following the Revolution, American Methodists led the way in what Nathan Hatch has termed "the crusade against Calvinist orthodoxy and control." In an age of progressive optimism and common sense, many Americans came to ridicule the complexity of Calvinist dogmatics and the implication that those "seeking salvation had to wait for the movings of an inscrutable and arbitrary God." This crusade against Calvinism was as much an attack on elite control as it was a theological or doctrinal campaign. Many of those who joined in the anti-Calvinist crusade between 1780 and 1830, ranging from Methodists to Mormons, shared little in common other than a deep resentment of elite privilege. The Methodist conception of prevenient grace resonated with the prevailing democratic notions of the day in a way that Calvin-

Figure 1.3. Charles Giles, from his autobiography, Pioneer *(New York, 1844). Courtesy of the Billy Graham Center Museum, Wheaton, Illinois.*

ism's apparent denial of human free will simply could not. The sometime Methodist preacher Lorenzo Dow spoke for many when he reduced Calvinism to a jingle: "You can and you can't—You shall and you shan't—You will and you won't—And you will be damned if you do—And you will be damned if you don't."[64]

The experiences of Charles Giles and Billy Hibbard are instructive here. Born in 1783 to hardworking Connecticut farmers, like many New Englanders Giles's early religious views were dominated by popular conceptions of predestination. His autobiography contains a lengthy description of Calvinist doctrine that, if nothing else, demonstrates the importance that he once attached to understanding it. Methodist Arminianism, with its universal offer of salvation to all who would seek it, provided Giles with a powerful intellectual counterpoint to the Calvinism of his youth.

But the appeal of the Methodist message went much deeper. For many, the rejection of Calvinist theology implied a sweeping critique of long-dominant social structures and cultural conventions as well. Giles rejected "the doctrines of predestination, particular election, and reprobation" as notions resting on little more than "the respect and reverence . . . for the supposed infallibility of the learned clergy . . . as if their faith were 'the end of all perfection.'" In contrast, Methodist preachers impressed him by speaking "plainly and forcibly." "Experimental religion was a lucid theme to them. They spoke from the deep emotions of their own hearts—told us what they knew and how they felt." This appeal to commonly available personal experience, rather than to a remote system of learning, was what ultimately drew Giles to Methodism. As was the case for a great many Methodists of this period, an intricate series of prophetic dreams and visions played a significant part in his conversion. These served to validate his experience, functioning in the place of assurances from a learned clergy.[65]

The testimony of Billy Hibbard is remarkably similar in this regard. The son of a tanner and shoemaker, Hibbard was born in Norwich, Connecticut, in 1771. His conversion involved not only a series of dreams and supernatural impressions but also rejection of the advice of a local gentleman, "Capt. B," and the town minister, both of whom attempted to school Hibbard in Calvinist doctrine. When his neighbors "came to dispute" his newfound Methodist beliefs, Hibbard did not begin with theological arguments, but with "the experience of religion."[66] In typical Methodist fashion, he was less interested in doctrinal precision than in a practical piety available to all and unmediated by an educated elite.

The pragmatic bent of American Methodism is also evident in the way that Americans related to John Wesley's authority. Though Wesley's only visit to America as a young missionary during 1736 and 1737 was a decided failure, the Methodist movement would indirectly make him a profoundly influential figure in the early American republic. But because Wesley's influence in America was so circuitous, it was clearly limited from the start. In general, American Methodists accepted Wesley's authority only in matters of doctrine, and then only so far as his guidance seemed practical.

Wesley's most original theological innovation was his doctrine of "Christian perfection" or "entire sanctification," which he considered central to the Methodist way of salvation. He clearly believed that there were degrees of faith. One could be truly Christian without being fully Christian; faith is a gift from God, but one that we might neglect. While justification frees us from the penalty of sin, sanctification liberates us from the plague of sin. Hence, salvation is a therapeutic process that does not end with conversion. While Wesley often described sanctification as a progressive journey, he also held out the possibility of instantaneous Christian perfection in this life.[67]

Following Wesley's lead, sanctification was a central theme of the earliest Methodist preachers in America. Writing in 1778, William Watters professed that he did not believe any sermon complete that did not dwell on sanctification and "exhort believers to go on to perfection." Similarly, during his preaching career from about 1773 to 1795, Benjamin Abbott was frequently "much drawn out to preach up sanctification to the people," and to "press them to seek after sanctification."[68] But by the early nineteenth century it seems clear that Methodists were preaching less on sanctification than they had only a few years before, and far less than John Wesley would no doubt have preferred. While retaining Wesley's emphasis on salvation as a progressive journey, many Americans eventually chose to minimize his concept of Christian perfection. Though perfectionism remained a conspicuous aspect of American Methodism, over time it clearly came to mean less to most American Methodists than it had to Wesley. For many, sanctification was simply too much at odds with the doctrines of America's other leading denominations. Just as Wesley insisted that experience was a legitimate source of doctrinal judgment, American Methodists were quick to rely on *their* experience in shaping Wesley's system for its new setting.[69]

2 *The Methodist Connection*

There is nothing out today
but crows and Methodist preachers.

—Nineteenth-century proverb
for inclement weather

*I*n 1802, twenty-six-year-old Jacob Young took on the task of forming a new circuit along the Green River in Kentucky. With little preparation or prospect of outside assistance, Young suddenly found himself responsible for a vast and growing region of central Kentucky. Knowing that he could count on little direct help from his supervising elder, John Page, a millwright who divided his time between building mills and itinerating, Young devised his own strategy for evangelizing the region: "I concluded to travel five miles, as nearly as I could guess, then stop, reconnoiter the neighborhood, and find some kind person who would let me preach in his log-cabin, and so on till I had performed the entire round." Near the end of one dreary day he came upon a solitary cabin in the woods. Seeing a woman in the doorway he asked for lodging, but the woman refused. Desperate, Young exclaimed, "I am a Methodist preacher, sent by Bishop Asbury to try to form a circuit." "This information appeared to electrify her," recalled Young. "Her countenance changed, and her eyes fairly sparkled. She stood for some time without speaking, and then exclaimed, 'La, me! has a Methodist preacher come at last?'" The family were North Carolina Methodists who had recently migrated to Kentucky. Their home soon became a regular preaching appointment on Young's circuit.[1]

On most days Young managed to find a place to preach. Several times he found groups already gathered, eagerly awaiting the rumored appearance of a preacher. On other occasions he was aided by local preachers who had settled along his route. Wherever possible, Young established new class meetings to carry on in his absence. At a place called Fishing Creek, he discovered a Methodist society under the leadership of an African-American slave named Jacob. With the assistance of several local women, Jacob preached regularly and had organized a class meeting. Young was impressed with what he saw. Though Jacob was illiterate, Young noted that he "could preach a pretty good sermon," and that "his society [was] in excellent order."[2] Within three weeks Young had forged enough appointments for a four weeks' circuit. On one occasion he preached in a bar room. On another a man began shouting at the top of his voice, "Young Whitefield!, young Whitefield!"—comparing him to the famous eighteenth-century evangelist. "I thought I was one of the happiest mortals that breathed vital air," wrote Young. He named his new circuit the Wayne circuit, after general Anthony Wayne. By the end of the conference year he had taken in 301 new members, receiving all of $30 for his labors.[3]

Jacob Young's experience illustrates the way in which the creation of early American Methodism was at heart a cooperative endeavor requiring the active participation of both clergy and laity. In 1805 Charles Giles arrived at his new appointment on the Seneca circuit near Cayuga Lake in western New York "faint, weary, and depressed in mind." The area was completely new to him, but he was encouraged at his first appointment to find a congregation already assembled, anxiously awaiting his message. He was equally pleased by a quick offer of lodging following the meeting, and to find this pattern repeated many times over as he made his first round of the circuit. "Though I came here a stranger," wrote Giles, "I was not a stranger long: I found friends—real friends everywhere, whose prayers and solicitude for my welfare consoled my heart, and animated me in my arduous labour."[4] Half way across the new nation, Lovick Pierce had a similar experience when he arrived on his first circuit appointment in South Carolina in 1804. Pierce did not even know where the circuit was until he stumbled across a family who told him that he was already within its bounds, and had just missed a preaching appointment. The family took Pierce in for the night, and the following day led him to his next scheduled appointment.[5]

Whether in Kentucky, New York, or South Carolina, the Methodist system allowed and encouraged both preachers and people to use their imaginations and creative resources to extend the movement and to evangelize those within their reach. The way in which Jacob Young was aided by local preachers and lay people who organized preaching appointments and class meetings, sometimes before he even knew of their existence, is particularly remarkable considering that he was fashioning an entirely new circuit. His experience suggests how the Methodist system thrived by continually pushing outward to engage America's rapidly expanding peripheries, drawing, as Francis Asbury wrote in 1797, "resources from center to circumference."[6]

In its basic design, the administrative framework of American Methodism evolved along the lines of its British parent.[7] Prior to the arrival in 1769 of Wesley's first official missionaries, Richard Boardman and Joseph Pilmore, American Methodism was a tiny, loosely organized lay association.[8] From 1769 it was structured around preaching circuits, class meetings, and quarterly meetings, to which a single annual conference was added beginning in 1773. The class meetings in particular provided a foundation for Methodist solidarity and served to identify and cultivate new leaders. Along with the quarterly meetings, these weekly small-group gatherings were the most important grassroots organizational units of early American Methodism, as we shall see in chapter 4.

Prior to 1784 Methodists in America were officially long-distance members of Wesley's English movement. For his part, Wesley always maintained that Methodism was simply a society within the Anglican Church. He deliberately intended Methodist worship to be incomplete outside of the established church. Hence, the first American Methodists were expected to seek out an Anglican minister to obtain the sacraments. But as the movement in America grew and the Revolution intervened, few Americans found this to be a workable arrangement, especially in regions where the Anglican Church maintained only a tenuous foothold. Even in the South, where Anglicanism was strongest, Methodists shared few social or cultural values with most Anglicans and would remain for the most part genuinely suspicious of them throughout the revolutionary era. "We are thoroughly convinced, that the Church of England, to which we have been united, is deficient in several of the most important Parts of Christian Discipline; and that (a few Ministers and Members excepted) it has lost the Life and Power of Religion," declared the American *Discipline* of 1787.[9] By the late 1770s there was a strong movement among American Methodists to begin ordaining their own ministers and administering the sacraments of baptism and the Lord's supper. Indeed, the movement narrowly avoided schism over this issue in 1779 and 1780.

The sacramental crisis had much to do with the separation of English and American society reflected in the Revolution. When the southern preachers, mostly Virginians, met for the 1779 annual conference in Fluvanna County, Virginia, neither Asbury nor any other northern preacher except for William Watters attended because of the war. At the Fluvanna conference the southern preachers voted to ordain one another to administer the sacraments of baptism and the Lord's supper. This represented a clear break from Wesleyan practice, indicating among other things how little authority Asbury actually commanded in the South at the time.[10]

Prior to the Fluvanna meeting, Asbury had called a preparatory conference in Kent County, Delaware. There, the sixteen preachers present voted Asbury the title of General Assistant in America, and gave him a veto over all conference debates. During the remainder of 1779 and early 1780 the two sides drifted further apart. In the South there were dramatic increases in the number of adherents, which, according to Jesse Lee, only served "to confirm the preachers in the belief, that the step they had taken was owned and honoured of God." "At that time there was very little room to hope that they would ever recede from their new plan, in which they were so well established," concluded Lee.[11] With little contact between the two sides because of the war, Asbury and the northern preachers met for their annual conference in Baltimore in April 1780. Along with passing the first resolutions against slavery, this conference voted to censure and, in effect, expel the southern preachers, declaring, "we look upon them no longer as Methodists in connection with Mr. Wesley and us till they come back." The conference then appointed Asbury, Freeborn Garrettson, and William Watters to attend the next Virginia conference and inform them of their actions. At this point the likelihood of a split seemed overwhelming. "It was like death to think of parting," wrote Asbury after the 1780 Baltimore conference.[12]

When Asbury, Garrettson, and Watters arrived at the southern annual conference, held in Manakintown, Powhatan County, Virginia, in May 1780, they proposed, as a last effort to avoid schism, that the southern preachers suspend administering the sacraments for one year, with the two sides to meet again the following year to weigh their options. But after two days of debate, the southern preachers rejected the offer. Defeated, Asbury prepared to leave the conference "under the heaviest cloud I ever felt in America."[13] Then, during the night, a majority of the preachers unexpectedly had a change of heart, voting to agree to the suspension and to, in a measure, recognize Asbury's authority over the movement both North and South. The immediate crisis was passed, although it would be four years before Wesley provided for the ordination of American preachers.

This episode indicates at least two important things about the movement's development during the war. First, it demonstrates how firmly Asbury and many others held to the basic framework of the Wesleyan system, even to the point of risking schism with the movement's fastest growing region. Second, it indicates the degree to which a great many American Methodists felt the need to establish their own identity independent of English oversight, particularly from the Church of England. Though the southern preachers did most of the compromising in this instance, their more innovative demand for an independent American church would eventually win out.

By 1784 Wesley was willing to concede the inevitable, granting American Methodists a wide measure of freedom, including the ability to ordain their own preachers to administer the sacraments. These concessions led directly to the establishment of the independent American Methodist Episcopal Church at the so-called Christmas conference of 1784. Independence positioned American Methodists to compete on an equal footing with other sects and churches in the early republic without requiring them to jettison their Wesleyan heritage. While remaining Wesleyan, after 1784 American Methodism ceased to be ostensibly Anglican. Though the Methodist Episcopal Church's administrative structure now became fully separated from its English parent, its methods and message remained essentially the same, and its doctrines and theology continued to rely first and foremost on Wesley himself.[14]

As the movement grew, its organizational complexity increased. After 1779 there were dual and then multiple annual conferences to accommodate American Methodism's rapid geographic expansion. In addition to the yearly conferences and quarterly meetings, quadrennial general conferences were instituted beginning in 1792 in Baltimore, the movement's unofficial capital. By 1792 as many as 20 yearly conferences were being held in various places. The 1796 General Conference reorganized these into set annual conferences with official titles and defined boundaries. By the early nineteenth century annual conferences were composed of districts, divided into circuits and societies, which in turn encompassed a number of class meetings comprising about two dozen people each. The annual conferences were supervised by the bishops, the districts by the presiding elders, the circuits and societies by the itinerant preachers, and the classes by local preachers, lay stewards, and class leaders.[15] Hence, nearly every Methodist was, in a sense, integrated into a truly national network. This is why American Methodists themselves continued to refer to their movement as a "connection" long after it had become a recognized church. As Francis Asbury traversed the nation in 1805 he was "happy to find, one spirit animates the whole, for 1700 miles, the same Hymns, prayers & language, salutes my Ears & heart."[16]

Though ostensibly arranged on a rigidly hierarchical model, on the ground the Methodist connection operated with a truly remarkable degree of flexibility. The leading architect behind the Methodist system in America was Francis Asbury (1745–1816), the church's foremost bishop from its inception until his death in 1816. Born near Birmingham, England, Asbury came to America in 1771 and was the only one of Wesley's official missionaries to remain through the war. Within the broad confines of Wesleyan tradition, Asbury and his colleagues used a pragmatic trial-and-error approach to construct and extend an organizational system designed to balance individual initiative with centralized control. Connectionalism allowed the movement to maintain its popular ap-

Figure 2.1. Francis Asbury, by Charles Peale Polk, 1794. Courtesy of the Lovely Lane Museum, Baltimore, Maryland.

peal on the local level, while at the same time efficiently channeling its expansionist energy into new areas of the rapidly growing nation. It encouraged a great deal of local prerogative and lay leadership while still maintaining an economical national framework of itinerant preachers and administrative conferences obligated to meet the needs and demands of their constituents. Asbury would undoubtedly have bristled at the suggestion that he and his preachers were "packaging" American Methodism to suit the tastes and demands of a new kind of consumer. But this, in fact, is exactly what was happening.[17] Along the way, ineffective ideas and institutions were discarded in favor of more popular policies and practices. It is worth noting that the 301 new members taken in by Jacob Young in the episode given at the beginning of this chapter came at a cost to the church of just $30, or about 10 cents per new member.

In many respects, the Methodist connection was a remarkably *decentralized* system. While American Methodism had a well-defined central hierarchy, the clergy never dominated the movement in the late eighteenth and early nineteenth centuries. Because American Methodism was a thoroughly voluntary association, and, perhaps more important, because the circuit riders only visited each society an average of about once every two weeks, local congregations shared much of the responsibility of regulating the day-to-day affairs of the church. In sharp contrast to colonial patterns of church polity, a wide variety of lay leadership positions were open to ordinary Methodists (even, at times, to women and African Americans) who wanted an official part in shaping the movement's future. Unprecedented numbers eagerly took advantage of these opportunities. By creating so many avenues for lay men and women to participate in the church's leadership, American Methodists diffused much of the traditional tension between clergy and laity. The movement had a place for just about everyone who could adhere to its broadly evangelical doctrines and discipline, or at least aspired to.

Every Methodist preacher was familiar with Wesley's injunction that "it is not your business to preach so many times, and to take care of this or that Society: but . . . to bring as many sinners as you possibly can to Repentance, and . . . to build them up in that Holiness, without which they cannot see the Lord."[18] While itinerants were expected to stay within the bounds of their circuits and to keep the appointments made by their predecessors, the culture of Methodism demanded individual initiative. Ezekiel Cooper's circuit notebooks reveal that he never made exactly the same circuit twice. Like all Methodist preachers, Cooper exercised a great deal of freedom in choosing where he would preach, omitting places where he met with an unfriendly reception and adding others where prospects were more encouraging.[19] The New York local preacher James P. Horton once declined the offer of a horse to use in meeting his appointments. Though Horton was often gone for weeks at a time and sometimes walked up to 40 miles a day, he feared that a horse would cramp his style. "I found it more convenient to be on foot," wrote Horton, "for I could visit all the houses I saw from the road, without the trouble of letting down bars, and opening gates." Horton's practice was to stop "a dozen or twenty times at different houses along the road to sing a hymn, and pray in each, and sometimes give an exhortation to the people."[20]

In 1785 Thomas Ware met a colleague in New Jersey whose method of arranging preaching appointments was no less freewheeling and given over to the leading of the Spirit. "His manner was, to let his horse take his own course, and on coming to a house, to inform the family that he had come to warn them and the people of their neighbourhood to prepare to meet their God," recalled Ware. After this introduction, Ware's colleague would announce when he would return to preach, carefully noting the date in his appointment book, and then would ask the often startled family to gather their neighbors for the

Figure 2.2. James P. Horton, from his autobiography, A Narrative of the Early Life, Remarkable Conversion, and Spiritual Labours of James P. Horton *(1839).*

event. Finally, "if he found they were not offended," he sang and prayed with whomever would join him, and then rode on.[21]

Preachers were not the only ones to use this sort of tactic. William Watters recalled that in the early 1770s, when there were only three Methodist preachers in all of Maryland, the members of his society would often divide into "little bands" and canvass nearby neighborhoods, singing, praying, reading scripture, and talking to whomever would listen. "In one sense we were all preachers," concluded Watters. Similarly, Abner Chase's conversion occurred during a series of dramatic meetings in April 1801 entirely organized and conducted by a group of single, young adults in Saratoga and Montgomery counties, New York. By the second day, these meetings had produced so much excitement throughout the community that "at an early hour, there was a general rush to the appointed place of meeting." The third day Chase and "two or three young persons . . . took a circuit, extending some two or three miles from the centre, and invited all, young and old, rich and poor, to attend the meeting." When a Methodist itinerant preacher finally arrived on the scene, he was delighted to find 60 to 70 new converts ready to join the church.[22]

What is perhaps most remarkable about this style of loosely regulated evangelism was how commonplace it had become by the early nineteenth century. A generation before, this kind of activity would have been unheard of in many regions of America and vigorously opposed by the established churches in others. But the new ideologies of the post-revolutionary era presented new opportunities. Seizing on the democratic and leveling impulses of the age, American Methodists offered new roles for zealous lay men and women as local preachers, lay exhorters, class leaders, and a host of other semi-official positions. Within a remarkably short period of time these new roles became an accepted part of America's religious landscape, helping to redefine the role of the clergy for American evangelicals.

Methodists drew a technical distinction between exhorting and preaching, and between local and itinerant preachers. In theory, exhorting consisted of simply telling one's testimony of conversion or relating life experiences in the faith, with the goal of imploring one's listeners toward greater holiness and fuller service. Preaching and exhorting were often used together, so that a preacher's sermon might be followed by an exhortation from someone else. While exhorters could be licensed, any Methodist or recognized adherent, man or woman, black or white, young or old, could, under the right circumstances, be invited to give a public exhortation. Preaching, on the other hand, consisted of "taking," or reading, a text of scripture and then explaining the meaning of that passage. Only licensed preachers were supposed to exercise the privilege of taking a text.

In practice, however, this distinction often became blurred almost beyond meaning. Preachers sometimes chose perfunctory texts that served only as launching pads for what were really exhortations. One itinerant of this era was known to have preached from passages such as: "Shem, Ham, and Japheth" (Gen. 5:32); "There are six steps to the throne" (1 Kings 10:19); "I have put off my coat; how shall I put it on?" (Song of Sol. 5:3); "Woe to the women that sew pillows to all armholes" (Ezek. 13:18); and "Ephraim is a cake not turned" (Hos. 7:8).[23] Conversely, Alfred Brunson, who preached and exhorted more than 10,000 times during his career, noted that exhorters were often allowed to "*steal* a text." According to Brunson, an exhorter "had no right to sing and pray and take a text, giving book, chapter and verse: but might, after singing and prayer, begin to introduce a subject, and bring in a text that he wished to explain, but not tell where it could be found." For Methodist preachers, "topical preaching and exhortation are so nearly allied as to be inseparable," concluded Brunson.[24]

"To commence speaking by exhortation is doubtless the best mode of procedure for a young man who is intending to preach extemporaneously," agreed the itinerant Charles Giles of New York. "A great exhorter, in the high sense of the term, is truly a great preacher; for he preaches much in his exhortations." Added Giles: "To declaim, to advise, to warn, to persuade, to entreat with tears, all are comprised in the ample range of exhortation. And, in doing this awfully sublime work, the depths of human learning may be opened, the wide field of revelation explored, its doctrines brought up, its promises spread out, together with the rousing of Sinai's thunder, and the blood and groans of Calvary."[25] Exhorting allowed for a greater degree of spontaneity and permitted the speaker to concentrate more fully on establishing a rapport with his or her listeners. Hence, at times exhorting seemed better suited for communicating the Methodist message and took precedence over preaching at Methodist meetings. "This I say, we ought to be wise as serpents, in the management of our meetings," wrote Francis Asbury to Daniel Hitt in July 1805. Under some circumstances, Asbury advised Hitt that "Preaching ought to give way to Exhortation." He noted that at the recent New York Conference "We had all preaching & very little Exhortation," with less than satisfactory results. But in a similar gathering in Lynn, Massachusetts, "Exhortation prevailed & the work went on." At the Massachusetts conference some 100 exhortations were given with the result that "Lynn was thunder struck." Meetings lasted till midnight, and Asbury was delighted to report that even the five a.m. meetings were crowded.[26]

Though all Methodist exhorters and local preachers were supposed to be licensed by their quarterly meetings before launching out on their own in public, many began to speak without waiting for formal sanction, often with the hearty approval of their audiences. While it is true that the Methodist system allowed prospective preachers to test their abilities before seeking a license, some clearly went beyond a simple trial run of their speaking gifts. In 1774 or 1775 John Littlejohn and two other recent converts organized neighborhood "prayer meetings" in Alexandria, Virginia, because there was no regular preaching nearby. "The house where we met being too small we made use of a large thatched pen, where some hundreds came to hear us pray—this led me to speak a little," recalled Littlejohn, "& so greatly were many affected, & deeply wounded & amidst their cryes & tears my voice was often lost." Spurred on by this response, Littlejohn began to "exhort" regularly in public before obtaining any kind of license, though he eventually did so. In 1775 he became a class leader in Fairfax County, Virginia, and in 1776 began an itinerant career under the guidance of William Watters.[27]

Jacob Young began to speak in public in much the same manner soon after his conversion. "Although I had no license to preach I became the servant of all, holding prayer meetings, exhorting, and preaching whenever I was called upon, both among the Methodists and Baptists," recalled Young. Likewise, Billy Hibbard began exhorting before even joining the Methodists, Elijah Woolsey began preaching and making appointments "somewhat in the form of a circuit" before being licensed to preach, Lovick Pierce never received a license until, several years after joining the itinerancy, he was ordained a deacon, and Philip Gatch preached, exhorted, and formed a small circuit in Maryland and Pennsylvania, all without official sanction. After preaching at one appointment, the people asked Gatch to speak again in the afternoon, but he declined because he had already given the only sermon he knew! When the itinerant John Brooks's health failed in Tennessee, he "picked up three fine young men," who were nevertheless unlicensed, sending them out to "hold the meetings and exhort and hold class-meetings." Under this system, "shocks of divine power continued with us every where; conversions at every place," reported Brooks. "The whole church was fully in the work." [28]

In practice, the most important distinction among Methodist preachers was between local and itinerant, or circuit-riding, preachers. In 1799 Jesse Lee estimated that there were 850 local preachers but only 269 itinerant preachers active in the United States. Ten years later Francis Asbury counted 1610 local preachers, compared to 597 itinerants. [29] While the itinerants were salaried, voting members of their respective annual conferences, local preachers were not. Typically, a preacher's career followed a progression from class leader, to exhorter, to local preacher, to itinerant preacher, and, more often than not, back to local preacher when he married or his health failed.

Local preachers, as the name implies, lived in a given community, farmed or worked at their trade or profession, were usually married or widowed, and received little or no financial support from the church. Their role within Methodism was analogous to that of the Baptist farmer-preacher. They commonly preached on Sundays and often led prayer and class meetings during the week. The task of nurturing members between visits by the itinerant preacher almost always fell on any local preacher who happened to reside near a Methodist society.

In many cases local preachers migrated into newly settled regions or unreached rural or village pockets before these areas could be reached by regular circuit riders. While forming a new circuit in south-central Ohio in 1799, the itinerant Henry Smith discovered a total of 10 local preachers settled along his route. In 1800 when no itinerant was appointed to the Miami, Ohio, circuit, the four or five local preachers living in the region took it upon themselves to maintain the circuit. According to Philip Gatch, "they systematized their operations, preached not only on Sabbath, but also on other days, held two days' meetings, and kept up a routine of quarterly meetings." Local preachers were, in the words of the long-time itinerant James Quinn, "very often the pioneers of Methodism in forming new circuits in the West."[30]

As long as the itinerancy persisted, local preachers also found ample opportunities to preach and lead in more settled regions. As a local preacher for better than 16 years, Benjamin Abbott built up his own circuit of appointments in New Jersey, Pennsylvania, Delaware, and Maryland. Once established, the more successful of these appointments were often taken into nearby circuits by regular itinerant preachers. Abbott's preaching tours kept him away from home as much as six weeks at a time. On one extended tour through eastern Pennsylvania, he preached 29 sermons and saw scores converted. On another occasion he preached so often and so stridently that he lost his voice for two months. Yet, like all local preachers, Abbott received no regular financial support from the church. Nor did he ever wear black or any other kind of clerical garb, a trait which in most cases probably only served to enhance his affinity with his listeners.[31] In much the same manner, following his conversion in about 1799, the New York shoemaker and local preacher James P. Horton spent more than 30 years dividing his time between making shoes to support his wife and 13 children, and preaching wherever he felt led to go. Like Abbott, Horton's preaching tours often kept him away from home for weeks at a time, and he became a fixture at camp meetings in his region of New York. Indeed, there was a certain freedom to the life of a local preacher. When James Jenkins left the itinerancy in 1806 he felt like "one of the freest men in the world. I could now make my own appointments, and attend what meetings I pleased." The fact that he now had "young men over me," did not trouble Jenkins because "it was not by their will I was to be governed, but by the discipline of the church."[32]

Though the itinerants defined the Methodist system and held it together, the contributions of the local preachers were clearly indispensable. Had local preachers insisted on being paid for their services, the movement would have had far fewer preachers at its disposal and could not have expanded as rapidly as it did. So deeply ingrained was the concept of local preachers ministering for free that John Littlejohn steadfastly refused to be paid after he located. In 1818, when he learned that the people of Louisville were raising a salary for him, he "begged it might be stopted[.] I could not think of prostrating the charrecter of a Local Methodist Preecher for Money." Had he accepted a salary, Littlejohn feared that his conscience might not have been free to preach as he saw fit: "It might have shut my mouth agst that plainness of speech I thot it my duty to use in my preeching to this people."[33]

On the local level, lay exhorters, local preachers, class leaders, and circuit stewards did much to assure that the movement would remain in touch with its constituents even as it grew at an unprecedented pace. On the national level, the itinerant system provided an overarching framework connecting each Methodist circuit and society to the larger whole, making it possible to efficiently distribute the movement's resources wherever they might have the most telling impact. Without a strong itinerancy, American Methodism would have quickly lagged behind the nation's rapid geographic expansion, as most Methodists clearly perceived. It is not surprising, then, that the itinerancy was the most revered of Methodist institutions.

Wesley himself was convinced that were he to preach a whole year in one place, "I should preach both myself and most of my congregation asleep." "Nor can I believe it was ever the will of our Lord that any congregation should have one teacher only. We have found by long and constant experience that a frequent change of teachers is best. This preacher has one talent, that another. No one whom I ever yet knew has all the talents which are needful for beginning, continuing, and perfecting the work of grace in an whole congregation."[34] American Methodists were no less certain of this principle, carefully preserving the itinerancy as one of the cornerstones of the movement in America. "*Our grand plan*, in all its parts, leads to an *itinerant* ministry," wrote Francis Asbury and Thomas Coke in their notes to the *Discipline* of 1798. "Our bishops are *travelling* bishops. All the different orders which compose our conferences are employed in the *travelling line*; and our local preachers are, *in some degree*, travelling preachers. Every thing is kept moving as far as possible; and we will be bold to say, that, next to the grace of God, there is nothing *like this* for keeping the whole body alive from the centre to the circumference, and for the continual extension of that circumference on every hand."[35]

In an era when most Americans lived on scattered farms or in small and often remote villages, itinerancy provided preaching, the sacraments, and ecclesiastical structure to communities that would not otherwise have been able to attract or afford a minister. In 1795, 95 percent of Americans lived in places with fewer than 2,500 inhabitants; by 1830 this proportion was still 91 percent. Thomas Ware noted that when he was appointed to the New River circuit in Virginia in 1788, "there was not within the bounds of our circuit a religious meeting except those held by us." Similarly, in 1790 Freeborn Garrettson noted that in New York, "hundreds, if not thousands, in the back settlements, who were not able to give an hundred a year to a minister, and could seldom hear a sermon, may now hear a sermon at least once in two weeks; sometimes oftener," thanks to the presence of Methodist circuit riders. The long-time itinerant William Beauchamp expressed a common sentiment among Method-

Figure 2.3. Thomas Ware, from Abel Stevens, History of the
Methodist Episcopal Church in the United States of America
(New York, 1867).

ists when he declared: "Itinerancy is the life of Methodism; the great spring
that keeps every part of the machine in operation; the vital principle which
imparts animation, health, strength, and vigour throughout the whole body.
Destroy this, and you will destroy Methodism."[36]

Itinerant preachers initially joined a conference on a trial basis. This probationary period usually lasted for one or two years, after which the preacher
became a full member of the conference. Ordination was a separate matter. In
1784 Wesley provided for the ordination of deacons and elders to administer
the sacraments in America. The office of deacon was something of a transitional ordination, allowing deacons to baptize, marry, bury the dead, and assist
in administering the Lord's supper.[37] The General Conference of 1796 stipulated that traveling deacons be eligible for election as elders after two years.[38]

Itinerants usually received their appointments at the annual conferences.
In most instances these appointments were for one year. The annual confer-

ence of 1774 recommended that preachers rotate assignments every six months, but this procedure was soon abandoned as the movement grew. In 1804 a time limit was first placed on appointments to stations and circuits. Thereafter, no itinerant preacher was to remain in the same station for more than two successive years, except for the presiding elders (whose tenure had been limited by the General Conference of 1792 to four years), those connected with the book business, and supernumerary and superannuated preachers.[39]

Convinced that preachers ought to circulate widely, Francis Asbury often made it a point to move promising young preachers far outside their home regions. "It will never do for preachers to rise up in a district and never move out of it for three or four years," wrote Asbury in 1792.[40] Most of the early itinerants agreed, believing that prolonged appointment in one region would foster parochialism, eventually endangering the integrity of the entire connection. Most accepted their yearly reassignment without open protest—though there were always exceptions—even when these appointments took them far from home. In 1795, Jesse Stoneman, who had grown up on the Ohio frontier, was appointed to the Litchfield, Connecticut, circuit, far from "my own country." Connecticut was quite a shock to Stoneman, but he did not intend to give up, despite "days of sore trials." "My resolutions, & determinations are at present, to spend and be spent in the glorious cause, I have embarked in," he wrote to fellow itinerant Daniel Hitt, who was then riding the Redstone circuit in western Pennsylvania. "Brother, this is a fine school; I am not sorry that I came to this land; I am satisfied the hand of GOD was in it; I have seen good days, & hope to see greater."[41]

A typical Methodist itinerant was responsible for a predominantly rural circuit, 200 to 500 miles in circumference. He was expected to complete this circuit every two to six weeks, with the standard being a four weeks' circuit. His partner, if he had one, usually did not travel with him, but either followed or preceded him on the circuit. Hence, on a four weeks' circuit the people could expect preaching from a circuit rider about every two weeks, but only rarely on a Sunday. As the number of Methodists in cities and larger towns grew, an increasing number of itinerants were assigned to "stations" in these communities. There the routine of a Methodist preacher more closely resembled that of a traditional clergyman. On rural circuits, the itinerants made preaching appointments for nearly every day of the week, sometimes both morning and evening, with only a few days per month allotted for rest, reflection, and letter writing. Along with preaching, circuit riders usually met and examined the classes at each appointment, all of which could take three to four hours a day apart from traveling. Quarterly meetings held at a centralized location added variety to this routine, with a camp meeting often replacing one of the quarterly meetings beginning in the early nineteenth century.

Immediately subordinate to the bishops in the church hierarchy were the presiding elders, a position created and defined in the 1780s and 1790s. Appointed by the bishops, the presiding elders were responsible for supervising the preachers and societies within a given district. Ideally, the presiding elders served as the bishops' "eyes, ears, and mouth, and pens," acting as liaisons with the preachers and people.[42] Many of the presiding elders of this period accepted their appointments only with great reluctance, which is not surprising considering the responsibilities the position entailed. Often there was little in the post to make it attractive for the average circuit rider, other than the opportunity for a wider field of service. Presiding elders received the same pay as the preachers under their supervision, and were generally required to travel more extensively. Elijah Woolsey's first district as a presiding elder in 1803 was 800 miles in circumference, requiring eight to nine weeks to traverse.[43] As a presiding elder Woolsey was responsible for managing all quarterly and camp meetings in the district, collecting receipts from the sale of books (which were often short), handling the toughest disciplinary cases, administering the sacraments throughout the district if none of the other preachers were ordained, and recruiting and evaluating candidates for the ministry. When Charles Giles was appointed to the Chenango district in western New York in 1818, his responsibilities embraced 11 circuits, 18 traveling preachers, and over 4,500 members. During the next four years he supervised a remarkable 164 quarterly meetings.[44]

James Jenkins accepted his appointment as presiding elder over the South Carolina district in 1801 with the soberness of one who fully understood the difficulty of the task set before him. "In every advance I made in the church I wished to make corresponding improvements in piety and usefulness" recalled Jenkins, "and when I looked over the field, which was extensive and laborious, I felt the responsibility of my charge, and concluded that *now* I must almost kill myself." He was not mistaken. At the end of Jenkins's first year, Asbury was disappointed that he had made only three rounds of his district rather than four. "I told him if I had been quartered, and each part made to travel, then I might have done it," replied an exasperated Jenkins. "My rule was, to visit every part of the district, to travel, preach, meet the societies, &c., nearly every day. I had hardly a rest day a month."[45]

Along with reshaping clerical roles, American Methodists redefined sacred space. By 1785 only 60 Methodist chapels had been purchased or built, but there were more than 800 recognized preaching places.[46] Before the proliferation of Methodist church buildings, meetings were held in homes (where the majority of weekday sermons were delivered), court houses, school houses, the meetinghouses of other denominations, barns, or in the open. While riding the St. Lawrence circuit in 1813, Benjamin Paddock regularly preached in a dry goods store in Potsdam, New York. In 1810 on the Delaware, New York, circuit, Abner Chase regularly preached in a ballroom connected to a tavern along the banks of the Schoharie River. According to one account, Robert R. Roberts once preached in a tavern in northwestern Pennsylvania, though not without difficulty. Partway through Roberts's discourse a drunkard in the audience awoke, calling out, "Landlord, give me a grog!" When Roberts protested granting the man's request, the tavern owner replied, "Mr. Roberts, you appear to be doing well; I would thank you to mind your own business, and I will mine." Benjamin Abbott likewise once tried preaching in a tavern near Albany, New York, but gave up when he "saw the people frequently running in and out of the bar room."[47]

At some places Methodists built union meetinghouses in cooperation with other denominations. But these were often the cause of far more contention than union, and were therefore relatively few in number. At Litchfield, on the Utica, New York, circuit the Presbyterians, Baptists, and Methodists pooled their resources to build a meetinghouse. But on one occasion a member of one of the other denominations arrived early in the morning, took one of the doors off its hinges, laid it on the floor, and sat on it to prevent the Methodists from holding a love feast.[48] To overcome problems such as this, and to reach a broader spectrum of the unchurched, the *Discipline* of 1784 called on the preachers not to neglect field preaching whenever the weather permitted. "Our call is to save that which is lost. Now we cannot expect them to seek *us*. Therefore we should go and seek *them*." Added the *Discipline:* "The greatest Hindrance to this you are to expect from rich, or cowardly, or lazy *Methodists*."[49]

On city stations and in more densely settled areas where they might preach and travel less, the itinerants were charged with visiting members regularly in their homes. "Family religion is shamefully wanting, and almost in every branch," advised the *Discipline*. "We must, yea, every Travelling Preacher must instruct them *from House to House*. Till this is done, and that in good earnest, the Methodists will be little better than other People."[50] While stationed in Fayetteville, North Carolina, William Capers's practice was to visit each family in his charge once a week. He set aside 9 A.M. to 1 P.M. five days a week for this purpose, allowing half an hour per visit.[51] In much the same way, Dan Young called at every house in Lynn, Massachusetts, once a week while stationed there in 1808.[52] Earlier, while stationed on the Grantham, Vermont, circuit, Young employed a similar pattern of house-to-house visitation. There, his usual practice was to "start as early in the morning as I could, and visit every family on the way to my appointment." At each home, he would first announce that he was "a preacher of the Gospel," and then ask the head of the household to gather the family together for prayer and possibly an exhortation, or even individual exhortations for each member of the family. At times, Alfred Brunson adopted the same formula of visiting house-to-house while itinerating in Ohio, as did Charles Giles in upstate New York.[53]

Whether he was appointed to a city station or a rural circuit, the fact remained that the life of a traveling preacher was often an overwhelming and exhausting affair, and that not all the circuits were equally attractive. In 1809 Jesse Lee estimated that of the 988 preachers admitted into full connection between 1769 and 1806, fewer than 90 had died while itinerating, and fewer than 300 were still traveling. The vast majority of the remaining 600 itinerants had married and located at some point in their career. Furthermore, Lee estimated that during this same period 251 would-be preachers were admitted on trial but quit traveling before ever joining into full connection. More recently, William Warren Sweet has estimated that of the 1616 preachers who joined the itinerancy prior to 1814, 821 had located, "most within a relatively few years after their admission," 131 had died while traveling, 34 had been expelled, and 25 had quit the church.[54]

The Methodist itinerancy was a demanding system, but one that could yield enormous dividends for both preacher and church. When Abner Chase first considered joining the itinerancy in 1810, the former itinerant Eber Cowles warned him that "the itinerant life is a good school, but it is a severe one—you have but a gloomy prospect before you for the present life—I think a young man in your circumstances can do better."[55] Thomas Ware spoke for many when he wrote, "I thought our [itinerant] system too severe. It called us in youth to sacrifice all means of acquiring property, and threatened to leave us dependent on the cold hand of charity for our bread in old age."[56] But few doubted the system's effectiveness. Indeed, what Ware considered a flaw, James Quinn pointed to as a cause for celebration. "Methodist itinerancy, as a system, has hitherto had no place for loungers, and may Heaven forbid it ever should," concluded Quinn near the end of his career. "This plan calls for men to cut loose from the world, and cast it behind. Let us have the men who are constrained by the love of Christ, moved by the Holy Ghost—men who can walk hand in hand with poverty, for twice twenty years; then leave their widows to trust in the Lord, and their fatherless children to be provided for and preserved alive by him."[57] Quinn himself itinerated for 44 years, and Ware for more than 40. Despite its hardships, the itinerancy offered unique opportunities for middling young men in search of souls and personal fulfillment. "I know of no employment or situation this side of heaven that I would prefer before that of an *itinerant Methodist preacher*," declared Abner Chase, who joined the traveling connection as a young man despite Cowles's warning.[58]

The hallmark of the Methodist episcopacy was the appointive power of the superintendents, or bishops.[59] The church's four early bishops were Francis Asbury (1784–1816), Thomas Coke (1784–1814), Richard Whatcoat (1800–1806), and William McKendree (1808–1835). While the annual conferences ostensibly retained the right to admit new candidates to the ministry, the bishops held the authority to ordain and to make all circuit appointments. Moreover, since Coke never spent enough time in the United States to be taken seriously as a bishop, and Whatcoat and McKendree deferred to Asbury whenever possible, the latter for all practical purposes retained the right to appoint almost every traveling preacher wherever he saw fit until relatively late in his career.[60]

This remarkable concentration of power was at the heart of James O'Kelly's protest at the General Conference of 1792, and led to American Methodism's first major schism. Born of Irish ancestry either in Ireland or Virginia, O'Kelly served in the American army during the Revolution. By 1778 O'Kelly was itinerating on trial in the Virginia conference. From 1779 to 1784, he traveled the New Hope and Tar River circuits in North Carolina, and the Mecklenburg, Brunswick, and Sussex circuits in Virginia. When the Methodist Episcopal Church was organized at the Christmas Conference in 1784, O'Kelly was ordained one of its first elders.[61] A gifted and popular preacher with little formal education, O'Kelly built a large following in eastern Virginia.

O'Kelly's final break with the Methodist Episcopal Church came at the first General Conference in 1792, which he had largely been responsible for promoting. At the 1792 conference he motioned that "after the bishop appoints the preachers at conference to their several circuits, if anyone thinks himself injured by the appointment, he shall have liberty to appeal to the conference and state his objections; and if the conference approve his objections, the bishop shall appoint him to another circuit."[62] But when brought to a vote, the motion was defeated by a large majority. Dismayed, O'Kelly and some 30 preachers left the Church and, in 1794, founded the Republican Methodists.

Throughout his controversy with the church's leadership, O'Kelly framed his arguments in republican terms and maintained that what he was really fighting against was the "spurious episcopacy" of Francis Asbury. Asbury's "ecclesiastical monarchy . . . makes a bad appearance in our Republican world," argued O'Kelly. "Francis was born and nurtured in the land of kings and bishops, and that which is bred in the bone, is hard to be got out of the flesh." Even the apostle Paul, quipped O'Kelly, "did never exercise the authority Francis doth. He did not . . . send a minister but by his free consent."[63]

Asbury's supporters, on the other hand, quickly came to believe that they could detect other motives behind O'Kelly's railings and to view him as a misguided eccentric who was determined to "be head or nothing."[64] He certainly did not appear to have been the victim of much tyranny. From 1782 to 1792 he was stationed almost constantly in his homeland, the heart of old Virginia, "presiding over a large district of the very best circuits in the connection." He had also been a charter member of Asbury's short-lived council of presiding elders established in 1789.[65] Many eventually concluded that O'Kelly left the church for four reasons: (1) overwhelming personal ambition; (2) disappointment at not being appointed a bishop; (3) bitterness at having a manuscript rejected for publication; and (4) fear of being expelled for holding Unitarian beliefs.[66]

However valid both perspectives may have been, the key to understanding the O'Kelly schism is in appreciating the tension between O'Kelly's concept of local sovereignty on the one hand and traditional Methodist connectionalism on the other. In effect, O'Kelly's plan would have allowed each preacher, and therefore each congregation or circuit that could pay his support, to have the final say on where that preacher would be stationed. Asbury and his supporters, on the other hand, wanted to maintain what Donald Mathews has referred to as Methodism's "dialectic between locality and universality."[67]

When the debate on the O'Kelly motion opened at the 1792 conference, the majority of the preachers were initially supportive of the idea. They assumed there would be few of the kind of appeals O'Kelly's motion addressed. "For myself, at first I did not see any thing very objectionable in it," recalled Thomas Ware.[68] But Ware and many of his colleagues soon became alarmed at the severity of the arguments advanced by O'Kelly's supporters. "O Heavens! Are we not Americans!" exclaimed Hope Hull at one point during the debate, "Did not our fathers bleed to free their sons from the British yoke? and shall we be slaves to ecclesiastical oppression?"[69] As the debate progressed, Ware and others became convinced that what O'Kelly and his followers really intended was to undermine and reformulate the itinerant system. What at first seemed a minor proposal to help assure fair treatment for all the preachers quickly took on a more ominous appearance. Many concluded that O'Kelly's underlying design was to remake Methodism into a loose association of nearly autonomous congregations, and in this roundabout way to secure his grip over the circuits of eastern Virginia. Methodism, O'Kelly would later write, ought to consist of "districts . . . formed in a kind of confederacy." He clearly held strong sectional prejudices that were diametrically opposed to Asbury's broader, more inclusive outlook.[70] Convinced of this, the preachers voted decisively to prevent O'Kelly's motion from succeeding.

Within the context of this debate, the majority of the preachers were not so much concerned with establishing a more democratic polity as they were

with maintaining the church's popular appeal and its ability to continue expanding. This, they believed, required that the itinerancy be kept strong and
viable. "We were *itinerants*," wrote Thomas Ware, reflecting on this period,
"The plan of a general superintendency had not only been submitted to, but
was universally approved by both preachers and people." William Watters
agreed. "The sacrifice that a preacher makes in giving up his choice, and going
wherever he is appointed, is not small. But no one is worthy of the name of a
travelling preacher, that does not cheerfully go any where he can, for the general good," wrote Watters. "Better many individuals suffer, than the work at
large should."[71]

In response to the democratic rhetoric of O'Kelly's followers, those in favor
of the existing system argued that O'Kelly's motion would result in "easy and
wealthy circuits" being "crowded with preachers, while poor circuits would be
left alone."[72] They quickly came to believe that making the stationing of
preachers a matter of personal preference and local initiative would fragment
the church and destroy its connectional character. "Methodism is a unit, and
should, if possible, be the same everywhere," asserted Henry Smith on another
occasion, but with the same issue in mind.[73] The defenders of connectionalism
also pointed out that the church was a strictly voluntary association, with
plenty of other denominational choices available for those offended by Methodist discipline. No one, they argued, could be really oppressed in a church
that he or she was at once free to leave.

The subsequent history of O'Kelly and the Republican Methodists bears
out the distinction between his notion of local sovereignty and traditional
Methodist connectionalism. The Republican Methodists never expanded far
beyond their original boundaries, and O'Kelly himself remained in Virginia
until his death in 1826. In 1809 O'Kelly's church, by then called the Christian
Church, began establishing ties with Elias Smith's Christians. Perhaps most
significant, though O'Kelly's church boasted as many as 20,000 members when
it linked with Smith's Christians, it never presented more than a localized
challenge to the Methodist Episcopal Church. In the short run, the connectional structure of episcopal Methodism proved more versatile and efficient
than O'Kelly's confederacy. For the majority of Methodist leaders and followers
alike, what counted most was the ability to reach the widest possible audience.
Measured against this standard, O'Kelly's charges against Asbury and the
church seemed largely irrelevant.[74]

Six years after the O'Kelly schism, episcopal connectionalism was more
fully defended in the notes appended to the *Discipline* of 1798. To the suggestion that the annual conferences be given the authority to station the preachers, Asbury and Coke responded that, since the annual conferences were only
concerned with affairs within their bounds, the inevitable result of doing so
would be to fragment the church. "The conferences would be more and more

estranged from each other for want of a mutual exchange of preachers," asserted Asbury and Coke, "and *that grand spring, the union of the body at large,* by which, under divine grace, the work is more and more extended through this vast country, would be gradually weakened, till at last it might be entirely destroyed. The connection would no more be enabled to send missionaries to the western states and territories, in proportion to their rapid population. The grand circulation of ministers would be at an end, and a mortal stab given to the itinerant plan."[75]

Furthermore, throughout this period the majority of the preachers remained convinced that Francis Asbury's powers were actually a good deal more circumscribed than O'Kelly and his supporters had implied. Asbury's authority was a complicated matter. He inherited the extraordinary appointive power that had been Wesley's, a precedent reinforced in the American church's *Discipline.* But Asbury would not have maintained such vast influence for long had he wielded it in broadly unpopular ways. Prior to 1808, the general conferences were theoretically all powerful. They could create or revise *any* statute they chose. They even had the power to dismiss a bishop without trial.[76]

At the famous Christmas conference of 1784 that organized the Methodist Episcopal Church, Asbury himself insisted that he be elected by the preachers rather than simply receive Wesley's consecration. By doing so, Asbury shrewdly garnered a mandate that was not mediated through Wesley or Coke, but came directly from the American conference. But Asbury surely had more in mind than simply shifting the source of his authority from Wesley to the American preachers. Even though conferences in 1779 and 1782 had already in large measure elevated him to the leadership of American Methodism, he must have known that in the democratic context of the early republic only the election of bishops would place them above the charge of spurious tyranny.

In fact, the trend throughout the early national period was to limit, not expand, episcopal power.[77] In 1806 William Watters wrote of Francis Asbury: "His power I confess is great, but let it be well observed, that it intirely respects the travelling preachers, and none else. It never can from the nature of things, be put into the hands of any man, but one in whom the whole have the highest confidence, and that no longer than he faithfully executes his trust."[78] Similarly, Thomas Ware noted that the annual conferences were careful to guard their independence. "To place the power of deciding all questions discussed, or nearly all, in the hands of the superintendents, was what could never be introduced among us," wrote Ware reflecting back on the period of the late 1780s.[79] As with so much else, when it came to the episcopacy, American Methodists thought first and foremost in pragmatic terms.

Most Methodists assumed that the main responsibility of the episcopacy was to preserve the itinerancy, and no one was more committed to the latter than Asbury. But this alone falls far short of explaining Asbury's immense stature in early American Methodism. Nicholas Snethen, Asbury's official defender in the pamphlet war with James O'Kelly, readily admitted that Asbury sometimes erred in the details of his administration of the church. But in the larger perspective, argued Snethen, Asbury faithfully reflected what American Methodism ought to be. In Asbury Methodists saw themselves, or, rather, their ideal of themselves. "In him we see an example of daily labour, suffering, and self denial, worthy of the imitation of the young preacher," argued Snethen.[80] Most Methodists agreed.

Asbury's travels set the standard for all early Methodist itinerants and left little doubt as to what he expected from his charges. The pace that he kept up during his 45 years in America, is astonishing given the hardships of travel at the time. Few could match his endurance. During his career Asbury rode more than a quarter of a million miles and crossed the Allegheny Mountains some 60 times. He visited nearly every state once a year and traveled more extensively, over a longer period of time, in the trans-Appalachian frontier than any other prominent American. By 1811 Asbury had taken it upon himself to ride 6,000 miles a year, preside over the eight annual conferences then in existence, preach 200 sermons, and station 700 preachers. "I think there is not a traveling preacher in the connection that goes through more fatigue," wrote Henry Boehm while on the road with Asbury in 1803. "His extreme toil and labor eclipses the most zealous among us." Preaching and traveling were Asbury's "element, his life; he could not live long without."[81]

Asbury usually rose at 4 or 5 A.M. to spend an hour in prayer, and fasted on Fridays. One biographer estimates that he stayed in 10,000 households and preached 17,000 sermons. He was more widely recognized than any person of his generation, and more than a thousand children were named after him. The itinerant John Dickins named his first son Asbury Dickins, while James Jenkins named his daughter Elizabeth Asbury (presumably after Asbury's mother), and Benjamin Paddock named his son Francis Asbury. Thomas Morrell also named his first son Francis Asbury, and when that child died in infancy, he named his second son after the bishop as well. Asbury was so well known by postmasters across the nation that British correspondents could send him mail addressed simply to "America."[82] It is worth noting that at the time Jacob Young proclaimed himself to be Asbury's representative in Kentucky (in the episode given at the beginning of this chapter), he had never even met the bishop. In all likelihood neither had the woman from North Carolina. But both knew of Asbury's reputation.

Though he is seldom remembered as a leading figure of Jeffersonian America, Asbury is perhaps a more fitting symbol of this period than any other

American. Part of his genius lay in his instinctive feel for the dynamics of the post-revolutionary religious marketplace. Asbury did not fear social leveling and boiling hot religion. He understood the transitional nature of American society just as Wesley understood that of English society. Asbury, according to Thomas Ware, "lived in the feelings . . . of both preachers and people."[83] He governed by building consensus, and by making his own career a model for other Methodists to follow.

Despite the church's phenomenal success, Asbury's lifestyle changed little during his 45 years in America, and his salary never exceeded that of an ordinary traveling preacher. Like George Whitefield and John Wesley before him, Asbury never fell prey to greed, womanizing, or the temptation of a life of ease and leisure. Indeed he had no private life outside his friendships with Methodist preachers and others whom he visited periodically in his travels. He rarely owned more than could be carried on horseback, maintaining that the equipment of a Methodist preacher was a horse, saddle and bridle, one suit of clothes, a pocket Bible, a hymn book, perhaps a watch, and, in Asbury's case, a pair of spectacles. Anything more would be an unnecessary encumbrance. "Of all men that I have known he is in my estimation, the clearest of the love of money, and the most free to give away his all, in every sense of the word," wrote William Watters in 1806.[84] Even as the movement grew beyond hope, Asbury continued to see himself as an ordinary itinerant first, a church leader second. As early as 1799 Asbury considered resigning from the episcopacy, and was still considering doing so as late as 1806.[85]

As a result of his relentless peregrinations and the advice of the presiding elders, until late in his career Asbury had a remarkable grasp of both the abilities of the individual preachers at his disposal and the needs of a great many communities and regions across the nation. He was known to have kept a private notebook in which he recorded assessments of each preacher's abilities.[86] One of the strategies Asbury employed was to appoint more refined preachers who had at least some idea of the more delicate nuances of polite society, such as Ezekiel Cooper, to important town pulpits. His more rustic charges were then assigned to rural and frontier areas. At the 1810 South Carolina conference, a young William Capers listened intently to Asbury's call for missionaries to venture into the frontier regions of Alabama and Mississippi. Deeply touched, Capers spent the entire night weighing the matter in prayer. The next day he sought out Asbury to offer himself for the new mission field. "Can't send you, Billy, sugar," Asbury quickly replied, without even pausing to consider the idea, "you won't know how to take care of yourself." Instead, Asbury appointed Capers to Charleston, South Carolina, a station far better suited for a son of the South Carolina gentry.[87]

But it is important to note that even Asbury was not above being challenged by preachers unhappy with their assignments. At the 1800 annual conference held in Kentucky, he attempted to appoint William Burke presiding elder over a district in Virginia. Burke flatly refused. "I told him it was out of the question; that I had returned to Kentucky, at his request, from Baltimore, in the spring; that I had rode down my horses; that I had worn out my clothes; that I was ragged and tattered; and last and not least, I had not a cent in my pocket."[88] Asbury relented and Burke stayed in Kentucky. Similarly, in 1803, at the urging of his presiding elder, Jacob Young defied Asbury and refused to change circuits, though he later came to believe that this had been a great mistake. That same year Asbury ordered Ezekiel Cooper, the church's book steward in Philadelphia for the past five years, to move to Baltimore. "I think of any preacher that has been stationed in Philadelphia for six or seven years, I would conclude it was time for him to be removed if he was not local, and altogether out of my power. I wish every person that can be moved to be moved," wrote Asbury to Cooper. Notwithstanding the earnestness of this appeal, Cooper refused to leave Philadelphia. In 1784 Freeborn Garrettson turned down Asbury's appointment to the Redstone circuit in western Pennsylvania, though he later "suffered much in my mind; wishing many times afterward, that I had taken up the cross." Henry Smith likewise refused appointments on at least two occasions, in 1800 and in 1806.[89]

In the end, what is perhaps most remarkable is not that Asbury was on occasion defied, but that he was so often obeyed. That this was so indicates not only how dedicated most of the early circuit riders were to the itinerant plan, but also how seldom Asbury attempted to appoint a preacher to a charge he was not likely to accept. The Methodist historian James Buckley has observed that the average tenure on a given circuit increased dramatically between 1794 and 1804. "Many remained *two* years, and several stayed *three* years," writes Buckley, "and Francis Asbury *could not* prevent it."[90]

As time went on and his responsibilities grew increasingly onerous, Asbury clearly realized that he was stretching himself too thin. In June 1809, for example, he presided over the New England annual conference at Monmouth, Maine. The conference ordained 21 deacons and 7 elders, admitted 17 preachers on trial, allowed 11 elders to locate, and readmitted one. In addition to overseeing these activities, Asbury had to station the conference's 82 preachers, all in about four days. "I have to lament my want of information respecting both the preachers and the circuits," he noted in his journal.[91] And this was only one conference out of seven that year. At times Asbury asked presiding elders to station the preachers for him at annual conferences. In November 1804, he wrote to Daniel Hitt asking him to do just this at the 1805 Baltimore annual conference. "I am in no doubt or fear but the Connection will do as well or better without me, as with me," wrote Asbury to Hitt, "the president elders have more local knowledge, they have more personal information of the preachers, and Circuits." But at other times he was not so sure. Whatever the merits of local control, in the end all such proposals were simply O'Kellyism revisited. In April 1806, Asbury once again wrote to Hitt, this time complaining about preachers who refused to accept backcountry appointments. "Before I establish two orders, one for the Cities, and the other for the Country," grumbled Asbury, "may the General Conference strip my authority of Superintendency over my head & off my head. If when they are sent to Circuits, they locate, or leave the connection, be it so."[92]

Asbury walked a thin line in exercising his appointive power. The task of stationing the circuit riders was never an easy one, but most Methodists of this period believed that it was crucial to the movement's vitality. They would have agreed with William Beauchamp's assertion that "the *power of appointment*, lodged in the hands of the Episcopacy, is the main-spring in this mighty machine, the Travelling connexion."[93] In exercising this role, Asbury often had to balance the desires of local societies and strong-willed preachers against the broader needs of the movement. At times he was reduced to little more than trickery to maintain order. Henry Boehm traveled some 40,000 miles with Asbury as his assistant from 1808 to 1813. Boehm noted that at the close of annual conferences Asbury often had his horse waiting at the door so that he could make a hasty departure immediately after reading the new circuit assignments. "He thus avoided importunity, and no one could have his appointment changed if he desired to," noted Boehm, "for no one knew where to find the bishop."[94]

That Asbury had to resort to such measures gives some indication of both the nature and limit of his authority. Dynamic and remarkably efficient, connectionalism was designed to channel the religious passions of ordinary believers into action. Everything about Methodist doctrine and practice demanded individual initiative and action. But the Methodist system also demanded order and cooperation. The movement's extraordinary growth is largely an indication of how successful early American Methodists were in balancing these two impulses.

In a 1783 election sermon, Ezra Stiles predicted that the Congregationalist, Presbyterian, Anglican, and Reformed churches would triumph over the American religious landscape in the years to come, leaving little room for groups such as the Baptists and "westleians." By 1816 Lyman Beecher realized that Stiles had wildly missed the mark, but his own perception of trends in American religion was little better. Beecher despaired that for a population of some 8 million, there were only 3,000 college-educated ministers in the United States. Worse yet, west of the Allegheny Mountains there were only 130 "regularly educated and settled ministers" to serve a population of 2 million, presenting, in Beecher's view, "a scene of destitution and wretchedness little realized by the more favored parts of New England." For Beecher, the future was indeed bleak. "Let the tide of population roll on for 70 years, as it has done for the 70 that are past," he fretted, "and let no extraordinary exertion be made to meet the vastly increasing demand for Ministers; but let them increase only in the slow proportion that they have done, and what will be the result? There will be within the United States seventy million souls—and there will be only six thousand competent religious teachers; that is, sixty four millions out of the seventy, will be wholly destitute of proper religious instruction."

Neither prediction, of course, even remotely reflected what was to come. What both Stiles and Beecher failed to discern was that new religious movements were fundamentally reformulating American religion in the generation following the Revolution. As Freeborn Garrettson pointed out in a reply to Beecher, the New England model of tax-supported churches would hardly have been acceptable to most Americans by 1816. Instead, popular religious systems such as the Methodist connection seized the opportunities offered by the free market of the early republic, devising strategies to succeed in that context. In West Chester, Putnam, and Dutchess counties of New York—an area Beecher referred to as a "moral wilderness"—Garrettson noted that the Methodists had 70 congregations and 3,000 members in 1816. "I fear your prejudices are local," Garrettson advised Beecher, "and in my opinion, it would be of great service to you, were you to travel awhile."[95]

3 *The Methodist Itinerant*

When I see a man preach
I like to see him act
as if he were fighting bees.

> —Abraham Lincoln, quoted
> in Charles A. Johnson,
> *The Frontier Camp Meeting*

The vernacular is the real test.
If you can't turn your faith into it,
then either you don't understand it
or you don't believe it.

> —C. S. Lewis to Harold Fey, 1958

*I*n 1855 the historian Philip Schaff wrote that the emergence of Methodism was almost as important a step in the development of Protestantism as the Puritan revolution of the seventeenth century. Though Schaff had little sympathy for the popular nature of American Methodism's early phase, he was a keen observer who could not help but acknowledge some of the factors that led to the movement's vitality and growth. Schaff, like so many commentators before and since, was particularly impressed by the effectiveness of the Methodist preachers. What Methodist preachers lacked in higher education they made up for with "a decided aptness for popular discourse and exhortation," and by "fidelity and self-denial." Added Schaff: "They are particularly fitted for breaking the way in new regions . . . and for laboring among the lower classes of the people."[1] Predominantly young, single-minded, and remarkably dedicated, Methodist itinerants forever changed the appearance and tone of American religion. In short, they were a different kind of clergy than had ever been seen before in America.

Methodist preachers of the early republic represented a distinct social class and came from remarkably similar backgrounds. Educationally and socially, these preachers were cut from the same fabric as their predominantly middling and artisan audiences. Hence, unlike their college-educated Congregationalist, Presbyterian, and Episcopalian counterparts, they were not burdened with the task of spanning social boundaries and comprehending unfamiliar anxieties and aspirations. They began with the advantage of a natural social affinity with their listeners. In many instances the only real distinction between a Methodist preacher and the bulk of his audience was which side of the pulpit each was on. Almost none of the first- or second-generation itinerants had anything more than a common school education. Until 1800 even a full-time itinerant's salary was limited to a mere $64 a year. In that year it was increased to $80 a year for an unmarried preacher. By comparison, the average annual income of a Congregationalist minister in 1800 was $400.[2]

Many, or perhaps even most, of the early itinerants and local preachers came from artisan and petty-merchant backgrounds. Before turning to preaching, Francis Asbury, Jacob Gruber, and Noah Levings were blacksmiths; Benjamin Abbott was apprenticed to a hatter and then farmed for a time; Henry Boehm was apprenticed in a grist mill, as was Nicholas Snethen; John Campbell Deem was a tanner, as were his father and the Methodist preacher who led him to conversion; James P. Horton, Alfred Brunson, and Enoch Mudge were shoemakers; Samuel Parker, known as the "Star of the West," was a cabinetmaker; John Littlejohn was a shopkeeper and saddlemaker; John B. Matthias was a carpenter, as were Sampson Maynard, who also spent some time at sea, and Robertson Gannaway, who also worked as a shopkeeper, blacksmith, and innkeeper; Thomas Morrell was a shopkeeper and Revolutionary War soldier; Thomas Rankin was a brewer and merchant; Henry Smith was a wagoner, while his father was a blacksmith; Dan Young, Benjamin Paddock, and Ebenezer Newell were common schoolteachers, the first in New Hampshire, the second in New York, and the third in Maine, New Hampshire, and Massachusetts; and Jacob Young was raised on the Pennsylvania and Kentucky frontiers and built brick houses for a time.[3] In 1802, in Winchester, Virginia, alone the itinerant James Quinn befriended two carpenters, two shoemakers, and a gunsmith, all of whom eventually became Methodist preachers.[4]

Only a portion of those preachers hailing from the deep South appear to have represented something of a distinction to this pattern. In contrast to the artisan beginnings of their northern counterparts, some of the preachers from the Carolinas and Georgia came from slave-holding families who owned small farms or were part of the minor gentry. Examples of this brand of preacher include William Capers, James Jenkins, and Joseph Travis, all from South Carolina. But most southern Methodist preachers probably came from backgrounds more like those of their northern counterparts. Lovick Pierce, for instance, came from a "poor, humble" South Carolina family that "lived by personal daily labor" and "never owned slaves."[5]

Far from being backward-looking traditionalists, most Methodist preachers were products of post-revolutionary America and felt comfortably at home among its rising middling classes. In particular, they knew the importance of mobility in an era of unprecedented expansion. Before entering the itinerant ranks, most already had an extensive history of geographic mobility themselves. They understood its economic promise for those seeking to better themselves as well as the risks and hardships frequent relocations entailed. Increasingly longer migrations not only physically removed both preacher and people from established religious structures, but also provided the psychological distance necessary to embrace new ideas and institutions.

Throughout Francis Asbury's tenure in America the typical appointment for a Methodist itinerant was only one year on any given circuit. In contrast, the ideal of New England clergy had always been life-time tenure at a single parish. Of the 550 graduates of Yale College who entered the Congregationalist ministry between 1702 and 1794, a remarkable 71 percent ministered for their entire career at only one church. Only 4 percent served more than three pastorates. In colonial New England, both pastor and people saw ordination as a long-term commitment to a single congregation.[6] Nothing could have been more foreign to the Methodist concept of an itinerant ministry.

A vivid example of the mobility and artisan training that characterized the early lives and careers of so many Methodist preachers is that of John B. Matthias (1767–1848). Born in Germantown, Pennsylvania, the sights and sounds of the war years were among his most poignant childhood memories. "I had the prinsebels of liberty stambt in my soul boath of state and church," recounts Matthias, "for my father insruckted me in all those princebeals."[7] Before leaving home, Matthias followed his parents' wish by joining the Dutch Reformed Church at age 18, though he professed to have little understanding of its doctrines. Soon thereafter he began serving a four-year apprenticeship to a carpenter in Philadelphia, where he left off attending church and became a "great sinner." Before his apprenticeship was complete Matthias quit Philadelphia for New York City and joined the Freemasons.[8]

Hearing of the Methodists' reputation for loud and passionate preaching, Matthias sought out the John Street Methodist church. There he heard "thundering" John Dickins, "a plain dreast man and When he spock it came with all his might, and it suted me very well, for I allways love'd to hear preashears spack as if thay whar in ernest." For about a year Matthias attended Methodist preaching with a growing sense of conviction before suddenly becoming convinced that God had accepted him and that his conversion was complete. "This testomoney within was as plane to me as the phiseckel operations of the wind apon my Body without," recalled Matthias. "I becam varey zelous and I beleved that I should one day becom a travling preaser [preacher]." He was then 23 years of age.[9]

Matthias immediately joined a class meeting and began to exhort in public. Though his exhortations were too boisterous and jarring to suit many New Yorkers, the stationed preachers often sent him to the outposts of Fort Lee and Brooklyn to hold meetings. But it would be more than two decades before he realized his dream of becoming a full-time circuit rider. In 1790 Matthias married Sarah Jarvis, a member of the John Street Church, and in 1793 he was licensed as a local preacher. Soon after, he moved to Peekskill on the Hudson, where he worked as a ship's joiner and preached up to three times each Sunday.[10]

In 1796 Matthias and his family moved to Tarrytown, New York, where he continued as both a joiner and local preacher. Since there was no Methodist preaching in Tarrytown at the time, Matthias announced a meeting in the village shortly after his arrival. When the townspeople "heard of this thay sead to one another[,] com and let us hear our Joiner preash, for som of them thought it streansh for a man to preash that work't all the weeck, and had not com from a colledge."[11] Indefatigable as he was, it still took Matthias four years to form a class meeting in Tarrytown. Subsequently, Tarrytown became a regular circuit appointment.

Not long thereafter Matthias spent a summer working on a sloop in Haverstraw, New York, where there also was no Methodist preaching. In a short while he succeeded in forming a class of nine members. That fall he "gave the church to sister wondil [Wendel], for she was the only one amongs them that knew anything about exsperemental godleness." He advised the class to meet at least once a week, and then returned to Tarrytown. When he returned to Haverstraw the following year to work on another ship, Matthias found the new class "in a vearey prospreas state." With encouragement from the presiding elder of the district, Elijah Woolsey, he expanded the Haverstraw work into a two weeks' circuit, joined 40 new members into a society, and eventually formed the outlines of a four weeks' circuit.[12]

By 1810, with three of his sons serving apprenticeships, Matthias was finally able to fulfill his long-time dream of riding a circuit as a regular Methodist itinerant. As such, he traveled various New York circuits until his retirement in 1841. His preaching was most effective in the rural, frontier areas of upstate New York. In 1825, Matthias volunteered to pioneer a circuit in the remote Highlands region. In that year alone he took in 248 new members. In many ways the Highland mission represented the apex of his career. "Thre are no popel better than those Highlanders," wrote Matthias. "The state of Religion is at presend vary prsperris [prosperous,] the classis are vary livly[,] thay are seeking for Holiniss of hart[,] som are mead perfcte in Love and othris groning so to be—I naver in joy'd my self so well in all my life."[13]

Matthias's career is remarkable when one considers how different it was from the traditional conception of the ministry. He obviously had little formal education and almost no contact with society's elites. For the more than two decades that he labored as a local preacher he received little or no financial support even from his own church, and following his accession to the itinerancy he was given mostly difficult, backcountry circuits. Yet for Matthias these issues were of relatively little concern. If anything, he turned these circumstances to his advantage, using first his occupational freedom to blaze new trails in areas of New York beyond the reach of the regular circuit riders and then his affinity with common folk to reach frontier settlers.

While Matthias entered the itinerancy relatively late in life, the early life and career of Alfred Brunson (1793–1882) were more typical in this regard. Though Brunson was a thoroughgoing Yankee who always retained a deep pride in his heritage, he, like Matthias and hundreds of other Methodist preachers of his time, led a peripatetic life both before and after entering the ministry. Born in Danbury, Connecticut, Brunson was apprenticed to a shoemaker, but ran away at age 15. Determined to work his way to Ohio, he instead experienced conversion at a Methodist meeting in Carlisle, Pennsylvania. Returning to Connecticut, Brunson bought out his apprenticeship, settled in Bridgeport, obtained a license to exhort, and married Eunice Burr, all by the age of 18. Believing that he had been called to preach by an audible divine voice, Brunson applied to enter the full-time itinerancy but was turned away because he was married and judged to be too brash even for a Methodist preacher. Disappointed, Eunice and Alfred moved to Trumbull County, Ohio, in 1812. Soon after their arrival, Brunson joined the army as a sergeant and spent a year in campaigns on the shores of Lake Erie. In 1817 he began traveling as something of an adjunct circuit rider in the Ohio Conference before the conference admitted him on trial in 1821. Thereafter, he itinerated extensively in Ohio and western Pennsylvania, eventually settling in Wisconsin. Brunson was popular for his pithy and combative preaching and for his prowess at handling camp meeting rowdies. Known in his younger days as the "boy preacher," he never lost the shop-mechanic edge that made him a favorite with many on his circuits.[14]

Like the majority of their colleagues, John B. Matthias and Alfred Brunson began their preaching careers, not with a classical education, but with a firsthand knowledge of the challenges facing middling people in the volatile postrevolutionary years—their daily hopes and fears, their ultimate aspirations. Their pilgrimages into the Methodist itinerancy followed a familiar pattern of artisan training, broken apprenticeships, and emotion-laden conversions. Like Matthias and Brunson, most early circuit riders were accustomed to frequent relocations and understood the sense of rootlessness engendered by the unprecedented geographic expansion of the early American republic. It was from this base of understanding that Methodism launched its campaign to evangelize the nation.

Not only did most of the early Methodist preachers begin life in similar social circumstances, they also by and large shared a common beginning to their religious lives. Most experienced conversion at a relatively young age, often in dramatic fashion, and subsequently began preaching early in adult life. The vast majority could remember the exact date and time of day at which they were converted. Their conversions formed a base of experience without which no Methodist could hope to obtain a public platform.[15]

The conversion of Jacob Young (1776–1859) was typical in many respects. Born in Allegheny County, Pennsylvania, of "poor but respectable parents," Young moved with his family to Kentucky in 1797, where they purchased a tract of uncultivated land. Though his father was "violently opposed to the Methodists," Young began attending Methodist preaching out of "curiosity" soon after his arrival in Kentucky. He quickly discovered that these meetings were unlike anything he had ever witnessed before. At one gathering "the congregation was melted into tears; I could compare it to nothing but a storm of wind . . . the congregation nearly all rose from their seats, and began to fall upon the floor like trees thrown down by a whirlwind." Young looked on with amazement: "my tears flowed freely, my knees became feeble, and I trembled like Belshazzar; my strength failed and I fell upon the floor."[16]

The next evening Young sought out the woman at whose house the meeting had been held and asked her to pray and sing with him. No sooner had they begun to sing than Young once again fell to the floor, lying there for "many hours, having no recollection of any thing that passed, only that my mind was dark, and my soul greatly distressed." Then, about midnight, a "light appeared to shine from the south part of heaven, and God, in mercy, lifted up the light of his countenance upon me, and I was translated from the power of darkness into the kingdom of God's dear son." Recovering his senses, Young stood up and began to shout and cry aloud. A few days later he gained assurance of his conversion through a prophetic dream in which Christ showed him his name written in the Book of Life.[17]

All of these elements—family opposition, boisterous meetings, falling in a swoon, shouting, and prophetic dreams—were common parts of early Methodist conversions. Indeed, few preachers of Young's day passed through this stage without similar experiences.

Perhaps no Methodist experienced a more dramatic conversion than did Benjamin Abbott (1732–1796). Born on Long Island, New York, Abbott was apprenticed to a hatter in Philadelphia after the death of both his parents. Leaving the hatter before his term had expired, he next went to work on his brother's farm in New Jersey. Later he married, rented a farm of his own, and joined a Presbyterian church. At age 33 Abbott had a startling dream in which he died and was carried to hell, "a large place, arched over, containing three apartments with arched doors to go from one apartment to another."

> I was brought into the first, where I saw nothing but devils and evil spirits, which tormented me in such a manner, that my tongue or pen cannot express. I cried for mercy, but in vain. . . . Being hurried into the second apartment, the devils put me into a vice, and tormented me until my body was all in a gore of blood.—I cried again for mercy, but still in vain. . . . I was soon hurried into the third apartment, where there were scorpions with stings in their tails, fastened in sockets at the end thereof: their tails appeared to be about a fathom long, and every time they struck me, their stings, which appeared an inch and a half in length, stuck fast in me, and they roared like thunder. . . . I was hurried through this apartment to a lake that burned with fire: it appeared like a flaming furnace, and the flames dazzled like the sun. The devils were throwing in the souls of men and women . . . and the screeches of the damned were beyond the expression of man. . . . When it came my turn to be thrown in, one devil took me by the head and another by the feet, and with the surprise I awoke and found it a dream. But oh! what horror seized my guilty breast.[18]

Five or six weeks later Abbott had a second dream in which an angelic guide conducted him on a tour of heaven. There, peering through a door, he "saw the Ancient of Days sitting upon his throne, and all around him appeared a dazzling splendour. I stood amazed at the sight; one stepped forward to me arrayed in white, which I knew to be my wife's mother and said to me, 'Benjamin, this place is not for you yet,' so I returned, and my guide brought me back. I awoke with amaze at what I had seen, and concluded that I should shortly die."[19] Despite their vividness, these dreams had little immediate impact on Abbott. Then, seven years later, in 1772, he attended the preaching of a Methodist itinerant at the urging of his wife. "The preacher was much engaged, and the people were crying all through the house," he later recalled. "This greatly surprised me, for I never had seen the like before."[20] Immediately the memory of his dreams seven years previous returned, and his sense of conviction grew.

Abbott and his wife now became devotees of Methodist preaching in their area. At one meeting "the word reached my heart in such a powerful manner that it shook every joint in my body," recalled Abbott. "Tears flowed in abundance, and I cried out for mercy." On another occasion he was "taken with fainting fits," and neighbors began to fear that he was going mad. Yet another intricate prophetic dream finally led to Abbott's conversion shortly thereafter.[21]

Conversions such as those of Abbott and Young laid the foundation for a deep sense of personal piety characteristic of virtually all late eighteenth- and early nineteenth-century Methodist preachers. Like Wesley before them,

American Methodists continued to see salvation as a progressive journey. John Littlejohn (c. 1756–1836) was typical in this regard. Born in England, Littlejohn arrived in Maryland in 1767 with his new master, storekeeper Thomas Broomfield, on a brig whose company included 65 indentured servants and 14 convicts. After leaving Broomfield, he worked as a saddlemaker, storekeeper, and shop foreman in Norfolk, Annapolis, and Alexandria. A prophetic dream led to his conversion in 1774.[22] At the beginning of his preaching career in November 1776 Littlejohn listed the following nine resolutions in his journal:

1st Every night to exam[ine] myself.

2d To rise every morng before or by the peep of day, & to have family prayr where practicable the 1st thing that the Blacks may attend; & to engage heads of Families to do so.

3rd To avoid talkg of Worldly things as much as possible[;] others may yea must[,] I need not.

4th To converse with all I can on the Salvatn of their souls. Rich & poor.

5th Never to stay at any place longer than necessary.

6th To avoid lightness & reprove those who joke & laugh to excess.

7th Strictly to enforce the rules on every membr of Society Rich or poor.

8th Never to triffel or while away time, & to guard ag[ain]st talkg too much.

9th To read the Bible & notes every Morng & eveng wth prayr to God & to read other books occasionally[.] O Lord do thou be my helper.[23]

These kinds of resolutions appear frequently in the journals of early Methodist circuit riders. The first *Discipline* of 1785 advised preachers to rise at 4 A.M. and spend an hour in prayer, meditation, and reading the writings of John Wesley, and to do the same again from five to six in the evening. When possible, preachers were further urged to spend the entire morning in reading and study.[24] This was essentially the pattern followed by the South Carolina itinerant James Jenkins. "It was my usual practice to read the Bible in the morning, and spend some time in prayer and meditation before going to my appointments," wrote Jenkins. "In the afternoon I read other religious books, and, sometimes, retired into the woods for prayer and meditation." Jenkins often spent evenings talking with whomever he was lodging with, noting that "in these private exhortations, I have frequently seen the power of God manifest in the awakening and conversion of souls."[25]

The combination of a peripatetic artisan background and a deeply felt practice of piety created a potent mixture. The early itinerants rode their circuits with the belief that bringing the lost to Christ was the highest calling on earth, that their reward in heaven would more than compensate for their sufferings on earth. Spurred on by this belief, they willingly ventured into unfamiliar regions of the country, far from family and friends, often enduring a grueling pace of riding and preaching, prayer and class meetings, all for a meager salary that often barely covered their expenses. For these men the itinerancy held many allures, including the appeal of being recognized as a minister, albeit a Methodist preacher. Though the foundations of ministerial authority had begun to crack in the post-revolutionary years, ministers were still among the most respected people throughout the new nation. Moreover, though Methodist preachers were often ridiculed and threatened, they were seldom ignored. It must have been exhilarating for a former carpenter or blacksmith to ride into town and instantly draw a larger audience than the local Congregationalist or Episcopalian minister. Few other endeavors offered middling-born men the potential for such instant recognition. Nonetheless, this kind of explanation alone falls short of explaining the tenacity of the early itinerants without an appreciation for their heart-felt religious motivations and their affinity to common folk.

In many parts of the new nation Methodist preachers suddenly seemed to be everywhere, leading one New Yorker to exclaim in 1788, "I know not from whence they all come, unless from the clouds."[26] Their exploits soon became the stuff of legend among their supporters, and the cause of deep foreboding among their competitors.[27] The Presbyterian minister Joseph Huber was amazed as he traveled the mountains of southeastern Kentucky to discover how thoroughly Methodist circuit riders had canvassed the region. "I at length became ambitious to find a family whose cabin had not been entered by a Methodist preacher," recalled Huber. "For several days I traveled from settlement to settlement, on my errand of good, but into every hovel I entered, I learned that the Methodist missionary had been there before me."[28] According to another account, on the Tombigbee, Alabama, circuit in 1812 or 1813, Richmond Nolley followed fresh wagon tracks to the camp of a family newly arrived in the area. "What!" exclaimed the father when he discovered Nolley's identity, "have you found me already? Another Methodist preacher!" The man had already left Virginia and Georgia in hopes of breaking the church's hold on his wife and daughter and was dismayed to encounter a circuit rider on the upper reaches of the Tombigbee River "before my wagon is unloaded." Nolley offered him small comfort, telling the man that not only were the Methodists everywhere in this world but that there would undoubtedly be Methodist preachers both in heaven and in hell.[29]

The Methodist onslaught embraced nearly every region of America's demographic periphery. In 1806 the family of John Campbell Deem (1802–1879) moved from Kentucky to Butler County, Ohio, to escape the "curse of slavery" and an uncertain land title. At that time, Butler County was an "almost unbroken forrest" containing so many wolves that shortly after their arrival the family's two large dogs opted to return to Kentucky, swimming both the Miami and Ohio Rivers on the way. Deem's father built a 16 by 20-foot log cabin on their new tract of land, which at the time they moved in did not have a chimney, windows, or a floor. Yet within days of their arrival, a solitary figure on horseback rode up in the rain asking "if there was a Methodist family living there." According to Deem, his mother's "heart was swelled with emotion" to discover that one of the twin pillars of her life (the other being her family) had preceded her into the new country. As was customary, the preacher stayed for dinner and then led the family in prayer and singing. Not only did the Deems remain staunch Methodists, but John Campbell eventually became a circuit rider himself.[30]

Half a continent away, Nancy Caldwell (1781–1865) recalled that there was no regular preaching in North Yarmouth, Maine, until the itinerant Joel Ketchum made a foray into the area in 1795. Deeply affected by the preaching of Ketchum and subsequent itinerants, Caldwell, her parents, and siblings all joined the Methodists. "I valued a meeting more than my necessary food," remembered Caldwell. For the Caldwells and thousands like them, the Methodist Church became the one social institution outside the family that gave meaning to their daily struggles and on which they could depend. There was not only the offer of eternal salvation but also the prospect of entertainment and the promise of someone to turn to in times of crisis.[31]

But this kind of growth did not come without risk. First-generation preachers were often threatened with physical attack, particularly during the Revolutionary War when Methodists were generally suspected of Loyalist sympathies, and before the movement had attained any appreciable degree of social legitimacy. American-born Philip Gatch was attacked and beaten on several occasions. In 1775 he was tarred near Baltimore, the hot tar permanently damaging one eye. Between 1778 and 1780, Freeborn Garrettson was beaten, nearly shot, threatened with hanging, and thrown in jail. In 1778 John Littlejohn came close to being tarred and feathered "by some of the bettr sort, as they suppose they are," because they mistakenly assumed he was a Loyalist. "Being denounced from the pulpit as illiterate, unsound in our principles, and enthusiastic in our spirit and practice—in a word, every way incompetent, and only to be despised," wrote the itinerant Thomas Ware reflecting on this early period, "the multitude, men and women, were imboldened to attack us; and it was often a matter of diversion to witness how much they appeared to feel their own superiority."[32]

No less a concern for many a first- and second-generation itinerant was the disapprobation of family members who thought that the young man in question could do better than to become a Methodist preacher, or who feared the consequences of challenging dominant ecclesiastical hierarchies. Dan Young's mother urged him to join the Presbyterians or Baptists rather than the Methodists, and John Littlejohn's mother threatened to disinherit him if he persisted in his preaching. Benjamin Paddock's father found the Methodists to be "about as distasteful to him as any thing well could be." Word that his son planned to join the itinerancy "frenzied him." John Cooper's father "threw a shovelfull of hot embers" on Cooper when he discovered him at prayer, but Cooper became a Methodist preacher anyway.[33] Even the audacious Billy Hibbard had his early doubts about the Methodists. Following his conversion, Hibbard was torn between his desire for respectability and his attraction to Methodism. "I wanted to be a Congregationalist, and to be respectable. But I wanted the love and seriousness of the Methodists," wrote Hibbard. His early public speaking was opposed by his wife, who was embarrassed at her husband's hubris, and by his father, who threatened to disinherit him, and who "reproved me for preaching, because I had not been educated at college."[34] Whatever else might be said in this regard, it is clear that most early itinerants were not pushed into joining the traveling connection by parents or family.

A further risk stemmed directly from the grueling pace of traveling and preaching undertaken by early itinerants. Inevitable risks included sickness and accident. Richmond Nolley died from exposure in 1814 after falling from his horse while fording a stream in a remote area of Louisiana. John Brooks labored so intensely during his first three years in the itinerancy that, he recorded, "I lost my health and broke a noble constitution, so that I have never seen one day since, clear of pain, and sometimes of indescribable sufferings." During one tempestuous revival Brooks lay "sick in bed," but the people "literally forced me out, and made me preach."[35]

The sheer size of many circuits and the number of appointments they included added a further dimension of hardship. Freeborn Garrettson claimed to have traveled over 100,000 miles between 1776 and 1793, while sometimes preaching up to four times a day. Benjamin "Green" Paddock's first two full circuits—the Lyons, New York, circuit in 1810 and the Northumberland, Pennsylvania, circuit in 1811—were both four weeks' circuits of 300 to 400 miles with some 30 preaching appointments per round. In 1812 his appointment was to the Chautauqua circuit, a vast charge covering all or parts of Cattaraugus and Chautauqua Counties in western New York, and Erie, Venango, Crawford, and Warren Counties in northwestern Pennsylvania. Like

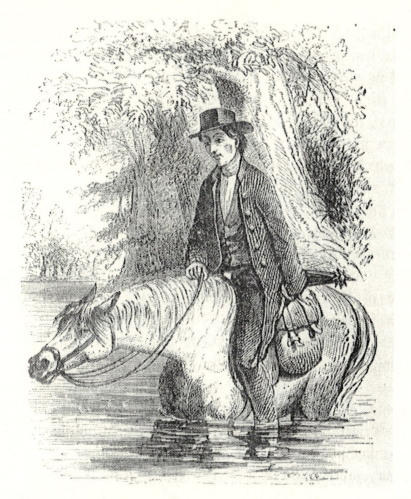

Figure 3.1. Jacob Gruber crossing a stream, from Lebensbilder aus der Ge-schichte des Methodismus (Cincinnati, 1883). *Courtesy of Donald Byrne.*

Paddock's previous two appointments, Chautauqua was a four weeks' circuit of some 400 miles with few roads, numerous streams to cross, and over 30 preaching appointments.[36]

In 1799 Billy Hibbard rode the Cambridge, New York, circuit, a 500-mile, four weeks' circuit with up to 63 preaching appointments plus the responsibility of meeting classes. During the same conference year Thomas Smith estimated that he traveled a remarkable 4,200 miles, preached 324 times, exhorted 64 times, and met classes 287 times on the Flanders, New Jersey, circuit.[37] Likewise, Jacob Young's first assignment was on the Salt River, Kentucky, circuit, a six weeks' circuit of some 500 miles. On his first round the new itinerant delivered 50 sermons in addition to meeting classes and holding prayer meetings. By the conference year 1806 Young routinely reported that he was averaging 30 sermons a month, in addition to class meetings, prayer meetings, and family visitations.[38]

The combination of preachers drawn from artisan backgrounds and integrated into a national network was unique to Methodism. In contrast, the Baptists relied on farmer-preachers, particularly in newly settled regions, who functioned on much the same level as a Methodist local preacher, preaching on Sundays and occasionally at weekday meetings or funerals. Often a Baptist preacher was paid a dollar per meeting, or about the going wage for many skilled workers.[39] Though some state and regional Baptist home missionary societies were organized in the first decade of the nineteenth century, it was not until much later that Baptists effectively banded together on a national level. Hence, the Baptists simply could not match the canvassing power of the Methodist itinerants who preached nearly every day. This was a major reason that while the Baptists grew impressively during the early national period, Methodist expansion was even more remarkable. Sociologists Roger Finke and Rodney Stark have estimated that while the Baptist share of religious adherents increased from 16.9 percent in 1776 to 20.5 percent in 1850, the Methodist share increased from 2.5 percent to 34.2 percent during the same interval.[40]

Along with a frenetic pace of traveling, preaching, and conducting quarterly, class, and prayer meetings, the circuit riders of this period frequently had to contend with poor or uncertain lodging. Most often, the itinerants stayed with sympathetic families along their route, though they sometimes lodged at inns or slept in the open. At the end of one weary day in the North Carolina backcountry, Thomas Ware sought shelter at the isolated cabin of a young couple. "The man gave me to understand, at once, that I could not stay there," recalled Ware. "I looked at him, and smiling, said, that would depend upon our comparative strength." Unwilling to wrestle the preacher, the couple relented, and in the morning Ware baptized their children.[41]

Like most of the itinerants, Henry Smith made it a policy to lodge at the homes in which he preached. But after preaching a funeral sermon in Ohio in 1801, even his resolve was put to a "severe trial." "For when bed-time came I was conducted to the room from which the corpse had been taken a few hours before, to sleep on the bedstead, perhaps the very bed, on which the young man had died, without the house having been scrubbed and properly aired." Smith stuck it out, but fleas and barking dogs kept him awake all night. Thomas Smith had a similar experience while riding the Asbury, New Jersey, circuit in 1807. On this occasion Smith found himself in the uncomfortable situation of having to sleep in the same room with the body of a man who had died that morning. Unlike Henry Smith, he did not last the night, opting instead to sleep outdoors curled up next to a tree root.[42]

Similar experiences led Jacob Young to eventually give up on the policy of always staying where he preached, but not without being challenged by a colleague who accused him of excessive pride and ambition. Young replied that he "would visit the people as far as practicable, catechise them, and pray with them, but, when I could avoid sleeping among fleas and bed-bugs, I intended to do it."[43] The fact that Young had to defend this decision at all indicates the strength of the early circuit riders' commitment to maintaining a close rapport with the people to whom they preached. It was this commitment, perhaps more than anything else, that endeared them to their listeners. Looking back on his career, Henry Smith observed: "If I was but poorly qualified for a missionary in every other respect, I was not in *one thing*; for I had long since conquered my foolish prejudice about eating, drinking, and lodging. I could submit to any kind of inconvenience when I had an opportunity of doing good. . . . My call was among the poor, and among them I could feel myself at home."[44]

The popularity of Methodist preachers among the church's adherents was also, no doubt, in part the result of their small salary. Even so, there were frequent shortfalls. For the fifteen years James Jenkins itinerated, he received $22, $44, $64, $54, $64, $64, $64, $64, $64, $64, $64, $64, $80, $160, and $140, respectively. The long-time itinerant James Quinn traveled for more than 40 years beginning in 1799, mostly in and around the Ohio country. He estimated that at the end of his career the church owed him some $2600 in unpaid salary and expenses. Dan Young likewise realized a $200 shortfall in five years in the itinerancy, and Peter Cartwright calculated his shortfall over the course of his career at $6,400. Nor were things likely to improve with retirement. "I have long since learned that a superannuated Methodist preacher is usually a much more welcome guest in heaven than any where on earth," concluded Quinn at the end of his career. But in the end the financial uncertainty of the itinerancy was perhaps no worse than that faced by most Americans of the period. In many instances shared hardships only served to strengthen the bond between both the preachers themselves, and between preacher and people. "I have observed," wrote the itinerant Benjamin Lakin in 1810, "that where I have suffered most, I always find it hardest to part with the people."[45]

Perhaps Freeborn Garrettson best captured the essence of the resiliency of the early itinerants when he wrote in reference to upstate New York, "I feel for the preachers in these back settlements, for although the people are kind, yet they often have hard fare, and seldom a private room; but it is a most growing country."[46] Growth, that was the measure of success. It required sacrifice, but it also held great promise. Offsetting the rigor of the itinerancy was the potential of getting in on the beginning of something big. It was this potential on which the Methodist system thrived. As a group, the early Methodist preachers were well suited for reaching newly politicized middling Americans. Willing to endure the hardships of the itinerant life, they kept pace with the nation's territorial expansion, remaining both geographically and socially close to their constituents and to potential converts.

As a result of their common social background, similar religious experience, and shared adversity, the itinerants of the early national period not surprisingly developed close personal ties with one another.[47] Cut adrift from family and community, they turned to each other for fellowship, solace, and advice. For many, these friendships lasted a lifetime. "Of all beings on earth, Methodist preachers should love each other," wrote the southern itinerant Joseph Travis. "Their toil, their privations, their self-sacrificing and laborious calling, should ever create a unison of feeling and of sentiment towards each other."[48] The long-time Methodist preacher William Burke, who began his preaching career in 1791 in western Virginia and Tennessee, concluded that the early circuit riders were "like a band of brothers."[49] Sentiments such as these abound in the journals and memoirs of Methodist preachers from every region. "We loved one another," wrote New York's Elijah Woolsey. "We felt willing to live, to suffer, and to die together."[50] Methodist preachers may have ridden their circuits alone, but through quarterly meetings, camp meetings, and annual conferences, and, perhaps most important of all, through a vast correspondence network, they developed and maintained close friendships.[51]

A rare window into how this communications network functioned is afforded to us by a collection of letters written to Daniel Hitt. Born in 1770, Hitt was throughout much of his career a thoroughly average Methodist preacher. He entered the itinerancy in 1790 and traveled extensively in western Pennsylvania, Virginia, and Maryland. In 1795 he was appointed presiding elder over the region encompassing most of western Pennsylvania. In 1807 Hitt became Francis Asbury's traveling companion for one year, and then for eight years served as one of the church's book agents. Thereafter he served as presiding elder over various districts in or near Pennsylvania.[52]

The surviving collection of letters to Daniel Hitt includes 335 letters written between 1788 and 1806 by some 100 people. Some of the letters are from family or former parishioners, but most are from some 50 colleagues. While a small portion of the letters are short notes concerning preaching appointments or other points of business, most are familiar in tone. More than anything else they reveal a vast fraternal network spanning the length and breadth of the

United States. For the circuit rider who changed locations every one or two years, the fellowship of the preachers often provided his most important reference point.

Along with family news and reports on their health, those who wrote to Hitt communicated news of revivals and trials from across the new nation. In 1794 the Methodist preacher Thomas Lyell wrote concerning the Lancaster, Virginia, circuit (a circuit Hitt himself had ridden in 1790): "I can with sorrow inform you that a great declension (greater than ever I expected) prevails:— The friends (if I may call them) are much in the spirit of *Slavery*.—some buying & others repenting that they ever let theirs go free."[53] Lyell's views on slavery were at odds with many on the Lancaster circuit, but he knew he could count on Hitt for a sympathetic ear. And for Thomas Lyell, in many respects this was more important. His association with the people of the Lancaster circuit was, after all, temporary and local; that with his fellow itinerants was lasting and national in scope.

Hitt's correspondents freely shared both their trials and triumphs. In a February 1797 letter, the itinerant Michael H. R. Wilson, then riding the Tioga, Pennsylvania, circuit, informed Hitt that, "My circuit was & is in a disagreeable condition: I turn out ten, where I take in one . . . my labor is not much blest in this place, unless it is blest in turning out disorderly persons." Daniel's brother Samuel Hitt, himself an itinerant, was even less delicate in his assessment of the Harford, Maryland, circuit. "I have accomplished a round on the circuit," wrote Samuel in January 1797, "& find it wants a great deal of pruning and manuring."[54]

Hitt's correspondents also sought and gave advice freely. In February 1796 the Methodist preacher Seely Bunn wrote to Hitt from Baltimore lamenting his own "bashfulness." "I have the greatest power over them in the pulpit & class room: but when I attempt to discharge my duty to individuals in private, they beset me." "Is it so with thee brother?" asked a perplexed Bunn.[55] While Bunn was looking for advice on how to handle contentious members, the itinerant Amos Garrett Thompson was ready to dish some out in a May 1790 letter to Hitt. Thompson, who fancied himself something of a home-grown poet, closed his letter with a composition designed both to admonish Hitt and to warn him against the temptation to marry.

> John saith to the Christians, Live in Love
> And I the saying must approve:
> Love is the prize I hope to gett.
> The prize is free for Daniel Hitt.
> Paul saith believe, but oh for faith,
> That I may find the narrow path;
> Some times I fear I've not a bit,
> How is it with you Brother Hitt?

James saith believe & work also,
One by itself will never do:
Both in concert are sure to get,
True peace for me & Brother Hitt . . .

If I creep slow, let Daniel know;
It's dangerous for to Tarry;
Think of this too, it will not do.
For you or me to marry.

Vexation & strife, and probation & Life,
Our all here on earth is but short;
But a sharp Edged knife, or if you please a Wife:
If it cuts us, it will make us to snort.
Let me & thee, or Hitt or miss,
Go see & be, an heir of bliss
And cry & die, & Spout & stamp,
And try & fly, and rout the camp.

The Devil is a suttle fox
He'll try to get us in a box;
To get our feet into the stocks
And then to shear us of our locks.[56]

Marriage was one of the few immediately perceptible threats to the bond that existed between the traveling preachers. Hence, it is not surprising to find that Thompson was not the only one who wrote to Hitt on this subject. In 1794 Caleb J. Taylor wrote from Kentucky decrying a "marriage Fever" that seemed to be sweeping the ranks of the preachers. "Though I expect you are no misagomist," wrote Seely Bunn later that same year, "[I hope] you will remain in a state of celibacy, yet awhile."[57] Whatever the effect of these persistent warnings, Hitt never married.

The degree of collegiality reflected in the letters to Daniel Hitt persisted as long as the itinerancy remained a viable institution. But over time the itinerancy underwent a gradual transformation, beginning first in the cities and more densely populated regions. By the middle third of the nineteenth century, as fewer preachers willingly moved outside their immediate regions and some even demanded long-term or virtually permanent appointments, the sense of a truly national fellowship among the traveling preachers had begun to fade.

Marriage represented a special challenge for the itinerant system. Most of the first-generation Methodist preachers considered celibacy a necessity, if not a

Figure 3.2. William Capers, from William H. Daniels, Illustrated History of Methodism *(New York, 1880).*

duty. Marriage usually necessitated locating, since the people on most circuits either could not or would not provide enough extra financial support for a preacher's wife or children. So, while marriage was not an outright sin, it was clearly an abdication of a higher calling. Preachers who married and located usually continued as local preachers, though as such they forfeited membership in their conference, becoming something of a second-class citizen. William Capers captured the antagonism toward marriage among first-generation preachers in a speech by the presiding elder Lewis Myers at the South Carolina conference of 1811:

A young man comes to us and says he is called to preach. We answer, "I don't know." He comes a second time, perhaps a third time, even a fourth time, saying, "A dispensation of the gospel is committed unto me, and woe to me if I preach not the gospel." Then we say to him, "Go and try." He goes and tries, and can hardly do it. We bear with him a little while, and he does better. And just as we begin to hope he may make a preacher, lo, he comes again to us, and says, "I must marry." We say to him, "If you marry, you will soon locate: go and preach." "No, I must marry, I *must* marry." We say to him, "A dispensation of the gospel is committed to you, and woe be unto you if you preach not the gospel." "But no," he says, "I *must marry*." And he marries. It is enough to make an angel weep![58]

"In those days of long rides and little quarterage, with no allowance for family expenses, it was deemed vastly imprudent for a young preacher to marry, should he even get an angel for his wife," concluded Capers. Indeed, he discovered just how true this was after marrying Anna White in January 1813. That year the Capers were stationed in Wilmington, North Carolina. Their expenses for "subsistence of the most frugal kind" were $300, while their income was less than $200. Capers located the next year and took up farming. As late as 1809 the Virginia Annual Conference was known as the "Bachelor Conference," since of the 84 preachers present only three were married.[59]

Hence, the decision of whether or not to marry was a difficult one for many preachers and their prospective wives. Some, such as Freeborn Garrettson in the North and James Jenkins in the South, delayed marrying for many years so as not to impede their ministries. Though Jenkins was "strongly tempted" to marry and locate in 1795, in the final analysis, "when I looked over the work and saw the harvest so great, and the labourers so few, I could not reconcile it to my conscience to quit while I was able to hold on." Similarly, Garrettson withdrew a marriage proposal in 1775 after he received what he believed to be a divine impression in the night, saying, "You are about to do your own will; I have a greater work for you: you must go out and preach the gospel."[60] Henry Boehm likewise waited until he was 43 to marry Sarah Hill in 1818, Thomas Ware did not marry until age 38, and Henry Smith waited until 60.[61] All the same, many more married at a more customary age and located to farm or practice a trade. Perhaps no one agonized over this decision more than John Littlejohn.

Almost from the beginning of his itinerant career in 1776, Littlejohn had been considering the possibility of marrying and settling down. Early on he wrote to the veteran preacher George Shadford asking his advice. Shadford wrote back that "he did not approve of my locating."[62] In June 1778 Littlejohn made a dangerous pilgrimage (dangerous because many regarded Methodists as Loyalists at the time) to see Francis Asbury in Delaware and opened his heart to him on the matter. Whatever else he may have said, Asbury promptly sent Littlejohn back to preach on the Baltimore circuit. Soon after, Littlejohn consulted Philip Otterbein, who "gave it as his opinion that I ought to preach, that my call was sufficient," and also the Methodist preacher Philip Gatch, who "wrote to me, to let me know, he wished it was with him as in times past, meang before his marriage."[63] Indeed, about the only person who did not want Littlejohn to continue itinerating was his mother, who threatened to disinherit him if he continued. Not surprisingly, amidst all this dithering his prospective bride grew "much disatisfied wth my intentions."[64]

His doubts notwithstanding, Littlejohn married Monica Talbott of Fairfax County, Virginia, in December 1778, settling soon thereafter in Leesburg, Virginia. "My purpose was to follow my Trade for a support," wrote Littlejohn. "I had no difficulty in deciding to Locate as I then reviewed it improper for a Methodist Preecher to travel the Circuit after they were married."[65] In all likelihood, more than two-thirds of the late eighteenth- and early nineteenth-century itinerants followed a course similar to John Littlejohn's.[66]

But as time went on, more and more preachers continued to itinerate even after marrying. Some of their wives became more involved in their ministries, rather than simply living with relatives or friends while their husbands traveled, while others singlehandedly ran their households during their husbands' long absences. Most were as committed to the spread of the Methodist message as their husbands were, if not more so. A case in point is Betsey Roye Lakin. In February 1796, Benjamin Lakin wrote in his journal, "Was much exercised about Marrying, an object presented herself before my mind, many delights appeard in that state of life; But I believe I can serve God and be more useful in my present state." But by March 1798 Lakin had changed his mind, and in April of that year he married Betsey Roye and located. Two years later, at Betsey's urging and following a series of prophetic dreams and omens, Lakin rejoined the traveling connection, accepting appointment to the Limestone, Kentucky, circuit. Lakin continued to travel for the next 20 years, with Betsey often accompanying him. Frequently plagued by self-doubts, it is unlikely that Lakin would have reentered or remained in the itinerancy without Betsey's unflagging support. Once, after a run-in with his presiding elder, he decided to quit the itinerancy. "But when I came to inform my wife of my intentions she opposed me in my plan, and insisted that I was not traveling for the President Elder But for God and if God had called me to the work I aut [ought] not to quit it."[67]

Much as Benjamin Lakin had done, Elijah Woolsey married in 1797 and reentered the traveling connection in 1800. Woolsey's wife often assisted in his meetings by "praying with and comforting the mourners." Similarly, Joseph Travis continued to itinerate after marrying Elizabeth Forster in 1811, as did Jacob Young after marrying Ruth Spahr and Lovick Pierce after marrying Ann Foster, both in 1809. In 1812 while Young was in charge of the Ohio district, he noted that, because of the economic impact of the war, some of the itinerants "felt discouraged, and some thought of retiring from the work, but their

courage revived again, their wives were zealous for the good cause, and exhorted their husbands to weather the storm."[68] Sibbel Hibbard consistently
offered this kind of support to her husband, the itinerant Billy Hibbard.
Though she opposed Billy's public speaking early on, by the time he launched
his itinerant career in 1797 Hibbard could write, "My dear wife instead of
desiring me to stay at home, exhorted me to trust in the Lord, and be faithful
to do my duty; she assured me that nothing could induce her to give me up."
During the succeeding years Sibbel took in weaving and spinning, earning
$300 over one three-year stretch, and briefly ran a school for some 30 children.

Alfred Brunson, whose wife once ran a boarding house to augment the
family income, even argued that marriage was an advantage for a Methodist
itinerant because it served to more firmly "fasten" him to the local community.
Writing in the 1840s, the long-time itinerant Henry Smith also argued in favor
of itinerants marrying:

> We take up a young, inexperienced man, and admit him on trial, with the
> expectation that he will lay aside the spirit and study of the world, and devote
> himself wholly to his religious studies, and the work of the ministry, to which
> he solemnly professes to be called. But the first or second circuit he goes to,
> he seems to forget his solemn pledge, and enters prematurely into matrimonial
> engagements, and fills the circuit with more talk about his courtship than his
> usefulness, or the number of souls converted through his instrumentality. This
> may afford some amusement to the young and chaffy professors, but it rolls
> trouble upon the hearts of the more serious and zealous of the flock of Christ,
> over which he is made an overseer, and thus ends his call to itinerate; for he
> drives down his stake, and enters into other business.

"Better take one well made, well married, laborious, enterprising minister of
Jesus Christ, than half a dozen such fickle-minded boys," concluded Smith.[69]

Analyses such as Smith's and Brunson's represented a subtle, yet profound
shift in American Methodism, and indeed in much of the larger culture as
well.[70] The post-revolutionary years had been a period of unprecedented upheaval in which only the most basic elements of past religious structures and
practices seemed immune to change. In this atmosphere, American Methodism
both nurtured and relied on a cadre of zealous young preachers willing, at least
for a time, to sacrifice all in their quest to evangelize the nation. Methodist
preachers were liminal figures in regards to their celibacy, but unlike the Shakers, Mormons, and Oneida Perfectionists of the 1830s and 1840s, their practice
did not lead to some new, radical concept of marriage and the family.[71] The
celibacy of the itinerants was never an overt attempt to redefine sexual relations and the family, but rather a matter of pragmatic expediency during the
movement's most volatile, formative years. When the immediate need for celibacy faded, so too did the practice among Methodist preachers.

In their marriage practices and attitudes toward the family, Methodist preachers never operated very far outside the prevailing values of middling Americans. By the 1810s and 1820s, as Methodist societies became more numerous and more prosperous, and the church in general became more socially respectable, fewer preachers were willing to forgo marriage and a settled home life, and fewer of their parishioners saw it as a preacher's duty to do so. Married preachers were able to continue itinerating, but only because in most regions of the country circuits became more compact, closer to one another, and less difficult to travel, while salaries increased and became more dependable—in short because the itinerancy did not demand the same sacrifices that it once had.

This transition can be seen in the autobiography of Mary Orne Tucker (1794–1865), a rare first-person memoir by the wife of a Methodist preacher. Born in Corinth, Vermont, Tucker's parents farmed out their children to relatives early on because of financial pressures. Mary was thus raised by a relatively well-to-do aunt and uncle on a farm near Charlestown, New Hampshire. Tucker's religious curiosity was first aroused when Francis Asbury visited her home, and later stimulated by an elderly wayfarer whom the family took in on a stormy winter night. Before retiring to bed, the man sang from a Methodist hymnbook, prompting Mary to ask, "Do tell me, old man, what makes you look so happy? You are poor, and you came here on foot in this severe storm; I am certain that you possess but little to render life cheerful, yet you seem perfectly so." The man simply replied that he was a Methodist, but this was enough to arouse Mary's curiosity about what at that time seemed a mysterious and shadowy sect.[72]

Mary was converted in 1812, and in 1816 married Thomas Wait Tucker (1791–1871), despite the "opposition of near and dear friends who . . . thought me rash and foolish in uniting my destiny with that of a penniless Methodist preacher."[73] That year Thomas was appointed to the Athens, Vermont, circuit, a three weeks' circuit of 160 miles. During Thomas's first tour of the circuit Mary boarded with a family in Athens. But when Thomas returned, she insisted on accompanying him, over his objections, by riding two to the horse. "We set out in rather awkward style, which afforded a little amusement to some of the lookers on, but it did not disconcert me, as I expected to improve by practice. It was not a very comfortable mode of traveling, but a perfectly safe one for me, as I was young and nimble as a squirrel. . . . We were every where received with the greatest cordiality, and my first essay at circuit travelling was successful."[74]

Combative and energetic, Mary would need all these qualities to persevere through the trials of the early rural itinerancy. At one house, holes in the walls and roof allowed enough snow to blow into their bedroom so that it became ankle deep by morning. On another occasion the Tuckers were invited to share a dinner being cooked on the same fire over which an old horse that "had recently died a natural death" was being boiled for soap grease. Mary noted with dismay that the contents of the two kettles occasionally frothed over into one another.[75]

In time, material circumstances gradually improved for the Tuckers, though Thomas never rose above ordinary stature as a preacher and often suffered from poor health. Stage travel became more widespread and the Tuckers were routinely appointed to one after another of the rapidly multiplying city stations in New England. In 1818 and 1819 Thomas was stationed in Bristol, Rhode Island, and in 1820 and 1821 in Somerset, Massachusetts, followed by appointments in New London, Connecticut; Milford, Massachusetts; Lisbon, New Hampshire; Weymouth, Massachusetts; Newport, Rhode Island; and Wilbraham, Massachusetts. In 1837 Mary, who wanted to be near her grown children, accompanied Thomas to the annual conference in Springfield, Massachusetts. When Thomas's station was announced as a town in lower Rhode Island, she went to bishop Elijah Hedding and had the appointment changed to Millbury, Massachusetts.[76] This of course was a far cry from the way things had been done in the days of Francis Asbury, as Tucker herself fully realized, and was indicative of how settled and comfortable Methodism was becoming by the second quarter of the nineteenth century.

Shifts in Francis Asbury's attitude about marriage also reflect this same trend toward a settled clergy. Always concerned with maintaining the movement's popularity and its ability to reach the broadest possible audience, Asbury initially opposed his preachers marrying. "No man I ever knew cherished a higher Christian regard for the female character than he," wrote Thomas Ware concerning Asbury's stance on marriage circa 1790, "yet, for the sake of the itinerancy, he chose a single life, and was doubtless well pleased with those preachers who, for the same reason, followed his example."[77] "Some men marry fortunes, and go to take care of them; some men marry wives, and go to make fortunes for them; and thus, when, for the time, we should have age and experience in the ministry, we have youth and inexperience," Asbury remarked to James Quinn in 1803.[78] As late as 1805, when Asbury heard of Thomas Coke's marriage in England, he wrote, "Marriage is honourable in all—but to me it is a ceremony awful as death. Well may it be so, when I calculate we have lost the travelling labours of two hundred of the best men in America, or the world, by marriage and consequent location."[79] But as it became easier for a married preacher to itinerate, and, indeed, as the people began to expect their preachers to marry, Asbury at times gave his blessing to a circuit rider's marriage. Hence, in 1803, he gave his blessing to James Quinn's marriage at the age of 28, and at the 1804 Virginia Annual Conference he defended admitting the married Samuel Monnett on trial, stating, "Better take preachers well married, than be at the trouble of marrying them after you get them."[80]

However strong his misgivings about a settled clergy may have been, Asbury could not deny that, like Mary Tucker, many preachers' wives worked tirelessly in support of their husbands and the church. "With youthful ardor and sanguine expectations," wrote Tucker after 30 years of marriage and itinerancy, "I set out upon life's great journey, determined if I could not labor like my husband in a public manner, I would devote all my energies to smooth his rough paths, and strengthen his hands for the great work of saving souls." However confining this role may seem from our perspective, it was one that Tucker readily and gladly accepted. Despite the sacrifices demanded of an itinerant's wife, she enjoyed a strong relationship with Thomas throughout their married life. "It may be thought by some, of cold practical natures, that the old and gray headed should have done with romance . . . that the happiness of wedded love is a thing of the past," wrote Mary in the late 1840s. This, she admitted, might be true for those whose marriage was based only on "sentiment." But "those whose affections are founded upon true love and esteem, and nurtured by constancy and unselfishness, grow in strength with each succeeding year . . . the silken cord that first bound such hearts together is gently drawn tighter, and the crosses and afflictions shared in common bind them the more firmly."[81]

Indeed, by the 1820s and 1830s the strong but domesticated faith of Mary Tucker was in many ways more representative of American Methodism than was that of Francis Asbury. It is telling that after Asbury's death in 1816, the two men elected bishops in his place, Enoch George and Robert R. Roberts, were both married.[82]

The development of close personal ties between the preachers formed the foundation of Methodist ministerial training. In many respects the Methodist system was based on the artisan concept of apprenticeship. Unwilling to submit to lengthy, traditional programs of theological education, newly licensed Methodist preachers were tutored on-the-job by more experienced colleagues. In place of any kind of seminary or college training, less experienced preachers were often paired with better seasoned itinerants on the same circuit.

Though early Methodists rejected traditional theological education, they by no means rejected learning per se. "We do not despise learning," declared the itinerant Thomas Ware, "on the contrary we hold it to be desirable. But we do not deem it an essential qualification of a gospel minister. Grace, rather than human learning, qualifies a man to preach." And grace, as the itinerant William Beauchamp was fond of pointing out, could most readily be measured by the conversion of souls. Hence from the very start Methodist preachers were judged in the eyes of their colleagues and congregations by the results of their preaching. Early Methodist sermons invariably emphasized the practical, the immediate, and the dramatic. "People love the preacher who makes them feel," concluded Ware.[83]

Despite their aversion to formal schooling, one of the by-products of conversion and entrance into the ministry for a number of early itinerants was a newly awakened desire to read. "Such was my thirst for knowledge," wrote Alfred Brunson, reflecting on his early career, "that when I could not get lights in the house, I have sat for hours out-of-doors and read by moonlight." Similarly, following his conversion, Jacob Young "began to feel an intense thirst for knowledge . . . the desire to improve my mind increased daily." He pored over the Bible, read Freeborn Garrettson's journal, Fletcher's *Appeal* and *Works*, Baxter's *Saints' Everlasting Rest*, and Wesley's *Sermons*.[84] Like Young and many of his contemporaries, Billy Hibbard embarked on a similar course of reading early in his career. "Though I had only a small degree of education, barely a common school education," wrote Hibbard, "yet I could sometimes read one hundred pages in a long winter's evening, and the next day work hard at farming business, dressing flax, threshing grain, chopping wood; working with my hands, that I might not be chargeable to any, and have something good to feed the Methodist preacher and his horse."[85] From the beginning, Wesley had placed a premium on encouraging his preachers and people to read, and literacy remained an important part of the Methodist experience in America. Like Wesley, Asbury and his colleagues believed strongly in the power of the written word. If a preacher claimed "I have no *Taste* for Reading," the 1784 *Discipline* advised him to "Contract a Taste for it by Use, or return to your Trade."[86]

Indeed, an impressive number of the late eighteenth- and early nineteenth-century preachers improved their literacy dramatically following their conversions, as the life of Sampson Maynard illustrates. The son of a carpenter, Maynard was born in England about 1757. Early on he was apprenticed to a butcher, but soon ran away, eventually learning carpentry from his father. When the Revolutionary War broke out, Maynard again ran away, this time to join the British navy. After five years at sea he returned to England, leaving the navy and returning to carpentry once again. "I rambled from town to city, and worked at my trade," he wrote, "for I hated the name of a lazy fellow, nor could I bare to go in rags as I saw some of my shop-mates. . . ."[87] His conversion was the result of an intense visionary experience in which Satan confronted him in his shop. In 1795 Maynard left England for New York, where he was ordained as both a deacon and an elder, all as a local preacher while still working at his trade. Maynard reported that he could barely read when converted, but by the end of his career he was able to compose an autobiographical work of some 252 pages. Likewise, Benjamin Abbott's autobiography is nearly 200 pages, Billy Hibbard's is 368 pages, Jacob Young's is 528 pages, and Alfred Brunson's stretches to more than 800 pages.

What is perhaps most important to understand in this respect is that though almost none of the early Methodist preachers had a classical education, most were at least as well educated as the bulk of their audience. They had enough learning to make them respectable to their listeners, but not so much as to make them appear distant or irrelevant.

The autobiography of William Capers (1790–1855) sheds additional light on the training of young Methodist preachers and the bonds that formed between them. Capers's account is particularly valuable because, though he became a thoroughgoing Methodist preacher, his upbringing, conversion, and career were in many respects atypical. Hence, his background demanded that he reason through what most early itinerants took for granted. The son of a slave-holding plantation owner and a former Revolutionary War officer, Capers was born in January 1790 near Charleston, South Carolina. Unlike most Methodist itinerants he grew up in relative affluence. As a youth, he attended boarding schools, entering South Carolina College in 1805 with the ability to read some Latin and Greek. Eager to make a name for himself in local politics, he dropped out of college in 1808 and began studying law.[88]

Prior to this time, Capers had attended camp meetings in 1802, 1803, and 1806 near his home. At the first two of these meetings he witnessed first hand the "jerks," the "jumping exercise," and other forms of convulsive enthusiasm often associated with turn-of-the-century revivals. At all three meetings Capers saw large numbers fall in a swoon, appearing "senseless, and almost lifeless, for hours together; lying motionless at full length on the ground, and almost as pale as corpses." He came away from these meetings with a deep sense of conviction, but remained unconverted. "I did not fall at any time, as I saw others do," he later recalled. "I kept myself aloof, I knew not why."[89]

In 1808 Capers was again convicted of his lost spiritual state following yet another camp meeting. As a result he gave up studying law and looked for an opportunity to join the Methodists. "I longed with intense desire for the time to arrive when, by joining the Church, I should formally break with the world, and identify myself with those who . . . for being the most spiritual and least worldly, were regarded the most enthusiastic and least rational of all the sects of Christians." Capers did in fact join the Methodists in August 1808, but an incident from this event reveals how little he actually understood of the movement at the time. Following the meeting, Capers, who was dressed "in the point of fashion, with a deep frill of linen cambric and a full-sized breastpin at my bosom," went to the home of an "old Methodist." There he was advised that he should quit wearing ruffles and breastpins, or at least find a way to "hide them." At first he was "profoundly puzzled"; why would anyone want to hide fine clothes? But he soon caught on, and proceeded to "rip off the frill from my bosom, which my sister kept, as a memorial of those simple-hearted times, for many years." Later, Capers would even forgo wearing suspenders because they struck some of his listeners as too pretentious.[90]

On the day that Capers joined the church, the itinerant William Gassaway asked him to accompany him on his circuit. Capers agreed and, much to his surprise, was immediately called on to exhort following Gassaway's sermons. Why would someone who was still unsure of his conversion be afforded such treatment? Most likely Gassaway simply could not resist the temptation to have a member of the local gentry by his side, or pass up the opportunity to draw someone of social distinction further inside the Methodist orbit. If so, the tour had the desired effect. As he traveled with Gassaway, Capers gradually became confident of his own conversion, though he never had the kind of dramatic encounter so typical of early Methodist preachers. He also felt increasingly called to preach, and proposed that he should embark on "a regular course of divinity studies, which I should pursue without interruption for several years." Gassaway objected, telling him that the Methodist way was "to study and preach and preach and study, from day to day."

> He admitted that on my plan he might learn more theology, and be able to compose a better thesis, but insisted he would not make a better preacher. In this argument he insisted much on the practical character of preaching: that to reach its end, it must be more than a well-composed sermon, or an eloquent discourse, or able dissertation. It must have to do with men as a shot at a mark; in which not only the ammunition should be good, but the aim true. . . . And the force of preaching must largely depend, under the blessing of God, on the naturalness and truthfulness of the preacher's postulates; arguing to the sinner from what he knows of him. . . .

"The true question was as to usefulness, not eminence," concluded Capers.[91]

Capers eventually came to accept what most new itinerants realized up front: Methodist preachers were literally trained on-the-job, learning by observation and through coaching from their more experienced colleagues to preach forceful, pragmatic, vernacular sermons. "The traveling preacher finds himself providentially initiated into a great theological school, where study and practice move on together," wrote Charles Giles. "What he gains by study is brought into daily use; and hence it becomes deeply printed on the memory. . . . So he must pursue his course of learning through life, and graduate on the day of his death."[92]

Seasoned preachers like Gassaway often made a practice of taking junior colleagues under their wings. Alfred Brunson looked to Shadrach Bostwick as his mentor. Bostwick had begun itinerating in 1791 and located in 1805. Thereafter, "his house was a theological school," wrote Brunson, "where he gave many lectures and model sermons, from which we [the younger preachers] obtained much useful knowledge pertaining to our holy calling."

In addition to mentoring by senior colleagues and presiding elders, the younger itinerants also evaluated and advised one another. While appointed to the same circuit, Brunson and Calvin Ruter agreed to critique each others sermons. "No one step in my life contributed so much to correct my language in public speaking as this," wrote Brunson. According to William Capers, the younger preachers of his day were rarely together for any length of time without exchanging this kind of advice. "It might be in their pronunciation of such or such a word, some article of dress, or the way the hair was combed," recalled Capers, "or it might be something more serious, touching their spirit or manners; so that we were always watching over each other, and, as I believe, for good."[93]

Some of the better educated and more experienced preachers were of course capable of producing subtle, well-crafted sermons. Ezekiel Cooper (1763–1847)

Figure 3.3. Ezekiel Cooper, from Abel Stevens, History of the Methodist Episcopal Church in the United States of America (New York, 1867).

was known as one of early American Methodism's outstanding preachers and debaters. Born in eastern Maryland, Cooper left home in 1783 to become a joiner, but reluctantly agreed, at the insistence of Francis Asbury, to take up the Caroline, Maryland, circuit in 1784. Like many itinerants, he kept both a journal and a circuit notebook. For each year, the notebook contains a listing of each preaching place, plus the dates and sermon texts for each appointment. These notebooks reveal that on rural circuits Cooper preached up to 400 times a year. On the East Jersey circuit in 1786–1787 he preached 345 times, but used only 73 scripture passages, or texts. Twelve of these texts were used 10 or more times. Mark 13:37 and I Thessalonians 5:19 were Cooper's favorites that year; he used each at least 20 times. Both Mark 13:37 ("And what I say unto you I say unto all, Watch.") and I Thessalonians 5:19 ("Quench not the Spirit.") are short, cryptic passages that could no doubt be turned to several purposes. Nonetheless, Cooper's sermons on these passages could be memorable events. Elijah Woolsey distinctly remembered Cooper preaching from Mark 13:37 more than four decades after the event, describing the sermon as "a dagger to my heart."[94]

After Cooper had spent only four years on rural circuits, Asbury began stationing him in important town pulpits. In these settings Cooper honed his skills as an orator. Here he spent more of his time meeting classes and calling on members, and less time preaching. He also did not have the luxury of being able to repeat himself as often. In Annapolis, Cooper preached only 185 times during the conference year 1789–1790, but used 120 texts.[95]

But most of the early itinerants were less inventive than Ezekiel Cooper. Twenty-nine of Thomas Smith's preaching texts for 1798 through 1802 are recorded in his memoirs. Of these, nine are from the book of Matthew. Indeed, during Smith's first year of itinerating it seems he read or preached from little else! In the ensuing years Smith expanded his sights to include the writings of Paul, the other gospels, and a handful of Old Testament books, but the majority of the Bible never found its way into his preaching.[96] Thomas Morris's journal for January 1816 to February 1817 on the Marietta, Ohio, circuit reveals a similar pattern of repetition and selectivity. Apart from the Psalms, the newly licensed Morris preached almost exclusively from a limited number of New Testament passages.[97]

Of itself, this pattern did not represent a failing on the part of either Smith or Morris. The first *Discipline* of 1785 stated that the goal of Methodist preaching was to deal with an audience "so as to get within them, and suit all our Discourse to their several Conditions and Tempers: To chuse the fittest Subjects, and to follow them with a holy Mixture of Seriousness, and Terror, and Love, and Meekness."[98] In other words, as Philip Gatch pointed out, the goal was to aim "more at the heart than the head," to link the concerns of everyday life to the ultimate fate of one's eternal soul. Gatch's sermons relied heavily on anecdotes, leading Henry Smith to describe him as a "close home preacher." "Sound Wesleyanism," according to James Quinn, was best represented by "a truly evangelical sermon—no philosophical chaff or metaphysical froth."[99] Charles Giles remembered that the early Methodist preachers in upstate New York spoke "plainly and forcibly." Their sermons were rarely "formal and lifeless, but close, alarming; pointed, and practical." Added Giles: "It is a lamentable fact, which cannot be concealed, that there are many ministers in the different churches, famed for their talents and learning, who have attracted much attention, and often obtained the applause of men, but never have made a Felix tremble, or caused an infidel to blush, or converted one sinner from the error of his ways. No signs follow them but worldly honours, pride, affluence, and moral death."[100]

However partisan this assessment may be, the early Methodist preachers were clearly cut from different cloth than many of their counterparts in the established churches. Anning Owen, an itinerant who spent most of his 20-year career from 1795 to 1814 in western New York, was known as "Bawling Owen" because of his vociferous preaching style. Lovick Pierce reportedly could preach three 3–hour sermons in a day, "and then sing the doxology with as clear a tone as when he rose in the morning." James Meacham most often used the word *cry* in his journal to describe his own sermon delivery, as in "many precious souls, to whom I cryed . . . " Likewise, when the itinerant Jimmy Jenkins prayed, it was said that his "soul, voice, strength, all went in. The sound was as the roar of a tempest, ablaze with lightning, and pealing with thunder." In this regard, Owen, Pierce, Meacham, and Jenkins were simply following the advice of Francis Asbury, who once urged one of his preachers to "feel for the power, feel for the power, brother."[101]

Sometimes a preacher's illustrations could be dramatic. Benjamin Abbott once preached a funeral sermon to the accompaniment of a violent thunderstorm: "I lost no time, but set before them the awful coming of Christ, in all his splendour, with all the armies of heaven, to judge the world and to take vengeance on the ungodly! It may be, cried I, that he will descend in the next clap of thunder! The people screamed, screeched, and fell all through the house." Abbott's sermons (at times he claimed to be given sermon texts in his dreams) were often the occasion of such emotional outbursts. At one particularly boisterous meeting, people shouted and fell to the floor while others rushed the door or jumped out of windows to escape the mayhem inside. In the midst of it all a woman cried out that Abbott must be a devil to cause such a stir, but Abbott himself was quite pleased with the whole affair.[102] Similarly, Joseph Everett once preached a sermon during a storm in which he twice entreated God to "send thy thunder still nigher." According to one account, the next day a man attempted to get a legal injunction against Everett's preaching, stating that "he verily believed that had Mr. Everett called the third time, they would all have been struck dead."[103] This last embellishment may well be apocryphal, but it nonetheless illustrates the emotional appeal associated with early Methodist preaching.

Clearly the Methodist style of preaching was new and even shocking at first for many Americans. According to Jesse Lee, when Robert Williams first preached in Norfolk, Virginia, in 1772, "the general conclusion was, that they never heard such a man before: for they said, sometimes he would preach, then he would pray, then he would swear, and at times he would cry." Explained Lee: "The people were so little used to hearing a preacher say hell, or Devil in preaching, that they thought he was swearing, when he told them about going to hell." But by the early nineteenth century the Methodists had helped to alter the tone and appearance of both sermon and preacher to such a degree that this kind of preaching was widely recognized, if not universally welcomed. According to Abner Chase, two lawyers once happened upon a meeting at which the itinerant William Keith was about to preach. Seeing Keith, one lawyer quipped, "If that is the preacher, I think we shall get but little to-night." "Don't be hasty in making your conclusion," replied the other, "you can never tell how far a toad will hop from his appearance."[104]

Because Methodist preachers were largely judged by their ability to evoke a heart-swelling response and their willingness to endure the rigors of itinerant life, rather than for their theological polish, many began their preaching careers at a remarkably young age. Seth Crowell and Benjamin Paddock began exhorting at ages 14 and 16, respectively, and were appointed to their first circuits at 18 and 20; George Gary began itinerating in 1809 at age 15, as did Martin Ruter in 1800 at 16, both in New England; Lovick Pierce joined the South Carolina conference as a traveling preacher in 1804 at the age of 19, despite never having attended school more than six months in his life; and Seth Mattison was licensed to exhort in 1805 at age 17 and as a local preacher at 19.[105] In June 1801 Laban Clark attended his first annual conference in New York City. As he gazed at the assembled preachers, Clark noted with approval that "the conference was composed mostly of young men in the prime of life and none past the meridian and vigour of manhood . . . looking at them I said to myself[,] with such men we can take the world."[106]

The typical early circuit rider preached from a basic set of scripture texts embellished with anecdotes and analogies from everyday life. The doctrinal content of his sermons was no doubt consistently Wesleyan, and both his character and beliefs were subject to an annual review. But what few expository skills he may have utilized were largely gleaned from the sermons of his colleagues. He learned to preach with what the itinerant Henry Smith referred to as an irresistible "holy 'knock-'em-down' power."[107] Nothing would have been more unthinkable to a Methodist itinerant than the dispassionate reading of a prepared sermon. They invariably preached extemporaneously, without the aid of notes or manuscript. In the ardently egalitarian and turbulent post-revolutionary years, the itinerants succeeded in both establishing a rapport with their audiences and stunning them with an apocalyptic vision of impending divine judgement. Largely self-educated, they instinctively understood the importance of speaking in the vernacular. They were both familiar and frightening—homespun heralds of a gospel that was attune to everyday life and common experience, and unsettling in its larger implications. This proved to be an alluring combination.

This appeal was something the famous evangelist Charles Finney clearly understood. "Look at the Methodists," wrote Finney relatively early in his career. "Many of their ministers are unlearned, in the common sense of the term, many of them taken right from the shop or the farm, and yet they have gathered congregations, and pushed their way, and won souls every where. Wherever the Methodists have gone, their plain, pointed and simple, but warm and animated mode of preaching has always gathered congregations." "We must have exciting, powerful preaching, or the devil will have the people, except what the Methodists can save," concluded Finney.[108] Early Methodist preachers popularized American religion not so much out of ideological conviction but because it was the only world they knew. They were natives in the early republican world of egalitarianism, geographic mobility, and the religious free market—a world in which the older denominations were still but immigrants.

4 The Social Principle

Christianity is essentially a
social religion . . . to turn it into
a solitary one is to destroy it.

—John Wesley, from "Upon Our
Lord's Sermon on the Mount"

*L*ike all popular religious movements,
American Methodism was, at heart, a local event. Its itinerant plan ensured
both that each community would have some direct connection with the movement as a whole and that lay members would have a remarkable degree of
input in shaping the character of the church. On the standard four weeks'
circuit, an itinerant might visit each society only twice a month, and then
only rarely on a Sunday. At all other times the administration of the church
was in the hands of local preachers, lay exhorters, stewards, and class leaders.[1]
The continuity of the class meetings, quarterly meetings, love feasts, and camp
meetings, and the constancy of Methodist discipline, all acted as a counter-
weight to the transience of the itinerancy. Together, these community events
did much to define the "movement culture" of Methodism's connectional system.[2] They prevented American Methodism from either splintering into a series of disjointed revivals or turning to congregationalism. No other religious
movement of the period, including the Baptists, could call on such a uniform
set of nationally recognized institutions. No labor association could match the
national scope of Methodism's appeal among artisans and middling folk of the
early republic.

The fundamental institutional building block of American Methodism was
the class meeting. Originating under John Wesley in the 1740s, these gatherings were partially modeled after the late seventeenth- and early eighteenth-
century religious societies of the Church of England and the communal piety

of the Moravian Bands. Wesley had direct experience with both, incorporating elements of each into the design of the class meeting.[3] But like many Methodist institutions, the immediate origins of the class meeting were more pragmatic in nature. Beginning in 1739 the Methodist society at Bristol had gone into debt to build a new meeting room. In February 1742 while Wesley was in Bristol, a Captain Foy suggested that the debt could be retired if each member would give a penny a week. When someone objected that some of the members were too poor to give even this, Foy proposed that about ten or twelve of these be assigned to him. Each week he would collect what they could give, making up the balance himself. Others made the same offer, and Wesley divided the Bristol society under these leaders.[4]

Wesley quickly discovered that what began as a financial expedient had far greater possibilities. One of the Bristol leaders soon informed Wesley that while making his rounds he had found a man quarreling with his wife and another drunk. "This is the thing; the very thing we have wanted so long," thought Wesley. "The Leaders are the persons who may not only receive the contributions, but also watch over the souls of their brethren." Wesley soon introduced the Bristol system in London, and thereafter wherever Methodism spread. Hence, from the 1740s on, the class meeting was the foundation of both Methodist finances and Methodist corporate piety and discipline.[5]

From the beginning, class meetings were an integral part of the Methodist connection in America. Like Wesley, American Methodists often referred to class meetings as the "sinews of Methodism." Thomas Rankin began visiting all the classes in New York City soon after his arrival in America in 1773. In May 1774 he did the same again, and was happy to report that "their number increases and I hope their grace also." John Littlejohn's journal indicates that during his brief itinerant career in Maryland, Delaware, and Virginia from 1776 to 1778, he, like all Methodist circuit riders of his day, spent as much time meeting classes as he did preaching. The same was true of James Meacham, whose journal for the years 1789–1797 includes almost as many references to meeting classes as to preaching. "I have so often observed the blessed Effects of the class Meeting that I highly esteem it, one of the richest pastures we enjoy," wrote Meacham in 1789. "It appears if we were not to enjoy that privilege our people (would) soon be a lump or body of formality."[6]

Assuming an average of 30 members per class meeting, by 1815 there would have been more than 7,000 Methodist classes in the United States. This organizational strength far exceeded that of any other comparable movement of the time. The class meeting was the basic building block of early American Methodism, and without it the movement would not have been nearly the same. Neither the itinerancy nor the Methodist brand of piety could have long survived the movement's rapid, predominantly rural-based expansion without the grassroots support generated through the class meetings.

Many, if not most, of the early itinerants began their careers as class leaders, remaining committed to the institution ever afterwards. Henry Boehm was a class leader for more than two years before joining the itinerancy. "To the class-meeting I am greatly indebted," reflected Boehm near the end of his career. "There I was 'strengthened,' 'stablished,' 'settled.' "[7] "Our classes form the pillars of our work," declared Edmund S. Janes, "and . . . are in a considerable degree our universities for the ministry."[8] After joining the church in South Carolina in 1789, the future itinerant James Jenkins and his brother regularly rode 12 miles to their class meeting. Even though they had to cross a river and a swamp, "it was a rare thing to miss our meeting." "Class-meetings assisted me in various ways," recalled Jenkins. "Here I was drilled and instructed, warned and comforted; and so fond was I of them, that I would rather miss hearing an ordinary sermon than neglect my class." Henry Smith similarly concluded that no matter how awkward he might have felt while preaching, "I was always at home in class meeting."[9]

Without the class meetings, many Methodist converts would undoubtedly have drifted into other denominations or demanded some sort of settled clergy. "No institution of Methodism is more important than that of the classes—not even the itinerancy," wrote Leonidas Rosser at mid-century, "for the evangelical fruits of the itinerancy cannot long be preserved without the use and help of the classes." Churches with a settled ministry might not need such an institution, but for an itinerant ministry it was indispensable. "Let the classes be disbanded, and the Methodist Church is dissolved," argued Rosser. "Let this institution be abolished, and Itinerancy, the glory of constitutional Methodism, is powerless, and must soon be exchanged for some other method of preserving and superintending the church."[10]

In America throughout the late eighteenth and early nineteenth centuries, as in England, membership in a class largely defined who was, and who was not, a Methodist. Methodists were not so much members of societies, circuits, or districts as they were of a particular class. New members were received on a six-month probationary basis. Apart from curious seekers, who were customarily allowed to attend three or four meetings before joining, attendance at class meetings was both required of and limited to members in good standing.[11] This exclusiveness formed the foundation of Methodist solidarity and communal identity. It was also responsible for much of the curiosity and even suspicion that class meetings often aroused when introduced in new regions.

When class meetings were first formed along the banks of the Little Miami River in Ohio, they kindled a great deal of excitement. Henry Smith recalled that at one meeting held in a second-floor room, "so great was the curiosity to see and hear what was done in class meeting, that the stair steps were crowded, and some got upon the trees that stood round the house, to look through the windows." Prejudices against the class meeting were stronger and more enduring in New England than perhaps anywhere else in the nation. There, the concept of state-sanctioned religion under the control of society's elites was staunchest, and upstart sects with an air of secrecy or exclusivity were viewed with great suspicion. The itinerant Dan Young, a native of New Hampshire, recalled that during Methodism's early days in New England, class meetings were often "represented . . . as the scenes of the worst crimes, the place where plans of treason were concocted, and politics, with all their bitterness, dragged in."[12]

Class leaders were usually lay men and women chosen or approved by the itinerant preacher in charge of the circuit or city station. Unlike Congregationalists, Episcopalians, or Presbyterians, Methodists encouraged artisans, farmers, petty merchants, and, at times, women and African Americans to participate in the leadership of the church as class leaders and stewards. In late eighteenth- and early nineteenth-century Baltimore, as Charles Steffen has noted, most class leaders were successful mechanics—shoemakers, carpenters, shipwrights and so forth—with assessed assets of more than $1,200, or double the average for all Baltimore mechanics. In New York City, the majority of class leaders in 1812 were small masters, journeymen, master craftsmen, and shopkeepers. Hence, while not elites, class leaders tended to be the more successful and respected members of their neighborhoods and villages.[13] Though perhaps more ambitious than most, they were still very much a part of the local Methodist community. Like the circuit riders, they were cut from the same cloth as their fellow Methodists, and could readily understand their hopes, fears, and deepest aspirations.

Besides conducting the weekly meeting, class leaders were generally responsible for keeping attendance records, collecting and recording contributions, visiting sick and delinquent members, bringing new itinerants up to speed on the character and status of each member, and pointing out to the circuit riders or presiding elder potential candidates for licensing as exhorters or local preachers. By the early nineteenth century class leaders were also official members of their respective quarterly meeting conferences, participating in the yearly reviews of exhorters and local preachers, and in disciplinary trials.[14] Early American Methodists were inveterate record keepers, anxious to judge their success or failure in terms of numbers of conversions, new members, and the like. But the position of class leader was fundamentally much more than simply an administrative one. In their notes on the *Discipline* of 1798, Asbury and Coke wrote that the office was "of vast consequence. The revival of the work of God does perhaps depend as much upon *the whole body of [class] leaders*, as it does *upon the whole body of preachers*." Every class leader, according to Coke and Asbury, "is, *in some degree*, a gospel minister." Each "should not only be deeply experienced in divine things, but *have a measure of the gift of preaching*, so as to feed the flock of Christ under their care in due season."[15]

A typical class meeting included singing, prayer, and an examination of each member, and might proceed as follows. After the group had gathered, the meeting would be opened with a hymn, with those present being encouraged to "sing *lustily,* and with a good courage."[16] If the hymn was unfamiliar to some, the leader would first "line out," or read, the hymn, and the group would then bawl it out together. Next, the leader would offer an opening prayer, praying specifically for each member in turn. Class meeting prayers were always extemporaneous, and early Methodists were encouraged to be both specific and informal in their prayers. Many would have agreed with Sampson Maynard's observation that "it is always a grief to me when I hear a long formal prayer, perhaps for fifteen or thirty minutes, and nothing is said concerning the person who is or ought to be the subject of that prayer."[17] After prayer the group would once again be seated (early Methodists almost always knelt to pray), and the leader would offer a confession of his or her own spiritual condition, of how he or she had fared during the past week. The leader would then examine each member in turn, asking him or her to reveal their troubles and triumphs, offering direction, counsel, or encouragement as might seem appropriate. Leaders were encouraged to "leave time for the members to express their feelings, to ask questions on any subject about which they are perplexed, and for special intercession for any one who may be afflicted."[18] Rather than stage another preaching occasion, the intent of the class meeting was to foster an atmosphere of communal fellowship.

Classes were originally supposed to include about 12 members each, a size thought best to promote intimacy, openness, and discipline. But almost from the beginning they exceeded this size. Women and men were segregated into their own meetings in some places, but in others the meetings were mixed. Likewise, at times African Americans had their own classes (though often with a white leader), while at others they met with whites. Since, on average, more women than men joined the church throughout the early republic, they also constituted a numerical majority of those attending class meetings. In 1805 in Poughkeepsie, New York, there were 24 women and 19 men enrolled in the town's class meeting.[19] Surviving records for the New Haven class in Worthington, Ohio, show that it included 20 women and 6 men in 1806. By 1808 the class had grown to include 22 women and 14 men, and by 1811 it had expanded to 54 members.[20] At times class meetings could grow exceptionally large. In 1802 in Kentucky, Jacob Young met a class of 100 members.[21] But in most places during the late eighteenth century and first decades of the nineteenth, class sizes appear to have been more uniform. The Baltimore city station records show that in 1800 there were 14 white women's classes with an average of 25 members each, 12 white men's classes averaging 19 each, and 11 African-American classes averaging 28 each. By 1804–1805 these averages had increased slightly to 26 members per white class and 31 per African American.[22] In New York City the average class size actually fell from about 27 members in 1793 to 20 in 1802.[23]

Though a great many class meetings were undoubtedly dull and tedious affairs, in general the institution was firmly embraced by early American Methodists. It was largely in these gatherings that Methodism developed its communal character. "Here," wrote Thomas Morris, who first joined the itinerancy in 1816, "where only pious friends are presumed to be present, where all would help and none would hinder us in the pursuit of spiritual life, we can freely talk over our hopes and fears, trials and deliverances, resolutions and prospects in the way to heaven. In a word, we may safely and prudently state our case as it is, whether encouraging or otherwise, and thereby secure the sympathizing prayers, counsels, exhortations, or admonitions of those in whom we have most confidence."[24] Though the class meeting's primary purpose was to improve each member's spiritual condition, it was readily acknowledged that it had a larger socializing effect as well. "*The social principle* is one of the grand springs in the soul of man," wrote Asbury and Coke in their notes to the *Discipline* of 1798. "It was not the design of christianity to annihilate this principle, but the very contrary—to improve it, to spiritualize it, and strengthen it."[25] Imagine how important it must have been for a woman who had just moved from tidewater Virginia to the Ohio frontier, or a journeyman recently arrived in one of the larger eastern seaboard cities, or a slave lately sold to a new plantation to find an intimate group of his or her peers, eager to welcome a fellow believer into their fellowship, to open their lives, to offer their assistance in meeting both the spiritual and temporal needs of the newcomer. The importance of this kind of communal bonding was vital to Methodism's growth in the turbulent world of the early republic. Shortly after his conversion, Billy Hibbard took his non-Methodist wife to a class meeting. After returning home, Hibbard asked her what she thought of the meeting. "She answered, 'O how they love one another, I never saw such love in all my life.'" "My dear," replied Hibbard, "that is our religion."[26]

The fact that so many spoke and prayed at each class meeting was central to its appeal. Testifying in class meeting could be an intimidating prospect for many, but it could also foster the kind of openness and intimacy that formed the foundation of larger revivalistic outbursts. Joseph Travis recalled that when he was stationed at Georgetown, South Carolina, in 1809, class meetings "would seldom break up before midnight." Benjamin Abbott, not surprisingly, presided over numerous emotionally charged class meetings, as did William Watters. At one gathering on the Sussex circuit in Virginia in 1778, wrote Watters, "The windows of Heaven were opened, and the Lord poured out such a blessing as our hearts were not able to contain. . . . We were so filled with the love of God, and over awed with his Divine Majesty, that we lay prostrate at his footstool, scarcely able to rise from our knees for a considerable time, while there were strong cries and prayers from every part of the house." At a subsequent meeting "the glorious presence and power of God, rested upon us in a manner I had never known before. For an hour and a half, we all continued constant in prayer and supplication to be saved from sin, that we might be able in our weak manner, while in this world to glorify God, in every breath." At yet another gathering, Watters attempted to close the meeting in prayer but his voice was "soon lost in the earnest cries of those around." "I was in agony, and my heart ready to burst asunder with longing after the blessing. . . . My cry was incessant—Father glorify thy name—pour out thy spirit. I felt a deep and awful sense of the Divine presence, and a calm within that words cannot describe."[27]

Jacob Young's conversion, recounted in chapter 3, was initiated at a class meeting in which many were "melted into tears," and fell to the floor "like trees thrown down by a whirlwind." "In a short time," recalled Young, "nearly all . . . were upon the floor, some shouting for joy, others crying aloud for mercy." Such displays of overt enthusiasm—people crying out or lying slain in the Spirit, unable to stand—were as common in class meetings as at larger public gatherings. In 1809 Alfred Brunson attended a class meeting in Carlisle, Pennsylvania, soon after his conversion. There, a young woman "of undoubted piety, rose to relate the state of her mind, in answer to the inquiry of the leader, and while speaking fell like a log set up on one end, striking her head on the iron foot of an old-fashioned ten-plate stove." Brunson caught his breath and "my flesh cringed . . . for I thought her skull must be broken, and if so, that death must ensue. Every joint and muscle in her frame appeared to have lost all elasticity, and assumed a rigidity, to me, unaccountable. A cold chill passed over my whole frame; and if I had not been sitting I should have sunk down upon my seat." But Brunson's tension was short lived, "for the good sister's present, who understood the matter, immediately raised her up, and the rigid state of her frame was gone and she went on with her sweet story of love to God and his cause, and of the peace and joy she felt in her soul. And when the meeting was out she walked off as sprightly as if nothing of the kind had occurred." Still amazed, Brunson later asked the woman if she had not been hurt, but was assured "that not even a bump was raised."[28] At the close of a subsequent class meeting, this same young woman "took a regular jumping shout," in which she repeatedly leaped into the air and fell to the floor, often striking her head "on the end of a table or chest which stood in the room, and then upon the uncarpeted floor." This continued for an hour or more, while Brunson "sat with astonishment and wonder . . . being now satisfied that her excitement and superhuman strength were produced in some mysterious way, to me unknown, by the influence of the Divine Spirit."[29] While most class meetings were no doubt more subdued, this kind of enthusiasm set the stage for the better known emotionalism of the camp meetings and other Methodist revivals.

But as the nineteenth century progressed, the class meeting outlived its usefulness in the eyes of an increasing number of Methodists. Beginning first in the cities of the eastern seaboard, multitudes of American Methodists eagerly strove to participate in what Richard Bushman has called "the refinement of America." As Methodists adopted the "vernacular gentility" of the emerging middle class, the class meeting lost its allure. Its artisan-like concepts of intimate self-disclosure and emotionalism simply did not fit in a world of fashionable parlors and measured decorum. Admittedly, a large portion of Methodists did not find their way into polite society until near mid-century, but many were keen on the possibility of doing so long before.[30] Though a residue of communal openness and vulnerability long remained in the movement, the pattern of change is unmistakable. As refinement and religion grew increasingly "intertwined as values of nearly equal standing," it seemed less and less appropriate to require members of standing to weekly bare their souls before a collection of mechanics, small farmers, or clerks.[31] Hence, with little formal discussion or doctrinal debate, antebellum American Methodists gradually, almost silently, abandoned the class meeting in search of a more respectable faith.

Along with the class meeting, three other communal events were pivotal in shaping the rise of American Methodism: the love feast, the quarterly meeting, and the camp meeting. Like class meetings, Methodist love feasts originated in England under John Wesley and were patterned, to an extent, after a similar Moravian practice.[32] The love feast was directly connected to the class meeting for much of this period in the sense that none could attend the former without having passed a quarterly examination by the circuit preacher in the latter. At times the circuit preachers gave out admission tickets to identify those who had been duly examined. These tickets were in use in America as early as 1769. Printed on small pieces of paper, they were dated by either the month or the season of the year, and usually included a passage of scripture or a picture depicting a biblical scene.[33]

A love feast often served as the climax to a quarterly meeting on Sunday morning, along with the sacrament of the Lord's supper. As the tickets were designed to assure, none could attend the love feast except members in good standing and perhaps a few select earnest seekers who had been given permission (sometimes in writing) by a preacher or other local leader. The meeting itself included prayer, singing, the eating of a small portion of bread and drinking of a little water in imitation, not of the sacrament, but of the communal fellowship of the early saints, and, most important, unrehearsed individual testimonies of struggles and triumphs in the faith, of what God had done in the lives of those present.[34] "We sat together in heavenly places," wrote William

Watters of a love feast on the Baltimore circuit in 1779. "I was as in a little Heaven below, and believe Heaven above will differ more in quantity than in quality. Never did I hear such experiences before. Our eyes overflowed with tears, and our hearts with love to God and each other."[35]

As with the class meeting, the exclusivity of the love feast often aroused a great deal of excitement and suspicion. In early nineteenth-century Georgia, "The shutting of the doors in class-meetings and love-feasts, and turning all others out, gave great offense to all and was much spoken against by all other denominations," according to John Brooks.[36] In New England the closed doors of the love feast were, as Dan Young put it, a "bugbear" for many.[37] At an 1810 Connecticut love feast, according to Alfred Brunson, one rowdy pushed his way past the three "good stout men" assigned to guard the door, seating himself at the front of the assembly to observe the proceedings. The people then gathered in "thick and fast" so that the man was "soon hemmed in on both sides by the devout worshipers." When the house was full, the door was barred and the three guards stood with their backs against it. Meanwhile, the meeting began with prayer and singing. "Great power was manifested from the throne above, and some were jumping, and others falling to the floor," Brunson recalled. As the pitch of the meeting increased, the rowdy "became frantic." At that moment one of the jumpers fell across his lap, and "he rose, and with one bound went head foremost out of the window, leaving his hat behind, and lighting on the ground some ten or twelve feet from the window."[38]

As with the class meeting, the closed-door policy of the love feast helped create for those present the sense of security and confidence necessary to develop strong group cohesiveness and the homogeneity of expectations in which discipline could be enforced. "Where else," but in love feasts and class meetings, asked Edmund S. Janes, "is found such Christian intimacy, such stated seasons of fellowship, such familiar conversation on religious experience, such spiritual sympathy, so much helping of each others faith, and such watching over one another in love?"[39] Fostering this kind of communal intimacy was a key to Methodism's success from the beginning. As early as July 1776 Thomas Rankin attended a large love feast on the Virginia–North Carolina border lasting some three to four hours. "Many testified that they had 'redemption in the blood of Jesus, even the forgiveness of sins.' And many were enabled to declare, that it had 'cleansed them from all sin,'" wrote Rankin in a letter to John Wesley. "So clear, so full, so strong was their testimony, that while some were speaking their experience, hundreds were in tears, and others vehemently crying to God for pardon or holiness."[40] What Rankin experienced in 1776 would remain characteristic of American Methodism well into the nineteenth century.

Without this foundation of corporate fellowship, it is unlikely that American Methodism's more public events, most notably the camp meetings of the early nineteenth century, could have sustained the energy that they did. "It is manifestly our duty to fence in our society, and to preserve it from intruders," wrote Asbury and Coke in their notes to the *Discipline* of 1798, "otherwise we should make our valuable meetings for christian fellowship cheap and contemptible, and bring a heavy burden on the minds of our brethren."[41] In response to the suggestion that easing the rules might result in people thronging to the church, Thomas Morris replied, "Perhaps they would. That is what we are afraid of, and what we aim to prevent; for then persons without piety, without religious principle even, would readily avail themselves of the influence arising from Church membership, because cheap; it would require but little sacrifice of worldly pleasure; there would be but few crosses to bear, or duties to perform." "The church is of little use to such members," concluded Morris, "and they are of no use to it."[42]

Quarterly meetings, like class meetings and love feasts, were a part of American Methodism from the beginning. Thomas Rankin, Wesley's chief representative in America between 1773 and 1778, spent most of his time in the colonies traveling from one quarterly meeting to the next. By the late 1770s, quarterly meetings (which met every three months, as the name implies) came to have two distinct components: an official business session and a larger set of public meetings. This division represented two distinct purposes. First, quarterly meetings were the primary administrative gathering of a circuit. Here, at the official business session, often referred to as the quarterly meeting conference, disputes and disciplinary cases were tried, candidates for the office of exhorter and local preacher were examined and licensed, candidates for the itinerancy were recommended to their respective annual conferences, and the contributions collected at the class meetings were distributed. Second, quarterly meetings were a collective event at which Methodists and others from the surrounding towns and countryside gathered for several days of preaching, singing, and socializing, all culminating in a love feast and communion.

Each circuit generally had its own quarterly meeting conference, whose official members, by the early nineteenth century, included class leaders, stewards, licensed exhorters, local preachers, the circuit preachers, and the presiding elder. Members of the August 1806 Hockhocking, Ohio, circuit quarterly meeting conference included the presiding elder, John Sale, the circuit riders James Axley and Peter Cartwright, 9 local preachers, 15 exhorters, 2 stewards, and 13 class leaders. Four years later, in September 1810, the conference members included Sale, the itinerants Benjamin Lakin and John Manley, 10 local preachers, 12 exhorters, 3 stewards, and 25 class leaders.[43]

Quarterly meeting minutes provide only a partial record of Methodist disciplinary practices. Most cases involving ordinary members would have been decided in class meetings, leaving little trace of the issues involved or their outcome. But quarterly meeting conferences often did hear the more serious cases or those involving preachers. Perhaps more than anything, these records reveal how carefully Methodists watched over one another. Disciplinary trials for the Hockhocking, Ohio, circuit from 1806 to 1815 ranged from cases of neglecting daily family worship to sabbath breaking to adultery. At the August 1806 Hockhocking quarterly meeting the local preacher John Williams was tried for traveling from a mill on the sabbath even though he had been offered accommodations by a fellow Methodist. Williams was found guilty and his license to preach suspended, though it was reinstated at the next quarterly meeting in November 1806. The August 1806 conference also recommended that Frederick Hood be licensed as a local preacher. Eight years later, in July 1814, Hood also found himself on trial for sabbath breaking, this time for making sugar on Sunday. After admitting his error, he was let off with a lecture from the presiding elder and a censure from the conference. At the July 1812 quarterly meeting conference held at Lakin's chapel in Ohio, Betsey Russel was found guilty of adultery and excluded from membership in her local society, the severest penalty available.[44] Though any one of these cases might seem trivial in isolation, taken together they reveal how close-knit Methodist communities could be.

Cases from other circuits follow a similar pattern. On the Paint Creek, Ohio, circuit 1811–1815 charges brought before the quarterly meeting conference included "immoral conduct" and a case involving financial debt. In the latter instance, the May 1814 conference ordered John Thompson to pay Nanny Warner the "just sum" of $54.61.[45] On the Union and Mad River, Ohio, circuits 1807–1814 charges included "repeated intoxication with ardent Spirits"; "writing an imprudent letter to Mrs. James"; "giving way to unholy tempers and using improper expressions"; "Hardness of Spirit"; slander; and injuring Thomas Cotton's horse "by shooting him with stones."[46]

Disciplinary cases on the Madison, Kentucky, circuit 1811–1820 and the Accomack, Virginia, circuit 1804–1820 were quite similar, with one notable exception. On each circuit, 13 of 18 recorded cases concerned members holding slaves. The conferences used these hearings primarily to determine how long a member might hold a slave, and to ensure that a legal deed of emancipation had been filed according to their decision (see chapter 6). Minutes indicate that the conferences exercised a considerable degree of discretion in determining how the remaining cases ought to be handled. At the August 1812 Madison quarterly meeting conference Jonathan Kidwell was charged with "not holding family prayer." Rather than expel Kidwell, the conference appointed a committee to "converse in a friendly manner with him on the subject." But other defendants did not fare so well. At the same 1812 conference David Hardesty was "charged of having inveighed against the Doctrine and Discipline of the Methodist Episcopal Church" and expelled. The conference also expelled Isaac McHenry in July 1815 after finding him "guilty of slandering the character of sister Carter." In much the same manner, the conference suspended the local preacher Cornelius Bowman's license to preach in July 1819 after Deborah Moore, Isabella Bowman, and Elenor Moore testified that he had threatened to "kill" William Strong if he "ever came on his place."[47] Non-slave-holding cases on the Accomack circuit revolved around similar issues, including charges of "immoral conduct," drunkenness, "backbiting," and the sexual harassment of school girls by a local preacher and school teacher.[48]

Apart from judging individual cases, quarterly meeting conferences at times issued general proclamations applicable to all Methodists under their jurisdiction. The August 1809 conference held at Tilmon Lueses's on the Hockhocking circuit declared "that the attending of barbacues and Drinking of toasts on the 4 of July is contrary to the Sperit of christianity and can not be don to the glory of god." Though this declaration was rooted in Federalist versus Republican political divisions within the church, it nevertheless indicates how tight the Methodist concept of corporate discipline could be. It also demonstrates the limits of Bishop Francis Asbury's control over quarterly meeting conferences, of which he was not an official member. In this instance, when a number of Hockhocking circuit members were expelled from the church for having celebrated the fourth, Asbury "had no power to redress the wrong, though he would gladly have done so."[49]

Renewing the licenses of exhorters and local preachers was an equally important task of the quarterly meeting conferences, as was the examination of new candidates for these offices and the recommendation of candidates for the itinerancy to the annual conferences. All of these functions, which did much to determine the fortunes of Methodism in a given region, were, by the early nineteenth century, carried out without the input of the bishops or the annual conferences.[50] Candidates were examined not only by the presiding elder and circuit riders but also by their class leaders and other peers who knew them well, thus giving each community a significant measure of control over the makeup of the church.

Most local leaders were subject to an annual review at their respective quarterly meeting conference. The August 1811 conference on the Madison circuit in Kentucky began with public examinations of the class leaders, all of whom were "found unreprovable." Next came the exhorters. Martin Green was also judged "unreprovable," but Cornelius Bowman was "found guilty of some improprieties." Though we are not told what these improprieties were, Bowman "made . . . acknowledgement and the Conference renewed his license." Robert Anderson did not fare so well. Anderson was "found blameless," yet the conference "thought best not to renew his License for want of abilities." After examining the local preachers individually, the conference moved on to consider new candidates for the ministry, each of whom had been recom-

mended by his respective class meeting. Jesse Weeks's class meeting had recommended him for a license to exhort. After questioning Weeks, the conference
agreed, granting the license. Next came John Murphy seeking a local preacher's
license, but for "certain reasons" the conference turned him away. The last to
be examined was Robert Hatton. After Hatton's "character, gifts and usefulness" were "inquired into," he was granted a license to preach.[51]

In a similar set of proceedings, the September 1808 Mad River quarterly
meeting conference voted to revoke Elijah Standiford's license to preach, giving him a license to exhort instead. The conference wrote a letter to Standiford (who apparently was not present) assuring him that "immoral conduct"
was not "the reason for this act, but an impression its the most proper station
for you at this time." Standiford's demotion may well have been precipitated
by complaints from the laity about his preaching. In a similar case at the Xenia
quarterly meeting conference in March 1812, Robert Sale testified "that he
believed Brother McGuire (a local Preacher) to be a bad man, and that he was
no more fit to preach the Gospel than his (the said Sale's) Dog Ranger, and
that he also believed that said McGuire told lies." Though the charges against
McGuire were eventually dismissed, what is perhaps most remarkable about
this case is that Sale, an ordinary layman, had his day in court at all, and that
his testimony was duly considered and recorded.[52]

Quarterly meetings provided ordinary Methodists with access to the
church's leadership, thus inviting them to participate in the shaping of the
movement's character. The importance of these kinds of proceedings can
scarcely be overemphasized. Working together, the presiding elder, circuit
preachers, and local lay leaders did much to determine the future of a circuit
through their appointments of class leaders, exhorters, and local preachers.
Moreover, since these positions served as gateways into the itinerancy, the
collective actions of the quarterly meeting conferences had powerful repercus-
sions for the Methodist movement as a whole.

Along with their administrative tasks, quarterly meetings fulfilled equally
important social and religious functions as well. From the late 1770s on, quarterly meetings were two-day affairs (an American innovation), usually held
over a Saturday and Sunday.[53] On Saturday, while the official conference members conducted the administrative affairs described above, Methodists gathered
from the surrounding communities and countryside to hear preaching, sing
favorite hymns, and fellowship in a festive atmosphere. Sunday usually cli-
maxed with the love feast, celebration of the Lord's supper, and more preaching. Often, large crowds of non-Methodists also came to join the festival-like
proceedings. At one such meeting near New Brunswick, New Jersey, in 1792,
the itinerant Richard Swain records that it "seemed as if" non-Methodists
"would over run us for awhile. For they broke the door open once or more,
and a number of them a selling watermellons and cake, and beer, and rum

etc. through the whole Meeting."[54] Though in this case the presence of non-Methodists was problematic, it nonetheless indicates the way in which quarterly meetings often drew in outsiders. Hence, as Russell Richey has noted, three constituencies commonly gathered at quarterly meetings: the official conference delegates, the Methodist faithful, and crowds of curious onlookers.[55] "Our quarterly meetings were noted seasons, which excited general interest," wrote the itinerant Charles Giles of the early nineteenth century. Apart from the official deliberations of the conference, "the members of the church, coming from all directions, and from various distances, bring some of their unconverted friends and neighbors with them . . . add[ing] much to the importance and interest of these occasions." At these gatherings, friendships were formed that would be renewed from time to time, news was exchanged, and participants generally came away feeling that their faith had been renewed and they had gained a broader perspective on the world. "Indeed," concluded Giles, "quarterly meetings then were accounted great seasons, not only by our own church, but by many others in community."[56]

As a public event, quarterly meetings drew people out of their normal routines and focused their attention on matters of the spirit. They had a concentrating effect that could lead to dramatic results. In 1801 Elijah Woolsey was on his way to his third quarterly meeting on the Flanders, New Jersey, circuit when he dreamed "that I went a fishing, and that I cast my net in the water and caught a great many fish." Interpreting this as a good omen, Woolsey exclaimed upon awaking, "My Lord, *this is* a quarterly meeting indeed!" He was not to be disappointed. The Saturday meeting continued all night, with Woolsey estimating that 6,000 were present on Sunday. "There was preaching from the pulpit, exhorting from the windows, and sinners crying for mercy in the house and out of it," recounted Woolsey. The impact of this meeting was felt for many months to come throughout New Jersey.[57]

The impact of successful quarterly meetings could be extended into other Methodist gatherings, particularly the class meetings. In 1806, James Poynter wrote to Daniel Hitt from the Wyoming circuit in northeastern Pennsylvania that he had "labored with a gloomy prospect until our third Quarterly Meeting held in a neighborhood called Brier-Creek." Though only 10 were converted at the Brier Creek meeting, it sparked a revival that fed into the class meetings, with one class increasing from 17 to 69 members and another from 17 to 34. In all, 135 new members joined the church on Poynter's circuit during the conference year.[58]

At times quarterly meetings seemed to take on a life of their own. In 1798 presiding elder Thomas Ware led a quarterly meeting at a chapel built by Henry Boehm's father in Lancaster, Pennsylvania. On Saturday, "the work of revival commenced, and such were the cries of distress, the prayers for mercy heard all over the house, in the gallery as well as the lower part," recalled

Boehm, "that it was impossible for Mr. Ware to preach." The meeting lasted all day and most of the night. On Sunday morning, "they attempted to hold a regular love-feast, but all in vain. The cries of the mourners, the prayers for mercy, and shout after shout as one after another passed from death unto life, made it impossible to proceed."[59] Reflecting on this period, Ware noted that as numbers increased, "we knew not what to do with the thousands who attended our quarterly meetings."[60] Increasingly meetings had to be held outdoors, even though the camp meeting, as such, had yet to be invented.

The numbers who often thronged quarterly meetings both taxed Methodist resources and demonstrated the depth of Methodist unity and hospitality. "Our quarterly meetings were high times," wrote Henry Smith, "and people came to them from far and near."[61] In 1801 Abner Chase attended a quarterly meeting in Montgomery County, New York, at which he and 30 to 40 others stayed at the home of William Bentley. "As was the custom of those days," recalled Chase, "the brethren from abroad were entertained by the families in the vicinity of the meeting, not in pairs, but by dozens." At this meeting, services were held in a barn, with women sitting on the floor, and men in the loft.[62] In southern Ohio, Philip and Elizabeth Gatch often hosted quarterly meetings, boarding 50 to 100 at their home (the men sleeping in the barn), with other neighbors doing the same.[63] The same pattern prevailed in the South. The 29 members of the South Carolina conference who attended the conference's annual meeting in December 1806 almost all stayed in the home of John Lucas, where the conference was held.[64]

The homes at which meeting goers and circuit riders lodged came to be known as "Methodist taverns," or "Methodist harbors."[65] Methodists themselves stubbornly maintained that this sort of hospitality brought far more rewards than hardships. In a story typical of many, Alfred Brunson tells of a father who upbraided his son for keeping so many Methodists, telling him that he "would soon be eaten out of house and home." But the son claimed that his fortunes had increased since Methodist preachers had begun frequenting his home. How could this be? asked the father. "Why, father," replied the son, "the Methodist preachers come to my house with their horses; they make manure; I put that on the land, and that makes the grass grow."[66] But of course there was a limit to the number of people that any Methodist community could support.

For this reason, camp meetings were a godsend for Methodism, and Methodism for camp meetings.[67] As the movement grew both in numbers and geographical extent, camp meetings provided a way to continue holding large-scale meetings over several days without overwhelming local resources. In turn, the Methodist tradition of extended and often dramatic quarterly meetings provided a firm foundation on which the camp meeting movement could build in the early years of the nineteenth century.

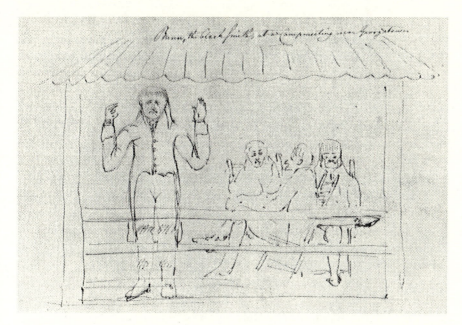

Figure 4.1. "Bunn the Blacksmith at a Camp Meeting near Georgetown," pen-and-ink sketch by Benjamin Henry Latrobe, 1809. This may well be the Methodist itinerant preacher Seely Bunn, who was stationed in nearby Baltimore in 1809. Courtesy of the Maryland Historical Society, Baltimore, Maryland.

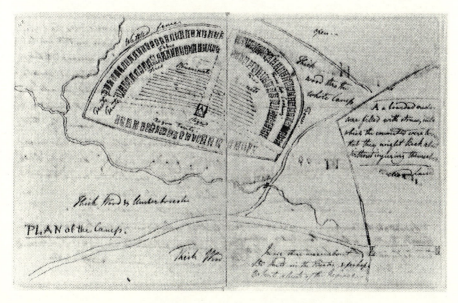

Figure 4.2. "Plan of the Camp," sketch by Benjamin Henry Latrobe, 1809. Courtesy of the Maryland Historical Society, Baltimore, Maryland.

The importance of camp meetings in the Methodist scheme has long been acknowledged, perhaps to excess. Books such as Charles A. Johnson's *The Frontier Camp Meeting* (1955), Dickson D. Bruce's *And They All Sang Hallelujah* (1974), and Bernard A. Weisberger's *They Gathered at the River* (1958) have stressed the importance of the camp meeting for early American Methodism, and, in the absence of counterbalancing works on other components of the Methodist system (class meetings, quarterly meetings, and the like) have given the impression that camp meetings were of singular importance to Methodist growth. These studies also tend to distort the picture by giving the impression that camp meetings were intrinsically linked to the frontier and thrived there in a way which could not be reproduced in more settled regions. Neither conclusion is valid. First, Methodism's most explosive period of growth came before the advent of the camp meeting; the movement's basic structure was already well established before camp meetings emerged at the turn of the century. Second, large and enthusiastic meetings were a familiar and consistent component of the Methodist movement throughout the new nation, not only on the frontier. Some of the most explosive Methodist meetings of the first years of the nineteenth century occurred on the Delmarva Peninsula, a region settled long before.[68] (Bounded on the west by the Chesapeake Bay and on the east by the Delaware River and the Atlantic Ocean, the penin-

Figure 4.3. Camp meeting, lithograph (c. 1820) after painting by A. Rider. Courtesy of the Billy Graham Center Museum, Wheaton, Illinois.

sula was early known as the "Garden of Methodism." It is divided among the states of Delaware, Maryland, and Virginia, hence the name.) It is precisely because camp meetings were so readily adaptable to existing Methodist style and practice that they became so quickly an important part of the movement.

Beginning after the turn of the century, a camp meeting was often held in place of the summer or fall quarterly meeting, and at times in conjunction with an annual conference. Building on the foundation of well-established quarterly meetings, camp meetings were quickly and easily integrated into the Methodist system, often with dramatic results. According to Henry Boehm, the first camp meeting on the Delmarva Peninsula occurred in 1805, with others quickly following. "It is now almost impossible to realize what great times we had at our early camp-meetings," wrote Boehm, reflecting on this period. "They did much in breaking up the strongholds of the devil, and almost revolutionized the Peninsula."[69] While riding the Dover circuit on the peninsula in 1806, Boehm reported 1,100 converted at a camp meeting in June, another 1,320 converted at a July camp meeting, and yet another 900 converted at a subsequent July meeting.[70] In Georgia, membership more than doubled from 1,663 members in 1801 to 3,702 in 1803, largely as a result of the introduction of camp meetings.[71]

By December 1802 Francis Asbury was writing to presiding elder Thornton Fleming that camp meetings "have never been tried without success . . . this is field fighting, this is fishing with a large net."[72] Asbury urged that order be observed at every camp meeting, but at the same time he was careful not to quench the Spirit. Describing an 1803 camp meeting, he wrote that "we have great order and attention," but also noted with unconcealed relish that many fainted and fell, "crying for mercy."[73] By 1811 American Methodists were conducting 400 to 500 camp meetings annually. While Asbury's estimate that these gatherings drew 3 to 4 million Americans is surely exaggerated, it is reasonable to assume, as Nathan Hatch has suggested, that more than 1 million annually attended Methodist camp meetings by this time.[74]

Early American Methodism was a profoundly community-oriented event. In the turbulent years of the early republic it reached out to ordinary Americans in a way unequaled by any other religious group (at least on such an extensive, nationwide scale), drawing them into a well-defined system of social activities: class meetings, love feasts, quarterly meetings, and camp meetings.[75] As the movement grew, success bred success. Large quarterly meetings and camp meetings producing throngs of converts helped assure the Methodist faithful that God had taken their part, that their church had the power to transform society. Emboldened by their own achievements, most Methodists readily embraced the notion that their continued advance hinged on maintaining the discipline of a well-honed army.

The promise of discipline formed a major component of the appeal of early American Methodism. Because of the Wesleyan emphasis on personal experience and conversion as an ongoing process, doctrine could not be separated from discipline.[76] Moreover, the breakdown of time-honored social patterns in the wake of the American Revolution and the unprecedented mobility of ordinary people, brought about by rapid territorial expansion, made the early national period a time of both great optimism and uncertainty. Though the full meaning of the market revolution would not be evident until after the War of 1812, its beginnings were visible long before.[77] Many eagerly migrated to new areas following the Revolution, embracing the opportunity to own their own store, shop, or farm in western New York, Ohio, Kentucky, Tennessee, or Georgia. Even for those who stayed behind, the constant arrival of new faces and departure of familiar ones cast an often bewildering shadow over otherwise familiar towns and villages. With the abandonment of so much that had been a familiar part of colonial American society, Methodist discipline promised to provide a much needed supplement to family, community and church ties, a way for ordinary people to re-order and control their own lives. Though the Baptists, Presbyterians, and others also at times established relatively strict standards of collective discipline, the Methodist connectional system was exceptionally well suited for the task of maintaining uniform practices.[78]

It is not surprising, then, to find that the majority of class leaders were the more successful members of their peer groups, in terms of both worldly accomplishments and spiritual progress. Imagine, as Charles Steffen has suggested, "a master mechanic who had undergone an apprenticeship of seven years, lived frugally as a journeyman and banked his savings, and by the age of thirty had opened his own shop, married, and started a family." After watching others fall behind to become permanent wage earners and even drunkards, Methodist discipline would make sense to such a man, and to his wife. It offered, as Donald Mathews notes, "the persistent strain of self-discipline that enhances the self-esteem of persons who have the power of making themselves new."[79] The church's *Discipline* condemned indebtedness, intemperate drinking, swearing, ostentatious dress, gossiping, discord, gluttony, gambling, bribery, and taking "treats" when voting at civil elections, a message frequently reinforced by Methodist preachers.[80] In particular, early American Methodists considered diligence and hard work moral imperatives. "Something should be always under the hammer," proclaimed Charles Giles. "To labour then is no disgrace. It is commendable and beneficial every way. It strengthens the physical powers of man, makes his food relish, his sleep quiet and refreshing."[81] Of course, there were inevitably those who became disgruntled with intrusions into their private affairs by a class leader or circuit preacher. But on the whole the practice of discipline was an aid to vitality and growth, rather than a deterrent.[82]

From the beginning, upholding Wesleyan standards of discipline constituted one of the cornerstones of American Methodism. In 1773, Wesley sent Thomas Rankin and George Shadford from England to direct the movement in America largely because he had reports that Joseph Pilmore and others were failing to adhere to Methodist standards. Rankin found that Wesley's fears were true, and immediately began enforcing the discipline of the class meeting, love feast, and quarterly meeting. While visiting Philadelphia in December 1773, he wrote: "What trouble do I find by the members of the Society here, and at New York, but by not having our discipline enforced from the beginning! This has given me pain, and it is likely to cause more."[83] Pilmore, the most cosmopolitan of Wesley's preachers in America, remained unrepentant and unreformed, but his views were clearly in the minority. On June 4, 1773, the day after Rankin and Shadford's arrival in America, Pilmore sat glumly through Shadford's sermon entitled "True Old Methodism," in which Shadford "seemed to intimate the people had wanted it till now." Realizing that Rankin and Shadford enjoyed Wesley's full support, Pilmore left for England in January 1774, not returning to America again until 1785, when he would be ordained a priest in the new Protestant Episcopal Church.[84] For his part, Rankin continued campaigning for Wesleyan discipline, noting in July 1774, "I am more and more convinced that unless the whole plan of our discipline is closely attended to, we can never see that work nor the fruit of our labours, as we would desire."[85]

From his first days in America in 1771, Francis Asbury closely followed Rankin's style of discipline. In fact, putting into practice uniform Wesleyan discipline was perhaps Asbury's greatest concern during his first several years in America. Once established, he clung fiercely to the Wesleyan system. Under his leadership, the movement's basic organizational structure remained unchanged between the Revolution and the second decade of the nineteenth century. " 'Tis order, 'tis system—under God—that hath kept us from schism, and heresy, and division," Asbury wrote to James Quinn in 1812, reflecting on the merits of the polity he had spent his life building.[86] The uniformity of Methodist discipline gave the movement a cohesiveness unknown to any other large-scale religious movement of the time.

Like Asbury, nearly all of the early Methodist preachers eagerly embraced the call for a well-ordered church and well-ordered lives. "The truth is, that the preaching of the word of God, and the administration of discipline, are the two parts of the same great work," asserted the itinerant William Beauchamp.[87] "As to the discipline of the Methodist Church," wrote William Watters in 1806, "though I have no doubt but it has its defects, yet I do think that it is by far the most scriptural and the most primitive, of any I have ever seen, and the best calculated to spread the genuine Gospel, and to keep up the life and power of godliness in the Church of God."[88] When forming a new class meeting or society, Methodist preachers frequently took the prospective group of new members aside and read them the rules for membership, or portions of the

Discipline, as Freeborn Garrettson did in Delaware in April 1779. After several successful preaching engagements, Garrettson "appointed a day to read, and explain the rules of our society; and many came together." On this occasion, Garrettson thoroughly examined and admitted about thirty, "but being weary, I declined taking any more at that time."[89]

Making sure that new members lived up to Methodist standards was one of the primary responsibilities of all preachers and class leaders. Frequently this involved expelling recalcitrant members, the stiffest penalty available to the church. As a young itinerant, Asbury found himself in this position after preaching at Portsmouth, Virginia, on October 13, 1775. "Well may the kingdom of heaven be compared to a net, which is cast into the sea, and gathereth all, both good and bad," reflected Asbury in his journal that night. Of the 27 members of the Portsmouth society, he expelled 15, the last a woman fond of "excessive drinking." "Unless the discipline of the church is enforced," wrote Asbury in defense of his actions, "what sincere person would ever join a society, amongst whom they saw ungodliness connived at?"[90]

However unpleasant the enforcement of disciplinary standards might have been, well-ordered societies formed a necessary foundation for growth. Before taking on the Flanders, New Jersey, circuit in 1801 Elijah Woolsey dreamed that he went in search of springs of living water with a crowbar on his shoulder. Finding some springs that were clogged with mud, he proceeded to clean them out. "The water then ran as clear as crystal, and the barren places became pools of water." During his first quarter on Flanders, Woolsey saw the first part of his dream fulfilled, as he expelled "a great number," without taking in any. The second quarter he turned out "a number more," and accepted only one new member. It was then, on his way to the third quarterly meeting, that Woolsey dreamed he went fishing and "caught a great many fish." It was this meeting that drew up to 6,000 participants, and during the year the total membership on the Flanders circuit grew from 221 to 375.[91]

At times African-American Methodists managed to gain a measure of independent disciplinary control over their own classes and societies. In 1794 William Colbert came across a society of slave and free African-American Methodists who "not only have their Class meetings, but their days of examination in order to find out anything that may be amiss among them[,] and if they can settle it among themselves they will." Only disputes that could not be settled internally were brought before the circuit preacher. "Their seciety is very numberous and very orderly," concluded Colbert.[92]

Though the overall impact of establishing communal discipline was to stimulate growth, attracting those in search of a stable and reliable church, there were of course times when doing so led to a great deal of local conflict and unrest. While stationed in Annapolis during the 1805 conference year, Thornton Fleming had a difficult time enforcing Methodist standards. "I turned out two last Sunday; one for immoral conduct, & the other for not attending to the class meeting," he wrote to Daniel Hitt on June 25, 1805. "I hope it will make some fear, if not Love." The task was not a pleasant one, and by the time of his letter to Hitt some of the town's Methodists would not even speak to Fleming. Nevertheless, membership in Annapolis grew from 305 to 333 during the year.[93] While stationed on the Seleuda, South Carolina, circuit in 1795, James Jenkins launched a campaign against the local practice of distilling fruit into brandy. This so angered the locals that they gave him only eight dollars for the one quarter he spent on the circuit.[94] Alfred Brunson had a similar experience while forming the Huron circuit in northern Ohio along the banks of Lake Erie. After learning that 20 or more couples within the bounds of the new circuit were living in adultery, having left husbands or wives back East, he began to "cry aloud and spare not." Managing both to enrage the targets of his accusations and to "stir up the moral sensibilities of the virtuous," Brunson's preaching led both to threats on his life and to a grand jury investigation of the charges of adultery.[95]

Maintaining a dress code further worked to promote Methodist solidarity and communal identity. The *Discipline* of 1784 declared that "this is no Time to give any Encouragement to Superfluity of Apparel. . . . In visiting the Classes, be very mild, but very strict. . . . Allow no excempt Case, not even of a married Woman. Better one suffer than many. . . . Give no tickets to any that wear High-Heads, enormous Bonnets, Ruffles or Rings." Accordingly, those who joined the church in early nineteenth-century Georgia "had to become plain and simple in their dress; all ruffles, bows, rings and feathers, whether worn by gentleman or ladies, had to come off," noted the itinerant John Brooks. If a member "became fashionable" after joining, "they were talked to by the class and class leader, if they did not reform, they were dismissed from church; for members were never suffered to follow the ever varying fashions of the world."[96] One early itinerant was said to have "preached against the practice of powdering the hair" because "it was wicked to waste the beautiful grain which God had provided to sustain life in marring the beauty of one's hair." Similarly, in the early days of Methodism in Troy, New York, "a woman or girl having a ruffle around her neck was not allowed to participate in a lovefeast."[97]

Along with injunctions against swearing, drunkenness, pretentious dress, sexual immorality, and neglecting class meetings, it is worth noting that Methodist preachers were actively interested in promoting such middle-class values as cleanliness. While riding the Wateree, South Carolina, circuit in 1809, William Capers stopped at an "exceeding[ly] dirty" home immediately after having read the passage in the *Discipline* urging preachers "to recommend everywhere decency and cleanliness." Summoning all the tact he could muster, Capers began a discussion with his hostess about the merits of pewter plates, eventually remarking, "I have seen things that looked clean when they were not, and these plates are clean, I am sure, though they look rather darker than you would like to see them." He went on to describe how he had seen pewter plates cleaned using fine sand or brick dust. The woman took the hint, and, according to Capers, "I never afterwards found that a dirty house."[98] "Keep your cabins clean, for your health's sake, and for your souls' sake," James Quinn once heard Asbury proclaim during a sermon on the Ohio frontier. "There is no religion in dirt, and filth, and fleas."[99]

Discipline was as much a part of the early American ethos as was the itinerancy or the camp meeting. The discipline of the class meeting, love feast, and quarterly meeting provided the most tangible link between Methodist spirituality and the conspicuous success of many Methodists in the market revolution of the early republic. Those who could meet the demands for individual accountability and performance in the church stood a good chance of succeeding in the world as well. "To reach a mountain top we must expect to find an up-hill road," wrote Charles Giles, catching, perhaps better than anyone else, the essence of the connection between spiritual and worldly success. Such a road, explained Giles, is only traveled slowly and tediously. "The road to eminence, in any thing is up hill; and the only way to succeed well is to select a course and pursue it," turning neither to the right nor the left. "Keep the grand object always in view, and direct all your energies to accomplish it," advised Giles. "Perseverance in any good cause will make a man famous in that one thing. One man cannot be great in everything, nor is it necessary that he should be."[100] Though Giles primarily had spiritual advancement in mind here, his formula, if applied to other areas of one's life, might easily lead to worldly prosperity as well.

From the beginning, Methodist discipline was in harmony with the most cherished values of ordinary Americans. By adhering to the church's rules, early Methodists carved out both a religious and a social identity for themselves, establishing themselves as a recognizable community. Despite inevitable conflicts over the particulars of individual cases, most early Methodists firmly supported the church's rules. Most would have agreed with George Wells's conviction, expressed in a letter of 1791 to Daniel Hitt, that "I find it is & will [be] a blessing to keep up strict Discipline, without it our church will fall."[101] Methodism's success as an upstart movement led by farmers and artisans taught people not to fear innovation and ingenuity; its discipline taught them to lead well-ordered lives, diligently earning and frugally saving. In short, Methodism encouraged the new values necessary for "improvement" in a market-driven society, imbuing ordinary people with the belief that they as individuals and as communities could overcome folly and vice and improve their lot. It was these characteristics that meshed so well with life in the early republic and that helped create Methodist success and prosperity.

The career of Calvin Fletcher (1798–1866) vividly illustrates the irony of this pattern. The eleventh of 15 children, Fletcher was born into a Vermont Congregationalist family whose fortunes had declined since the Revolution. With little formal education behind him and $20 in his pockets, Fletcher struck out on his own in 1817, eventually landing in Urbana, Ohio. There he taught school, read law, gained admission to the bar, and married Sarah Hill. In 1821 he and Sarah moved to Indianapolis, where through "unyielding perseverance" Calvin became a prominent lawyer, banker, land speculator, and a leader in the Whig Party. Early in his career Fletcher wrote that he had "a thirst for improvement," adding, "Of all fears that of poverty I most dread." By 1835 he had laid at least this fear to rest, having amassed between $40,000 and $50,000 worth of property.[102]

Yet financial success did not completely quiet his spirit. Fletcher had largely abandoned his Congregational roots when he left Vermont, turning into, in his own words, "almost an infidel." But after attending several Methodist class meetings in 1828 he became "st[r]ongly impressed with the great importance of religion." Following a short but intense inner struggle, he was converted on New Year's Eve 1828 at a Methodist watchnight meeting in Indianapolis. Thereafter he became a pillar of the Methodist Church in Indianapolis.

Calvin Fletcher's subsequent career reveals the tensions that beset so many Methodists who began on society's geographic and social peripheries, but soon found themselves a part of its rapidly expanding core. Soon after his conversion Fletcher fretted that "I have always let my law business drive me, I never have drove my business. This neglect has done me much serious injury. It has made me often captious & Jealous towards my professional opponants and rendered me very unhappy. . . . It has been often suggested to me this winter that I could not live up to my religious professions for the want of time."[103] And yet he remained engrossed in business and worldly concerns for several decades to come. It is significant that though his conversion tempered his temporal ambition somewhat, it by no means required Fletcher to renounce his former professional and civic dealings. Methodism was simply too tightly bound to the youthful ambitions of a burgeoning city like Indianapolis for that. Experiences such as Fletcher's were not universal, but they were common enough. While most Methodists may not have climbed so high, a great many were driven by the same desires. In the end, Fletcher settled for what must have been the sentiment of many Methodists of his time: "Should God spare me I hope to be diligent in prayer & constant in business."[104]

5 *A Boiling Hot Religion*

I went on to church, and the brothers and
sisters prayed around me. Then, like a
flash, the power of God struck me. It
seemed like something struck me in the
top of my head and then went on out
through the toes of my feet. I jumped, or
rather, fell back against the back of the
seat. I lay on the floor of the church. A
voice said to me, "You are no longer a
sinner. Go and tell the world what I have
done for you."

—An ex-slave, from
God Struck Me Dead

*I*n October 1789, after a journey of some 46 days from Massachusetts to Baltimore and then on to Muskingum, Ohio, Thomas Wallcut sat down to write a letter to James Freeman, a Unitarian minister in Boston. Everywhere he went, Wallcut reported, one topic seemed to dominate conversation—the spread of Methodism. It seemed that wherever two or three were gathered together, "you would certainly hear something about Methodists—sometimes one of the Company would defend them, but I most generally fell among those that disliked & spoke against them." From what he could discern, the spread of Methodism in Virginia and Maryland seemed "unparrelled & astonishing." "Some go so far as to say that full half the People are Methodists already & that Methodism will be the established Religion of Virginia in a few years," wrote Wallcut. Though he doubted that this would ever be the case, he was nonetheless alarmed at the "enthusi-

Figure 5.1. Freeborn Garrettson, from Abel Stevens, History of the Methodist Episcopal Church in the United States of America *(New York, 1867).*

asm & intemperate zeal" of the Methodists. Methodist meetings, recounted Wallcut after witnessing several, were "attended with all that confusion, violence and distortion of the body, voice & gestures that characterizes such a boiling hot religion." "No Jack Tar in his cups appears to me more irreverend in profaning the name of the Deity than these noisy bellowers when they call upon him." [1]

Thomas Wallcut was not alone in his observations about American Methodism in the early national period. Methodists and non-Methodists alike agreed that much of the movement's astonishing success could be traced to the way in which American Methodists took advantage of the revolutionary religious freedoms of the early republic to release, and in a sense institutionalize, elements of popular religious enthusiasm long latent in American and European Protestantism. In England such popular religion was relegated to the pe-

Figure 5.2. Catherine Livingston Garrettson, from The Ladies Repository, *vol. 24 (June 1864).*

ripheries of society by the force of the church-state system. Only in America did it work its way deep into the predominant culture of the nation.

The enthusiasm of the camp meetings is well known, but what is less frequently acknowledged is that a great many early Methodists believed in the efficacy of prophetic dreams, visions, and supernatural impressions and were not afraid to base day-to-day decisions on such phenomena. Examples of this kind of supernaturalism abound in the journals and autobiographies of Methodist preachers and lay men and women. Freeborn Garrettson firmly believed in the veracity of supernatural impressions, prophetic dreams and even divine healing. So did his wife, Catherine Livingston Garrettson, who led an almost mystical existence before her marriage. In 1773, even before his conversion, Garrettson prayed for his brother John who was "dangerously ill." "Instantly the disorder turned," and he soon recovered. John later told Freeborn that while ill he had seen "death," and been "summoned to appear in the world of spirits," but that Freeborn's prayer had saved him. Later, while itinerating in Pennsylvania and the Jerseys in 1779, Garrettson noted that many "thought the Methodists could work miracles." Indeed, only a few months earlier, in Delaware, he had prayed for rain to end "a great drought" with the result that "a few minutes after the congregation was dismissed, the face of the sky was covered with blackness, and we had a plentiful shower; which greatly surprised and convinced the people."[2] Though others scoffed at looking to dreams and visions for guidance, Garrettson defended the practice, stating, "I know, that both sleeping and waking, things of a divine nature have been revealed to me." His dreams were often graphic and detailed and he took great care to record their contents in his journal. One night as he slept, Garrettson entered "eternity" through a "narrow gate." There he was met by a guide who led him on a tour of hell: "It appeared as large as the sea, and I saw myriads of damned souls, in every posture that miserable beings could get into. This sight exceeded any thing of the kind that ever had entered into my mind. . . . Was I to attempt to describe the place as it was represented to me, I could not do it. . . . I cried to my guide, it is enough." Garrettson then asked to see heaven, but was told "not now, return; you have seen sufficient for once; and be more faithful in warning sinners, and have no more doubts about the reality of hell."[3]

Given their common mystical bent, it is little wonder that Freeborn Garrettson and Kitty Livingston fell so immediately in love. Though she hailed from one of New York's leading families and he was a poor, wandering preacher, their visionary experiences bound them together. During their courtship they read each other's journals and even had dreams in common.[4] Catherine's own dreams and visions were no less vivid than Freeborn's. Shortly after her conversion she had a vision in the night:

> My bed stood beside the east window. It was a moonlight night and I suddenly awoke and directed my eyes to the east. As I looked a bright beautiful star shot thru the casement across the foot of my bed to the opposite side of the wall and then returned back thru the same window and disappeared. Instantly a diadem of stars bright, but not dazzling, took the same direction, and on its return was thrown over the looking glass between the two east windows where it remained while I contemplated its indescribable beauty and could distinguish every bright star of which it was composed, with astonishment, and with delight, as my future crown if faithful unto death.

"Many would say it was the power of imagination, enthusiasm, wild-fire," admitted Catherine of her vision, "but no, it was wonderful, yet true, and I shall ever think it a most gracious display of mercy, love and power to a poor sinking soul who was seeking God with every power and faculty and to whom the whole world, without His presence, was but a waste desert."[5]

Another Methodist woman who placed great confidence in dreams and other forms of supernatural leading was Mary Bradley (b. 1771). In 1793 Bradley was debating whether or not to marry David Morris. She could think of many reasons for not accepting his proposal: "he was not a professor of religion—a great disparity in our age—his comparative poverty. . . . And the greatest objection was, I did not love him—I never had any inclination for any acquaintance with him." Moreover, her family was decidedly against the match. But as a final test Bradley decided to "cast lots, to see how the matter would appear. I did so, and nine times running were for it." Based largely on this result she went through with the marriage.[6]

Much like Bradley and the Garrettsons, Benjamin Abbott described supernatural impressions leading to his conversion, was deeply impressed by dreams, and presided over some of the most explosive Methodist meetings on record. While itinerating near Wilmington, Delaware, in the early 1780s, Abbott discovered that some feared to sit too near him, "having been informed that the people on the circuit fell like dead men" when he preached.[7] Indeed, people fainting during his sermons was the hallmark of his career. On one occasion a "young man was struck to the floor, and many said that he was dead." Abbott, who had seen similar episodes many times before, assured the people that the man was not dead. But after three hours even he became alarmed. The man's skin grew cold and his fingers were stiff and could not be straightened. Abbott "concluded to go home, and not proceed one step further, for killing people would not answer." But eventually the man revived, "prais[ing] God for what he had done for his soul," and restoring Abbott's confidence in his ministry.[8]

In much the same manner, James P. Horton's, Sampson Maynard's and Billy Hibbard's autobiographies are filled with stories of dreams, impressions, shouting, and divine healing. Hibbard's memoir even includes an account of a woman apparently raised from the dead. Fanny Newell, the wife of a Methodist minister and a gifted preacher in her own right, had numerous visions, prophetic dreams, and supernatural impressions. Newell even predicted the death of an apparently healthy child only days before the event. Likewise, Lorenzo Dow was widely renowned for his ability to tell fortunes, and Valentine Cook, Philip Gatch, Noah Fidler, and Joshua Thomas gained reputations as healers whose prayers sometimes brought miraculous results.[9]

Other Methodists for whom these kind of experiences formed an integral part of their world view include Nancy Caldwell, the preachers Francis Asbury, Seth Crowell (whose ministry style was much like Benjamin Abbott's), Thomas Smith, Jacob Young, John Littlejohn, Henry Boehm, Alfred Brunson, Charles Giles, Abner Chase, Elijah Woolsey, James Jenkins, Joseph Travis, John Brooks, and Dan Young, and the African Americans Jarena Lee, Zilpha Elaw, George White, and John Jea.[10]

One of the most compelling and enigmatic figures of this period was John A. Granade. Born in North Carolina about the time of the Revolution, as a young man Granade became "perfectly reckless," rambling through Kentucky and the Cumberland country before settling in South Carolina to teach school. Distressed over his fallen spiritual condition, he soon made his way to Tennessee, where for two years he was plagued by "voices" and "tormenting whispers." "Day and night, through snow and rain," during the winter and spring of 1797–1798, Granade wandered about the woods "howling, praying, and roaring in such a manner that he was generally reputed to be crazy." Throughout the western states Granade was known as the "wild man." He wrote this poem at about this time:

> Alas! alas! where shall I go,
>   Jesus from me has gone;
> A child of sorrow, grief and wo,
>   Forevermore undone.
> The gospel too, is hid from me,
>   Tho' often I do hear
> The law denounces death on me,
>   And thunders out despair.
>
> My hope is fled, and faith I've none
>   God's word I cannot bear.
> My sense and reason almost gone,
>   Fill'd with tormenting fear:
> What next to do, I cannot tell,
>   So keen my sorrows are—
> Without relief I sink to Hell,
>   To howl in long despair.[11]

Finally converted at a camp meeting, Granade immediately channeled his spiritual energy into preaching. "I would sing a song or pray or exhort a few minutes," he later recalled, "and the fire would break out among the people, and the slain of the Lord everywhere were many." At one point Granade declared himself to be a prophet and was suspended from preaching for three months, but this probably only increased his appeal. Crowds began to follow him from place to place, "singing and shouting all along the road." Some claimed he had a secret "powder" that he threw over the people to enchant them, while others believed he worked "some secret trick by which he threw them down." At one meeting so many people fainted and "lay in such heaps that it was feared they would suffocate, and that in the woods." Exhausted after only three years of preaching, Granade located in 1804, studied medicine, married in 1805, and died in 1807.[12]

The enthusiasm of early American Methodism appealed to a broad spectrum of Americans for at least two reasons. First, its self-validating quality gave those furthest on the margins of organized American religion, particularly women and African Americans, the means with which to exercise greater influence than they had ever been allowed to command in the more established churches. Second, it answered the yearning of many for a more direct contact with the supernatural in everyday life, for the freedom to work out their own salvation outside the confines of traditional ecclesiastical structures. This was particularly appealing in an age enamored with democratic ideology, in which traditional religious institutions seemed to be crumbling and failing on every hand. The itinerant Jacob Young discovered this on his Kentucky circuit in 1803. Young was no prude, and later in life counted Lorenzo Dow as one of his closest friends, but in 1803 his Kentuckians were almost too much for him. "They became great enthusiasts," he later recalled, "and very superstitious in their notions—looking for miracles and things out of the common order. They expected God to tell them every thing they ought to do."[13]

It should be noted at the outset that what I have in mind by terms such as "enthusiasm" and "supernaturalism"—what Ronald A. Knox called "ultrasupernaturalism"—are a cluster of beliefs and practices that place great stock in dreams, visions, supernatural impressions, miraculous healings, speaking in tongues, and gatherings at which people fall in a swoon and are left lying in a trance, sometimes for hours or days. Enthusiastic religion offers a more interactive faith in which the believer and God actively work together to meet life's daily challenges and in which God communicates directly with the believer or community of believers. Because of its individualistic and self-validating nature—who can say if another person has really seen a vision or not?—this kind of supernaturalism often works to circumvent established patterns of hierarchy.[14]

But while enthusiastic religion may challenge established ecclesiastical structures, it must do so in culturally acceptable ways. Even enthusiastic religion must be broadly isomorphic with the larger culture if it is to win adherents.[15] Hence, it is not surprising to find that, in general, such practices are rife in times of broad cultural distress. Uncertain times, apocalyptic visions, and militant enthusiasm often go hand in hand.[16]

Despite Methodism's phenomenal growth, the full depth of its popular appeal has yet to be appreciated. Methodism's attraction went far beyond the intellectual appeal of Arminianism to include new concepts of how to mediate one's daily relationship with God. It may not be an exaggeration to say that this quest for the supernatural in everyday life was the most distinctive characteristic of early American Methodism.[17]

In helping to create the religious hothouse of the early republic, American Methodism drew on a wide range of popular religious practices from both Europe and America.[18] In England, Methodist splinter groups such as the Primitive Methodists and the so-called Magic Methodists of Delamere Forest were decidedly more enthusiastic than the Wesleyan parent body.[19] Because English Methodism was initially largely a movement from within the lower and middling orders of society it was especially susceptible to syncretization with folk beliefs, particularly in rural areas and on the fringes of English society. In his pathbreaking study of nineteenth-century south Lindsey, James Obelkevich concludes that even though Methodism dominated the religious life of the district, it never established a monopoly on religious beliefs. "Villagers might attend both church and chapel," writes Obelkevich, "but their religious realm extended beyond the churches, indeed beyond Christianity, to encompass an abundance of pagan magic and superstition." Such was the nature of religion in south Lindsey that many of the villagers apparently saw nothing wrong with combining militant Methodism with belief in witches, wise men, and a wide range of "low-grade magic and superstition."[20] The same was true in the early nineteenth-century mining communities of Cornwall. There, historian John Rule observes, "Methodism did not so much replace folk-beliefs as translate them into a religious idiom."[21] But in Britain, unlike in America, such popularly based beliefs were never allowed to advance much beyond the margins of society.

Along with these European antecedents, American Methodism was free to draw on the long tradition in American popular religion of putting great stock in signs, wonders, and ecstatic experiences. Religious enthusiasm could be found in all regions of colonial America. Charles Woodmason, an Anglican missionary to the Carolina backcountry in the 1760s, described one of his congregations as "a Gang of frantic Lunatics broke out of Bedlam. . . . One on his knees in a Posture of Prayer—Others singing—some howling—These Ranting—Those Crying—Others dancing, Skipping, Laughing and rejoycing."[22] Even colonial New Englanders lived in an enchanted universe where ghosts visited people in the night and neighbors dreamed prophetic dreams. In short, as David D. Hall has suggested, theirs were "worlds of wonder" in which it was not unreasonable to assume that the supernatural impinged on everyday life. Though increasingly opposed by the clergy as the eighteenth century waned, this supernaturalist tradition was far from dead on a popular level when the Methodists burst on the scene.[23] Given the decidedly enthusiastic cast of eighteenth- and early nineteenth-century religion, it is hardly surprising that the enthusiasm of early American Methodism had such widespread appeal.

All of these cultural precedents, along with the egalitarianism born of the Revolution, provided fertile ground for American Methodism. To a great extent, the early Methodist itinerants were not burdened with the task of converting their audiences to a new worldview. They had only to tap into powerful undercurrents of popular belief that had heretofore found little institutional recognition. Among Wesley's directly appointed regular preachers in America, only Francis Asbury seems to have perceived that in America the religious and cultural peripheries were in many respects stronger than the center. Asbury recognized that the enthusiasm so endemic to American Methodism was not an unfortunate anomaly but the very lifeblood of the movement. This becomes readily apparent when he is compared to Joseph Pilmore and Thomas Rankin, two of Wesley's chief early representatives in America.

In a sense, Joseph Pilmore's life was one long pilgrimage up the social ladder, as a brief review of his career demonstrates. Born in 1739 in Yorkshire, England, he attended Wesley's Kingswood school near Bristol, joining the English connexion on trial in 1765 as an itinerant preacher. Along with Richard Boardman, Pilmore was one of the first preachers Wesley sent to America, arriving in October 1769. In January 1774 both Pilmore and Boardman returned to England. There, Pilmore resumed itinerating for a time, not returning to America until 1784 when he was ordained a deacon in the Protestant Episcopal Church. From 1794 to 1804 he was rector of Christ's Church in New York City. In 1804 he became rector of St. Paul's Church in Philadelphia, remaining there until his death in 1825.[24] Though he remained friendly to Methodism throughout his life, Pilmore's ambition was to advance to the center of respectable society. "My province seems to be where there are many to hear," he wrote in 1771, "as I have always the most liberty in great congregations, and among sensible people."[25]

But even given his thirst for improvement, Pilmore was not strictly opposed to the popular enthusiasm he encountered in America. Though his sights were set on social advancement, Pilmore breathed the same air as his fellow Methodists. He clearly looked for his own preaching to have a visible impact on his listeners, and it often did. For example, he recounted with approval in his journal that in New York City in 1770, "a Woman, who fel down in the Chapel while I was speaking, came into our House, and told us with an heart full of love, and her eyes flowing with tears of joy, that *she had found the Lord*."[26] Similarly, after preaching in Trenton, New Jersey, in 1772 Pilmore recorded that "the people cried about me in such a manner that my voice was nearly lost."[27]

Pilmore also looked to God to speak to him directly concerning daily affairs and to intervene tangibly on his behalf. In May 1772, he began a truly remarkable one-year solo journey from Philadelphia to Georgia and back. Most often he traveled alone, on poor roads, with little idea of what lay ahead. Throughout his trip he relied on supernatural impressions to order his way: "My plan was to follow the leading of Providence, and go wherever the 'tutelary cloud' should direct."[28] Moreover, Pilmore was ready to admit that God could speak to anyone, even those traditionally excluded from authority. Hence, it is not really surprising to find that he probably appointed the first female class leader in American Methodism, Mary Thorn.[29]

But Pilmore, refined churchman that he hoped to become, had his limits. In Gunpowder Neck, Maryland, he encountered an especially enthusiastic society that was more than he could bear: "In the evening I had much conversation with some who think they are called to preach and are as hot as fire, but it is dreadfully *Wilde* and *Enthusiastic*. God has undoubtedly begun a work in these parts . . . but there is much danger from those, who follow a heated imagination rather than the pure illumination of the Spirit, and the directions of the word of God."[30] Though Pilmore was disturbed by what he found at Gunpowder Neck, it did not shake his belief that ordinary believers could discern "the pure illumination of the Spirit." "Wherever I go," he concluded, "I find it necessary to bear my testimony against all wildness, shouting, and confusion, in the worship of God, and at the same time, to feed and preserve the sacred fire which is certainly kindled in many hearts of this Country."[31]

In the end, Pilmore's brand of Methodism, aimed at combining a moderate measure of enthusiasm with a greater concern for social refinement, did not immediately take root in America. The bulk of American Methodists could not abide Pilmore's synthesis, which seemed to smack too much of elitism. Pilmore himself soon realized this. By becoming an Episcopalian he found a church whose outlook more closely matched his own.

In 1773, Wesley sent Thomas Rankin and George Shadford to America to shore up the leadership of American Methodism, mostly because he had become concerned by reports that Boardman and the ecumenically minded Pilmore were not adhering to Methodist discipline. So he sent Rankin to enforce the Methodist system of probationary membership, class meetings, and quarterly meetings. It was an assignment for which Rankin was well suited. Unlike Pilmore, Rankin had few aspirations toward social or professional advancement. He was far more concerned with the vitality of local Methodist institutions, and more at home in the countryside than in Philadelphia, New York, or Baltimore.

But Rankin was not the cold and dour person he is sometimes represented as. In fact, his journal presents a picture of someone more introspective and spiritually intense than does Pilmore's. The son of a brewer, Rankin was converted in his late teens after a series of dramatic dreams and visions. The climax of these events came one day when, after having despaired over the condition of his soul to the point of considering suicide, he fell into a deep trance. "Sleeping I was not, and waking I was not," he later wrote. "Some may think or suppose, what I am going to say was only a dream; but of the contrary of this, I am as much assured of, as I know I am at this moment a living man." Having not yet experienced conversion, Rankin firmly believed that he was a sinner destined to hell. In his vision he "clearly saw, my soul doomed to everlasting flames. . . . Around my bed, stood with eager looks, a company of damned spirits, ready to conduct my soul to endless torments." His vision, however, did not end with his demise into hell, but with a revelation of Christ. "In the twinkling of an eye, I beheld the heavens open and part asunder and the appearance of the glorified humanity of the Son of God. I thought I cried aloud, 'There is the Lord Jesus Christ! There is the Redeemer of lost and undone mankind!' "[32] It was an experience that Rankin never forgot, and the veracity of which he never doubted; it became the beacon of his life.

With this kind of background it is hardly surprising to find that Rankin was not categorically opposed to the enthusiasm he encountered in America. In fact, his own meetings were sometimes the scene of extraordinary emotional outbursts. While Rankin preached at one gathering in 1774, "it seemed as if the very house shook with the mighty power and glory of Sinai's God. Many of the people were so overcome, that they were ready to faint, and die under His almighty hand. For about 3 hours the gale of the spirit thus continued to break upon the dry bones. . . . As for myself, I scarce knew whether I was in the body or not: and so it was with all my brethren."[33]

But like Pilmore before him, Rankin found more in the way of enthusiasm in America than he could tolerate. In June 1776 he was present for a powerful revival at Bushill's chapel in Virginia at which "many fell to the floor" and "little could be heard, except groans and strong cries to God for mercy." Despite the conversions this outburst produced, Rankin was troubled by the accompanying enthusiasm. When he returned two weeks later, he was determined to quiet things down. According to the Methodist preacher and historian Jesse Lee, at this subsequent meeting, Rankin "gave us a good discourse in the forenoon and tried to keep the people from making any noise while he was speaking." But when Rankin went to "get his dinner," as soon as he left "the people felt at liberty, and began to sing, pray and talk to their friends, till the heavenly flame kindled in their souls, and sinners were conquered, and twelve or fifteen souls were converted to God." Rankin returned to preach again in the afternoon, though most of the congregation seems to have regretted that he bothered. When he could not stop the people from crying aloud and shouting out prayers as he spoke, he finally gave up and turned the meeting over to George Shadford, who embraced the assembly's emotional energy such that "in a few minutes the house was ringing with the cries of broken hearted sinners, and the shouts of happy believers."[34]

Thomas Ware, one of the earliest American-born preachers, records that in a similar incident in North Carolina, Rankin "so violently opposed" a revival that "it soon declined."[35] Soon after, at one of the conferences, Rankin declared that he "was alarmed at the noise—which he had witnessed in the southern states; that a stop must absolutely be put to the prevailing wild-fire, or it would prove ruinous to all we held sacred;" and that while he had done all he could to suppress it, he "was ashamed to say that some of his brethren the preachers, were infected with it." Dismayed at these "imprudent remarks,"

Francis Asbury "interposed to put a stop to them in a way which was alike gratifying to the preachers generally, and mortifying to the person concerned."[36] Both Asbury and Rankin realized that at issue was a distinguishing characteristic of the American movement. "The friends of order may allow a guilty mortal to tremble at God's word . . . and the saints to cry and shout, when the Holy One of Israel is in the midst of them," declared Asbury. "To be hasty in plucking up the tares, is to endanger the wheat." Ware believed that this dispute over the "spirit of the Americans" was one of the causes of Rankin's and Asbury's well-known animosity toward one another.[37] Had the Revolution not intervened, debate over the limits of enthusiasm may well have led to one of the first major disputes between American and English Methodism.

American Methodism's militant supernaturalism was a product of popular religion in the sense that it was largely supported and propagated by the laity. But this is not to say that it represented the religion of the people as opposed to that of the clergy.[38] Within American Methodism the line between clergy and laity was blurred as it had seldom been before in Europe or colonial America. While the career itinerants are the most celebrated figures of early Methodism, their contribution was equaled, if not exceeded, by a vast cadre of local preachers, lay exhorters, and class leaders.

A vivid example is James P. Horton. Born in 1769 in Dutchess County, New York, Horton was a sometime shoemaker, sometime preacher, and all-time enthusiast known as "Crazy Horton" and later in life as "Uncle Jimmy." He confessed that a tendency toward excessive enthusiasm was "my weakness" and something that offended his more refined listeners. "I made such a dreadful time of it, according to their notions, whenever I prayed, or exercised. I hallowed so loud it would frighten the devil's children."[39]

Following his conversion Horton spent the next 30 years dividing his time between making shoes to support his wife and 13 children, and preaching wherever he felt led to go. His meetings were filled with shouting, falling and fervent prayers, and his life with supernatural impressions and prophetic dreams. Horton was also a proponent of divine healing, believing that he himself had been miraculously cured on at least two occasions.[40] Not surprisingly, his beliefs and style aroused a degree of opposition and even fear in some. One woman went so far as to lock herself in her room when she heard that "Crazy Horton" would be attending a meeting in her house.[41] But his style also endeared him to a broad spectrum of people. Freeborn Garrettson paid Horton's way to several camp meetings, and others so frequently did the same that he became a fixture at these events in his region of New York. The Garrettsons also allowed Horton and his family to live on a portion of their land for a time.[42]

Horton's career illustrates the way in which early American Methodism enabled seemingly ordinary people to reach beyond themselves, whether it be in preaching the gospel or in some more secular pursuit. One can argue to what degree his dreams and impressions were simply mental devices that allowed him to cope with the uncertainties of life, but Horton himself would have scoffed at such an explanation. He believed his revelations had a thoroughly divine origin. What was important for Horton was that he had the highest possible mandate to pursue his calling. Almost predictably, his calling as a local preacher was confirmed to him in an intricate prophetic dream.[43]

Although the early itinerants occasionally stayed at inns or slept out in the open, their usual practice was to lodge with sympathetic families along their circuit. In this way Francis Asbury traveled the length and breadth of the new nation for more than 40 years without ever having a permanent residence or owning much more than he could carry on horseback. Under these conditions, family devotions led by visiting circuit riders could be dramatic and memorable events, as a description of John Granade illustrates.

Granade was remembered as having a voice "full and musical; his eye keen, *piercing*; and, when speaking, his jesticulations were violent." In Knox County, Tennessee, Granade lodged with a local family after having preached in the area. Following dinner, the family and some nearby relatives assembled and Granade began by reading a scripture passage, singing a hymn, and praying. As one observer recounted, "He then gave an exhortation, in which he waxed quite warm, frequently moving the table forward before him, till at the close of his exhortation it stood near the center of the room." This was enough to intimidate some of the adults present and cause one of the children to hide in the empty fireplace, but Granade was only getting warmed up. He sang another hymn, and then proceeded to speak personally to each individual present as the rest of the household looked on. At one point he stood before the father of the house:

> Rubbing his hands briskly, lifting his feet alternately, and letting them down with no very slow or light tread, breathing deep inspirations drawn through his teeth, he almost literally danced, like David before the ark. After indulging for some moments in this ebullition of feeling, in which not a word was spoken, his full soul found vent in an outburst of blessing and thanksgiving to God that, though the harvest was large, and the laborers so few in that region, he had found one who was laboring faithfully in the wilderness to prepare the way of the Lord.

The entire session lasted some two hours with one of the participants concluding, "I wept, I loved him; for I really believed he wished us all to be saved."[44]

This was not the sort of performance that most Americans had been accustomed to seeing from their ministers, and it is not difficult to appreciate why Granade made such a lasting impression on many.

Early Methodism's supernaturalism primarily took root in these kinds of intimate encounters, whether they occurred in rural cabins or in village class meetings. Henry Boehm, one of Asbury's long-time traveling companions, was convinced that such informal, small-group gatherings did more to advance Methodism than better known public meetings. "Is it not generally known," wrote Boehm, "that the greatest displays of divine power and the most numerous conversions were in private houses, in prayer-meetings?"[45]

Preachers such as Granade and Horton set the stage for the explosive public gatherings that remained characteristic of American Methodism from its founding into at least the second decade of the nineteenth century. These emotion-laden revivals took place not only on the frontier but also in rural areas long since settled and in the major towns and cities of the eastern seaboard. In 1787 a remarkable revival engulfed the Sussex and Brunswick circuits in southern Virginia. During the revival, according to Jesse Lee, meetings often lasted five or six hours, and sometimes all night. "Thousands" attended and "above one hundred" were converted at a two-day quarterly meeting at Mabry's chapel in late July. At a subsequent outdoor meeting in the same vicinity the people "roared and screamed so loud that the preacher could not be heard, and he was compelled to stop." "Many scores" of both whites and African Americans "fell to the earth," where they stayed "in the deepest distress" until late in the evening. Among those struck down were a number of the local gentry, who could be seen "lying in the dust, sweating and rolling on the ground, in their fine broad cloths or silks, crying for mercy." Altogether, more than 4,000 people were converted on the Sussex, Brunswick, and Amelia circuits alone during this revival.[46]

Though the Virginia revival was unusual in its intensity, it was not unique. Beginning in the late 1790s, a remarkably similar revival broke out on the Delmarva Peninsula. There, the itinerant Thomas Smith saw nearly 1,100 people join the Methodist Church from his circuits between 1800 and 1802. Among these was Thomas Burton of Accomack County, a member of the landed gentry. On New Year's Day, 1801, Burton invited Smith to preach at his home to a large gathering of people. The result was nothing short of spectacular. "This night, this memorable night, never to be forgotten, excelled all I had ever seen," Smith later wrote: "At the very commencement of the meeting the Spirit of the Lord came as a rushing, mighty wind—the people fell before it, and lay in heaps all over the floor. The work continued all night, nor did it stop in the morning, but continued for thirteen days and nights without interruption; some coming, some going, so that the meeting was kept up day and night."[47] One result of this protracted meeting was a new class of 55 whites and another of 40 African Americans, all of whom were new members. Even allowing for a fair amount of exaggeration on Smith's part, the meeting must have been one of intense spiritual energy. Nor was this meeting an isolated incident on the peninsula during the years 1798–1802. At a meeting on the Dover circuit in 1802, Smith attempted to close the service at midnight by sending the people out of the meetinghouse. When they refused to leave the yard, Smith preached a sermon by the light of a full moon while standing on a grave and then let the people back into the chapel. The result of this meeting was another 85 new members.[48]

Taken as a whole, Methodism's new cultural precedents had the unanticipated effect of dramatically empowering those previously held at arms length by organized religion, particularly women and African Americans. Even on the Delmarva Peninsula, where a relatively large proportion of the landed gentry were sympathetic to Methodism, in most cases it was women who led the way in supporting the Methodists and their husbands, brothers, and sons who followed along. Women were a clear numerical majority of Methodist adherents and formed the backbone of the early Methodist movement. Methodism attracted these women in part because it offered the kind of direct opportunity to help shape the religious and moral character of their families and communities often unavailable in the more established denominations.

Thomas Ware records the case of a Church of England clergyman who arrived on the eastern shore of Maryland in 1784 and was shocked by the inroads made by the Methodists. During his candidacy sermon the clergyman unleashed a "flood of invective upon enthusiasm," labeling John Wesley the "prince of enthusiasts." This kind of attack by gentlemen clergy was not at all uncommon in this period. William Watters tells of a Norfolk parson who, in 1772, preached a violent sermon against the Methodists calling them "enthusiasts and deceivers." "His text, for this noble purpose," records Watters, "was, 'Be not over righteous.' " "Amongst other things he told his people (what none of them would have otherwise suspected) that he knew from experience the evil of being over righteous."[49] Not surprisingly, this sermon did little to stem the tide of Methodism in Norfolk. Ware's clergyman met with little better success. Even as he railed against the Methodists, a woman in the congregation cried out, "Glory to God! if what I now feel be enthusiasm, let me always be an enthusiast!" Nor could the officers of the clergyman's prospective parish offer him much encouragement since many of their wives and daughters were Methodists.[50]

Like white women, African Americans not only were attracted by the enthusiastic nature of early Methodism but did much to shape its character. In all likelihood, elements of traditional African religion that closely resembled forms of early Methodist enthusiasm survived in the memory of many slaves.[51] Nowhere was this more apparent than in the slave spirituals. Not only the songs themselves but also the way in which they were sung—using a wide range of emotive expression—worked to break down the barrier between the realm of the supernatural and everyday life, to open the believer's heart to the voice of the Holy Spirit.[52] Writing in 1819, John F. Watson, himself no friend of enthusiasm, gave the following account of worship among African-American Methodists:

> In the *blacks'* quarter, the colored people get together, and sing for hours together, short scraps of disjointed affirmations, pledges, or prayers, lengthened out with long repetition *choruses*. These are all sung in the merry chorus-manner of the southern harvest field, or husking-frolic method of the slave blacks; and also very like the Indian dances. With every word so sung they have a sinking of one or other leg of the body alternately, producing an audible sound of the feet at every step, and as manifest as the steps of actual negro dancing in Virginia, etc.[53]

Initially, some white Methodists found this kind of worship not only intensely disagreeable but also frightening. The itinerant John Littlejohn recorded an instance that took place in Richmond, Virginia, in 1777 in which he preached to a house crowded with both African Americans and whites: "Towards the close the poor Africans could forbear no longer but wth strong cryes & tears called for mercy; most of the Whites frightend, left the house, in confusion & dismay as if the great deep was going to overwhelm them, I pause till they had got into the Street, & continued to point the Blks to Jesus as their only ark of safty fm the storm."[54]

But by the early nineteenth century, enthusiastic worship permeated much of American Methodism, becoming for many middling Americans an accepted part of their religious lives. For example, as a young boy, William Cooper Howells (father of William Dean Howells) moved with his family to Ohio in 1813, eventually settling in Steubenville. Since there were no Quaker meetings in Steubenville, the Howells began attending Methodist meetings. "I shall never forget the terror with which the 'exercises' inspired me," Howells later recalled. "At the first prayer I knelt down with others; while the tone of supplication of the man who prayed waxed louder and louder." Knowing that "amen" was customarily said at the end of a prayer, Howells waited, "shaking till my knees rattled on the floor with fear." "I thought those around me were likewise affected, and were crying *amen* as an inducement for the brother to stop; when in fact they were only encouraging him. I regarded it as an awful time." Yet it was not long before Howells, like most early Methodist adherents, "got used to" this form of prayer and worship and "learned to regard it as what was just right."[55]

But critics remained, particularly those disturbed by the increasingly African-American character of Methodist worship. On the Harford circuit in

Maryland in 1791, William Colbert recorded in his journal that while he preached at one appointment, "a black woman cry'd out for sanctification, and I have no reason to believe she did not receive that great blessing, but I expect the noice she made offended some of my delicate hearers."[56] While touring Virginia that same year, Thomas Morrell also drew a direct connection between the presence of African Americans and enthusiasm in public worship, noting that the people were "fond of noisy meetings[,] particularly the blacks."[57] Blaming "such gross perversions of true religion" on African Americans, Watson noted with alarm that at camp meetings it had become common for large groups to stay up all night "singing tune after tune, (though with occasional short episodes of prayer) scarce one of which [is] in our hymn books. Some of these, from their nature, (having very long repetition choruses and short scraps of matter) are actually composed as sung, and are indeed almost endless."[58] Not surprisingly, Methodist enthusiasm aroused the most strident opposition from those most worried about maintaining traditional order. Along with the charge of religious miscegenation, more refined opponents of Methodism relished pointing out that women were more likely to fall in a swoon during Methodist meetings than were men, and often tied their criticisms to issues of class. John Watson was convinced that Methodist enthusiasts were mostly persons of "credulous, *uninformed* minds; who, before their change to grace, had been of rude education."[59]

Foreign travelers were also quick to pick up on these themes, which had long formed the core of anti-Methodist propaganda in England. In 1802 Francois Andre Michaux attended a camp meeting in Lexington, Kentucky, and noted that during the course of impassioned sermons sometimes 200 or 300 were overcome and fell. "This species of infatuation happens chiefly among the women," he observed, "who are carried out of the crowd, and put under a tree, where they lie a long time extended, heaving the most lamentable sighs." In 1806 the British traveler John Melish was offended by the intensity of Methodist meetings in Georgia, especially "the practice they often have of thumping and making a noise in the time of divine service, thereby converting the temple of the Lord into a scene of confusion and discord, exciting the laughter of the profane, and distracting the serious." Particularly shocking to Melish was the example of Dorothy Ripley, a "preacher" who "had the art of playing upon the passions so effectually, that she would sometimes trip half a dozen of her hearers."[60] These kinds of impressions fixed themselves in the minds of race- and class-conscious European travelers. In 1819 Swedish Baron Klinkowstrom was drawn to an African-American Methodist church in Brooklyn by the noise and intensity of a meeting. "I can not now describe for you the effect it had on me to see twenty or thirty Negresses, who thought they were full of the Holy Ghost, behave like regular furies," he later wrote. "Their bellowing, dancing, and jumping on benches was hideous and extremely bar-

Figure 5.3. Jarena Lee, from her autobiography, Religious Experience and Journal of Mrs. Jarena Lee *(Philadelphia, 1849). Courtesy of the Billy Graham Center Museum, Wheaton, Illinois.*

baric." "The Methodists in America," added the British traveler Isaac Holmes in 1823, "appear determined to take heaven by storm." What undoubtedly disturbed all of these observers was the way in which traditional lines of authority were being redrawn before their very eyes.[61]

Perhaps no group had a more enduring attachment to militant Methodist supernaturalism than African-American women. Methodism not only resonated with their heritage of black spirituality but also legitimated their spiritual experiences in a way that transcended conventional standards of education, social standing, gender, and race. Since most Methodists believed in the reality of divinely inspired impressions, dreams, and visions, it was not so easy to protest when women, be they white or African American, manifested such experiences in acceptable and apparently authentic forms. The journals of Jarena Lee and Zilpha Elaw provide two of the most vivid examples of the validation provided by Methodist supernaturalism in the lives of African-American women. While the scope of their ministries was perhaps extraordinary, the nature of their spiritual experience was by no means exceptional.[62]

Jarena Lee was born in 1783 at Cape May, New Jersey, and Zilpha Elaw in Pennsylvania about 1790. Both were dramatically converted through direct revelation. Elaw's search for spiritual meaning began with a dream at age 14. "It was a prevailing notion in that part of the world with many," she later recounted, "that whatever a person dreamed between the times of twilight and sunrise, was prophetically ominous, and would shortly come to pass."[63] After attending Methodist meetings for some time, Elaw believed her prayers were answered one night when she "distinctly saw" Jesus approach her "with open arms, and a most divine and heavenly smile upon his countenance. As He advanced towards me, I felt that his very looks spoke, and said, 'Thy prayer is accepted, I own thy name.' " She was sure that this was no mere illusion because the cow she was milking at the time also "bowed her knees and cowered down upon the ground" when Christ appeared.[64]

Both Elaw and Lee eventually launched successful preaching careers. Elaw conducted preaching tours not only in the Northeast but also in the slave states of the upper South and in England as well. Widely known and accepted as an exhorter Lee preached in homes and Methodist churches, to slaveholders and magistrates, to congregations of both African Americans and whites. In 1835 alone she traveled over 700 miles and preached almost as many sermons.[65] Moreover, in a journal of only 21 printed pages, Lee records numerous instances of supernatural impressions, dreams, and visions. She believed that God gave her these "uncommon impressions" to make up for her lack of formal education. As the other senses of the blind are said to be enhanced, "so it may be with such as I am, who has never had more than three months of schooling; and wishing to know much of the way and law of God, have therefore watched the more closely the operations of the Spirit, and have in consequence been led thereby."[66] For both Lee and Elaw, their mystical experiences provided a confirmation of their calling that was available from virtually no other source.

The same was true for Rebecca Jackson. A free African American, Jackson was born in 1795, converted under the Methodists, and eventually became a Shaker eldress. During her Methodist phase she concluded that since "there was no mortal that I could go to and gain instruction, so it pleased God in His love and mercy to teach me in dreams and visions and revelation and gifts." Jackson not only had frequent prophetic dreams and visions but also claimed to have an extraordinary gift of healing, along with other supernatural powers. Like Lee and Elaw, she too was a popular preacher among both African Americans and whites.[67]

For African-American male preachers, enthusiastic experiences played much the same role that they did for women, as the career of John Jea demonstrates. Jea was born in Africa in 1773, brought to America as a slave, experienced conversion at age 15, and began preaching two years later. He had frequent prophetic dreams and visions, and claimed to have been taught to read in a single night by an angel who came to him with a "large book open, which was the Holy Bible, and said unto me, 'Thou hast desired to read and understand this book, and to speak the language of it both in English and in Dutch; I will therefore teach thee, and now read.'" Soon after, Jea, who identified most closely with the Methodists, gained his freedom and traveled the Atlantic world as a sailor and popular itinerant preacher.[68]

While early American Methodism cannot be reduced to enthusiasm, neither can it be understood without it. Early Methodism without enthusiasm would be like *Hamlet* without the ghost or *Macbeth* without the witches. For believers who found themselves struggling to come to terms with unprecedented social and cultural changes and with frequently hostile resistance from the broader society, visions, dreams, and supernatural impressions not only held deep religious meaning but also served to validate the Methodist system. Methodists did not invent this brand of religiosity, nor was it unique to Methodism in America. But they were far more willing to embrace and advance religious enthusiasm than were the leaders and members of any other cohesive, large-scale religious movement before 1820.

This kind of militant supernaturalism formed an integral part of the Methodist message in every region of the post-revolutionary United States. If it was stronger in the South and West, this was only because Methodists were less restricted by cultural and societal precedents in these areas. State-sponsored religion under the control of educated elites was receding in all parts of the new nation, but it held on longest in New England. Yet even in places such as Massachusetts and Connecticut, Methodist enthusiasm made a dramatic impact. Writing from Salem, Massachusetts, in 1805, the Jeffersonian clergyman William Bentley complained that "the excentricities of the Methodists [tend] to every disorder," including "fainting, shouting, yelling, crying, sobbing, [and] grieving." In a similar fashion, the author and publisher Samuel Goodrich vividly remembered that in post-revolutionary Connecticut the Methodists raised "sudden and irregular storms of fervor" in which "the very air at last seemed impregnated with [an] electric fluid." Many years later Goodrich could still clearly recall hearing Lorenzo Dow preach in such a setting.[69]

Not surprisingly, this ethos of enthusiasm persisted among Methodism's more marginalized groups, notably African Americans, longer than among its more upwardly mobile members. So powerful was this tendency toward enthusiasm among African Americans that W. E. B. Du Bois concluded that "the Frenzy" was one of the three fundamental characteristics of black religion (the other two being "the Preacher" and "the Music").[70]

But such was not predominantly the case for white Methodists. By the 1820s and 1830s in the mostly white Methodist Episcopal Church there was a noticeable shift away from overt enthusiasm.[71] In 1826 the board of the Ithaca Methodist Episcopal Church met to discuss an upcoming camp meeting. A prominent local merchant, David Ayres, recommended that since they could not "break up the meeting, and prevent its being held," they at least should maintain a respectable distance from the rural Methodists. He proposed that the Ithaca Methodists hold their own separate prayer meetings and that they "request our colored members all to stay in our prayer-meetings." In this way, concluded Ayres, "if the Methodists from the country become disorderly, we will not suffer, as the public can see the difference between the Ithaca Methodists, and the ranting Methodists from the country."[72] This shift on the part of those who, like Ayres, rejected the movement's earlier enthusiasm, corresponded exactly with an overall rise in social status for the church as a whole. Radical enthusiasm began to fall from favor among mainstream Methodists at precisely the same time that the majority of Methodists were beginning to feel fully at home in America. As we shall see more fully in chapter 8, this transformation of Methodist spirituality was part of a much larger trend.

6 *Slavery and African-American Methodism*

The man who robs me of my earnings
at the end of each week meets me as a
class-leader on Sunday morning, to show
me the way of life.

> —Frederick Douglass, *Narrative
> of the Life of Frederick Douglass
> an American Slave*

The African's Hymn

Ye sons of Africa, rejoice
Your Saviour calls, O hear his voice;
In prayer stretch forth your hands to God,
And wash by faith in Jesus' blood.

God sends our Ethiopian race
The blessed news of gospel grace;
O let us now his praises sing.
And shout the honours of our King.

Here is a fountain open'd free,
Come wash, and you may cleansed be;
Your souls may be made clean and white
And you be children of the light.

In bondage long your tribes have been
To men and devils, flesh and sin;
But now the gospel does proclaim
A freedom through the Saviour's name.

Come brethren, let us burst our chains,
And triumph on the gospel plains;
Assert our freedom, and improve,
Rich blessings, granted by God's love.

> —Camp-Meeting Hymn Book, 1818

On February 14, 1807, the itinerant Seth Crowell preached at "the African meeting-house" in New York City. "The Lord manifested his presence in a glorious manner," he noted in his journal following the meeting. "I have always found it good to preach to that people: God is with them—he has no respect to persons—all colours and persons are alike to him, if they fear him and work righteousness." Crowell was impressed not only with the African Americans' piety, but also with their methodical administration and well-regulated discipline. "The Africans here form a very respectable society; are decent in their appearance, and strictly religious and moral in their deportment," noted Crowell. "A number of the African preachers are men of sound judgement, good sense, and decent education: on the whole, they are an honour to the methodist cause."[1]

Two decades before Crowell's sermon in New York, the itinerant James Meacham preached to a racially mixed congregation on the Greensville, Virginia, circuit on a Sunday in August 1789. Meacham's sermon sparked a stir in the congregation such that "the Lord was all over the church . . . the Spirit of the (Lord) was great." Amid the outcry, "the dear black people was filled with the power & spirit of God and began with a great Shout to give Glory to God." Enraged by the sight of slaves worshipping so freely, a group of white men "eagerly ran into the Church with sticks[,] clubs and caines—abeating and abusing the poor Slaves[,] them outcast of Men[,] for praising of God." The mob was led by a magistrate who "with bitter oaths and gnashing of teeth . . . put up a prayer that we the preachers was all in Some Miserable Infernal Place." Virginia-born Meacham was sickened by what he saw. As he looked out the window he saw "a poor black bro. [who] lucked me in the face, and cryed, this is what I have got for praising of my dear Jesus.—It reached my poor heart, I begged him to bare it for Christ Sake, he would Soon (if he was faithful) be out of the reach of their Clubs." "O how can I rest when I see my bro unhumanely [treated]," reflected Meacham. "O America. America; blood and oppression—will be thy overthrow."[2]

In many ways, these two scenes are representative of the tension that tore at the heart of early American Methodism. As both accounts illustrate, African Americans constituted a large proportion of Methodism's earliest and most sincere adherents and contributed much to the shaping of the movement. Like Seth Crowell and James Meacham, many white Methodists welcomed their presence. But others resented both their influence on the movement (particularly on Methodist worship) and the inevitable question their presence raised:

if black and white Methodists were spiritual equals, why should they not be equals in all facets of life?

It must be remembered that the widespread Christianization of African Americans began not with the Anglicans, Congregationalists, and Presbyterians of the colonial era, but with the Methodists and Baptists of the early republic. Prior to the American Revolution, Anglican missionaries in South Carolina managed to convert only a small percentage of slaves despite considerable effort.[3] Churches in other regions did little better. But Methodism was different in this regard from the beginning. African Americans were among the first to respond to the Methodist message in large numbers. As early as 1771 the itinerant Joseph Pilmore noted that African Americans regularly attended Methodist meetings in New York City. "God has wrought a most glorious work on many of their souls," wrote Pilmore, "and made them witnesses that he is no respecter of persons." The itinerant Thomas Rankin likewise frequently noted the participation of African Americans in Methodist meetings as he traveled throughout the upper South and mid-Atlantic region between 1774 and 1776. In May 1774, for instance, he recorded that "some of the poor black people, spoke with power and pungency of the loving kindness of the Lord" at a particularly moving love feast in New York City.[4]

In 1786, the first year that annual conference records distinguished members by race, black Methodists accounted for 9 percent of total membership. By 1790, slaves and free African Americans constituted 20 percent of the Methodist Episcopal Church, with this proportion holding steady through 1815, and then declining to 16 percent by 1820. On at least one Maryland circuit African-American Methodists outnumbered white members as early as 1786. By 1800 African Americans represented 45 percent of Maryland's Methodists.[5] White Methodists simply could not ignore this response and its implications for the church, especially in the Chesapeake region.

Why did African Americans turn to Methodism in such great numbers after other churches had failed to win their allegiance? To begin with, social forces within the African-American community itself rendered many blacks more receptive to Christianity. In the Chesapeake region, slave imports peaked in the 1740s, declining sharply through the 1790s. As a result, adult sex ratios evened out, black community life became more settled and more distinctively African American (as opposed to African), and the influence of African religious systems declined, all of which worked to open African Americans to the Christian message.[6] Much the same was true in other regions.

There were also significant changes in the way that the Methodists, the Baptists, and others presented Christianity to African Americans. First, as Nathan Hatch suggests in his brilliant study *The Democratization of American Christianity,* these groups "earned the right to be heard."[7] A significant number of Methodist preachers condemned slavery and even racism in uncompromising terms from the 1770s well into the nineteenth century. One of the first Methodist preachers in America, Robert Williams, was interrupted while preaching at the courthouse in Norfolk, Virginia in 1772 by town officials who fretted that "if we permit such fellows as these to come here we shall have an Insurrection of the Negroes."[8] Though exactly what Williams said on this occasion is unknown, his message was clearly threatening to slaveholders, a fact that any African Americans who heard him would not have missed. Both slaves and their masters understood the potential connection between Methodist preaching and slave unrest. When the leaders of Gabriel's rebellion laid their plans for an attack on Richmond, Virginia, in 1800, they agreed that "all the whites were to be massacred," except for Quakers, Frenchmen, poor women who did not own slaves, and Methodists, whom the rebellion's leaders considered "friendly to liberty."[9]

In some places black and white Methodists worked closely together to spread the gospel. In Wilmington, North Carolina, the Methodist preacher William Meredith joined with African Americans to establish a large independent Methodist church in the 1790s. The church was characterized by "good order" and the congregation was said to be "deeply pious" and "well disciplined." Nonetheless, many Wilmington whites felt threatened by Meredith's ministry, subjecting him to "all manner of annoyances" and having him thrown in jail on at least one occasion. When arsonists burned down the church in 1798, a "much larger" church and adjoining house were built "by means of penny collections among the negroes" who "almost exclusively" composed Meredith's congregation. Following Meredith's death in 1799 his congregation joined the Methodist Episcopal Church, adding 231 African Americans and 48 whites to the church's membership roles.[10]

William Meredith's career illustrates the degree to which a significant number of early Methodist preachers moved beyond simply patronizing the African Americans to whom they preached. Though the Methodist Episcopal Church never managed to institute a meaningful national policy against slavery, the rules of many annual and quarterly conferences throughout the North and upper South represented what for their time were radical challenges to the foundations of perpetual race slavery. The Methodist commitment against slavery was always mixed and uneven, but many African Americans readily recognized that at times it was passionate and sincere.[11]

A second reason that African Americans responded so readily to Methodism was that the Methodists proclaimed a Christianity "that was fresh, capable of being readily understood and immediately experienced."[12] Methodist preachers invariably preached extemporaneously and instinctively understood

Figure 6.1. Richard Allen, founder of the African Methodist Episcopal Church, from a steel engraving by John Sartain of Philadelphia. Courtesy of the Billy Graham Center Museum, Wheaton, Illinois.

the importance of speaking in the vernacular. Their message was framed in terms that made sense to the multitude of both whites and African Americans. Richard Allen, founder of the African Methodist Episcopal (AME) Church, believed that the Methodists were "the first people that brought glad tidings to the colored people" in a way that they could understand. "All other denominations preached so high-flown that we were not able to comprehend their doctrine."[13]

"Boiling hot" Methodism embraced popular religious enthusiasm in a manner that did away with the need for elite education and traditional ecclesiastical hierarchy. The Methodist willingness to accept divinely inspired impressions, dreams, and visions as evidence of the work and call of God circumvented conventional assumptions about education, social standing, gender, and race. A nineteenth-century historian of Allen's church noted that more African Americans did not become Presbyterians because "Presbyterianism disregarded too much the emotional character of experimental religion—it laid too great stress upon the head . . . it strove to lift up without coming down." [14] In this regard Methodism was far more open to African-American spirituality. Since all were equal in the world of religious experience, Methodism offered unparalleled opportunities for many otherwise ordinary African Americans to take an active role in Methodist gatherings.

The third and "most critical" reason that African Americans joined groups like the Methodists, observes Hatch, was the emergence of black preachers and exhorters. [15] Like the emergence of "uneducated" white circuit riders, the appearance of large numbers of African-American preachers was a post-Revolutionary War phenomenon. In large measure, Methodism both created the climate in which these preachers could flourish and restricted their ministries. Some African-American preachers, such as Richard Allen and Harry Hosier, were well-known public figures. Probably born a slave and later manumitted, the immensely popular Hosier traveled and preached with Francis Asbury, Thomas Coke, Richard Whatcoat, and Freeborn Garrettson during the 1780s and 1790s. [16] Coke believed that Hosier was "one of the best Preachers in the world." Whites as well as African Americans crowded in to hear him preach "not only because he was a colored man, but because he was eloquent." [17] On one occasion while traveling through New England with Garrettson, Hosier's audience numbered more than a thousand. [18] "He was unboundedly popular," recalled the itinerant Henry Boehm, "and many would rather hear him than the bishops." [19] Similarly, Richard Allen was a widely recognized public figure in Philadelphia. His AME Church formed the basis of one of the most important African-American institutions of the nineteenth century. [20]

But the vast majority of African-American preachers were little known outside their immediate region and, as individuals, are almost invisible to us. African-American preachers were never licensed for the itinerancy and seldom appear in otherwise meticulous Methodist records. Their ministries are visible to us only through the most indirect sources, such as in advertisements for runaway slaves. In January 1798 the *Maryland Gazette* carried an advertisement for a runaway slave named Jem, who "is or pretends to be of the society of Methodists, he constantly attended the meetings, and at times exhorted himself." Two years later, in September 1800, the *Maryland Gazette* carried notices for a runaway named Jacob who "professes to be a Methodist, and has been in the practice of preaching nights," and for a slave named Dick who "is a Methodist preacher." Similarly, an August 1800 advertisement for a fugitive slave in the *Newbern Gazette* noted that "he is a Methodist preacher, and can read and write. . . . The most probable method to catch him, will be at Methodist meetings." [21] While riding the Salem, New Jersey, circuit in June 1792 the itinerant Richard Swain recorded in his journal that he "went and preached at Wm. H's and conversed with a black man that exhorts here," adding, "he seems gifted."[22] As with many such references, this is all we are ever likely to know about this unnamed exhorter.

But while the individual identities of most early African-American Methodist preachers and exhorters remain obscure, their collective impact is much clearer. Following the American Revolution "The Preacher" became a leading, if illusive, figure in African-American communities across the nation. He was, in the words of W. E. B. DuBois, "the most unique personality developed by the Negro on American soil. A leader, a politician, an orator, a 'boss,' an intriguer, an idealist—all these he is, and ever, too, the center of a group of men, now twenty, now a thousand in number."[23]

Largely as a result of the ministries of such preachers, African Americans took an active role in shaping the early Methodist movement. Consider Henry Evans, a free African-American shoemaker, licensed local preacher, and the "father" of Methodism in Fayetteville, North Carolina. Described as "the best preacher of his time in that quarter" and "the most remarkable man in Fayetteville," Evans's early preaching was opposed by the town council. Ordered to stop preaching, he instead held secret meetings in the woods. Eventually his preaching led to such an improvement in the "public morals" of local slaves, "particularly as regarded their habits on Sunday, and drunkenness" that he was permitted to preach in town. By 1802 Evans's congregation had built their own church, meeting the expenses themselves. Evans soon became so popular that his church had to be enlarged because whites began crowding the African Americans out of all the available seats.[24]

Another good example in this regard is the career of George White (1764–1836), one of the few African-American Methodist preachers who wrote a detailed autobiography. White was born a slave in Accomack County, Virginia, and sold the following year to a master in Essex County, Virginia. He was sold again at age 6 to a master in Somerset County, Maryland, and yet again at 15 to a planter in Suffolk County, Maryland. George White knew the hardships of slavery first hand.[25]

White gained his freedom at age 26 when his master died. Shortly thereafter he attended a Methodist quarterly meeting and became "considerably alarmed with a sense of my sins." Though he had previously attended the Church of England, this was the first time that he had experienced deep religious convictions. White eventually made his way to New York City, where he was converted at a Methodist meeting in 1791. In many respects his subsequent career was typically Methodist. He had a number of vivid prophetic dreams and visions, after one of which he applied for an exhorter's license in 1805. "Having a desire to travel," White combined his occupation as an oysterman with preaching tours through Long Island and New Jersey. He soon experienced sanctification, and, with the help of his oldest daughter, learned to read and write.

But White's story is also uniquely African American. Despite his diligent service to the church, he had to apply five times before receiving a local preacher's license in April 1807. According to Graham Hodges, deliberations over his applications were not even recorded in the quarterly meeting minutes, as they surely would have been for a white applicant. White preached actively to African Americans in the Methodist Episcopal Church, and occasionally to whites, until 1820 when he left to join Richard Allen's AME Church.[26]

African-American preachers understandably connected with their audiences in a way that few white preachers could match. While stationed in Charleston, South Carolina, in 1811, the itinerant William Capers discovered that white preachers were "excluded, as if by some sentence of outlawry" from preaching on several plantations, but that certain "extraordinary" African Americans "were permitted to hold meetings with the negroes pretty freely." Capers and his colleagues simply could not penetrate this barrier. As a result, the white preachers devised a "plan" to "recognize" these preachers as "our agents" and to authorize them "to admit and exclude members," and keep class meeting records—a major component of Methodist discipline. "They were the only persons who for Christ's sake were zealous enough to undertake such a service, and who, at the same time, could get access to the people that that service might be rendered," according to Capers.[27] He insisted that these "agents" were under close white supervision, but this may well be an exaggeration. No doubt there was much about these all-black plantation meetings that Capers and his colleagues did not understand.

As these examples indicate, African-American preachers and people alike worked together to fashion their own distinctive religious tradition. Though black preachers contributed much to white religion, their greatest significance lay in the fact that, as Albert Raboteau notes, "black preachers took it upon themselves to minister to their own people, with or without license from whites."[28] In doing so, they made the church a pillar of their society and culture, second only to the family in importance. But this is not to imply that all African Americans shared a common, monolithic community. Even within Christianity, African Americans were often deeply divided, as the split between Richard Allen's AME Church and the New York–based AME Zion Church indicates.[29] African Americans participated in the early republic's religious free market in much the same way that white Americans did. The intense rivalry between black churches often only serves to demonstrate how committed partisans were to their group.

In choosing to place the church at the center of community life, African Americans did more than simply copy white practices. Instead, they fashioned a faith that spoke to their daily hopes and fears, much as white Methodists shaped their practices to fit their circumstances, placing special and understandable emphasis on the Exodus story of the Old Testament.[30] In her study of the Gullah people of the coastal lowlands and islands of South Carolina and Georgia, Margaret Washington emphasizes that Gullah acceptance of Christianity was both "eclectic" and "complex." Christianity not only inspired Gullah spirituality but "also built internal community regulation and contributed largely to cultural creativeness." White Methodists were among the first to bring the gospel to the Gullahs and had the greatest early impact on Gullah Christianity. But as whites increasingly "used Christian instruction to secure the plantation system," notes Washington, "slaves practiced selective disengagement by refashioning Christianity according to their reality and their collective historical vision."[31]

It was this sort of creative energy that gave African-American Methodism its life, that made it possible for ordinary African-American Methodists to shape their own communities of faith. As was the case with white Methodists, education and social status counted for less among African-American Methodists than heart-felt conviction and entrepreneurial zeal. While itinerating along the banks of the Potomac near Alexandria, Virginia, in 1794, William Colbert encountered an African-American society at Oxon Hill that had built its own meetinghouse. "God has blessed the[ir] labour in an extraordinary manner, their society is very numerous, and very orderly," observed Colbert, "and to their great credit with pleasure I assert, that I never found a white class so regular in giving their Quarterage." The society, composed of both free African Americans and slaves, conducted its own class meetings, recognized its own leaders, and administered its own discipline, holding "days of examination in order to find out anything that may be amiss among them." "They are so numerous the circuit preacher cannot meet them all," noted Colbert, "there are 2 leading characters among them, that fill their station with dignity."[32] Colbert's description, reveals a community both committed to Methodism—including paying their share of the white circuit rider's salary (no small matter from Colbert's perspective)—and determined to maintain a degree of autonomy—including choosing their own local leaders. In a similar manner, the itinerant Henry Smith tells of a "large society of colored people" not far from Bladensburg, Maryland, "converted and collected through the instrumentality of a few colored men in that neighborhood." This society had built its own meetinghouse, and was "Methodistical in doctrine and in discipline, with the exception of a few rules peculiar to themselves." Because the society was composed mostly of slaves, they "administered corporeal punishment for some offenses," and in other cases would not allow those under discipline "to come into the congregation," but required them to "sit or stand at the door for a season." "This was upon the whole a simple-hearted, devoted people," concluded Smith.[33] It is to congregations like these that the story of African-American Methodism in this period most properly belongs.

As large numbers of African Americans poured into the movement, questions revolving around race in general and slavery in particular deeply divided Methodists. The massive response of African Americans placed pressure on the movement to live up to their expectations. In some places white Methodists accepted slaves and free blacks as legitimate members of Methodist societies. But in many places this clearly was not the case.[34] The attitudes of most white Methodists toward slavery both mirrored and helped to create those of the larger society in any given region, which is not surprising given the movement's voluntary foundation. The "crime" of white Methodist leaders, notes a nineteenth-century historian of the AME Church, was in "acting upon the damnable policy of expediency—of doing what seemed to be necessary, but not just—of compelling the Church, the Church that should account to no man, and to no time, to succumb to the base prejudices of the human heart."[35] In the end, much of American Methodism came to reflect what Ira Berlin has identified as the often contradictory "larger themes" of the American Revolution: "the egalitarian impulse, the restraining presence of slavery, and the ubiquity of racial division."[36]

Methodists were not part of the earliest protests against slavery, either in America or in England.[37] But by the revolutionary era, Methodists increasingly joined with a growing number of Americans and Britons in the belief that slavery was a great moral evil, radically at odds with the word of God. During the 1770s antislavery tracts by Samuel Hopkins, Anthony Benezet, Benjamin Rush, and others began to multiply, and Quaker opposition to slavery solidified, as Methodists were readily aware.[38] In 1774 the Continental Congress first resolved to end the slave trade, the same year in which Wesley published his tract *Thoughts Upon Slavery*, insisting that "the African is in no respect inferior to the European," and that "liberty is the right of every human creature."[39] In August 1775 the itinerant Thomas Rankin was in Philadelphia, where he met "many members" of the newly formed congress and "could not help telling many of them, what a farce it was for them to contend for liberty, when they themselves, kept some hundreds of thousands of poor blacks in most cruel bondage."[40] In 1780, the same year in which Pennsylvania passed the first emancipation law in America, the annual conference held in Baltimore declared slavery to be "contrary to the laws of God, man, and nature, and hurtful to society." In an attempt to add bite to this denunciation, the conference demanded that all traveling preachers emancipate any slaves they owned.[41] This rule reflected the abolitionist convictions—largely formed out of the ideology of the Revolution—of an increasing number of Methodists in the North and the upper South, particularly Maryland. Writing in 1806, William Watters lamented that his brother had died in Maryland in 1774, "before there was much, if any, talk amongst us about the impropriety of holding our fellow creatures in slavery," and therefore had not freed his slaves.[42]

Though it may not have been so a decade before, by the early 1780s slavery had become a topic of household conversation among Methodists. The growing antislavery convictions of many Methodist preachers had much to do with their frequent contact with African Americans. Always on the lookout for a receptive audience, the preachers from this era often commented in their journals on both the integrity of African-American faith and the magnitude of the black response to Methodism. While preaching in Calvert County, Maryland, in 1781 the itinerant William Watters noted that "the eagerness to here and receive instructions amongst the poor blacks in these parts, is truly affecting, and exceeds any thing that I have ever seen in any place."[43] Many also saw preaching to African Americans as a chance to live out their antislavery convictions. One of the first Methodist preachers to free his slaves was Freeborn Garrettson, the son of a prosperous Maryland planter, who did so in June 1775 shortly after his conversion.[44] As part of his ministry, Garrettson "often set apart times to preach to the blacks," and adapted his message "to them alone." For Garrettson, these were "precious moments."[45] Other Methodist preachers adopted similar practices. The circuit rider Thomas Smith recorded that at a March 1801 quarterly meeting in northeast Virginia, while the presiding elder Thomas Ware "was preaching in the house on Sunday morning, I was preaching in the wood to at least three thousand people of color, where I believe much good was done." Three months later Ware and Smith repeated this arrangement, with Ware preaching in the chapel while Smith "repaired to the grove, and preached to, as some said, four thousand Virginia slaves."[46] By the fervency of their response, African Americans compelled many white Methodists to reconsider some of their fundamental assumptions about race and faith.

Apart from preaching to African Americans and against slavery, revolutionary-era Methodist preachers also published abolitionist letters, essays, and tracts. In 1805 Freeborn Garrettson published a 55–page pamphlet entitled *Dialogue Between Do-Justice and Professing Christian*, which explicitly argued for "the universal emancipation of slaves thro' the continent." In this work the abolitionist Do-Justice argues that "if to deprive a human being of a free gift of God, namely freedom, is not oppression, I know nothing of the just rights of man." After much debate, Professing Christian is finally convinced of the immorality of slaveholding and agrees to free his slaves. He is then renamed Real Christian.[47]

Other prominent Methodist preachers who wrote and preached against slavery extensively in the 1780s and 1790s included James O'Kelly and Ezekiel Cooper. Cooper was first aroused to enter the public arena after attending a session of the Maryland Assembly in November 1789. At that meeting he was delighted to discover that "the majority of the House appeared in favor of abolition in some way or other, believing it to be cruel to have a hereditary slavery entailed upon any part of the human race." "I had great satisfaction in finding the poor oppressed had so many on their side," concluded Cooper. The following July 4, Cooper preached a strident antislavery sermon in Annapolis on the text, "If the Son therefore shall make you free, ye shall be free indeed" (John 8:36). The sermon supposedly led one slaveholder to declare, "The matter's settled; mine go free." But others were alarmed and offended. In Anne Arundel County nearly half the population were slaves, and the fear of insurrection was never far from the minds of slaveowners. "If they fear, the ground of their fear must be their own injustice in keeping those poor creatures in slavery whom God made free," noted Cooper in his journal a few days later. "Let them fear and be alarmed as they may, I must plead the cause of the innocent."[48]

The following November 1790, Cooper wrote a stern abolitionist letter to the *Maryland Gazette* under the pseudonym "A Freeman," declaring that "the argument that the 'Negroes were providentially intended to be slaves' is a most groundless proposition, and I confess a surprise that any man should ever advance it." This letter was answered in the *Maryland Gazette* first by "A True Friend to the Union" and then by "Abaris," with Cooper replying to each in print. In 1791 Cooper published lengthy antislavery letters in the *Maryland Journal* and the *Virginia Gazette*. All of his compositions are well written, well reasoned, and uncompromising in tone. He even argued against deporting freed slaves on the ground that they had committed no crime worthy of the punishment. Besides, "where would you export them to?" asked Cooper. "They are as much Americans now as we; and we are as much Europeans as they are Africans."[49] In his mind, free African Americans had as much chance of becoming good citizens as free whites.

Similarly, in 1789 James O'Kelly, who freed his only slave in 1784, published an *Essay on Negro Slavery*. In it he argued that for ministers to own slaves "hath more the appearance of wolves than shepherds."[50] The fact that both Cooper and O'Kelly remained popular and effective preachers, the former in Annapolis and Alexandria and the latter in Virginia, at the same time that they were publishing and preaching against slavery indicates the degree to which many Methodists in these regions shared their convictions. When Thomas Morrell visited O'Kelly's area of Virginia in 1791, he noted with approval that "the preachers of this district bear a good testimony against Slavery & many of our people have liberated their Negroes."[51]

One region in which Methodist opposition to slavery undoubtedly had a dramatic impact was on the Delmarva Peninsula. Methodists represented a significant portion of the peninsula's population, greatly magnifying their influence. By the end of the Revolution almost one-third of all Methodists lived on the peninsula. By 1810 some 20 percent of peninsula whites were Methodists, as well as 25 percent of the peninsula's African Americans, who accounted for one third of all Delmarva Methodists.[52]

Early Methodist preachers on the peninsula were vigorous opponents of slavery. As early as 1781, while stationed on the Sussex circuit, Freeborn Garrettson was "in a particular manner, led to preach against the practice of slaveholding." "Several were convinced of the impiety of the practice," noted Garrettson in his journal, "and liberated their slaves," while many others began to treat their slaves more humanely. In the early 1780s, Joseph Everett (a peninsula-born itinerant) refused to eat with slaveholders until they freed their slaves. In 1797 an Episcopal rector in Talbot County observed that Methodist preachers "relish the manumitting subject as highly as the Quaker preachers and spread the evil far and wide." That same year, while in Somerset County, Maryland, Francis Asbury noted that "most of our members in these parts have freed their slaves."[53]

In 1801 William Colbert and Henry Boehm were teamed on the Annamessex circuit on the peninsula. There, according to Boehm, "we preached against slavery, and persuaded our brethren and those who were converted to liberate their slaves, and we were often successful." Colbert was particularly zealous in his convictions and often showed more respect for the religion of his "black friends" than that of white Methodists. On one occasion in 1801 when he met a slave trader on the road he "told him if he did not repent for what he was doing he would be damnd as sure as the devil was damn'd." Later that year he used one of his sermons as an occasion to "scorge the sons and daughters of oppression: those infernal drovers of the human race." "May we not suppose that clouds of vengeance are collecting over the heads of the inhabitants of this country, for their cruelty [to] the poore distressed Africans," added Colbert in his journal.[54]

As an increasing number of slaveholders were convinced to emancipate their slaves the free African-American population soared in the early national period, growing from approximately 32,000 in 1790 to some 108,000 in 1810. The bulk of this increase occurred in the upper South (particularly in Maryland), where there were 98,000 free African Americans in 1810.[55] In this region in particular, the Methodists were key proponents of emancipation.

The impact of Methodist abolitionism on the Delmarva Peninsula is borne out by data on manumissions in three Maryland counties: Caroline, Dorchester, and Talbot. As Kenneth Carroll noted some 30 years ago, the proportion of free African Americans in these three counties increased from about 3.3

percent of all African Americans in the 1750s to approximately 55 percent by 1860. The greatest number of manumissions came as a result of Methodist influences. Between 1791 and 1799, 999 slaves were freed, the majority by Methodists. From 1800 to 1809 there were 663 manumissions, and from 1810 to 1819 an additional 431 manumissions, again largely by Methodists.[56]

Though nonreligious factors may well have played a part in some of these manumissions, the sincerity of the religious convictions of many who freed their slaves is unmistakable. Among the Delmarva Methodists who freed their slaves was Andrew Barratt, an influential lawyer who held various political appointments from 1780 to 1820. Barratt freed his 13 slaves in January 1796, "being fully persuaded that liberty is the natural birthright of all mankind and keeping any in perpetual slavery is contrary to the injunction of Christ." Other members of the Barratt family who manumitted their slaves included Andrew's father Philip Barratt, his brothers Caleb and Elijah Barratt, and a cousin Samuel Barratt.[57] Another Delaware Methodist who freed his slaves, though not immediately, was Judge Thomas White, who had sheltered Francis Asbury at his home near Whitelysburg, Delaware, during the Revolution. In his will, White liberated all 21 of his slaves, writing, "I think it wrong and oppressive and not doing as I would be willing to be done by, to keep negroes in bondage or perpetual slavery." Thomas White's son Samuel, a U.S. Senator from 1801 to 1809, likewise manumitted his slaves in four separate deeds between 1799 and 1804.[58] In Dorchester County, on the eastern shore of Maryland, 22-year-old Thomas Haskins freed his only slave in 1782, the same year he entered the itinerancy.[59] In much the same manner, Thomas Hill Airey used a single deed dated March 25, 1790, to free his 30 slaves, the first immediately and the last in 1811. Airey's decision clearly reflected the weight of Methodist preaching against slavery. Stating "that the practice of holding Negroes in perpetual bondage and slavery is repugnant to the pure precepts of the Gospel of Jesus Christ," he acknowledged "that if I continued to hold them in bondage, I should never be received into that rest that remains for the people of God."[60]

Apart from freeing their slaves, significant numbers of Methodists from Virginia and Kentucky moved north to Ohio in order to further escape the stigma of slavery. Philip Gatch (an early itinerant turned local preacher) and his wife Elizabeth freed the slaves she had brought to their marriage in 1788 while living in Virginia. Gatch's deed of emancipation read: "Know all men by these presents that I Philip Gatch, of Powhatan County do believe 'that all men are by nature equally free,' and from a clear conviction of the injustice of depriving my fellow Creatures of their natural Right, do hereby emancipate, or set free, the following persons." The deed then lists the names of Gatch's nine slaves. Then, in 1798, the Gatches took the further step of moving to Ohio to escape living in a slave state altogether. "O what a country will this be," wrote

Gatch in his journal as he contemplated their move north. "What a Paradise of pleasures, when these fields shall be cultivated and the Gospel of Christ spread through this rising Republic unshackled by the power of Kings and Religious Oppressions on the one hand, and slavery, that bane of true Godliness, on the other."[61]

The strength of the convictions of Philip Gatch and other Methodists who moved north can be seen in a collection of letters written by a number of these migrants to Edward Dromgoole (1751–1835) between 1802 and 1812. An Irish immigrant to America, Dromgoole itinerated from 1774 to 1786 before locating in Brunswick County, Virginia. In an 1802 letter to Dromgoole, Gatch explained that he had been reluctant to leave Virginia, but had decided to do so because "I felt unwilling to lay my Bones there, and leave my Children whom I tenderly loved in a land of slavery not knowing what the Evils there of would amount to in there time." Other former Virginians wrote to Dromgoole likewise encouraging him to come to Ohio, even offering to help with the details of the move. In February 1807 John Sale, then presiding elder of the Ohio District, wrote that he had "been told you have had thought of coming to this country," adding, "we have a fertile soil & Sallubrious Air that is not contaminated with *Slavery*." Five months later, in July 1807, Frederick Bonner wrote to Dromgoole explaining his reasons for migrating to Ohio, much as Philip Gatch had done. "When the Legislature of Va has determined against liberty & our preachers & people will be purchasing Slaves without a prospect of liberating them," wrote Bonner, "what can we think will be the condition of the church in the state when slavery is encouraged and liberty suppresst, in a few years." This theme is repeated so often in the letters to Dromgoole that one can scarcely doubt its importance for many northern Methodists.[62]

Fueled by such convictions, the antislavery movement within Methodism steadily gained momentum during the early 1780s, leading to a brief but dramatic attempt to completely rid the movement of slavery. At the 1783 annual conference, Francis Asbury noted with satisfaction that "we all agreed in the spirit of African liberty, and strong testimonies were borne in its favour in our love feast."[63] Antislavery legislation for the Methodist movement as a whole reached its high water mark in 1784. To the question: "What shall we do with our friends that will buy and sell slaves?" the annual conference minutes of May 1784 answered: "If they buy with no other design than to hold them as slaves, and have been previously warned, they shall be expelled, and permitted to sell [their slaves] on no consideration." The conference also resolved to suspend those local preachers in Maryland, Delaware, Pennsylvania, and New

Jersey who refused to free their slaves, but to give those in Virginia one more year to consider the matter.[64]

The Christmas conference of 1784, at which American Methodism separated from its British counterpart, went even further in outlining a plan to rid the movement of slavery. "We view it as contrary to the golden law of God on which hang all the law and the prophets, and the unalienable rights of mankind, as well as every principle of the revolution, to hold in the deepest abasement, in a more abject slavery than is perhaps to be found in any part of the world except America, so many souls that are all capable of the image of God," declared the conference. Every Methodist slaveholder was given 12 months to execute a legal deed of emancipation, although the emancipations themselves could be delayed. Slaves between the ages of 25 and 45 years were to be freed within five years; those between 20 and 25, by the age of 30; those under 20, by the age of 25 at the latest. The preachers were called on to keep written records verifying compliance; those members who refused to follow the rule were to be expelled, as were any members who sold their slaves. If fully implemented, this plan would, of course, have systematically rid American Methodism of slavery and brought freedom to thousands of African Americans. But it was not to be.[65] The reaction to the 1784 rules exposed how deeply divided American Methodists really were when it came to issues of race. As Russell Richey perceptively observes, when it came to slavery what Methodism ultimately transmitted to the nation was "a troubled conscience."[66]

Within six months after the Christmas conference, outcry and resistance from southerners led to the indefinite suspension of the 1784 rules. For the next 11 years the topic was absent from annual and general conference minutes. Not until 1796 would northern Methodists again attempt to formulate a national policy with respect to slavery. In that year, the general conference once again took up the debate, declaring that "we are more than ever convinced of the great evil of African slavery," but stopping far short of expelling slaveholders. At the next general conference in 1800, motions to forbid slaveholders from joining the church, to guarantee eventual emancipation to slaves born after July 4, 1800—a date deliberately picked for its obvious significance—and to once again require all members to execute deeds of emancipation for their slaves were all defeated. A motion to prepare "an affectionate address to the Methodist societies in the United States, stating the evils of the spirit and practice of slavery, [and] the necessity of doing away with the evil as far as the laws of the respective states will allow," was passed, though its eventual impact was far different from what its supporters might have hoped. A motion by William McKendree to present yearly addresses to the various state legislatures calling for "a gradual abolition of slavery" was also passed, as was a motion to allow the bishops to ordain African Americans to the office of deacon. The latter measure, however, caused such an uproar among the southern preachers that it was not printed in the conference minutes or in the *Discipline*.[67]

But the Methodist position on slavery was far more complex than this summary suggests. As we have seen in the cases of Ohio and the Delmarva Peninsula, many Methodists remained deeply opposed to slavery well into the nineteenth century. Hence, in the absence of a movement-wide policy, individual annual and quarterly conferences often fashioned their own rules on slavery. For example, in 1810 the Philadelphia Annual Conference, which had jurisdiction over the Delmarva Peninsula, called on every preacher and quarterly meeting conference "to use their lawful and prudential influence to promote the freedom of slaves," and urged quarterly meeting conferences not to license slaveholders to preach or exhort. It also requested that no class leaders be appointed "who are unfriendly to the freedom of slaves."[68]

But even where antislavery sentiment ran relatively high, Methodists often remained deeply divided, as the quarterly meeting conference minutes from the Madison, Kentucky, circuit illustrate. Minutes are extant for 45 Madison circuit quarterly meeting conferences from 1811 to 1826. These records reveal an internally divided society struggling to strike a compromise between rejecting and accommodating slavery. During this period, Madison circuit conferences held hearings on 13 separate cases involving the purchase or sale of slaves. Madison circuit Methodists followed a set of rules stating that "no member of our society shall purchase a slave except in cases of mercy or humanity to the Slave purchased." Anyone who purchased a slave was required to "state to the next ensuing Quarterly meeting Conference the number of years he thinks the Slave should serve as a Compensation for the price paid." The conference could shorten the period of service if it thought the purchaser was asking for too much, after which the purchaser was required to "execute a Legal Instrument of manumission of such Slave at the expiration of the time determined by the Quarterly meeting Conference." Anyone refusing to abide by these rules was to be expelled from the church. The rules also forbade members to sell slaves "except at the request of the slave to prevent separation in families," and stipulated that children born to a slave "during the time of her servitude shall be free at the age of twenty one, if the Laws will admit so early a manumission and if not at such time as the laws will admit."[69]

At times Madison circuit Methodists appear to have closely adhered to these rules. Thomas Stewart stood before the August 7, 1813, conference to state that he had purchased a slave for $140 "in consequence of his grand father's requesting him to purchase him to retain him in the family." Stewart proposed to emancipate the slave after 11 years of service. The conference approved, agreeing that Stewart had acquired the slave "thro the principle of humanity."[70]

But other cases were not so easily settled. At the same August 1813 conference, Presley Morris reported that Nathaniel Tevis had purchased a slave but failed to notify the conference. Tevis subsequently failed to attend the next two conferences in October 1813 and April 1814. At the 1814 conference

J. L. McMahon reported that Tevis had told him that he intended to keep the slave for life. Hearing this, the conference moved to expel Tevis. Likewise, the January 1815 conference heard a report that John Bennett had purchased a slave. After confirming this report, the April 1815 conference expelled Bennett for failing to abide by the slavery rules. The following November Bennett finally appeared before the conference, reporting that he had purchased 18-year-old Sarah for $370, and proposing to free her after 20 years. The conference agreed, restoring Bennett's membership.[71] Sarah's case illustrates both the commitment of some Madison circuit Methodists to a—limited—antislavery agenda, and the circumscribed nature of their rules. Though Sarah was promised her freedom, she would have to wait another 20 years for it.[72]

On the Accomack, Virginia, and Dorchester, Maryland, circuits, disciplinary cases followed a similar pattern. Of the 18 cases brought before the Accomack quarterly meeting conference from 1804 to 1816, 13 involved members holding slaves. As on the Madison, Kentucky, circuit, the conference was primarily concerned with determining how long a slave should be required to serve, and with seeing that deeds of emancipation were filed.[73] Much the same was true on the Dorchester circuit. There, the March 1804 quarterly meeting conference ordered Levin Lecompt to record a deed of manumission for Cloe, a slave whom he had purchased for $200, freeing her on January 1, 1816. The following year the conference expelled Joseph Meekins for refusing to free two slaves after what was thought to be a reasonable length of service. Similarly, in 1806 it "disowned" Roger Robertson for "selling a negro for life, alleging ignorance of the rules of the society."[74]

Predictably, the range of opinion among white Methodists was generally much broader in the upper South than in the southernmost states, where throughout the postwar period planters developed a deepening commitment to slavery.[75] As southern attitudes in general began to harden, it became increasingly costly to speak out against slavery in places like the South Carolina lowcountry. There, publication of the address called for at the General Conference of 1800 caused an immediate uproar. Reaching the South as it did hard on the heels of Gabriel's plot in Richmond, Virginia, the address's timing could scarcely have been worse.[76] Methodist preachers in particular were targeted by pro-slavery advocates. In October 1800 the Methodist itinerant George Dougherty was seized by an angry mob in Charleston and held under a pump till he nearly drowned. The other Methodist preacher in Charleston, John Harper, was forced to burn his copies of the address. Soon after, Harper wrote to Ezekiel Cooper, stating that "some magistrates of the highest respectability have given it as their opinion that we need not expect peace in this State unless we abjure our principles respecting slavery." Added Harper: "It is the general opinion that if Mr. Asbury comes here it will be at the peril of his life." Asbury apparently took the threat seriously, not returning to Charleston until 1803.[77]

Southern Methodist preachers were dismayed by the furor that the 1800 address raised. James Jenkins claimed that the address so infuriated slaveholders in South Carolina that it "almost shut up the door of usefulness to these people." In Charleston, an ordinance aimed primarily at the Methodists forbade African Americans to assemble for any reason between sunset and sunrise. "O, what a change for the worse!" lamented Jenkins the next time he preached in the city. "I had been accustomed to see the galleries filled with coloured people, and to hear the most cheerful and delightful singing from these willing worshippers; but now there were not exceeding two or three heads to be seen, and they apparently afraid to show themselves." Jenkins concluded that the overall impact of the address was to wake "up the spirit of persecution against our people generally, and especially against the preachers; many of whom, and myself among them, suffered some gross insults repeatedly."[78] In much the same manner William Capers noted that while Methodism's initial introduction into the South Carolina lowcountry had been "as favorably received as anywhere else in the United States," by 1811 (when Capers was first appointed to Charleston) "we lay under the ban of suspicion as disorganizers who could not be trusted among the negroes."

Asbury himself was also alarmed and disappointed by reactions to the 1800 address. While traveling in South Carolina in January 1801 he recorded in his journal that he was "sure nothing could so effectually alarm and arm the citizens of South Carolina against the Methodists as the *Address of the General Conference*. The rich among the people never thought us worthy to preach to them: they did indeed give their slaves liberty to hear and join our Church; but now it appears the poor Africans will no longer have this indulgence. Perhaps we shall soon be thought unfit for the company of their dogs." The next month, while in North Carolina, Asbury met a certain Solomon Reeves who "let me know that he had seen the *Address*, signed by me; and was quite confident there were no arguments to prove that slavery was repugnant to the spirit of the Gospel." "If the Gospel will tolerate slavery, what will it not authorize?" lamented Asbury. "I am strangely mistaken if this said Mr. Reeves has more grace than is necessary, or more of *Solomon* than the name."[79]

In opposition to this rising tide of pro-slavery sentiment, the itinerant system offered a support network for antislavery preachers riding circuits in the South. Recall from chapter 3 that after surveying the Lancaster, Virginia, circuit in 1794, the itinerant Thomas Lyell wrote to Daniel Hitt (who had ridden the Lancaster circuit in 1790), "I can with sorrow inform you that a great declension (greater than ever I expected) prevails: The friends (if I may call them) are much in the spirit of *Slavery*.—some buying & others repenting that they ever let theirs go free."[80] Lyell was clearly at odds with many Methodists on the Lancaster circuit, but he knew that he could count on Hitt for support. The strength of the itinerant network served to bolster the resolve of antislavery circuit riders as they preached in areas of the upper South where sermons against slavery were seldom universally welcome among white audiences.

In 1818 the itinerant Jacob Gruber, a Pennsylvania abolitionist with a "rough thunderbolt manner," was arrested for preaching an antislavery sermon at a Washington County, Maryland camp meeting. Gruber's audience had included 4,000 to 5,000 whites and 300 to 400 slaves, seated separately, as usual, behind the stand. At the time, Gruber was the presiding elder over the district that encompassed Washington County, located in northwestern Maryland along the Pennsylvania border. Toward the end of his sermon he declared, "Is it not a reproach to a man to hold articles of liberty and independence in one hand and a bloody whip in the other; while a negro stands and trembles before him with his back cut and bleeding?" Then, in a fateful flourish, he added that while some masters might treat their slaves well, their children might not, so that "after you are dead and gone . . . may not the slaves thus abused rise up and kill your children, their oppressors, and be hung for it, and all go to destruction together?" Coupling the ill treatment of slaves with the possibility of insurrection was too much for the slaveholders of Washington County to bear. Gruber was soon indicted and arrested for "unlawfully, wickedly, and maliciously intend[ing] to instigate and incite divers negro slaves, the property of divers citizens of the said state, to mutiny and rebellion . . . to the great terror and peril of the peaceable citizens thereof."[81] At his trial, Gruber was successfully defended by a team of lawyers that, ironically enough, included Roger B. Taney, later chief justice of the U.S. Supreme Court and architect of the Dred Scott decision. Conceding that Methodist preachers were well known opponents of slavery, Taney argued that no one in his right mind would attempt to foment a rebellion before an audience of 4,000 to 5,000 whites, and that, knowing Methodist views on the matter, those masters who did not want their slaves to hear antislavery rhetoric should not have allowed them to attend the meeting.[82] The case demonstrates both how firmly many Methodist itinerants in the upper South held to abolitionist convictions well into the nineteenth century, and how strongly their views came to be opposed by slavery's supporters.

But in the southernmost states it was a different story. As abolitionism grew more unpopular, Methodist preachers in slave states became increasingly reluctant to speak out against the basic tenets of the institution, if indeed they questioned them at all, opting instead to try to work within the system's confines. They also became less willing to accept appointments outside their native region, which only served to increase sectional tensions within the church. Even in areas where African Americans formed a numerical majority among Methodist adherents, and, incredibly, paid the bulk of a preacher's support, Methodist itinerants were seldom willing to risk whatever degree of social respectability the church had obtained by appearing in any sense radical in their views on slavery.

Methodist ministers in the lower South continued to preach to slaves, but for the most part only in the paternalistic terms acceptable to southern whites.[83] If this approach enhanced Methodism's image in the minds of most white southerners, it had just the opposite effect on large numbers of slaves. In Georgia the combination of pro-slavery sentiments among white Methodists and the Baptist tradition of congregational autonomy led many African Americans to become Baptists. By 1800 African-American Baptists outnumbered African-American Methodists five to one in Georgia. When the itinerant William Capers was first stationed in Savannah, Georgia, in 1819 he was dismayed to discover that, unlike in the upper South, "there were very few negroes who attended Methodist preaching." Capers concluded that this was because "the policy of the place allow[s] them separate churches, and the economy and doctrines of the Baptist Church please them better than ours."[84]

Faced with Methodism's ambiguous record on slavery and racism, many African Americans rejected the movement outright. The famous abolitionist Frederick Douglass was well acquainted with Methodism's darker side. Several of Douglass's worst masters were Methodists. After one of these was converted at a camp meeting in Talbot County, Maryland, Douglass observed that "it neither made him to be humane to his slaves, nor to emancipate them. If it had any effect on his character, it made him more cruel and hateful in all his ways." Experiences such as this led Douglass to conclude that "the religion of the south is a mere covering for the most horrid crimes,—a justifier of the most appalling barbarity,—a sanctifier of the most hateful frauds,—and a dark shelter under, which the darkest, foulest, grossest, and most infernal deeds of slaveholders find the strongest protection."[85]

But other African Americans saw far more potential in the Methodist message. After his conversion, Richard Allen joined a Methodist class meeting and adopted Methodist-style discipline. He and his brother agreed to "attend more faithfully to our master's business, so that it should not be said that religion made us worse servants." The two kept their crops "more forward than our neighbors," attended public preaching once in two weeks, and class meeting once a week. Impressed by his industry and convicted by the preaching of Freeborn Garrettson, Allen's master was finally persuaded to sell him his freedom, though it took Allen another five years to earn the $2,000 his master required. Allen subsequently became a leader in Philadelphia's African-American community. Though he was well acquainted with the racism that existed in Philadelphia's white Methodist churches, he maintained that Methodism's "plain doctrine" and emphasis on "good discipline" could be separated from the racial prejudices of white Methodists. Indeed, Allen's own career served as a powerful example of the liberating influence of Methodist doctrine and discipline. In addition to his other accomplishments, he left an estate valued at $80,000 to his widow and six children.[86]

As white Methodism's commitment against slavery waned, African-American Methodists developed a number of strategies for preserving their religious integrity. In the North, free African Americans began to look toward establishing their own independent Methodist churches. One of the first of these was Richard Allen's Bethel Church of Philadelphia, launched in 1794 with Francis Asbury's backing. In 1816, under the leadership of Allen and Daniel Coker, the AME Church formally broke its ties with the Methodist Episcopal Church, as did a number of other African-American Methodist organizations in the first half of the nineteenth century. In this way free African-American Methodists in cities such as Philadelphia, Baltimore, New York, and Wilmington, Delaware, sought and gained control over their own local congregations. When forced to make a choice between tighter white control and establishing their own institutions, those African Americans who were free to choose understandably often opted for the latter. Independent African-American Methodist denominations characteristically tended to emphasize lay involvement, a strong stand against slavery, African-American autonomy over church affairs—particularly control over church properties—and, in some cases, the licensing of women to preach. Perhaps most important, these churches gained the ability to ordain their own preachers, who could then administer the sacraments and perform a full range of pastoral ministries.[87]

But most African-American Methodists remained within the framework of the Methodist Episcopal Church. There, they contributed significantly to the development of Methodist spirituality and worship, and sometimes succeeded in carving out their own local congregations or class meetings. Support for Methodism among African Americans was strongest in the upper South and in cities of the eastern seaboard. By 1815 on the Baltimore city station there were 8 African-American class leaders, 10 African-American exhorters, and 9 African-American local preachers. In 1810, Daniel Coker of Baltimore counted 15 African-American churches in the eastern United States. Of these, 11 were Methodist. In Dorchester County, Maryland, African Americans had 9 separate Methodist Episcopal churches by 1830, but no Baptist churches before the Civil War.[88]

Almost from the beginning, no one was more aware of the impact of slavery on Methodism, or agonized more over what to do about it, than Francis Asbury. Like Wesley, Asbury's antagonism toward slavery was not really awakened until the mid 1770s, several years after his arrival in America.[89] But as the

1770s wore on and he began to spend more time in the South, his conscience became increasingly troubled by the condition and treatment of slaves. More than any other Methodist, indeed, more than any other American, Asbury traveled extensively throughout the new nation, talking with a wide range of people, including slaves, free African Americans, abolitionists, and slaveholders. Like a great many Methodist itinerants, Asbury preached extensively to slaves and free African Americans and met with them privately in class meetings. He so won the respect of some slaves that he was sometimes referred to as "Moses" in slave spirituals.[90]

Asbury's friendly relations with Quakers in Philadelphia and other places on the mid-Atlantic seaboard also must have served to help formulate his views on slavery. Early in his career he sometimes lodged with Quakers, and they on occasion attended Methodist meetings. As early as 1772 Asbury met the abolitionist Daniel Roberdeau in Philadelphia. Twelve years later it was Roberdeau who arranged for Asbury and Thomas Coke to meet with George Washington in an attempt to convince Washington to sign a petition against slavery.[91]

By 1780 Asbury was ready to begin acting on his growing convictions, though he quickly realized that doing so would raise a great deal of controversy in the South. In June 1780 he was in Virginia, where he "spoke to some select friends about slave-keeping, but they could not bear it." "This I know," he later reflected, "God will plead the cause of the oppressed, though it gives offence to say so here." During the next four years, as the annual conferences enacted progressively tougher rules against slaveowners, Asbury continued to lobby against slaveholding in the South. In June 1783, for example, he stopped to lodge at the home of John Worthington in Maryland, "but I beheld such cruelty to a Negro that I could not feel free to stay; I called for my horse, delivered my own soul, and departed." Asbury never stayed with Worthington again, though he later visited his widow. A week later he lodged at John Wilson's in western Maryland, and had a "comfortable time" until the two became embroiled in an argument over slavery, which "well-nigh occasioned too much warmth."[92]

Even within the relatively friendly confines of Baltimore, Asbury could not escape the conundrum of otherwise pious Methodists owning slaves. Baltimore Methodism was similar to that of the Delmarva Peninsula in the sense that it included a small group of wealthy landowners and merchants and a much larger number of artisans, middling people, and slaves. Among the area's most prominent Methodists was Henry Dorsey Gough. Gough was a Baltimore merchant whose 1,100-acre estate, Perry Hall, included a mansion assessed at $9,000 in 1798. When the itinerant Henry Smith first visited Perry Hall in 1806 he was overawed, describing it as "the largest dwelling house I had ever seen."[93] Gough's wife, Prudence, was sister to Captain Charles Ridgely, who owned the Northampton iron works and whose estate, Hampton, encompassed 10,000 acres and included a mansion valued at $12,000 in 1798. Prudence Gough was converted in 1773 under Asbury's preaching, and Henry Gough was converted a few years later and eventually licensed as an exhorter. For the next 30 years Perry Hall was a favorite resting place for Asbury and many other Methodist itinerants. Asbury also became a confidant of Rebecca Ridgely, wife of Charles Ridgely and daughter of Caleb Dorsey, another prominent Baltimore area iron merchant and Methodist sympathizer. Rebecca Ridgely gave money liberally to Asbury, and, like Perry Hall, Hampton was a favorite stopping place for Methodist preachers.

Delighted as he was over the backing of prominent families like the Goughs, Ridgelys, and Dorseys, Asbury's satisfaction must have been tempered by the involvement of many of these elites in slavery. Henry Gough is said to have owned as many as 300 slaves at one time. In 1777 Thomas Rankin noted that Gough had about 70 slaves, but that soon after "he set all his slaves at liberty, and by doing so, gave a proof of the great things which God had done for his soul."[94] But if Rankin is correct, these emancipations were only gradual, since a 1798 tax assessment of Gough's property listed 11 slaves and an inventory after his death in 1808 still showed nine. In September 1785 Gough placed a notice in the *Maryland Journal and Baltimore Advertiser* for a runaway slave, an "ungrateful rogue I manumitted some years past, with a number of other slaves, who were free at different periods. . . . He is not free by manumission till next Christmas."[95] As this episode demonstrates, even those Methodists who manumitted their slaves often remained enmeshed in the slave system for years to come.[96] Even in Baltimore, Asbury could not escape the specter of slavery. It hung like an ever-darkening cloud over the movement.

In this connection, it is worth pausing to consider that Asbury and his colleagues were not above dividing the church over questions of discipline. Considering that they were willing to risk a schism in 1779 and 1780 over ordination and administering the sacraments, and indeed to divide Methodism in Virginia in 1792 rather than yield to James O'Kelly (see chapter 2), why did Asbury and his colleagues cave in so easily on slavery after 1784? Part of the answer lies in appreciating the differences between these issues. Both the ordination crisis and the O'Kelly schism were largely internal debates, pitting Methodists against Methodists, but not against the outside world. Though both had the potential to cost the church grave losses in numbers (O'Kelly probably drew away more than 4,000 Virginia Methodists alone) neither threatened the movement's social standing. Methodists could refuse to administer the sacraments in 1780 or to yield to O'Kelly in 1792 and still expect to succeed in American society.

But slavery presented a different kind of threat. To have held firm to the rules of 1784 would not only have split the church but also have destroyed its standing among whites throughout much of the South. Hence, after 1785 Methodist leaders became increasingly willing to sacrifice their antislavery convictions, and the trust of African Americans, for the sake of their reputations among southern whites. The fact that Methodism grew impressively in the South between 1780 and 1790, increasing from less than 2,000 to over 14,000 in Maryland and from less than 4,000 to over 16,000 in Virginia, only served to diminish the likelihood of any revival of the rules against slavery there.

Because of its popular and voluntary nature, American Methodism was both sustained and constrained by the beliefs and sentiments of its members in each locality. The genius of American Methodism was its popular nature, the way in which it enabled ordinary people to preach and lead, to take an active role in shaping the character and doctrines of their church. But allying the movement so closely to popular demands had its price. Reflecting on the Christmas conference of 1784, Thomas Ware observed: "We knew, and our people knew, that we were wholly dependent on them for our support; and that they could wield this check over us at any time they might deem it necessary." For this reason, recalled Ware, the conference was careful not to attempt any far-reaching changes in rules or doctrine, "except one relating to slavery which we could never enforce, and were obliged to rescind."[97]

At the 1804 general conference, a committee that included George Dougherty, who had nearly drowned while being "pumped" in Charleston, Henry Willis, Ezekiel Cooper, Freeborn Garrettson, and Thomas Lyell—all at one time dedicated abolitionists—failed to enact any meaningful rules against slavery. What is more, the conference approved a proposal to suspend the rules on slavery south of Virginia, and to print two versions of the *Discipline*—one with the rules on slavery for distribution north of the Carolinas, and one without for the southernmost states. It was at this conference that Asbury supposedly declared, "I am called upon to suffer *for Christ's sake*, not for slavery."[98] The 1808 general conference went even further, repealing all remaining restrictions against church members owning slaves, and leaving each annual conference to "form [its] own regulations, relative to buying and selling slaves."[99]

Though Asbury continued to abhor slavery, he became increasingly pessimistic about what could be accomplished in the South. "O! to be dependent on slaveholders is in part to be a slave, and I was free born," wrote Asbury while in Virginia during this period, adding, "I am brought to conclude that slavery will exist in Virginia perhaps for ages; there is not a sufficient sense of religion nor of liberty to destroy it; Methodists, Baptists, Presbyterians, in the highest flights of rapturous piety, still maintain and defend it." Gradually, Asbury, like the majority of Methodists, came to accept the fact of Methodists owning slaves and the church's inability to rid itself of the practice short of quitting the South. While in North Carolina in 1809, he fretted over the fact that many masters refused to allow Methodists to preach to their slaves.

"Would not an *amelioration* in the condition and treatment of slaves have produced more practical good to the poor Africans, than any attempt at their
emancipation?" wondered Asbury. "The state of society, unhappily, does not
admit of this: besides, the blacks are deprived of the means of instruction; who
will take the pains to lead them into the way of salvation, and watch over
them that they may not stray, but the Methodists?"[100]

Slavery haunted Asbury to the end of his life. John Wesley Bond, who
traveled with Asbury during the last two years of his life, records that Asbury
frequently spoke of slavery "with deep concern; and said he had examined it
every way of which his mind was capable," but that, "he did not see what we
as a ministry could do better than to try to get both masters and servants to
get all the religion they could, and get ready to leave a troublesome world."
Asbury never doubted that "avarice" was the true motive behind slavery, and
"that where this was the case, he considered the person to be a slave-holder in
soul; and that he could not see how a person who had a slave-holding soul in
them could ever get to the Kingdom of Heaven."[101] But, after the failed attempts of the 1780s, he became increasingly willing to divide his personal
convictions from his public pronouncements for the sake of popular appeal
among whites. "We thought," he is said to have remarked in 1812, "we could
kill the monster at once, but *the laws and the people* were against us, and we
had to compromise the matter, or lose the South."[102]

Northern white Methodists managed to sustain some opposition to slavery
and racism well into the nineteenth century, but throughout much of the
South the church accomplished far less in this regard than Asbury and many
of his colleagues had originally hoped. During the 1780s and 1790s, Asbury
had assumed that the Methodist message could quickly change the core values
of large numbers of Americans. Slavery proved how naive this assumption had
been. A popular movement cannot adopt a broadly unpopular position and
still maintain its influence, unless it can convert its followers to the new position. In regard to slavery, Methodism was able to do this to a significant extent
on the Delmarva Peninsula because other social and cultural forces were also
working to undermine slavery. But in the South Carolina lowcountry this was
not the case. Overall, by the early nineteenth century most white American
Methodists were as uncertain in their convictions as the itinerant Jacob Young,
who, though "never a rabid abolitionist," still claimed to be "antislavery, to all
intents and purposes."[103]

7 *Sisters and Mothers in Israel*

> We cannot divorce our wives and turn our
> daughters out of doors, because they have
> joined the Methodists.
>
> —A Maryland gentleman, 1784

*L*ike nearly all evangelical movements of the eighteenth and nineteenth centuries, women were a clear numerical majority among Methodist adherents and formed the backbone of the early Methodist movement.[1] In New York, Philadelphia, and Baltimore between 1786 and 1801 women constituted approximately 57 to 66 percent of the total Methodist membership.[2] In towns such as Poughkeepsie, New York, and Worthington, Ohio, they consistently accounted for the majority of class meeting members (see chapter 4). If Methodism was fundamentally a local event, then women were at its heart. Methodist women did far more than simply support an institution defined and run by men. Because of its voluntary and popular nature, early American Methodism primarily reflected the hopes, fears, and aspirations of its laity, the majority of whom were women. Like their fathers, husbands, and sons, Methodist women relished plain, forceful preaching, luxuriated in the free flow of the spirit, approved of the church's discipline, and valued the intimacy of the class meeting and the movement's strong communal bonds. Most Methodist women did not feel themselves marginalized by the movement's core beliefs. In many places women took the lead in establishing the church and defining what Methodism would mean to them and their community. As a movement, Methodism was created as much by women as it was by men.

Though the range of activities available to women in Methodism was by no means boundless, in its early phase the movement nevertheless offered many women a variety of opportunities unavailable in the more respectable denominations. Joining the Methodists must have been exciting for many of these women, expanding the horizons of their world. In her study of East Cheshire, England, Gail Malmgreen notes that not only could the Methodist chapel provide "a new form of community, a structured intimacy, even a surrogate family," it also offered women a much wider field of activity. "There was a kind of centrifugal force within the Connection," writes Malmgreen, "legitimating travel and new experiences, and breaking down the narrowness of provincial life."[3] Much the same was true in America. Methodism provided more than relief from the endless demands of mending, cleaning, cooking, and child care, though it surely did that as well. For hundreds of thousands of women throughout the new nation Methodism represented far more than a particular brand of creed. It encompassed a distinct and enticing subculture in which they discovered a new world of opportunity and obligation. It may be the case that Methodism had much to do with shaping the ideology of republican motherhood, at least as it was understood by ordinary women. The leap from mothers in Israel to mothers of the republic would have been relatively small indeed.[4]

Women's historians note that during the early national period most Americans drew increasingly sharp distinctions between public and private, men and women, the world and the family. While the Revolution had perhaps temporarily weakened the privacy of the household, in the war's aftermath American society became more clearly divided along gender lines than it had previously been, at least among ordinary people.[5] But this was a slow and uneven process. Though American Methodists clearly participated in this transition, what is most striking is not the degree to which men and women were separated in early American Methodism, but the extent to which they worked together. The Methodist system depended on women and men working in tandem.

While early Methodist women were almost never permitted to preach in a formal sense, in the movement's early years a small but significant number gained acceptance as gifted exhorters. Overall, early American Methodist women were generally acknowledged to be more "outspoken and assertive" than their Canadian counterparts.[6] Since only a thin line separated much of early Methodist preaching from exhorting, Methodist female exhorters undoubtedly used their public speaking opportunities to preach what were, in effect, sermons. In New England in particular, Methodist female preachers/exhorters were much like other female preachers among the Baptists, Christians, and smaller sects during the years 1780–1830. Like their male counterparts, these women, as Louis Billington points out, "were overwhelmingly the daughters of small farmer-artisans, possessed a common school education, and had grown up in a small-scale Yankee Protestant world where settlements were often recent and class lines fluid."[7]

As with white women, a handful of African-American women pursued active preaching careers in early American Methodism. Widely recognized as an extorter, beginning about 1819 Jarena Lee preached throughout the Middle Atlantic and northeastern states to racially mixed congregations. In 1835 alone she traveled over 700 miles and preached almost as many sermons.[8] Though recognized only as an exhorter, Lee explicitly claimed the right to preach. "For as unseemly as it may appear now-a-days for a woman to preach," declared Lee in her autobiography, "it should be remembered that nothing is impossible with God. And why should it be thought impossible, heterodox, or improper for a woman to preach? seeing the Saviour died for the woman as well as the man." "If a man may preach, because the Saviour died for him," continued Lee, "why not the woman? seeing he died for her also. Is he not a whole Saviour, instead of a half one?"[9] Like many female Methodist exhorters/ preachers, the theological core of Lee's message was quite similar to that of her male counterparts, concentrating on the basic Methodist doctrines of conversion and sanctification. Lee's message was unusual mainly to the degree that she defended female preaching, and (as an African American) condemned racial injustice.[10]

The vast majority of women who regularly exhorted remained unlicensed, making their activities difficult to track. Nonetheless, women exhorters were clearly an accepted part of the Methodist tradition in many places during the late eighteenth and early nineteenth centuries. As early as 1777, John Littlejohn tells of a sister Owings of Baltimore who felt "impressd wth an Ideal that God has called her to preech," and eventually succeeded in doing so on at least two occasions.[11] When a young woman stood up in the middle of one of Benjamin Abbott's sermons he stopped preaching and yielded the floor to her, "which I always judged was best, in similar instances" so that God could "send by whom he will send." "She went on for some time with great life and power," recounts Abbott, "and then cried out, let us pray; we all kneeled down and she prayed with life and liberty."[12] Like many Methodists of his day, Abbott saw nothing fundamentally wrong with a woman exercising this kind of prerogative in a Methodist meeting. Describing a sermon as having "great life and power" and a prayer as filled with "life and liberty" were the highest compliments that Abbott (a thoroughgoing enthusiast) could offer. At a camp meeting in 1819, Alfred Brunson recalled that sister Chamberlain exhorted for three hours "in one incessant flow of the most powerful and convincing eloquence." The fact that Chamberlain nursed her baby during part of her discourse did not bother Brunson in the least. "There was so much of heaven in it, and in her looks, that all who came within hearing were charmed to the spot."[13]

Nor was exhorting in this manner among early Methodists limited to lower class women. Catharine Van Wyck (b. 1751), the daughter of Joanna Livingston (of the powerful New York Livingstons) and New York Lieutenant Governor Pierre Van Cortlandt, was known as "a gifted woman, a shouting Methodist, who would exhort with great effect."[14] According to Dan Young, in the early days of Methodism in New England, "pious and talented sisters often exhorted with much effect." Daniel Waldo, a Rhode Island Congregationalist minister, discovered this much to his dismay in 1818 when he visited a Methodist meeting and was shocked to learn that "the women prayed and exhorted."[15]

For the most part, Methodist women operated within the movement's preaching tradition, a tradition they helped to create. The style and content of the exhortations given by Methodist women differed little from those given by men. The response that the most skilled of these preaching women elicited from their audiences seems to have equaled that of the movement's most dramatic male preachers. Benjamin Bishop, who joined the New England conference in 1805, regularly traveled with his wife, a deeply devout woman and gifted speaker who "uniformly" exhorted after Benjamin preached. According to at least one account, "she was so effective and happy in this effort of love," that the people were "much interested in listening to her."

An equally bold New England exhorter was Hannah Herrington, whom the itinerant Dan Young described as having "a most extraordinary gift of public speaking." When Herrington spoke, "her ideas seemed to flow by inspiration, everybody would be moved; you could not command your feelings; you would find yourself drawn along by an impulsive torrent, and the whole assembly would soon be bathed in tears." "I have never heard one who could produce such favorable effects as she would; and I would rather have her talent for speaking than be emperor of the nations," gushed Young.[16]

Perhaps the best known of the New England Methodist female exhorters was Fanny Butterfield Newell (1793–1824). Following a pair of vivid visions in which Christ appeared to her, Newell experienced conversion under the preaching and counsel of the itinerant Henry Martin in October 1808, immediately joining a class meeting in her hometown of Sidney, Maine. Newell first exhorted publicly at her baptism, standing for "some time in the water," and speaking to "the numerous congregation which crowded round the shore."[17] The following June, Newell attended her first camp meeting at Monmouth, Maine. There she was struck with a vision of paradise lasting three or four hours, during which she "was entirely insensible to all that passed around me in this world." Recovering her senses just before Bishop Francis Asbury ascended the platform to preach, Newell immediately jumped to her feet and began to exhort the assembly. "The first I knew of any thing around me I was standing upon my feet and praising God in the midst of the people with my tongue," Newell later recounted. "All were silent until I had closed my message and sat down." With hardly a pause, Asbury then preached his sermon, no one seeming to have doubted the authenticity of Newell's inspiration or the propriety of her actions.[18]

Jarena Lee delivered her first sermon in remarkably similar fashion and with nearly the same results. Her request for a license to preach having been rebuffed eight years before by Richard Allen, she attended a meeting at Bethel Church in Philadelphia in 1819 to hear Richard Williams preach. Williams took as his text Jonah 2:9, "Salvation is of the Lord," but "as he proceeded to explain, he seemed to have lost the spirit," Lee later recounted, "when in the same instant, I sprang, as by an altogether supernatural impulse, to my feet." For eight years, Lee told the congregation, she, like Jonah, had shirked her duty to preach the gospel. During the course of her message, "God made manifest his power in a manner sufficient to show the world that I was called to labour according to my ability." Still, even as she finished speaking Lee feared that she might be expelled from the church on the spot for her hubris. Instead, Allen stood and acknowledged the authenticity of Lee's call to speak, and her abilities as an exhorter.[19]

In 1810 Fanny Butterfield married Ebenezer Newell, a former school-teacher and local preacher, at a quarterly meeting in Sidney, Maine. Fanny exhorted before the wedding, which was conducted in true Methodist fashion, "without any more ceremony than necessity required."[20] The two almost immediately began riding Ebenezer's circuits together, with Fanny often exhorting after Ebenezer's sermons. Following the birth of their two children, Fanny continued to occasionally accompany Ebenezer on his rounds, sometimes bringing the children along, sometimes leaving them behind. She clearly believed that her public speaking ought to serve as a complement to Ebenezer's preaching, that her primary duty was "to help and not hinder him in the great work of the ministry." But within this context she had little doubt about the propriety of her call. "Whatever may be said against a female speaking, or praying in public, I care not," declared Newell, "for when I feel confident, that the Lord calls me to speak, I dare not refuse."[21]

On a Sunday in 1816, with the children in tow, the Newells held a meeting in a schoolhouse on the Durham, Maine, circuit. The opposition of the town's Congregationalist minister, who "bitterly opposed females talking or praying in public," only served to heighten local curiosity, such that by meeting time, "the house was crowded, and more stood round the door." Immediately after Ebenezer's sermon Fanny rose and took a text (the sign of a sermon, rather than an exhortation), cleverly choosing, "Come and see a man that told

me all things that ever I did; is not this the Christ?"[22] Tears streamed from
her eyes, and "the whole congregation appeared moved as the forest moves in
a storm," as Fanny reminded her audience that these were the words of a
woman spoken publicly to her neighbors. "If all women would talk as that
woman did last night," the Congregationalist minister is reported to have said,
"I would say, speak on!" Though this last embellishment may well be apocryphal, it nonetheless underscores the popularity of Fanny's preaching, as does
the fact that more than 10,000 copies of her autobiography were sold within
ten years of her death.[23]

But Fanny Newell's story also underscores the marginal status of female
preaching among Methodists. Though Newell continued to preach after her
marriage, it is clear that this was of only secondary importance. Of those
women who did speak in public, most were like Nancy Caldwell of Maine,
whose life revolved around a wide variety of church-related activities, but who
exhorted only on rare occasions.[24] For some, the movement did work to circumvent the binary opposition of gender relationships. Jarena Lee firmly believed that the obligation to preach had little to do with one's sex. As an
African-American woman, it is not surprising that Lee disagreed with the dominant gender ideology of this period. But most Methodists were more willing
to see essential differences between women and men in this regard. The exaggerated terms that male contemporaries used to describe women like Hannah
Herrington and Fanny Newell clearly indicate that they considered these
women extraordinary, something far from the norm. The question was not
whether or not God could speak through women; he surely could. The question was whether or not it was right for more than a few women to forsake the
calling of wife and mother to spend their lives in a masculine pursuit. In the
years following the Revolution, Methodists increasingly concluded that it was
not.[25]

Though the contributions of preaching women to the movement's appeal
should not be dismissed, by the 1810s and 1820s female exhorters would be
less welcome in most Methodist churches than they had been before the turn
of the century.[26] In this regard female preaching and the celibacy of the itinerancy are in some sense analogous. Recall from chapter 3 that the celibacy of
the early circuit riders was largely a pragmatic concession. Early American
Methodists did not mean to redefine the role of marriage or family for their
clergy. Circuits were simply too large and the countryside too untamed to allow
an itinerant to travel with a family. Similarly, allowing women to exhort and
preach in the early, more fluid days of the movement did not mean that most
Methodists ultimately envisioned radically redefining gender categories. Rather,
most believed that they were living in extraordinary times—times that demanded extraordinary measures, including female preaching. Under these circumstances, a relatively small number of gifted women could function as "dep-

uty preachers" (to paraphrase Laurel Thatcher Ulrich's concept of a "deputy husband" in colonial New England), temporarily performing a task for which they were suited, but one that lay outside the calling of most women. But just as the concept of deputy husbands fell from favor in the post-revolutionary years, so too early nineteenth-century Methodists gradually turned their backs on the concept of female deputy preachers.[27]

While few Methodist women preached, a far greater number participated in the movement's early development as class leaders, unofficial counselors to young circuit riders, network builders, extra-legal activists, and financial patrons. In many ways these activities were as integral to the life of the movement as was the preaching of the circuit riders. Sarah Roszel (1751–1830) of Virginia exemplifies many of the roles that women assumed in early Methodism apart from preaching. In the absence of a circuit rider—which would have been the case for most societies on all but a few Sundays a year—Roszel regularly conducted the only Sabbath meetings in her neighborhood in a schoolhouse. She typically opened these meetings with singing and prayer, read one of Wesley's sermons, gave an exhortation, concluded with more singing and prayer, and then afterwards held a class meeting, of which she was the appointed leader.[28] In much the same manner, Mrs. Smallwood organized the first Methodist class meeting in Springfield, Ohio, in 1805 in order to counter "the evils of personal combat, intemperance, and Sabbath breaking," and to foster a "better moral sentiment" in the community. Smallwood and her husband, a blacksmith, had moved to Ohio from Virginia in the spring of 1804. Mrs. Smallwood's class, which represented the beginning of Methodism in Springfield, was soon officially recognized by John Sale, then presiding elder of the Ohio District, with Smallwood as the appointed class leader.[29] In each case these women were responsible for establishing or maintaining Methodism in their communities largely independent of male initiative.

As these examples indicate, Methodist women at times served as class leaders, though in the absence of detailed community studies it remains unclear as to how extensively they did so. Mary Thorn of Philadelphia was probably the first female class leader in American Methodism, appointed by either Joseph Pilmore or Richard Boardman sometime in the early 1770s.[30] The fact that class meetings were often segregated by sex must have been a blessing to some women, allowing them to build friendships and construct support networks largely independent of male supervision. Many would no doubt have agreed with Mary Bradley, who counted her class meeting "a privilege which I greatly enjoy, and a work in which I delight to direct, encourage, and urge my Christian sisters, in their heavenly journey." Like Roszel and Smallwood, Brad-

ley herself eventually became a class leader.[31] A number of women distinguished themselves as class leaders. According to the itinerant Henry Smith,
at the Fells Point station near Baltimore in 1807, Sister Shaeffer "had the
largest female class in the station; it increased to overflowing, and it was necessary to divide it, which was a great trial to them all, for they were very much
attached to her." "And no wonder," adds Smith, "for she was one of the most
devoted and faithful leaders I ever knew." Like any good class leader, Shaeffer
was sure to look after any member who was absent, and if any were sick or "in
distress," she "went through all kinds of weather to visit them."[32]

One activity open to all Methodist women was praying in public. Becky
Browning, wife of the itinerant Jeremiah Browning, was known to be "much
in the spirit of the work, gifted and spiritual in prayer." "O that all the preachers' wives could pray and labor as did Becky Browning!" exclaimed Henry
Smith after being teamed with the Brownings on the Winchester, Virginia,
circuit in 1803 and 1804. In Chillicothe, Ohio, Rachel McDowell, a class
leader known to be "peculiarly gifted" in prayer, was often called on to lead
public prayer meetings. At Rhinebeck, New York, Billy Hibbard recalled that
Sally Schyler's "gift in prayer, at all times, surpassed all I ever heard, of man or
woman." Likewise, Thomas Ware remembered that his sister, who lived in New
Jersey during the 1780s, was "eminently gifted in prayer, so much so that many
of the preachers remarked they had seldom known her equal." Prayer was central to the Methodist worship experience; no Methodist meeting would have
been complete without extensive, heartfelt, extemporaneous prayer. For this
reason, women's participation in public prayer was far from a trivial matter.
Moreover, most Methodists assumed that women had a special aptitude for
prayer, if for no other reason than that their lives kept them further removed
from the corrupting influences of the world. "I am sure that I do not exagger-
ate," asserted Peter Cartwright, "when I say I have often seen our dull and
stupid prayer-meetings suddenly changed from dead clog to a heavenly enjoyment, when a sister has been called on to pray."[33]

Speaking at love feasts was another activity open to Methodist women of
this era. One reason for excluding non-Methodists from the love feast, argued
a contributor to the *Christian Advocate and Journal*, was that some "do not
believe it proper that women should speak in public. Our sisters, if they knew
such were present, would feel much embarrassed in attempting to speak."[34]
But even here, the right to speak in public was often qualified by gender distinctions. According to at least one account from early nineteenth-century
Ohio, if during a love feast "some good sister moved by the Spirit of God"
went beyond "narrating her religious experience" and "undertook to exhort her
neighbors . . . to seek a deeper work of grace, it was quite likely that a zealous
narrow-minded preacher or layman would begin to 'sing her down,' "—in other
words, begin singing a hymn to drown the sister out.[35] This kind of conflict is

not really surprising considering that the line between "narrating" and exhorting was indeed quite thin, but the underlying assumption that women ought to limit themselves to the former when speaking in public would have been increasingly clear to most Methodists by the early nineteenth century.

While the notion that women were the primary guardians of piety and morality placed considerable restrictions on women, it also promoted the idea that they possessed a certain moral virtue independent of the aggressive, politically minded prejudices of their male counterparts. As Ann Braude has recently suggested, the growth of this idea may well have led to a "vast increase in the spiritual status and role of women" in nineteenth-century America, allowing them to "criticize, and sometimes control, men's behavior." The Methodist itinerant John Brooks expressed a common sentiment when he stated that "I have long been convinced that the fate of the church is in the hands of the fair ones; let them become corrupt, and the present generation, as well as future generations, with a few exceptions . . . are damned above ground." [36] At times, Methodist women used this moral authority to protect vulnerable preachers, thus shielding the movement as a whole from the opposition of other male-dominated religious and social institutions. In 1779 on the Sussex, Delaware, circuit, Freeborn Garrettson and a group of Methodists were waylaid by a company of men, one of whom was armed. Anti-Methodist sentiment ran high during the early war years, but on this occasion Garrettson was saved by the women of his party. "Several of the women who were with us surprised me," recounts Garrettson in his journal, "they were in an instant off their horses, and seizing hold of his [Garrettson's assailant's] gun, held it until I passed by." [37]

John Littlejohn had a remarkably similar experience while conducting a love feast in Virginia in 1778. "The sisters" present so "shamed" a "posse" of men sent to arrest Littlejohn that the men fled and made no further attempt to detain him. [38] The fact that these women were able to shield Littlejohn simply by shaming his antagonists indicates the degree to which women were acknowledged to have a fuller measure of moral purity. In a similar account, while riding the Clinch circuit in Kentucky in 1803, Jacob Young reproved a man for "behaving rudely" during preaching. Offended, the man threatened to "beat" Young, and the next morning he and his brother came looking for the preacher at the Whitten home where Young was lodging. But Mrs. Whitten, "being a woman of great influence and authority, took the matter in her own hands . . . whipp[ing] him with more severity with her tongue than he could me with his fists." [39] As a result, Young went his way without further trouble.

Less dramatically, but no less significantly, Methodist women were the movement's primary community builders. [40] For many of these women, home and church were nearly synonymous institutions, with much of the life of the latter centered in the former. After Philip and Elizabeth Gatch moved to Ohio in the 1790s they frequently held quarterly meetings at their home. On these occasions Elizabeth entertained 50 to 100 guests at a time.[41] In 1802 when Jacob Young pioneered the Wayne circuit in central Kentucky, sympathetic women made him homespun cotton clothes to keep his appearance from becoming an embarrassment to all concerned. "I wore them quite contented," he later recalled, adding, "this was the best year of all my life." Three years later, in 1805, Young rode the Marietta, Ohio, circuit. After a bout with typhoid fever, a bedraggled Young stopped at the home of Ohio Governor Edward Tiffin, himself a Methodist deacon and local preacher. Perhaps because of his appearance, Tiffin treated Young "rather rudely," judging him to be "an ignorant young man, and not worthy." But Mrs. Tiffin came to his rescue. "I found her to be a mother in Israel," Young later wrote. "If I had been her own son, she could not have paid me more attention."[42] Marietta was a difficult circuit, and without this kind of encouragement Young might well have quit. This was more than behind-the-scenes support on the part of both Tiffin and the Kentucky women. Both circuits were difficult assignments. Without the active intervention of these and other women, Young and many itinerants like him might well have gone home, eventually making the whole itinerant system untenable.

Widows, particularly those of independent means, and women whose husbands were sympathetic to the movement but were not themselves members, played an especially important role in early Methodism.[43] The itinerant Joseph Travis recalled that he regularly "put up" with the McNeils in Lumberton, North Carolina, while riding the Brunswick circuit in 1807. Though Mr. McNeil was a Presbyterian, "Sister McNeil" was a "zealous Methodist" and "her house ever afterwards was my home for many years."[44] Francis Asbury's favorite lodgings included the homes of numerous widows scattered throughout the nation. One such widow was Mary Withey of Chester, Pennsylvania, who, according to Asbury, "kept one of the best houses of entertainment on the continent," and who regularly sheltered Methodist preachers for more than 20 years.[45] For itinerants who, like Asbury and Travis, were unmarried and traveled incessantly, these women often took on the role of surrogate sisters and mothers. "Be a mother in Israel . . . help me sister by your prayers," Asbury wrote to Ann Willis, another widow at whose home he periodically lodged, "watch on, pray and suffer on, believe on, fight on, like a *woman!* . . . be Frank's [Asbury's] *sister* and his *mother* and prompter to all good."[46]

Though these examples lack depth, they could be multiplied many times over, demonstrating that even if the experiences of women were rarely recorded in detail, their influence in shaping the early Methodist movement can scarcely be overestimated. These women were as committed to the Methodist system as the preachers themselves. Methodism was not the preachers' invention alone; it was women's as well. Methodist women might not be permitted to preach, acknowledged the itinerant James Quinn, "but they could read, and sing, and shout, walk some distance to meeting rather than not attend, talk in class and love-feast, encourage mourners, and pray as if they would bring heaven and earth together."[47] In this regard their activities were little different from those of most Methodist men, but nonetheless crucial. The trajectory of a voluntary, popular movement is largely controlled by its adherents. This was particularly true of early American Methodism because it aimed for such a broad constituency. Even when they tried, Methodist leaders were unable to sustain unpopular policies, as was the case with antislavery rules in the South. Since women constituted the majority of Methodist adherents, often joining independent of male family members, it seems only fair to assume that the church necessarily came to broadly reflect their views.[48] Even an institution as apparently male dominated as the itinerancy was shaped and sustained in important ways by women who acted as advisers and financial patrons to the stream of young circuit riders who passed through their doors.

Two of the women who assumed the role of hostess, counselor, and confidante to early circuit riders were Sarah Ennalls and Mary White. Sarah and her husband Henry Ennalls of Dorchester County were prominent members of eastern Maryland's landed gentry and dedicated Methodists. Soon after beginning his itinerant career on the Dorchester circuit in 1800, Henry Boehm stopped to lodge at the Ennalls' home. Sarah quickly discerned that Boehm was deeply troubled, fearing that he had "mistaken" his "calling" and worrying that he did not have what it took to be a Methodist circuit rider. "Ingenuously she asked me a great many questions, till she drew from me the real state of my mind," Boehm later recalled. "When she found out that I was discouraged, and about to give up my work in despair and return home, she gave me such a reproof as I shall never forget." Ennalls lectured Boehm in a "most emphatic manner" that he must not quit, indeed that his eternal salvation might depend on his continuing in the itinerancy. Boehm never again had similar doubts, later writing, "Her wise counsel has had an influence upon me all my days; it shaped my destiny for life."[49] Two years earlier Thomas Smith had a similar experience at the Ennalls' home. Like Boehm, Smith was seriously considering quitting the itinerancy when he lodged with the Ennalls in October 1798. But after receiving a "godly admonition in tenderness and love" from Sarah, Smith gave up any thoughts of quitting and soon found himself in the thick of perhaps Methodism's most dramatic revivals on the Delmarva Peninsula.[50]

Much like Sarah Ennalls, Mary White, originally of Sussex County, Delaware, was a member of Delaware's influential landed gentry. Her husband, Thomas White, was a state judge from 1776 to 1792 and their son Samuel was a Federalist U.S. Senator from 1801 until his death in 1809. It was at the White estate near Whitelysburg in Kent County that Francis Asbury took refuge for more than two years during the Revolutionary War, and the family later sponsored a Methodist meetinghouse known as White's Chapel. On one occasion, while entertaining some 20 Methodist preachers bound for a quarterly meeting, Mary White found the time to encourage a despondent Benjamin Abbott, taking him by the hand and "exhorting me for some time." "Sister White, I believe, was an Israelite indeed, in whom there was no guile," Abbott later wrote.[51] Like nearly all his colleagues, Abbott periodically doubted the value of his preaching and quailed under the hardships of the itinerancy. Though the circuit riders turned to one another for solace and advice whenever possible, they were seldom together for very long. Perhaps unwilling to appear weak in front of the local male leadership of their circuits, some of whom may have been considerably older and come from a higher social class, itinerants like Abbott frequently turned to women like Mary White to rejuvenate their faith.

Social constraints often left women more freedom to join the movement than men. In particular, prominent women joined the Methodists much more frequently than did their male kin. While the path to social status often prohibited men from experimenting with upstart sects, women were freer to choose the church that best articulated their immediate concerns.[52] Recall from chapter 5 that when a Church of England clergyman arrived on the eastern shore of Maryland in 1784, he was shocked to discover how many women had independently become Methodists. When the clergyman complained, a "gentleman" member of the church replied, "we cannot divorce our wives and turn our daughters out of doors, because they have joined the Methodists."[53] A number of other gentlemen present agreed, defending their wives' decisions to join the Methodists, though they themselves did not feel at liberty to do the same. A similar pattern prevailed in early nineteenth-century North Carolina. There, notes Richard Rankin, a significant number of genteel women abandoned the Episcopal Church to affiliate with the Methodists, independent of their fathers, husbands, and sons. Definitions of social status worked differently for these men than they did for their wives and daughters. Francis Asbury recognized this pattern while in Charleston, South Carolina, in 1795. "The white and worldly people are intolerably ignorant of God; playing, dancing, swearing, racing; these are their common practices and pursuits," grumbled Asbury. "Our few male members do not attend preaching . . . the women and Africans attend our meetings and some few strangers also."[54]

But prominent women were surely not the only ones to offer support and direction to young circuit riders. While riding the Calvert, Baltimore, and Harford circuits in eastern Maryland from February 1790 to May 1792, William Colbert lodged at the homes of 24 different women, 19 of whom are identified in his journal as widows, most of whom were of quite ordinary social status.[55] Many of these were homes at which Colbert stayed regularly on each round of his circuit. Although Colbert does not record many details about these visits, it seems reasonable to assume that along with the essential necessities of room and board, these women would have often provided emotional encouragement, lively conversation, and, on occasion, extra financial aid. Such was the case with Sarah Roszel. Henry Smith first met Roszel in about 1793, while traveling away from home but before entering the itinerancy. Roszel, "a woman of a strong mind, and deeply experienced in religious matters," spotted Smith waiting out a storm under a neighbor's porch and guessed that he was a Methodist. One of the many widows who watched over young Methodist preachers of the time, she invited Smith into her home. Their friendship lasted for many years thereafter. Roszel was "a lover of hospitality, and a mother to the preachers," recalled Smith. "Her house must have been the preachers' home for more than sixty years, and a house of God for the neighborhood." "I always felt myself as a mere child in the presence of this mother in our Israel," added Smith.[56]

In the context of these relationships between older women and young circuit riders, each person was filling what they viewed as a meaningful and obviously gendered role. In their own homes, these women felt a kind of authority, based on their age, their religious experience, and in some cases their social standing, that the younger circuit riders who sought their advice readily acknowledged. It is difficult to image how the early itinerant system could have successfully operated without these sorts of relationships. Moreover, to the extent that these women might have been aware of the ideology surrounding the concept of republican motherhood, acting as a mother of the church and a mother of the republic were quite similar callings.

Mary White's efforts further demonstrate the way in which Methodist women worked to construct the movement's community networks. Some years before the episode with Abbott described above, White introduced Francis Asbury to Richard Bassett. Bassett, whose inheritance included 6,000 acres of Bohemia Manor in Delaware, married Ann Ennalls, sister of Henry Ennalls. One night in 1778, when Bassett stopped to see Judge Thomas White, he noticed that the house was filled with black-cloaked men. These turned out to be a group of Methodist preachers whom Mary was entertaining. Alarmed, Bassett, whose opinion of Methodist preachers was not nearly as high as Mary White's, prepared to leave. But Mary convinced him to stay, and his impression of at least Francis Asbury quickly changed. Bassett was soon converted, becoming an integral part of the growing network of Methodist gentry on the Delmarva Peninsula.[57] For more than 30 years he remained one of Asbury's most influential and ardent supporters, bound to the movement both by conviction and through a web of marriage and community ties.

Along with the institutions of the class meeting, quarterly meeting and the like, the unofficial diplomacy and networking of women like Sarah Ennalls, Mary White, and Sarah Roszel kept American Methodism from splintering and disintegrating under the force of its own advance. In the movement's early, more fluid days, such extra-institutional activities were vital to maintaining Methodism's cohesiveness. Though American Methodism is often character-ized as a rigidly hierarchical institution from its beginning, the wide range of roles that women actually assumed is another indication of the decentralized, more flexible nature of the early movement. But as American Methodism be-came more uniformly defined beginning in the 1810s and 1820s, the kinds of informal networking and community building I have described here was in-creasingly marginal to the church's institutional structure. Predictably, as the church's social status rose, its center of activity moved out of the home into the world of church buildings, settled clergy, and increasingly rigid ecclesiasti-cal hierarchy. When this happened women did not abandon the movement, but their center of activity necessarily changed.

Two others whose lives provide insight into the experiences of early Methodist women are Elizabeth Henry Campbell Russell and Catherine Livingston Gar-rettson. Though both came from prominent and wealthy families, each at least in part renounced the social privileges of her upbringing to join the Method-ists, clinging fiercely to the core of traditional Methodist beliefs. In doing so, they help to reveal both the kinds of activities that were permissible for Meth-odist women, and those that were not.

Elizabeth Henry (1749–1825), the sister of Patrick Henry and wife of two Revolutionary War heroes, William Campbell and William Russell, was born in Hanover County, Virginia. Elizabeth's was a deeply religious background, associated with some of the most famous names in colonial religious history. Her uncle, the Anglican rector of Saint Paul's Parish in Hanover County for whom her brother Patrick was named, invited George Whitefield to preach in his church in 1745. Two years later her mother, Sarah Winston Syme Henry, experienced conversion under the preaching of the Presbyterian Samuel Da-vies.[58]

In the spring of 1776 Elizabeth married Captain William Campbell, whose inheritance included 1,000 acres in the Holston River valley of western Vir-ginia. Campbell was a dashing figure and a renowned Indian fighter. He once wrote to his "dearest Betsy" from Williamsburg that his party had scalped 27 Indians and that "I now have the scalp of one which I shall bring you," though exactly what she was supposed to do with it is hard to imagine.[59] When Eliza-beth first arrived in western Virginia with Campbell, the locals were so awed to have the legendary Patrick Henry's sister in their midst that they insisted she stand on a stump and turn pirouettes so that all could see her. Like her famous brother, Elizabeth was said to have had "the same fertile and vivid imagination, the same ready command of language and aptness of illustration, the same flexibility of voice and grace of elocution."[60] William Campbell was soon elected a Fincastle County magistrate and commanded the American forces at the Battle of Kings Mountain. Their daughter Sarah Buchanan Campbell was born in April 1778. When Campbell died in 1781, Campbell County was named for him. In recognition of Campbell's war service, his heirs received a patent for 2,666 acres, and Elizabeth inherited still more wealth following the death of her mother in 1784.[61]

In 1783 Elizabeth married Colonel William Russell, a future Virginia state senator who also had a county named for him. In 1788 William and Betty, or Madam Russell, as Elizabeth had come to be known, moved to Salt Lick in Smyth County, Virginia.[62] In May of that year the Russells attended a Methodist meeting near their home and were soon converted, "in the old-fashioned Methodist manner, with ardent prayers, agonizing soul searchings, confessions of sin, tears of repentance, trembling bodies, and, finally, repeated shouts of joy."[63] Both William and Elizabeth quickly became committed Methodists whom Francis Asbury counted as steadfast friends, though William Russell's conversion may have been less complete than his wife's. He still retained a quick temper, which led William Campbell's brother Arthur to have Sarah Buchanan Campbell removed from the home to live with a guardian in 1789.[64] But Madame Russell was renowned for her piety.

After William's death in 1793, Elizabeth immersed herself more fully in the Methodist movement. While her home remained a welcome sanctuary for weary circuit riders, she moved to strip herself of superfluous worldly possessions. In 1795 she relinquished her control over Russell's estate and gave her daughter Sarah Preston her dower rights in Campbell's estate. In that same year, "to the horror of her friends and neighbors, [and] against the advice of the most prominent men" of the community, Elizabeth freed the one slave she owned outright and liberated the six that she held by dower for the duration of her life.[65] These she provided with gardens and homes until they were reenslaved under her daughters' estates after Elizabeth's death. Throughout the remainder of her life Russell liberally funded Methodist chapels in Virginia and Tennessee, including donating the land in Saltville, Virginia, on which the present Madam Russell Memorial United Methodist Church is located.[66]

While her daughter Sarah and her husband Francis Preston used Sarah's inheritance to build a lavish brick mansion known as Preston Hall, Mother Russell continued to live in a simple log house. The house included a "prophet's chamber" for visiting circuit riders that could be converted into a chapel for preaching. When large numbers arrived for meetings, Russell stowed them away "as the Methodists divided their congregation, the women and children in one room and the men and boys in the other." "[A]m much pleased to find you are coming to See us on Your way down Holstein," she once wrote to the itinerant Stith Mead in February 1794. "Dear Brother bring as many preachers as you can with you, be assured, you will all be welcome at a house of mine."[67] Russell dressed in plain Methodist fashion, wearing dark calico in warm weather, and at other times a gray flannel-like material extending to the top of her shoes, along with a cambric handkerchief around her neck and a small cambric cap with a narrow frill.[68] She never kept a carriage, always insisting on riding her own horse, much like the circuit riders for whom she had such affection.[69] In dressing plainly, living modestly, practicing hospitality, and working to circumvent slavery, Elizabeth Russell was following a model of early Methodism that applied equally to women and men. But in other ways her actions were more decidedly those of a Methodist woman.

Like so many other Methodist widows, Mother Russell readily assumed the role of counselor, confidante, and patron to all the Methodist itinerants who stopped at her door. While stationed on the Holston circuit in 1804 at the age of 28, Jacob Young was thoroughly impressed by Russell's eloquence and erudition. Seeing that Young was "young and bashful," she gave him "great attention," including insisting that he scribe a letter for her, apparently as an exercise aimed at improving his writing.[70] For Young and dozens like him, Russell's tutoring provided a rare avenue into the world of learning and polite society in a way that few other Methodist women could match. But the plain, sincere hospitality and straightforward advice that Russell offered to every Methodist preacher who crossed her path were equaled by countless other Methodist women across the early republic.

Catherine Livingston Garrettson (1752–1849) shared much in common with Elizabeth Russell. Born into the stunningly wealthy, politically powerful, and religiously respectable Livingston clan of New York, Garrettson, even more so than Russell, was raised amid the best that elite society had to offer. The combined fortunes of her parents, Judge Robert R. and Margaret Beekman Livingston, included over 750,000 acres along the Hudson River south of Albany. Since both sons and daughters were to share equally in the family estate, Kitty and her nine siblings were assured of a lifetime of extraordinary wealth. Margaret Livingston was a faithful Dutch Calvinist, while Judge Robert was an Anglican; together their piety was "reasonable, orthodox, and measured."[71] Everything about the Livingston clan carried an air of aristocracy and family solidarity. "Nothing could exceed the cheerfulness of our family circle, the happiness of Clermont [the Livingston estate] was almost proverbial," Catherine later recalled.[72]

Livingston family connections extended to the top of New York society. Catherine's father, Judge Robert Livingston, a well-respected member of New

York's privileged legal and political fraternity, was appointed to the province's Supreme Court in 1763. Of the 12 New York delegates to the Second Continental Congress in Philadelphia, 3 were members of the extended family. Catherine's brother Robert served on the committee that drafted the Declaration of Independence (though he contributed nothing of substance to the document), delivered the oath of office to George Washington at his presidential inauguration in New York, and laid the diplomatic groundwork for the Louisiana Purchase while minister to France in 1803. Growing up, Catherine socialized with George and Martha Washington, Alexander Hamilton, foreign ministers, French officers, and other luminaries of revolutionary society.[73]

Yet, in a familiar pattern, Catherine grew increasingly dissatisfied with the direction of her life. "There was something wanting," she later recalled. While living in Philadelphia in 1782, she and a friend, Mary Rutherford, "would sit up after returning from brilliant Balls, and gay parties, and moralize on their emptiness, till it really became burdensome to accept of invitations, for such was the dissipation of the day that we had been asked to five private Balls in one week, but made it a rule never to go to more than one."[74] In October 1787, after the death of several close friends, including Rutherford, Catherine experienced conversion while reading the Book of Common Prayer alone in her room. "I was received and made unspeakably happy. A song of praise and thanksgiving was put in my mouth—my sins were pardoned, my state was changed; my soul was happy . . . All things were become new."[75] Her mother's housekeeper introduced Catherine to Wesley's writings, but for much of the next two years she was alone in her search for faith.

Then in 1788 the Methodist itinerant Freeborn Garrettson made a foray into the Hudson River valley, preaching the gospel and inadvertently stealing Kitty's heart. As their courtship unfolded, Margaret Livingston was scandalized. A match between her daughter and a wandering preacher from a disreputable sect of wild-eyed enthusiasts was unthinkable. Simply out of the question. As Diane Lobody notes, while the Livingstons had participated fully in the war, Garrettson had been beaten and jailed as a pacifist; while they continued to hold slaves he had freed his; while they meticulously guarded their wealth he had given much of his away. But Catherine held firm, and, after the intervention of several family members, Margaret relented and the couple were married June 30, 1793.[76]

Shortly thereafter the Garrettsons bought an old Dutch farmhouse in Rhinebeck, New York. While Freeborn continued to itinerate, Catherine settled down to raise their daughter, Mary Rutherford Garrettson, born September 1794, and to create a recognizably Methodist home. But Catherine also "began an extraordinary correspondence with a network of like-minded evangelical women . . . gathering similar women from New York into a circle of holy sisterhood."[77] In many ways this communications network mirrored that of the circuit riders. Much as the itinerants found solace and fellowship through corresponding about their shared experiences, Kitty knit together a network of women who also had much in common and much to offer one another. Among this group was Kitty Few, with whom Garrettson corresponded for more than 50 years and with whom she collaborated on projects such as the Society for the Relief of Poor Widows with Small Children in New York City.[78] Though the range of activities that Garrettson devoted herself to was clearly extraordinary, the fellowship with other like-minded women that she discovered after her conversion was quite typical. Many Methodist women created networks in the context of their class meetings and local societies that for them served a similar function. Though few Methodist women of this period had anything like Garrettson's financial resources or the breadth of vision that was a product of her upbringing, her underlying motivations were discernibly Methodist.

After her marriage much of the energy of Catherine's earlier mystical introspection was turned outward toward her church and community. Throughout their lives together, Kitty and Freeborn enjoyed a remarkably intimate relationship. Catherine reveled in the activities open to a Methodist laywoman and saw these as a logical complement to her husband's preaching. In 1799, using money from Catherine's inheritance, the Garrettsons built Wildercliffe overlooking the Hudson, later dubbed Traveler's Rest by Asbury. Like so many other Methodist women, Garrettson turned her home into a sanctuary for weary circuit riders, adding to the normal fare good food, a library, and paintings. In this sense she was much like fellow New Yorker Mary Mason. After crediting Mason with founding the first Methodist Sunday school in New York (started in 1815), along with "several charitable societies to whose interests she devoted 50 years of her life," her gravestone recorded that "she brought up children, she lodged strangers, she relieved the afflicted, she diligently followed every good work." These latter accomplishments were ones that nearly all Methodist women could hope to achieve. They largely defined what it meant to be a Methodist woman.[79]

Women like Catherine Garrettson, Elizabeth Russell, Mary White, Sarah Ennalls, Sarah Roszel, and countless others whose lives are more obscure formed the backbone of American Methodism. It is impossible to imagine the movement without them. Through their unwavering support of the church as an institution, they largely defined what Methodism meant to their local communities. Without their devotion, the institutional pillars of the movement—the itinerancy and the class meeting—would not have stood as firmly as they did.

In this sense, Methodist women and Methodist preachers were natural allies, as Barbara Welter suggests women and ministers in general were during the first half of the nineteenth century, but not for exactly the reason Welter advances. Methodist women and their preachers worked together not so much out of a shared anxiety for secularization, but from the conviction that this was their hour, their chance to reform and strengthen their personal religious experiences, their families, their communities, perhaps even their nation.[80]

In her study of Baptists in New England, Susan Juster concludes that the revolutionary period was a time in which Baptist women lost ground. By the 1780s and 1790s, New England Baptists had retreated from an earlier tradition of gender equality that had grown out of the Great Awakening in order to become "political insiders rather than religious outsiders." The result, according to Juster, was that "women and their ineradicable femaleness became a metaphor for disorder in the revolutionary era." The comparisons between the experiences of Juster's Baptists and Methodist women of the early republic are instructive. Perhaps precisely because American Methodism was a post-Revolutionary War phenomenon, it did not have the same kind of earlier tradition of gender equality that Juster describes for New England Baptists. Nor does it appear that Methodist women were as thoroughly marginalized in the late eighteenth and early nineteenth centuries as Juster argues Baptist women were. Methodists did not see women as naturally disorderly, nor was there a comparable "feminization of sin" in Methodist disciplinary cases.[81]

If anything, the disciplinary cases decided before quarterly meeting conferences of this period indicate that Methodists saw men as the more disorderly element in their midst. Most disciplinary cases involving ordinary members would have been decided in class meetings, leaving little trace of the issues involved or their outcome. But quarterly meeting conferences often heard the more serious cases or those concerning preachers. Though relatively few of these cases involved women, the ones that did are worth considering. From July 1804 to August 1816, the Accomack, Virginia, circuit quarterly meeting conference heard 18 disciplinary cases, of which 13 concerned members holding slaves (see chapter 6). Three additional cases involved only men: in February 1806 Thomas Bradford, a licensed exhorter, was suspended for "immoral conduct"; in January 1808 Ezekiah Pitt was found guilty of "backbiting" and having "an unchristian spirit" and placed on probation for six months; and in August 1810 William Finney, a local preacher, was suspended for "immoral conduct."[82] Of the two remaining cases involving women, one is mentioned only in passing. In February 1814 Peggy Stockley was expelled from the church on unspecified grounds.

The more interesting case concerns the trial of the local preacher and schoolteacher William Melvin in December 1804. Six witnesses appeared against Melvin. John Long, age 18 or 19, stated that he saw Melvin "frequently Drink Spirituous Liquors in his school and behave very Indecently to the female sex." Next, 13-year-old Tabitha Dormas testified that Melvin "behaved

Immodest to her and others of her sex in his school," and 12- or 13-year-old Betsey Mitchell and 15-year-old Sally Mitchell similarly stated that Melvin's behavior was "indecent" toward the girls attending his school. Finally, 34-year-old Littleton Long testified that he had seen Melvin drunk, and Thomas Discon said that he had seen Melvin drink "half a Pint of Pure Spirits" in one sitting.

Three witnesses appeared on Melvin's behalf. His apprentice, 17-year-old Thomas Robinson, stated that while attending Melvin's school at the same time as the girls who had already testified, he "never saw Mr. William Melvin behave Indecently." Two other students, 19-year-old James Lambden and 14- or 15-year-old Peter Henderson, gave similar testimonies in favor of Melvin's conduct. Though we are told nothing of their deliberation, the committee of three men assigned to hear the case found Melvin guilty of "Immoral Conduct," suspended his license to preach, and expelled him from the church.[83] While this is only one case, it indicates that Methodists of this period willingly heard the testimony of women, even teenage girls, and considered it in the same light as testimony from men. Though Methodists took a very dim view of excessive drinking, it is clear from the trial record that the more serious charge against Melvin revolved around the issue of sexual harassment. And here the conference relied almost entirely on the testimony of young women.

Disciplinary cases on the Madison, Kentucky, circuit followed a similar pattern. As on the Accomack circuit, the majority of cases, 13 of 18, concerned members holding slaves.[84] Only one of the five remaining cases directly involved a woman, and again it was decided in her favor. In July 1815, Isaac McHenry was "found guilty of slandering the character of sister Carter" and expelled from the church. The same pattern holds for the Cumberland, New Jersey, circuit. There the available records before 1820 give only one case directly involving a woman, though it occupied at least three quarterly meeting conferences. As a member of the local preacher Michael Swing's class meeting in Fairfield, Doctor James B. Parvin "entered a complaint" against Hannah Howell sometime prior to December 1816. A committee from the class apparently ruled against Howell, whereupon another preacher, Solomon Sharp, appealed on Howell's behalf to the quarterly meeting conference. Both Howell and Parvin appeared before the March 1817 conference, and both presented written testimony in their defense. This included a letter from Howell's husband, apparently not a Methodist, "wherein he supports her character and justifies his wife." On March 15, 1817, the conference decided "in favor of Hannah Howells holding her membership," but the case would not end there.

Two days later Michael Swing charged another preacher, Daniel Parvin (the relationship to James B. Parvin, if any, is unclear), with slander in connection with Howell's case. The trial would consume the remainder of the March 1817 conference and much of the June 1817 meeting. Witnesses testified that

Daniel Parvin had said "that Hannah Howell's daughter is the daughter of the Reverend William S. Fisher deceased"; that following the death of Swing's wife, Howell and Swing were "together one fourth of their time passing and repassing"; and that "if Mrs. Howell did not take care she would have a Swing as well as a Fisher." In the end, after much acrimonious testimony, the conference decided in favor of Swing and Howell, expelling Parvin from the church. Though the details available here are admittedly sketchy, on the face of it the evidence against Howell was not inconsequential. At one point Parvin declared that Nancy Fasmine had told him "that on account of Mr. Swing, Mrs. Howell flew in Mr. Howell's face and scratched him."[85] But even this evidence failed to sway the conference. Throughout the proceedings there is little evidence that the conference ever assumed that either Hannah Howell or women in general were naturally disorderly or morally weaker than men. If anything, the conference seems to have given Howell the benefit of the doubt.

Records from other quarterly meeting conferences follow a similar pattern. Minutes from the Hockhocking, Ohio, circuit (August 1806–July 1815), the Union and Mad River, Ohio, circuits (May 1807–August 1814), and the Paint Creek, Ohio, circuit (December 1811–August 1815) all indicate that although women were at times expelled for adultery and other unspecified offenses, most slander and financial debt cases seem to have been decided in their favor.[86] Hence, it seems that at times Methodist quarterly meeting conferences and class meetings provided women with a source of legal remedy not readily available in the courts.

Methodist women of this period did not experience anything like gender equality, but neither were they confined to the movement's margins. Women were actively, often decisively, involved in shaping Methodism's most important institutions, including the class meeting and the all-male itinerancy.[87] Though some women felt called to preach and take up what were generally thought of as masculine activities, most believed that their proper role was a more domestic one.[88] Like the men around them, these women were destined to live in culture, not outside it. Though they believed fervently in women's spiritual equality—a thoroughly Wesleyan idea—few Methodist women argued for a leveling of gender distinctions.

In many rural areas and among urban artisans the movement retained much of its primitive character well into the nineteenth century. But throughout the antebellum period Methodism as a whole grew more refined, more respectable, more quintessentially American. Though few middle-class women would have rued the church's social advancement during these years, the consequences for Methodist women were far reaching.[89] Female evangelists, for example, were less welcome among middle-class Methodists than they had been among an earlier generation of adherents. Women were also apparently forced out of leadership roles as class leaders. By 1795 no female class leaders remained in New York City despite large growth in female membership. The same trend held for Philadelphia and Baltimore as well.[90]

Perhaps the most significant institutional changes occurred as the movement moved out of the home and into a growing number of increasingly impressive church buildings presided over by an ever more settled ministry. For many early Methodist women home and church had been closely intertwined, with much of the life of the latter taking place in the former. But as the character of the church changed, Methodist women necessarily turned to new kinds of activities, creating, for example, their own auxiliary missionary and benevolent organizations. As bourgeois Methodism became increasingly preoccupied with following the lead of groups like the Presbyterians and Congregationalists, younger generations of Methodist women increasingly experienced home and church as distinct and separate institutions.

8   *Methodism Transformed*

The Methodists represent the great middle class and in consequence are the most representative Church in America.

—Theodore Roosevelt

I have no wish to draw final conclusions and prophesy disaster. . . . That would be to croak like a raven.

—Fyodor Dostoevsky,
The Brothers Karamazov

By the spring of 1816 Francis Asbury was clearly dying, the more than 40 years of relentless traveling to which he had subjected himself finally taking its toll. In truth, his health had been precarious for quite some time. Asthma and rheumatism, particularly in his feet, troubled Asbury throughout much of his career. As early as 1802, Henry Smith met Asbury at a Tennessee conference and was dismayed to find the bishop's feet so swollen that he could not "walk a step without assistance," and had to be "lifted on his horse, and off again, like a child."[1] At other times Asbury was forced to resort to crutches. In 1809 Henry Boehm accompanied Asbury across the Allegheny Mountains in Pennsylvania. Boehm was amazed at his furious pace despite rheumatism so painful that he could not "stand, preach, kneel, or pray." From that time on Asbury could only preach resting against a table or chair. By 1812 Boehm had to carry him "in my arms" from the two-wheeled sulky in which he now traveled to each church or home, where the bishop would sit to preach. In 1814 Asbury was taken with a severe three-month bout of pleurisy, from which he never fully recovered. The illness left him so thin that his bones "appeared in da[n]ger of cutting through the skin."[2] Each day thereafter was "a living death, a perpetual martyrdom."[3] And yet Asbury continued to travel. He crossed the Allegheny Mountains four more times, visited New England, and made two trips to South Carolina and Georgia. As Boehm had so often done, Asbury's new traveling companion, John Wesley Bond, carried him from his sulky to each appointment.[4] Like so much about him, Asbury's health was a paradox, a seemingly impossible mixture of fragility and resilience.

By the 1810s Asbury's phenomenal stamina had made him a living legend throughout much of the nation. Everywhere crowds pressed close for a look at the famed preacher. Parents brought their children to see the bishop on horseback, much as their parents had brought them. Among Methodist preachers he had no rival. While the church's other bishops might be "loved" and "admired," only Asbury was "venerated."[5] Among all the preachers, Asbury, "by common consent, stood first and chief."[6] While all others were considered brethren, he was acknowledged as American Methodism's only father.[7] His renown spread far beyond the Methodist Church. Following Asbury's death in 1816, Jacob Young was delegated to take the bishop's horse, along with some of his books and clothes, to William McKendree in Wheeling, Virginia (now West Virginia). While alone in the mountains he was accosted by two men evidently intent on robbing him. But on hearing of Young's cargo, their countenances fell. "Is Bishop Asbury dead?" asked one. "I have seen and heard him preach in my father's house." The two men rode off without troubling Young, too respectful of Asbury's memory to carry out their scheme.[8]

Yet in many ways Asbury had outlived his time. He always wore knee buckles and gaiters, never approving of the new-style pantaloons, though nearly all his preachers wore them by the 1810s.[9] While Methodists throughout the nation grew ever more prosperous, Asbury clung steadily to the old ways. He "observed the most rigid economy in every thing that related to spending money," recalled Jacob Young. His clothes were plain and inexpensive, as were his horses, saddles, and saddlebags. He preferred to travel on horseback because it was simpler and cheaper, but if forced to use a carriage, it was always "of the plainest and cheapest kind." Even here Asbury allowed himself no luxuries, though he was very fond of horses and gave all of his names.[10]

As time went on, fewer and fewer Methodists were interested in following Asbury's example, however much they might admire his spirit. Early American Methodism tended to attract people on the make, anxious to advance their own temporal well-being as much as the spiritual cause of the church. For the Methodist movement in America, numerical growth and economic advancement were organically linked. Both were swift because of the way Methodists so readily adapted to American culture. The movement simply cannot be understood without an adequate appreciation for this connection. While economic opportunities were mixed, at best, for most Americans throughout the antebellum period, the fortunes of the Methodist Church improved dramatically. In all likelihood, the period between the Revolution and 1820 was one of growing economic inequality. While economist Lee Soltow argues that the overall distribution of wealth remained fairly constant between the Revolution and the Civil War, other studies indicate that between 1774 and 1860 the richest 10 percent of free wealth holders increased their share of total American assets from a little less than 50 percent to 73 percent, and the richest 1 percent more than doubled their holdings from about 13 percent of all assets to 29 percent.[11] While few Methodists of this period were among the truly rich, as a group they steadily advanced during ambiguous economic times. In cities such as Philadelphia, where "artisans were more likely to experience downward rather than upward mobility" during these years, Methodist journeymen were "glaring exceptions to this rule."[12] Clearly Methodists were prominent among the nineteenth century's emerging middle class.[13]

Methodists used their newfound wealth to build increasingly ostentatious churches. Eighteenth-century Methodists had most often met in homes and barns. What few chapels they erected were simple boxlike structures almost entirely devoid of towers, steeples, and other trappings of wealth. Much of American Methodism retained this primitive character well into the nineteenth century. But when compared to the Baptists and other upstart sects of the early national period, the Methodist rise to social prominence was relatively swift. In New York City, Methodists spent some $30,000 to rebuild the John Street Church in 1818. The first Methodist church built in Schenectady, New York, in 1814 cost approximately $600. Despite a decline in membership from 1814 to 1836, in the latter year Schenectady Methodists instituted pew rents to raise $5,600 for a new building—even going so far as to specify that pewholders could place only blue cushions in their pews. Similarly, there was little about the early meetinghouse in Providence, Rhode Island, "to distinguish it from a barn." But by the mid-1830s Providence Methodists had added a steeple, a bell, and an organ. Not surprisingly, by then pew rents, first introduced in 1816, were approaching those of the city's more respectable denominations.[14] Gone forever in most places were the days when ordinary Methodists exasperated their preachers by insisting on bringing their dogs to meeting.[15]

By 1850 American Methodists had constructed 13,280 churches, nearly 4,000 more than their closest rival, the Baptists. By 1860 the Methodists could claim nearly 20,000 buildings, almost 38 percent of all churches in the United States. These were valued at more than $33 million, nearly 20 percent of the value of all American churches.[16] By mid-century Methodists in major cities had begun building elegant gothic edifices that rivaled those of the Congregationalists and Presbyterians, filling them with "those anti-Methodistical things, pews [and] organs."[17] In Delaware in 1870 the total value of Methodist Church property nearly equaled that of all other denominations combined. In that year in Ohio, the Methodists owned 2,115 church buildings. Their next closest competitor, the Presbyterians, could claim only 625.[18]

Antebellum Methodists not only built churches, but also founded colleges and universities. American Methodism's most significant eighteenth-century foray into the field of higher education, Cokesbury College (named for Thomas Coke and Francis Asbury), opened in 1787. Located in Abingdon, Maryland, 24 miles north of Baltimore, this first ill-fated effort was perpetually in debt, finally burning in 1795. The college was almost immediately reopened in Baltimore, but the following year the new building also burned and the project was permanently abandoned, much to the relief of many Methodists and non-Methodists alike. "I see not," wrote the Episcopalian Devereux Jarratt in reference to Cokesbury, "how any considerate man could expect any great things from a seminary of learning, while under the supreme direction and controul of tinkers and taylors, weavers, shoemakers and country mechanics of all kinds."[19]

Though Asbury was disappointed at the financial loss and the destruction of the library, he was relieved to withdraw from the field of higher education. "The Lord called not Mr. Whitefield nor the Methodists to build colleges," he wrote after Cokesbury burned. "I wished only for schools—Doctor Coke wanted a college."[20] Asbury of course valued learning, but he clearly feared that colleges would ultimately serve to corrupt Methodism by luring it into the American cultural mainstream. As William Warren Sweet has noted, all of the schools that Asbury had a hand in founding eventually failed, at least in part because they were located in out-of-the-way places, far from the perfidious influence of cities, but also far from potential students and financial backers.[21]

But following Asbury's death in 1816, Methodists almost immediately launched a sustained campaign to found schools and colleges. They established more than a dozen of these before 1830, including McKendree College in Lebanon, Illinois, and Augusta College in Augusta, Kentucky. During the 1830s Methodists added another 40 schools and colleges, including Wesleyan University in Middletown, Connecticut, and Indiana Asbury (later DePauw) University in Greencastle, Indiana, named, ironically, for one who had grave reservations about the value of universities. According to one tabulation, between 1830 and 1860 Methodists founded more than 200 schools and colleges.[22] Asbury's successors obviously shared little of his fear about the corrupting potential of these institutions. Whereas Asbury had deliberately maintained distance between Methodism and America's educational elite, later Methodist leaders eagerly sought to win a place for themselves within that orbit.

With rising wealth and social prestige came increased political clout. By 1810 the movement could boast nearly 175,000 members and possibly eight times as many adherents. By 1820 membership had risen to more than 250,000, and by 1830 it stood at nearly half a million.[23] Though there are no comprehensive studies of Methodism and politics in the early republic, it is clear that in certain regions or states the Methodists formed a distinct, well-recognized voting bloc capable of deciding major elections.

In Delaware, no other denomination was as politically powerful as the Methodists. Early Methodist converts there included such prominent Federalists as U.S. Senator and later Governor Richard Bassett, Judge Thomas White, Allen McLane, and Philip Barratt. Following the lead of these powerful families, the vast majority of downstate Methodists remained loyal Federalists throughout the late eighteenth and early nineteenth centuries, particularly in Kent and Sussex Counties. "The more wealthy and influential part of the community in this state embraced Methodism at its rise," explained the itinerant Thomas Smith of this period. "This had a happy influence on the common people—they had less opposition from the world, and a more ready access to the means of grace."[24] Such was the success of Methodism in Kent County that on a Sunday in 1800 Thomas Rodney noted: "Great Methodist Meeting at Milford Today & no Preaching in Dover of any kind for the Methodists have so thinned the Church & Presbyterian Meeting that neither Congregation Can Support a Clergyman."[25] By 1850 the Methodists had 35 churches in Kent County; the Baptists, Episcopalians, Quakers, and Presbyterians had only 11 combined.[26] At times Federalist politicians attended camp meetings to electioneer. At other times Democrats attempted to break the Methodist-Federalist alliance by questioning the piety of individual Federalist candidates, but to no avail. As historian John Munroe notes, the Methodist vote was key in making Delaware a Federalist stronghold for nearly a third of a century.[27]

In Ohio, the Methodist experience was much different, but no less significant. The Ohio country opened up just when the Methodists were hitting their stride. Following the treaty of Greenville in 1795, the Washington administration tried, but largely failed, to establish a dominant Federalist government in Ohio.[28] Instead, much of Ohio politics and society soon came under the control of Jeffersonian Republicans, many of whom were Methodists or Methodist adherents. Methodists participated eagerly in the early migrations to the Ohio country. Billy Hibbard estimated that of the 300 converts on his New Rochelle, New York, circuit in 1807 and 1808, not more than half could "be reckoned as nett increase, because of the many that moved away." "In these times it seems all will move to the Ohio," explained Hibbard. "Great talk about that country, I fear too much."[29]

Whereas in Delaware the Methodists had become politically powerful by converting the existing gentry, in Ohio they rose from outsiders to become pillars of society. Dan Young, a former New England circuit rider and later a member of the Ohio legislature, noted that because there were few established religious-political alignments in early Ohio, there was also little "systematic opposition to Methodism."[30] Similarly, Alfred Brunson observed that as Methodist numbers grew in northern Ohio and northwestern Pennsylvania, local politicians "favored us, though they might be skeptical as to religion." In Meadville, Pennsylvania, for example, the result was that "their attending upon our ministry drew out others, so that the old court-house was usually filled with hundreds of attentive hearers."[31]

Though there are no definitive studies of the impact of Methodist voting in early Ohio, it seems apparent that the Methodist-Republican alignment helped to propel a number of Methodist candidates into office. Local preacher and former itinerant Philip Gatch was elected to Ohio's constitutional convention and served as an associate judge of Clermont County for more than 20 years. The Republican Thomas Worthington, a long-time Methodist and friend of Francis Asbury's, built a business empire out of Chillicothe and was later elected one of Ohio's first U.S. senators and then governor of the state. His brother-in-law Edward Tiffin, a Methodist deacon and lay preacher, was Ohio's first governor and later a U.S. senator. Thomas Scott, a member of the Ohio legislature and chief judge of the Ohio Supreme Court from 1810 to 1815, was a Methodist elder and preacher, and John Collins, a powerful Methodist preacher, was the printer and editor of the *Scioto Gazette*.[32] When a branch of the Republican-affiliated Tammany Society was organized in Chillicothe in 1810, Methodists were among its major boosters, with Tiffin serving as the society's "Grand Sachem."[33]

In parts of Connecticut, as in Delaware and Ohio, Methodist concerns played a central role in the political debate by the first decade of the nineteenth century. Here, as in Ohio, the majority of Methodists were Republicans, in opposition to Federalist elites. In Danbury, Connecticut, "The great mass, if not the entire, of the Methodist Church and her adherents were Republicans," recalled Alfred Brunson, adding, "and so were the entire infidel portion of the community." Hence, Republican politicians both "favor[ed]" and "protect[ed]" the church "not from any particular love for it, or for religion, but from motives of self-interest." "They would protect and defend, and even contribute to the support of the Methodist ministry, and occasionally hear them," adds Brunson, "from motives of policy, because every convert to Methodism, in those times, became a Republican, if he was not one before."[34] Much the same was true in the Maine backcountry, the Connecticut River valley of Vermont, and in other areas of New England as well.[35] For example, in Redding, Connecticut, in 1803 the Methodist itinerant Aaron Hunt petitioned for and received legislative exemption from taxation, though the petitions of other non-Congregationalist clergy were routinely rejected.[36]

By 1820 American Methodists had obtained a degree of political power undreamt of 40 years before. Thereafter, Methodists were seldom viewed as political outsiders, and in some regions they were a force to be reckoned with. In Indiana, Philip Schaff asserts that by mid-century Methodists "control[ed]" state elections.[37] Perhaps more important, evangelical success in mobilizing the masses caught the eye of politicians who copied their revivalistic style. By the 1840s, party organizers had "learnt much from revival preachers about reaching a mass audience through printing press and indoor and outdoor pulpit," writes Richard Carwardine, "about the efficacy of persevering, continuous, and dramatic effort, and about consolidating loyalties."[38]

American Methodists had long held a prominent role in the popular press, and they continued to expand their publishing and distribution activities throughout the early national period. Wesley's writings had been popular in America before his first preachers ever stepped ashore. By 1774 Wesley's *Primitive Physick: or An Easy and Natural Method of Curing Most Diseases* had gone through 20 printings, four of them in America. To Richard Rodda in America Wesley wrote: "You should take particular care that your circuit be never without an assortment of all the valuable books, especially the *Appeals*, the *Sermons*, Kempis, and the *Primitive Physick*, which no family should be without."[39] Thomas Rankin apparently set up the first American Methodist distribution system for books published in London. Under Rankin, by 1775 six or seven stewards had been appointed to oversee the distribution and sale of books on individual circuits, though this system apparently did not survive the war.[40]

In 1789 John Dickins accepted appointment as the church's book steward. Using at least some of his own money, he launched a new era in Methodist publishing from his headquarters in Philadelphia. The itinerant system provided Dickins with a ready-made marketing network, though one that emphasized distribution rather than profits. Dickins's early publications included an edition of the *Discipline*, Wesley's abridgement of Thomas à Kempis's *The Imitation of Christ*, Richard Baxter's *The Saints Everlasting Rest*, an extract from William Law's *Serious Call*, Freeborn Garrettson's journal, John Fletcher's *Works*, Wesley's *Primitive Physic*, *Notes Upon the New Testament*, and *Thoughts Upon Slavery*, part of Asbury's journal, and a pocket hymnbook.[41] Dickins sent books to hundreds of Methodist preachers on their accounts, even though he knew many would fail to fully repay him. "I am obliged to keep myself near £3000 in debt," he wrote in early 1794 to Daniel Hitt, who had proved exceptionally faithful in maintaining his account. "If every one with whom I deal were to show the same diligence [as you have], I should not be embarrassed as I am."[42] When Dickins died of yellow fever in 1798 the Book Concern was $4,500 in debt. But, as Lester Scherer notes, "In a situation where spiritual edification through maximum distribution was the goal of the book business, the debt was a testimony not to Dickins' failure, but to his success."[43]

Ezekiel Cooper was elected to replace Dickins with only two dissenting votes—one of them his own. Under Cooper's direction, by 1804 the Book Concern had printed over 170,000 items and had a net worth of $27,000. By 1808 Cooper had raised the net worth to $45,000. Expanding membership, growing institutional stability, and rising respectability all worked to fuel this newfound prosperity.[44] In 1802 Asbury could write to Cooper from South Carolina that the "cry" for Methodist books "is greater than ever, the Presbyterians would purchase and many others."[45] When Samuel Mills and Daniel Smith toured the regions west of the Allegheny Mountains under the auspices of the Massachusetts Missionary Society in 1814 and 1815, they were stunned by the popularity and availability of Methodist books. "This energetic Society sends out an immense quantity of these books," reported Mills and Smith. "We found them almost every where. In the possession of the obscurest families, we often found a number of volumes. . . . It puts to the blush all the other charitable institutions in the United States."[46] By 1831 the New York City–based *Christian Advocate and Journal* had the largest circulation of any weekly paper in the nation. By 1840, circulation of the *Western Christian Advocate,* published in Cincinnati, reached 14,000.[47]

Rapidly expanding membership, rising economic prosperity, growing political clout, a newfound desire to join America's intellectual elite, and continued success in popular publishing all pointed to a fuller integration of the Methodist movement into American society. Methodists everywhere could look with pride on the advances of their church. No longer was it likely that anyone would repeat the mistake of a Delaware gentleman who, on hearing of the construction of a Methodist chapel in 1780, declared, "It is unnecessary to build such a house, for by the time the war is over, a corncrib will hold them all."[48] Methodist gatherings were no longer routinely threatened by mobs of rowdies. Reflecting on the social status of Methodism in Tennessee, circuit rider John Brooks wrote, "I never knew a camp-meeting but it was necessary to have a large guard of respectable men to protect it, till 1820. From that time to this [1848], they have been but seldom requisite."[49]

Whereas British Methodism was largely relegated to the peripheries of society by the force of the church-state system and the rigidity of English class divisions, in America Methodists took advantage of the unprecedented religious, geographical, social, political, and economic "free space" created by the Revolution to become a part of the emerging core culture of the nation.[50] Methodists were at the center of the major economic changes of the revolutionary era, including the expansion of a commodity-based economy, the growth of "unearned" profits through land speculation, and the emergence of middlemen between agricultural producers and consumers.[51] Though the Baptists and other evangelical groups also bettered themselves during this era, no denomination gained as much social, economic, and political ground as the Methodists.[52]

But many discerned a darker side to Methodism's rising social status. Writing in 1875, the brother of the late Methodist itinerant Benjamin G. Paddock observed that "one of the results of Wesleyan Methodism has ever been the material thrift of those who have been subdued by it to the obedience of the faith. Just as soon as they have found pardon and salvation, every thing in relation to their fortune has taken an upward direction."[53] But what Paddock, writing from the vantage point of the post–Civil War years, saw as a comfortable and happy nexus, earlier generations of Methodist preachers decried as a bitter irony. Setting out to usher in the kingdom of God on earth, these first- and second-generation itinerants had ended up presiding over a relatively prosperous and all too often complacent church. So common were complaints about American Methodism's lost zeal that dissidents became known by the widely recognized label of "croakers."

In a sense, the whole genre of circuit rider autobiographies can be seen as a series of jeremiads, calling the church back to the zeal of its earlier, less refined days. Though mostly written after 1840, almost all focus on the period before 1820, giving the clear impression that something had since been lost. Peter Cartwright's autobiography is perhaps the best-known example of this genre. Cartwright loved the frontier because there, he believed, the church was less susceptible to the allure of refinement. Yet it is important to note that almost none of the croakers were embittered outcasts grousing about what might have been for them personally. Rather, they were loyal and, for the most part, successful Methodists who loved the church deeply from beginning to end.

Nor was this primarily a generational conflict. Old and young could be found on both sides of the issues that animated croakers and their opponents. Certainly the croakers were not reflexively biased against youth. "Never be afraid to trust young men," wrote Francis Asbury in 1813. "They are able, and you will find enough willing to endure the toils and go through the greatest labors; neither are they so likely to fail as old men are."[54]

Moreover, though croaker complaints were similar to the Puritan jeremiads of the seventeenth and eighteenth centuries, they were not exactly the same. Unlike colonial Puritan divines, Methodist croakers were not reacting against a loss of either ministerial prestige or respect for the church. They fully realized that any decline in Methodist spirituality was probably the result of too much success, rather than not enough. This was particularly true for the preachers themselves. Hence, unlike Puritan ministers, croakers were more likely to blame their fellow preachers rather than the people for failure and declension in the church. But at its heart, the croaker complaint shared much in common with that of colonial New England ministers. Like their Puritan predecessors, Methodist croakers were troubled by the conviction that amid Methodism's great success, "we are become a people very different from our Fathers . . . we have fallen from their exemplary piety and virtue, and from their regard to God."[55]

One of the issues that troubled croakers the most was the transformation of Methodist preachers and preaching. In his semicentennial sermon of 1826, Freeborn Garrettson affirmed his confidence in Wesley's doctrines, but wondered "what his people will be a hundred years hence." "They may be a numerous and a learned people; but it is possible that by slow degrees they may retrograde, until they have very little of the spirit of old Methodism." In particular, he worried that the clergy were in danger of trading zeal for social status. " 'Lay hands suddenly on no man,' " reminded Garrettson, "look more to genuine piety, and to [a] real call from God, than to any literary qualifications without it. . . . The fall of the primitive Church began with the clergy; and should we fall, our declension will begin here." [56]

Likewise, Peter Cartwright lamented that in earlier days, "You could know a Methodist preacher by his plain dress as far as you could see him," but that by mid-century such was seldom the case.[57] A poem published in this period in the *Conference Worker*, entitled "Our 'Sidin' Elder," expressed this same sentiment:

'Twas in the days of yore—the good old times
When men were simple-minded, and the lines
'Twixt worldly vanities and Christian livin'
Were closely drawn; each state its bound'ries givin'
With mathematical precision, so that
By cut of coat or trowsers, you could know that
A man had "got religion"—had the leaven
To "rise" his nature to the state of Heaven.

As Uncle Samuel's fightin' men all dress
In fightin' clothin'; so, a man might guess
With certainty, before these days of evil,
Whether a man was 'listed 'gainst the Devil.
But modern style, with its enormities
Hath blasted Christian *uniform*ities;
And, these days, should you go to shoot Philistines,
You'd, like as not, destroy a lot of Christians.[58]

For Charles Giles, one clear indicator of a declension in Methodist preaching was the growing custom of reading sermons. While some might consider a well-written sermon the mark of a sound education, Giles reasoned that learning ought to qualify "a minister to speak readily and eloquently" without reading a text. If Methodist ministers "become disgusted with zealous preaching and plain dealing, trust in their literary acquirements, and seek for fame, wealth, and popularity, they would lose all their secret strength, and become weak as Samson shorn of his locks," declared Giles. "Reading sermons will never convert sinners—will not produce reformations, nor aid the work of religious revivals," he flatly concluded.[59]

Figure 8.1. James Quinn, from his autobiography, Sketches of the Life and Labors of James Quinn *(Cincinnati, 1851). Courtesy of the Billy Graham Center Museum, Wheaton, Illinois.*

John McLean, editor of Philip Gatch's journal, shared Giles's misgivings. Early Methodist preachers "did not aim to preach great sermons, but sermons that would reach the heart, and cause it to overflow," asserted McLean. He noted that younger preachers often made light of "story-telling"—the habit of earlier preachers to fill their sermons with anecdotes and analogies from everyday life—preferring to rely on more closely reasoned treatises that reflected a greater degree of erudition. For McLean, there was little doubt as to which was better: "What we gain in learning we lose in power." As if to prove McLean's point, the itinerant James Quinn often told the story of a man whose chickens "took fright and ran into the weeds" whenever an early Methodist preacher came near. But in later years the chickens lost their fear because "the preachers appear so much like lawyers that the chickens don't know them."[60] "There is a greater effort now being made to please the ear than to reach the heart, and bring men to the foot of the cross," echoed the itinerant Abner Chase. "The sword of the Spirit being muffled with silken wreaths cannot penetrate the coat of mail with which sinners are clad." Like so many of his generation, Chase concluded that younger Methodist preachers relied too heavily on "fine-spun metaphysical or philosophical theories . . . which when thrown upon a congregation tend rather to suffocation."[61]

As noted in chapter 1, in general Methodists of this period preached progressively less on sanctification than their predecessors had. Writing from Kentucky in 1820, the long-time Methodist preacher John Littlejohn asserted that "the state of Religion in this Country . . . is very superficial." The main reason, concluded Littlejohn, was "the manner of our preaching which seems chiefly to be confined to the doctrines of Repent[ance] & Justification by faith[,] not pressing the believers to follow after that holiness without which no Man can see the Lord."[62] By the 1840s in Troy, New York, according to one account, "the Wesleyan doctrine of holiness . . . came to be very unpopular and the preachers very seldom made it the subject of their sermons. Some of the younger preachers went so far as to declare that 'Wesley was bosh.'" Whenever someone would rise in a public meeting to promote the doctrine, another would declare, "I never had any such experience when God converted me. He did it well, and I have no need to have it done over again."[63]

Antebellum croakers were also deeply troubled by what they saw as a steady abandonment of the itinerancy. In a letter to Abner Chase in 1821, Bishop Enoch George asked, "Are we not, as ministers, departing from the spirit of the itinerant plan adopted by our fathers and predecessors, who by voluntary sacrifices, zealous labors and perseverance, have taken the ground, and formed the greater part of North America into circuits and stations?"[64] The answer of course was obvious. Over time circuits had grown progressively smaller and city stations had proliferated. More important, an increasing number of the younger preachers were marrying, having children, demanding parsonages, and refusing to move more often than every two or three years. In short, Methodism was becoming more settled, less countercultural, more middle class.

For William Beauchamp, no part of the Methodist connection was as "all-important to the continuance of Methodism" as the itinerancy. The movement's past success under the driving force of "this wonderful machine, so simple in structure, so energetic in operation, so certain in effect" served as "a sure pledge of the accomplishment of what remains to be done—*if this connexion be preserved in original purity and vigor.*" Beauchamp believed that, for the minister, "*settled* life . . . affords more abundantly the means of gratifying the love of ease and self-indulgence . . . it offers more inducements to seek riches, and honours, and worldly enjoyments, it has a greater tendency to sensualize the soul, to darken the understanding, and to obscure the visions of faith—to diminish the sense of obligation, to destroy the consciousness of responsibility, to cool the ardour, and decrease the diligence of the minister, in the great work of evangelizing the world." Beauchamp argued that Jesus and the apostles had been traveling preachers, indeed that the whole Bible "breathes the spirit of Itinerancy." Above all, then, Methodists ought to fear "innovation." "If *repair* is mentioned, expect ruin; if *reform*, look for destruction," warned Beauchamp.[65]

By mid-century many of Beauchamp's fears had been realized. Writing in 1851 James Quinn acknowledged that many believed that the itinerancy "has had its day, and must go down." "Learned clergy, who study and write their sermons," could not be expected to "submit to the toils and privations of an itinerant life." When Methodists "have pews, and organs, and pay the choir to do their singing," when "the itinerant is snugly fixed in the village station, and the local preacher do[es] what little itinerant work is done," then, lamented Quinn, "my fears come on."[66] Similarly, in 1857 Jacob Young worried that "though the Church is not going down yet, there are strong indications that she is in extreme danger; and in that very day that itinerant preachers begin to love pleasure, ease and idleness, the Church will sink in their hands; and I am sorry to say there is a strong tendency in that direction."[67]

Along with the waning of the itinerancy, croakers also discerned an erosion of Methodism's most intimate community events—the camp meeting, the class meeting, and the love feast. The South Carolina itinerant Jimmy Jenkins argued that apart from better tents almost every aspect of the camp meeting had declined by the 1840s. "There is too much company in the *preachers' tent*; too much smoking of tobacco, and light, frothy, and trifling conversation." Between preaching there was "not enough of singing and praying in the tents and elsewhere. Preachers, exhorters, and class-leaders, together with stewards, do not take the lead in this matter as formerly," when private tents had often been "the scene of the most remarkable displays of divine power." Jenkins was also "grieved to see so much labour and parade about eatables, and such extravagance in dress." "I think we might do without pound-cake, preserves, and many other *notions*," opined Jenkins, adding, "and I am sure if our dresses were plainer, we would feel more comfortable; for then the mind would not be harassed so much with the care of preserving them from getting a little soiled." In the end, Jenkins despaired that camp meetings had become an almost purely social event at which many ate much better and dressed much finer than they did at home.[68]

James Horton shared many of Jenkins's misgivings. Writing from New York in the 1830s, Horton was particularly disappointed by the practice at some camp meetings of holding "select" prayer meetings. At these gatherings, only those selected by the preacher beforehand were permitted to pray. Few knelt at these gatherings, and long "handsome prayers" whose only value was that they "quiet[ed] the mischievous by putting them to sleep," replaced the extemporaneous outbursts of earlier years. For Horton, nothing could have been more diametrically opposed to the spirit of primitive Methodism.[69]

Like Horton, Charles Giles believed that behind this push for order and moderation was a fear of enthusiasm. Earlier Methodists had luxuriated in the free flow of the Spirit, but their successors saw such displays as an impediment to refinement and respectability. "Zeal and ardour," Giles believed, were being replaced by "mechanical ceremonies." "Being trained to this monotonous sameness, the minister appears to be afraid to move one step out of the beaten track, fearing he might possibly produce a degree of pious friction," wrote Giles, "and by that means some sparks of sacred fire might be elicited, and ignite the sleepy, stupid assembly; [and] so set the neighbourhood on fire." "Indeed, it is a lamentable fact that some preachers are too deficient in zeal and pathos to make the house of worship an interesting place," he concluded.[70]

Even more disturbing than the transformation of the camp meeting for most croakers was the diminution of the class meeting. "Just as sure as our preachers neglect their duty in enforcing the rules on class-meetings on our leaders and members," declared Peter Cartwright, "just so sure the power of religion will be lost in the Methodist Episcopal Church."[71] As with the circuit rider autobiographies, most of the class meeting handbooks published in the mid-nineteenth century were in reality jeremiads bemoaning the demise of the class meeting.[72] By the 1830s and 40s, as David Holsclaw has demonstrated, "the Methodist probationary system was crumbling." In many places regular attendance at a class meeting was no longer upheld as a condition of membership. In 1834 one minister even suggested that "wealthy members purchase immunity from discipline (especially concerning class meeting) by providing generous financial support for the church."[73] Such policies, croakers contended, could only lead to "lifeless and formal" religion. "Our doctrine and discipline are good, but they are not, I think, so much attended to as in former days," fretted John McLean. "There is a great failure in the attending to class meetings."[74] Even those class meetings still functioning seemed to be losing their vitality. Class leaders no longer stressed the duties of prayer, fasting, scripture reading, and family devotions as vigorously as they once had. Nor did they require members to be as honest and straightforward in their weekly testimonies as they previously had. In earlier times the preachers had "required the members to speak out," recalled James Jenkins. "We did not have to crawl about among the benches to hear their whispers."[75]

As the class meeting declined in popularity so too did the love feast. Henry Smith noted with chagrin that in some places love feasts had been essentially replaced with "large and expensive parties." "The Methodists had parties too in former days," wrote Smith, "but they might be said to be 'feasts of love,' for little, if any of the spirit of the world was among them; and religion and Christian experience was the chief subject of conversation. Their hearts were made to burn within them while they talked of Jesus and his love, and

Figure 8.2. Henry Boehm, from Abel Stevens, History of the Methodist Episcopal Church in the United States of America *(New York, 1867).*

compared their experience with the word of God, and the experience of each other."[76]

Underlying all of these complaints was a common perception that as early as the 1810s and 1820s Methodists had begun to compromise their core values in order to obtain wealth and social status. Among the first of the croakers to publish was Billy Hibbard. "Some are religious for the Lord's sake, and some for their own sake.—Some to repair a lost reputation, and some to save their souls. Some to get money; and some to serve God," wrote Hibbard in 1825. Religion had been "abused in all ages, and in all countries," but "by none more shamefully" than the Methodists and Quakers "because they profess so much perfection." "How many have we in the present day who put on a saintish appearance and roll up the eye with [a] solemn groan, as though they were greatly affected with a concern for the glory of God and the good of men," inveighed Hibbard. "How solemn they appear . . . and yet how they will lie or equivocate to get a good bargain."[77]

The itinerant John Brooks was convinced that 1821 marked a great divide, at least for Methodists on the Tennessee frontier. Before that time Tennessee Methodists deliberately distanced themselves from the world. They "read no books, kept no company, but such as led to the knowledge and love of God and man." They "dressed plain," not following the "ever changing fashions of the cut of dress." "In this way they lived, and went through all sorts of weather to their class meetings and prayer meetings," continued Brooks. "In these meetings, the young as well as those more advanced, prayed in public, with and for one another and for all men; they watched over one another in love, and then in kindness told each other their fears about one another, and exhorted each other to all faithfulness." What, then, had gone wrong? Brooks believed that the church was a victim of its own popularity. As Methodists grew progressively more comfortable in American society, they inevitably relaxed their discipline. The church simply could not be both respectable and countercultural. Eventually, it did not even represent a subculture of American life. "Thus we have made the world our pattern," concluded Brooks.[78]

Many others reached the same conclusion. Even Henry Ward Beecher, writing in 1857, exclaimed, "How I long for the good old Methodist thunder! One good burst of old fashioned music would have blown this modern singing out the window like a wadding from a gun."[79] Writing at the age of 91, Henry Boehm perhaps best captured the misgivings of the antebellum croakers. Boehm asserted that he "never belonged to the family of croakers." Yet he could not help but conclude that "there was a power among the fathers, both in the ministry and laity, that we do not possess." "In some matters I cannot but think that, as a Church, we have retrograded," continued Boehm. "The people and preachers in that day were patterns of plainess; we conform more to the world, and have lost much of the spirit of self-denial they possessed. Our fathers paid great attention to Church discipline, and their preaching was more direct; they aimed at the heart, and looked for more immediate results than we of the present day."[80]

This kind of complaint was, of course, not entirely new. The danger of riches had been one of John Wesley's favorite themes. "The Methodists grow more and more self-indulgent, because they *grow rich*," declared Wesley in a sermon of 1789. Although many Methodists were "still deplorably poor," continued Wesley, "yet many others, in the space of twenty, thirty, or forty years, are twenty, thirty, yea, a hundred times richer than they were when they first entered the society. And it is an observation which admits of few exceptions, that nine in ten of these decreased in grace, in the same proportion as they increased in wealth. Indeed, according to the natural tendency of riches, we cannot expect it to be otherwise."[81] Likewise, while in western Tennessee in 1797 Francis Asbury was struck by the obsession of westerners, presumably including a good many Methodists, with obtaining land. "I am of opinion it is as hard, or harder, for the people of the west to gain religion as any other," he wrote in his journal. "When I reflect that not one in a hundred came here to get religion, but rather to get plenty of good land, I think it will be well if some or many do not eventually lose their souls."[82] "I am for no trade but truth," wrote Asbury on another occasion. "I see no reason why we should not have a revival of Religion but for worldly prosperity."[83]

But as the nineteenth century progressed, such indictments failed to carry the weight that they once had. Fewer and fewer Methodists saw much to fear in wealth and social status. Many agreed with George Cookman who scoffed at "good old Methodism." "Good old Methodism indeed!" exclaimed Cookman in the *Christian Advocate and Journal* in 1841. "And is good old Methodism susceptible of no improvement? If our noble fathers, in the days of their poverty, *walked*, is that any sufficient reason why we, their sons, now that we can afford it, should not *ride*? What, sir, shall we be so wedded to old prejudices, that we must travel in an old Pennsylvania wagon, at the rate of two miles an hour, when all the world is flying by steam? . . . I trust, sir, that Methodism will repudiate all such prejudices, and keep pace with the spirit of the age." The issue, of course, as David Holsclaw notes, was not really transportation, but accommodation to the world.[84]

Perhaps no one embodied this transformation more than Nathan Bangs (1778–1862). After joining the church in typical Methodist fashion, doffing his long hair and removing his shirt ruffles, Bangs entered the itinerancy in 1801 on the Canadian frontier. In many ways his early career was thoroughly typical. A series of prophetic dreams that he carefully recorded in his journal deeply influenced the early course of his ministry. But as the church's potential for social advancement increased, Bangs became increasingly concerned with promoting its refinement. Appointed to New York City in 1810, he set out to stifle "boisterous" members at the John Street Church, exhorting New York Methodists to "be more orderly in their social meetings." Significantly, Bangs believed that his campaign against enthusiasm was validated by a prophetic dream in which he slew a great serpent symbolizing the "enemy" of order. Like Pilmore and Rankin before him, he never opposed "experimental religion," only the kind of enthusiasm that checked the church's advancement into respectable society. Certainly the success of New York City Methodism supported Bangs's actions. During his tenure in the city he saw membership rise from 2,200 to more than 17,000, and two or three humble buildings increase to some 60 churches, "some of them ranking among the best ecclesiastical edifices of the nation." Toward the end of his career, Bangs contended that Asbury's two principal errors were "that he showed not enough interest for the intellectual improvement of the preachers and too great a solicitude to keep them poor."[85]

Of course, the transformation that so worried the croakers and delighted Cookman and Bangs was by no means uniform throughout American Methodism. Predictably, the older character of the movement survived much longer in predominantly rural areas than in the cities of the eastern seaboard. Class divisions also complicate any attempt to date the metamorphosis of "old" Methodism to "new." William R. Sutton argues that well into the 1830s Methodism provided artisans and workers in cities like Baltimore and New York with "powerful, sometimes radical, explanations and critiques of the deteriorative aspects of industrial and capitalist developments, and inspired activist, sometimes militant, responses."[86] Yet what no one doubted was that American Methodism had changed dramatically between the Revolution and the second quarter of the nineteenth century.

The dramatic changes that swept through American Methodism in the early decades of the nineteenth century bring us finally to the question of Methodism's larger relationship to American society. In this study I have argued that Methodism was America's most significant large-scale popular religious movement of the antebellum period. I have also argued, less directly, that the popularization of American religion during this era was one of the most important cultural or social developments of the early republic. Methodism and American culture did more than develop in parallel, they were integrally linked. While neither was dependent on the other, it is also true that neither can be adequately understood in isolation. While the social revolution of the early republic exerted a strong gravitational pull on American Methodism, Methodism exerted a lesser, but by no means negligible, pull of its own. Neither Methodism nor the broader culture would have been nearly the same without the other. Startling as this claim may seem, Methodism's numerical growth alone makes it credible.[87]

In many ways the contours of this debate concerning the connections among religion, culture, and society have developed along Marxian and Weberian lines. Historians working from a Marxian perspective have often portrayed American religion as an "order-inducing, repressive, and quintessentially bourgeois" tool by which elites control dangerous classes.[88] Weber countered that under certain circumstances religion could stimulate economic change as well as simply sanction it. In short, Weber saw religion itself as active and decisive in the formation of social structures such as capitalism in America. From these two starting points a wide variety of interpretative frameworks have portrayed religion's role in the formation of American society as everything from a "passive register" to an "active innovator," sometimes remote and seemingly disconnected, sometimes deliberate and calculating.[89]

American Methodism in the early republic was seldom, if ever, a movement controlled by social elites.[90] Nor, as Nathan Hatch has noted, was it a vehicle by which workers resisted the emergence of capitalism by retreating to the outmoded village life of the eighteenth century.[91] Rather, early American Methodism produced change in American culture and society from the bottom up, influencing millions through its doctrines and practices, even as it adapted to the demands of America's cultural, economic, and religious marketplaces. Hence, there is some truth in William Warren Sweet's assertion that organized religion's greatest contribution to American life in the early republic was in bringing civilization to the frontier.[92] Methodism provided a great many Americans of the early republic not only with a source of spiritual meaning but also with fellowship and community, with comfort and aid in times of distress—in short, with the sense of belonging that all people crave. The extent to which Methodists were able to accomplish this is what most clearly distinguishes their movement from the other denominations of this period.

One measure of the strength of the connection between Methodism and popular culture is the degree to which American Methodism participated in, and even anticipated, the development of modern managerial styles. Drawing on the work of Alfred Chandler and JoAnne Yates, David Paul Nord has recently argued that the American Tract Society worked out an innovative management system in the 1840s involving "eight key elements: (1) centralized budgeting and accounting; (2) decentralized middle-level management by region; (3) systematic statistical fact gathering; (4) formal recruitment and training of line workers (colporteurs); (5) in-service training; (6) printed handbooks and instructions; (7) standardized financial reporting methods and report forms; and (8) a monthly magazine and other in-house communication media."[93] Both Chandler and Yates argue that this style of management—built around extensive and accurate record keeping, a far-flung network of middle-level managers, and what Yates has termed "control through communication"—did not come to characterize American business until after the 1840s.[94] If this is so, reasons Nord, then the American Tract Society "may well have been progenitors of it."[95]

Though Nord does not do so, his argument could easily be applied to early American Methodism, which antedated the American Tract Society's heyday by more than half a century. Early American Methodism's leaders understood the nature of the post-revolutionary cultural marketplace, in effect designing an innovative marketing strategy to master it. Their extensive membership statistics also anticipated what Patricia Cline Cohen has referred to as the "sudden popularity of numbers and statistics in Jacksonian America."[96] No merchant or company of the early nineteenth century could match Francis Asbury's nationwide network of class leaders, circuit stewards, book stewards, local preachers, circuit riders, and presiding elders, nor the movement's system of class meetings, circuit preaching, quarterly meetings, annual conferences, and quadrennial general conferences, all churning out detailed statistical reports to be consolidated and published on a regular basis.

Methodism's lack of success whenever it crossed cultural boundaries, as with Roman Catholics in Ireland and New Orleans or among Native Americans, is another indicator of the strength of the relationship between Methodism and a certain version of American popular culture.[97] In both Britain and America, Methodism's advance hinged on maintaining physical, social, cultural, and religious contact with its constituents. In the absence of any one of these four elements its appeal was dramatically curtailed.

But did American Methodism remain a popular religious movement—did it still offer what ordinary people were looking for—after about 1820? Put another way, did the changes that swept through Methodism between the Revolution and the age of Jackson represent declension? In terms of numerical growth, it would appear not. American Methodism's most spectacular growth dates from the years before about 1810. Yet, as impressive as the statistics from this early period are, they should not be overemphasized. When dealing with relatively small numbers, even a modest increase in absolute membership can translate into a large percentage gain. When Methodist membership is analyzed on a decade-by-decade basis, it turns out that combined growth rates for the denominations representing the antecedents of the United Methodist Church either approximated or exceeded increases in the aggregate American population until the 1950s, with the exception of the 1790s, 1860s, 1900s, and 1930s.[98] Though Methodism's share of all religious adherents in the United States began to decline after about the middle of the nineteenth century, as Roger Finke and Rodney Stark have recently demonstrated, Methodist denominations continued to grow at a healthy rate until well into the twentieth century.[99]

What set the antebellum croakers' teeth on edge was not a declension in growth but a clearly visible change in character. Yet it would seem that much of this transformation was almost inevitable given American Methodism's fundamental organizing principles. Much of early American Methodism's success depended on holding two competing ideas in tension. The first declared that Methodism was a countercultural force for change in American society, an outsider movement bent on reforming a degenerate nation. Much of early Methodism's energy derived from the feeling among Methodists that they were a people set apart in opposition to the world. The second was built around Methodists' firm conviction that theirs was first and foremost a religion of the people, one whose ultimate authority rested in the hands of ordinary members.

As long as American Methodists could clearly distinguish themselves from the rest of the world, it was possible to balance these two ideas. But as both Methodists and their church prospered, the boundary between Methodism and American society became ever more difficult to discern.

Popularity was a double-edged sword that could cut both ways, exacting a heavy price. More than any other religious movement of the antebellum period, Methodism succeeded in co-opting much of American popular culture for its own purposes, but not without compromise. Inevitably, as American Methodists discovered, co-opting works both ways. Attracting large crowds of ordinary Americans simply was not possible without catering to their most deeply held hopes, fears, and prejudices. In no instance did this become more obvious than in the movement's ongoing struggle to come to terms with slavery.

As large numbers of American Methodists became well entrenched in American society, they transformed their church from a counterculture to a subculture of American society. By mid-century both the church and its constituency had largely become a part of America's predominant culture. In the process, much of what had been distinctive about the early Methodist movement was jettisoned.

This process was not unique to America. British Methodism experienced similar changes during this same period. There, observes David Hempton, "the Wesleyan leadership, when confronted by rapid expansion in the years of high social tension between Wesley's death and Peterloo, and pressed hard by successive governments to eliminate its radical under class, tried to retain control by clamping down on religious revivalism, political radicalism, undenominational sunday schools and other popular causes. In the process Methodism became more centralized, more bureaucratic, more clerical and more respectable."[100] Following Wesley's death in 1794, Jabez Bunting and his colleagues acted decisively to move English Methodism toward increasing order at the expense of popular revivalism. In the frequently troubling decades after 1790, Methodist ministers often became "agitators for order."[101] This drift toward respectability "brought the movement more firmly into the male world of professional ministry, chapel finance, business meetings, and local courts," but not without its price.[102] Though English Methodism continued to grow faster than the population as a whole until 1840, by 1820 it had ceased to be a force in working-class culture and politics.[103] As in America, by mid-century English Methodism had become far less countercultural than it had once been. In 1873 British Methodist S. W. Christophers was dismayed "to find the world changing its style of enmity and opposition." "Its senseless, murderous clamours are hushed, its brute force is withdrawn, and even its vulgar laugh is not everywhere to be heard. Its voice now is insinuating, its approach is stealthy, soft, and almost viewless. The influence of its presence is subtle and witching. It affects respectful and even reverent manners. It offers to be friendly; proposes combination for unobjectionable purposes; and is very willing to share in the cultivation of all hitherto debatable and faintly-marked border-lines between itself and Christian society."[104]

Samuel Goodrich's recollections of the rise of Methodism in Connecticut are also instructive here. As Methodists began to gain ground in Connecticut, most of the established clergy bitterly denounced them as ignorant enthusiasts, "declaring that in religion, as well as in the affairs of life, a steady, tranquil devotion was better than sudden and irregular storms of fervor." But Goodrich's father, a Congregationalist minister in Ridgefield, Connecticut, was of a different mind. Instead of railing against the Methodists, he copied their most popular techniques. The senior Goodrich adopted evening meetings at private homes, he "put more fervor into his Sabbath discourses," and he invited deacons and laymen to "pray and exhort, and tell experiences in the private meetings." Soon both churches were thriving. Though Methodism, in Goodrich's words, "had its rise in a kitchen," it soon came to "comprise many respectable citizens," including a "full proportion" of women "who comprehend and employ the advantages of coquettish French bonnets, trimmed with wreaths of artificial flowers!" Though Goodrich's father may have been slightly ahead of his time in adopting Methodist practices, the end result was much the same everywhere: "orthodoxy was in a considerable degree methodized, and Methodism in due time became orthodoxed."[105]

However much Methodists might respect their past, they were fated to live in culture, not outside it. Though the croakers could remember the movement's early days, by mid-century most of them conceded that there was little hope of reclaiming that past for the majority of American Methodists. Itinerancy did not work in towns and more densely populated areas the way that it had along the rapidly expanding frontiers of the early republic. Weekly class meetings demanding intimacy and vulnerability did not comport well with emerging middle-class notions of privacy. Unpolished preachers, female exhorters, and emotionally charged gatherings at which worshippers shouted and fainted no longer satisfied Methodists who could afford to build elegant churches, who longed to be accepted by their more refined neighbors and colleagues in other walks of life. In short, as American Methodists went, so, to a large extent, went their church.

But even as the Methodist Episcopal Church came to increasingly represent the nation's stable middling classes in the years after 1820, its earlier, more countercultural legacy did not disappear. When Methodists largely abandoned the margins of American society and religion, new movements sprang up to take their place, including holiness groups emerging from within Methodism itself. Both the Wesleyan Methodist Church, founded in the 1840s, and the Free Methodist Church, established in 1860, arose at least in part as reactions against the increasingly bourgeois character of the Methodist Episcopal

Church. In particular, the Free Methodist schism, originating in Illinois and the Genesee Conference of New York, reflected "a deep sociological chasm between the relatively plain rural people who liked the old ways and the sophisticated city people who believed in progress."[106] The Free Methodists decried the allure of pews, choirs, organs, and the "abominable practice" of sitting during prayer, required members to be "exceedingly plain in their dress," to refrain from joining secret societies, and to abstain from using alcohol or tobacco, and held firmly to the doctrine of sanctification.[107] They also, in the opinion of Methodist Episcopal bishop Matthew Simpson, "encouraged a spirit of wild fanaticism, claiming the power of healing by the laying on of hands."[108] Many of these issues would continue to animate the holiness movement through the end of the nineteenth century.[109]

The dissatisfaction of holiness-minded Methodists with the trajectory of American Methodism also played a key, though less central, role in the rise of Pentecostalism.[110] Early American Methodists, nineteenth-century holiness advocates, and early Pentecostals were much alike. All three movements appealed to people estranged from society's dominant religious and social structures and buffeted by the complexities of a rapidly changing world. Each assented to the notion that ordinary members are better judges of their own religious needs than are society's elites.

Because of Methodism's spectacular success, in many ways its beliefs and practices came to define the context from which future popular religious movements in America would emerge. Early American Methodism demonstrated both the power of popular religious movements in post-revolutionary America's religious free market, and their fundamental limitation. It showed that well-organized, large-scale popular religious movements not only could thrive as countercultures and subcultures in American life but also could influence the basic character of American society. But the history of early American Methodism also demonstrates the degree to which popular religious movements are limited by the boundaries of the broader culture in which they take shape.

Appendix: Methodist Membership 1773–1810

*T*his appendix was constructed from the minutes of the Methodist Annual Conferences, beginning in 1773. From the start, American Methodists were inveterate record keepers. Unfortunately, for most years the membership statistics are reported by circuit, rather than by state, territory, county, or some other convenient system. Outside of major population centers, these circuits were usually named for rivers, creeks, or other prominent landmarks. Hence, reallocating membership figures by state requires rediscovering the locations of all circuits, which for some of the more obscure circuits is no simple task. Where circuits crossed state boundaries, I allocated a portion of the total members to each respective state.

Table A.1 Methodist Membership in 1773

State	Total Population (thousands)	Methodist Members	Percent of Total Population
New York	177.2	180	0.10
Pennsylvania	266.2	180	0.07
New Jersey	124.1	200	0.16
Maryland	215.5	500	0.23
Virginia	474.3	100	0.02

Table A.2 *Methodist Membership in 1780*

State	Total Population (thousands)	Methodist Members	Percent of Total Population
New Jersey	139.6	196	0.14
Pennsylvania	327.3	190	0.06
Delaware	45.4	512	1.13
Maryland	245.5	1767	0.72
Virginia	538.0	3871	0.72
North Carolina	270.1	1728	0.64

Table A.3 *Methodist Membership in 1790*

State	Residents (thou.)	Change from 1780, %	White Methodist Members	Black Methodist Members	Total Methodist Members	Change from 1780, %	Percent of total Residents
Conn.	238	15	180	1	181		0.08
N.Y.	340	61	3236	130	3366		1.0
N.J.	184	31	2274	89	2363	1106	1.3
Pa.	434	33	1526	55	1581	732	0.4
Del.	59.1	30	2183	811	2994	485	5.1
Md.	320	31	9849	4658	14507	721	4.5
Va.	748	39	12846	3402	16248	320	2.2
N.C.	394	46	7068	1735	8803	409	2.2
S.C.	249	38	2962	496	3458		1.4
Ga.	82.5	48	2110	184	2294		2.8
Tenn.	36.0	260	691	55	746		2.1
Ky.	73.7	64	1024	66	1090		1.5

Table A.4 Methodist Membership in 1800

State	Residents (thou.)	Change from 1790, %	White Methodist Members	Black Methodist Members	Total Methodist Members	Change from 1790, %	Percent of total Residents
Me.	152	57.2	1197		1197		0.8
N.H.	184	29.6	171		171		0.1
Vt.	154	81.2	1095	1	1096		0.7
Mass.	423	11.6	1571	6	1577		0.4
R.I.	69	0.4	224	3	227		0.3
Conn.	251	5.5	1546	25	1571	768	0.6
N.Y.	589	73.2	6140	223	6363	89	1.1
N.J.	211	14.7	2857	173	3030	28.2	1.4
Penn.	602	38.7	2887	300	3187	102	0.5
Del.	64.3	8.8	1626	867	2493	−16.7	3.9
Md.	342	6.9	6549	5497	12046	−17.0	3.5
Va.	886	18.4	10859	2531	13390	−17.6	1.5
N.C.	478	21.3	6363	2109	8472	−3.8	1.8
S.C.	346	39	3399	1283	4682	35.4	1.4
Ga.	163	97.6	1403	252	1655	−27.9	1.0
Tenn.	106	194	681	62	743	−0.4	0.7
Ky.	221	200	1626	115	1741	59.7	0.8
Miss.	7.6		60		60		0.8

Table A.5 *Methodist Membership in 1810*

State	Residents (thou.)	Change from 1800, %	White Methodist Members	Black Methodist Members	Total Methodist Members	Change from 1800, %	Percent of total Residents
Me.	229	50.7	3460	4	3464	189	1.5
N.H.	214	16.3	1933		1933	1030	0.9
Vt.	218	41.6	4401	18	4419	303	2.0
Mass.	472	11.6	2785	41	2826	79	0.6
R.I.	77	11.6	471	2	473	108	0.6
Conn.	262	4.4	3369	48	3417	118	1.3
N.Y.	959	62.8	19112	944	20056	215	2.1
N.J.	246	16.6	6314	525	6839	126	2.8
Penn.	810	34.6	9314	1307	10621	233	1.3
Del.	72.7	13.1	3772	2369	6141	146	8.4
Md.	381	11.4	15978	12073	28051	133	7.4
Va.	983	10.9	18742	4894	23636	77	2.4
N.C.	556	16.3	13429	4956	18385	117	3.3
S.C.	415	19.9	6801	5010	11811	152	2.8
Ga.	252	54.6	6663	909	7572	358	3.0
Ohio	231	409	6491	38	6529		2.8
Tenn.	262	147	6373	550	6923	832	2.6
Ky.	407	84.2	6084	424	6508	274	1.6
Miss.	31.3	311.8	263	97	360	500	1.2
Ala.	9.0	624	71	15	86		1.0
Ind., Ill., Mo., Mich.	61.3	933	1692	9	1701		2.8

Sources: Asbury, *Journal and Letters*; Raymond Martin Bell and Charles F. Berkheimer, "Methodist Circuits in Central Pennsylvania Before 1812," TMs, Washington, PA, 1963; Lester J. Cappon, ed., *Atlas of Early American History: The Revolutionary Era, 1760–1790* (Princeton: Princeton University Press, 1976); William Henry Foote, *Sketches of North Carolina, Historical and Biographical, Illustrative of the Principles of a Portion of Her Early Settlers* (New York: Robert Carter, 1846; reprint, Dunn, NC: Reprint Co., 1912); Garrettson, *American Methodist Pioneer*; F. G. Hibbard, *History of the Late Genesee Conference of the Methodist Episcopal Church* (New York: Phillips and Hunt, 1887); Ray Holder, *The Mississippi Methodists 1799–1983: A Moral People "Born of Conviction"* (Jackson, MS: Maverick Prints, 1984); "Letters to Daniel Hitt"; Methodist Episcopal Church, *Minutes of the Methodist Conferences Annually Held in America: From 1773 to 1813*; Elizabeth Kristine Nottingham, *Methodism and the Frontier: Indiana Proving Ground* (New York: Columbia University Press, 1941); Simpson, *Cyclopedia*; Wallace Guy Smeltzer, *Methodism on the Headwaters of the Ohio: The History of the Pittsburgh Conference of the Methodist Church* (Nashville: Parthenon Press, 1951); William Warren Sweet, ed., *Circuit-Rider Days Along the Ohio: Being the Journals of the Ohio Conference from Its Organization in 1812 to 1826* (New York: The Methodist Book Concern, 1923); Tennessee Historical Records Survey, Division of Professional and Service Projects, Work Projects Administration, *Outline of Development of Methodism in Tennessee* (Nashville: Tennessee Historical Records Survey, 1940); Williams, *Garden of American Methodism*; Bureau of the Census, *Historical Statistics of the United States: Colonial Times to 1970*, 2 vol. (Washington, D.C.: U.S. Department of Commerce, 1975), 2:1168; Donald B. Dodd, comp., *Historical Statistics of the States of the United States: Two Centuries of the Census, 1790–1990* (Westport, CT: Greenwood Press, 1993), 2–104.

Notes

CHAPTER I

1. By 1876 all the various branches of American Methodism included more than 29,000 itinerant preachers, some 24,000 local preachers, and nearly 3 million members. See Methodist Episcopal Church, *Minutes of the Methodist Conferences, Annually Held in America; From 1773 to 1813, Inclusive* (New York: Daniel Hitt and Thomas Ware for the Methodist Connexion in the United States, 1813), 612; Robert Emerson Coleman, "Factors in the Expansion of the Methodist Episcopal Church From 1784 to 1812" (Ph.D. diss., State University of Iowa, 1954), 363–399; Roger Finke and Rodney Stark, "How the Upstart Sects Won America: 1776–1850," *Journal for the Scientific Study of Religion* 28 (1989): 27–44; C. C. Goss, *Statistical History of the First Century of American Methodism: With a Summary of the Origin and Present Operations of Other Denominations* (New York: Carlton and Porter, 1866), 88; Matthew Simpson, *Cyclopedia of Methodism: Embracing Sketches of its Rise, Progress, and Present Condition, with Biographical Notices and Numerous Illustrations* (Philadelphia: Everts and Stewart, 1878), 880. For a broader comparison of Methodism with the other denominations of this period, see Edwin Scott Gaustad, *Historical Atlas of Religion in America* (New York: Harper & Row, 1962), part 2.

2. William Capers, "Autobiography," in *Life of William Capers, D.D., One of the Bishops of the Methodist Episcopal Church, South; Including an Autobiography*, ed. William M. Wightman (Nashville: Southern Methodist Publishing House, 1859), 140.

3. In 1811 Asbury even more exuberantly declared that "we congregate annually 3 if not 4 million in campmeetings." While this estimate is high, it is reasonable to assume that by 1811 there were 400–500 camp meetings held annually, with a total attendance of some 1.2 million. Francis Asbury, *The Journal and Letters of Francis Asbury*, ed. Elmer T. Clark, Jacob S. Payton, and J. Manning Potts, 3 vols. (Nashville: Abingdon Press, 1958), 3: 310 (March 8, 1805), 3: 453 (September 1, 1811); Nathan O. Hatch, *The Democratization of American Christianity* (New Haven: Yale University Press, 1989), 257, n. 1.

4. These figures include children and make no attempt to account for regional variations. Using the same eight-to-one ratio for 1815 and 1820 results in Methodist

adherents accounting for about 20 percent of the aggregate U.S. population in both years. But the eight to one ratio may be too high for these later dates, when it was becoming more respectable to join the Methodists. In 1824 Freeborn Garrettson estimated that there were half a million Methodist members and another million "quiet hearers beside, who sit under our ministry." (Actual membership in 1824 was 328,500.) Freeborn Garrettson, *American Methodist Pioneer: The Life and Journals of Rev. Freeborn Garrettson, 1752–1827*, ed. Robert Drew Simpson (Rutland, VT: Academy Books, 1984), 351; and Methodist Episcopal Church, *Minutes of the Annual Conferences of the Methodist Episcopal Church*, 2 vols. (New York: T. Mason and G. Lane for the Methodist Episcopal Church, 1840), 1: 448 (hereafter referred to as *Minutes of the Annual Conferences*). See figures in Robert Baird, *Religion in America*, abridged by Henry Warner Bowden (New York: Harper & Row, 1970), chap. 64; and George M. Marsden, *Religion and American Culture* (Fort Worth: Harcourt Brace, 1990), 87.

5. It should be noted here that this study focuses primarily on the white Methodist Episcopal Church. Other Methodist groups such as the United Brethren or the followers of Jacob Albright also deserve their share of attention. But because the Methodist Episcopal Church was the largest, most geographically diverse, and most representative Methodist body of this period, it provides perhaps the most appropriate case study for exploring the broader connections between Methodism and American life.

6. Russell E. Richey, *Early American Methodism* (Bloomington: Indiana University Press, 1991), 47–64. Also see Donald Mathews's pathbreaking *Religion in the Old South* (Chicago: University of Chicago Press, 1977).

7. William G. McLoughlin, *Revivals, Awakenings, and Reform* (Chicago: University of Chicago Press, 1978), 137. On southern religion and its relationship to the North, see Samuel S. Hill Jr., *The South and the North in American Religion* (Athens: University of Georgia Press, 1980), 1–45.

8. The O'Kelly schism is discussed in chapter 2, and the Methodist Episcopal Church's stance on slavery is dealt with in chapter 6.

9. Nathan O. Hatch, "The Puzzle of American Methodism," *Church History* 63:2 (June 1994): 175–189. Also see David G. Hackett, "Sociology of Religion and American Religious History: Retrospect and Prospect," *Journal for the Scientific Study of Religion* 27 (1988): 461–474; and Harry S. Stout and Catherine A. Brekus, "Declension, Gender, and the 'New Religious History,' " in *Belief and Behavior: Essays in the New Religious History*, ed. Philip R. Vandermeer and Robert P. Swierenga (New Brunswick, NJ: Rutgers University Press, 1991), 15–37. Scholars who participated in what Henry May announced in 1964 as "the recovery of American religious history" were, for the most part, intellectual historians concerned with "the great tradition of the American churches": the partnership between the established denominations and society's leading political and educational institutions. In this scheme, American Methodists simply could not compete with the literary achievements or theological sophistication of the New England Puritans, or their intellectual heirs. See Henry F. May, "The Recovery of American Religious History," *American Historical Review* 70 (1964), 79–92; Winthrop S. Hudson, *The Great Tradition of the American Churches* (New York: Harper and Row, 1953).

10. Hatch, "Puzzle of American Methodism." Perhaps the two best known works on American Methodism are Donald G. Mathews's, *Slavery and Methodism: A Chapter in American Morality: 1780–1845* (Princeton: Princeton University Press, 1965); and Timothy L. Smith's, *Revivalism and Social Reform: American Protestantism on the Eve of the Civil War* (New York: Abingdon Press, 1957; reprint, Baltimore: The Johns Hopkins

University Press, 1980). Two other valuable, more recent works on American Methodism are Russell Richey's, *Early American Methodism;* and A. Gregory Schneider's, *The Way of the Cross Leads Home: The Domestication of American Methodism* (Bloomington: Indiana University Press, 1993). A valuable collection of essays on the history of Methodism can be found in *Rethinking Methodist History,* ed. Russell E. Richey and Kenneth E. Rowe (Nashville: Kingswood Books, 1985). This volume was recently updated and revised as *Perspectives on American Methodism: Interpretive Essays,* ed. Russell E. Richey, Kenneth E. Rowe, and Jean Miller Schmidt (Nashville: Kingswood Books, 1993). One-volume histories of American Methodism include Frederick A. Norwood, *The Story of American Methodism: A History of the United Methodists and Their Relations* (Nashville: Abingdon Press, 1974); and Charles W. Ferguson, *Methodists and the Making of America: Organizing to Beat the Devil,* 2d ed. (Austin, TX: Eakin Press, 1983). Unfortunately, none of these works has received much attention in the larger historiography. For a good assessment of Methodist historiography as of 1984, see Kenneth E. Rowe, "Methodist History at the Bicentennial: The State of the Art." *Methodist History* 22 (January 1984): 87–98. Dissertations that focus on the dynamics of Methodist expansion include: Doris Elisabett Andrews, "Popular Religion and the Revolution in the Middle Atlantic Ports: The Rise of the Methodists, 1770–1800" (Ph.D. diss., University of Pennsylvania, 1986); Coleman, "Factors in the Expansion of the Methodist Episcopal Church"; Raymond P. Cowan, "The Arminian Alternative: The Rise of the Methodist Episcopal Church, 1765–1850" (Ph.D. diss., Georgia State, 1991); James W. May, "From Revival Movement to Denomination: A Re-Examination of the Beginnings of Methodism" (Ph.D. diss., Columbia University, 1962); Michael George Nickerson, "Sermons, Systems, and Strategies: The Geographic Strategies of the Methodist Episcopal Church in Its Expansion into New York State, 1788–1810" (Ph.D. diss., Syracuse University, 1988); and William Thomas Umbel, "The Making of an American Denomination: Methodism in New England Religious Culture, 1790–1860" (Ph.D. diss., Johns Hopkins University, 1992).

11. Major works by these historians include: Elie Halevy, *England in 1815,* trans. E. I. Watkin and D. A. Barker (First published in French in 1913; reprint, New York: Barnes and Noble, 1968); E. P. Thompson, *The Making of the English Working Class* (New York: Pantheon Books, 1964); Eric J. Hobsbawm, *Labouring Men: Studies in the History of Labour* (London: Weindenfeld and Nicolson, 1968); Bernard Semmel, *The Methodist Revolution* (New York: Basic Books, 1973); James Obelkevich, *Religion and Rural Society: South Lindsey 1825–1875* (Oxford: Clarendon Press, 1976); John Rule, "Methodism, Popular Beliefs and Village Culture in Cornwall, 1800–50," in *Popular Culture and Custom in Nineteenth-Century England,* ed. Robert D. Storch (London: Croom Helm and New York: St. Martin's Press, 1982), 48–70; Robert Colls, *The Pitmen of the Northern Coalfields: Work, Culture and Protest, 1790–1850* (Manchester: Manchester University Press, 1987); Gail Malmgreen, "Domestic Discords: Women and the Family in East Cheshire Methodism, 1750–1830," in *Disciplines of Faith: Studies in Religion, Politics and Patriarchy,* ed. Jim Obelkevich, Lyndal Roper, and Raphael Samuel (London: Routledge and Kegan Paul, 1987), 55–70; Deborah M. Valenze, *Prophetic Sons and Daughters: Female Preaching and Popular Religion in Industrial England* (Princeton: Princeton University Press, 1985); David Hempton, *Methodism and Politics in British Society 1750–1850* (Stanford: Stanford University Press, 1984); David Hempton, *Religion and Political Culture in Britain and Ireland: From the Glorious Revolution to the Decline of Empire* (Cambridge: Cambridge University Press, 1996); and Alan D. Gilbert, *Religion and Society in Industrial England: Church, Chapel and Social Change 1740–1914* (London:

Longman, 1976). Also see David Hempton and Myrtle Hill, *Evangelical Protestantism in Ulster Society 1740–1890* (London: Routledge, 1992), 3–142.

12. Paralleling developments in religious history, interest in the early American republic has expanded in recent years as scholars seek to unravel the story of how the tighter social confines of colonial America gave way to the more fluid and market-oriented outlook of the post-revolutionary years. But much like their counterparts in American religion, historians of the early republic have all too often dismissed American Methodism as the bland, bourgeois religion of the middle class, or as an agent of elite control, rather than as an authentic expression of the hopes, demands, and fears of ordinary people. Three of the most influential recent works on the early republic are: Richard L. Bushman's *The Refinement of America: Persons, Houses, Cities* (New York: Alfred A. Knopf, 1992); Charles Sellers's *The Market Revolution: Jacksonian America, 1815–1846* (New York: Oxford University Press, 1991); and Gordon S. Wood's, *The Radicalism of the American Revolution* (New York: Alfred A. Knopf, 1992). In recent years there has been a great deal of interest in the frontier in the early republic, particularly in its transition of capitalism. Fresh works on this topic include Robert D. Mitchell's pathbreaking *Commercialism and Frontier: Perspectives on the Early Shenandoah Valley* (Charlottesville: University of Virginia Press, 1977), and books by Andrew R. L. Cayton, Christopher Clark, Randolph Roth, and Alan Taylor. But although the Methodists crop up here and there in some of these fine studies, nowhere are they fully incorporated into the analytical framework. Moreover, in considering the rise of liberal capitalism and modern bourgeois society, a number of recent studies, including those by Stuart Blumin, Sean Wilentz, David G. Hackett, Terry D. Bilhartz, and Charles G. Steffen, have fleetingly noted the close connection between Methodism and the middling artisan classes in the early republic, but none have pursued this lead to a satisfying conclusion. Relevant works by these authors include: Terry D. Bilhartz, *Urban Religion and the Second Great Awakening: Church and Society in Early National Baltimore* (London: Associated University Presses, 1986); Stuart M. Blumin, *The Emergence of the Middle Class: Social Experience in the American City, 1760–1900* (Cambridge: Cambridge University Press, 1989); Andrew R. L. Cayton, *The Frontier Republic: Ideology and Politics in the Ohio Country, 1780–1825* (Kent: Kent State University Press, 1986); Christopher Clark, *The Roots of Rural Capitalism: Western Massachusetts, 1780–1860* (Ithaca: Cornell University Press, 1990); David G. Hackett, *The Rude Hand of Innovation: Religion and Social Order in Albany, New York 1652–1836* (New York: Oxford University Press, 1991); Randolph A. Roth, *The Democratic Dilemma: Religion, Reform, and the Social Order in the Connecticut River Valley of Vermont, 1791–1850* (New York: Cambridge University Press, 1987); Charles G. Steffen, *The Mechanics of Baltimore: Workers and Politics in the Age of Revolution 1763–1812* (Urbana: University of Illinois Press, 1984); Alan Taylor, *Liberty Men and Great Proprietors: The Revolutionary Settlement on the Maine Frontier, 1760–1820* (Chapel Hill: University of North Carolina Press, 1990); and Sean Wilentz, *Chants Democratic: New York City and the Rise of the American Working Class, 1788–1850* (New York: Oxford University Press, 1984). A notable exception to the pattern noted above is Mark Noll's recent textbook, *A History of Christianity in the United States and Canada* (Grand Rapids: Eerdmans, 1992), esp. chap. 7.

13. Finke and Stark, "How the Upstart Sects Won America." This is also a theme of Roger Finke and Rodney Stark's recent book, *The Churching of America 1776–1990: Winners and Losers in our Religious Economy* (New Brunswick: Rutgers University Press, 1992), esp. chaps. 1–3.

14. Wood, *Radicalism of the American Revolution*; and Alan Taylor, *William Cooper's Town: Power and Persuasion on the Frontier of the Early American Republic* (New York:

Vintage Books, 1995). Also see Michael Zuckerman, "A Different Thermidor: The Revolution Beyond the American Revolution," in *The Transformation of Early American History: Society, Authority, and Ideology*, ed. James A. Henretta, Michael Kammen, and Stanley N. Katz (New York: Alfred A. Knopf, 1991), 170–193.

15. George Eliot, *Adam Bede* (Leipzig: B. Tauchnitz, 1859; reprint, New York: Harcourt, Brace & World, 1962), 78.

16. Joyce Appleby, *Capitalism and a New Social Order: The Republican Vision of the 1790s* (New York: New York University Press, 1984), 78–101. On the connections between evangelical religion and revolution in northern Atlantic societies from the mid-eighteenth to the mid-nineteenth centuries, see Mark A. Noll, "Revolution and the Rise of Evangelical Social Influence in North Atlantic Societies," in *Evangelicalism: Comparative Studies of Popular Protestantism in North America, the British Isles, and Beyond, 1700–1990*, ed. Mark A. Noll, David W. Bebbington, and George A. Rawlyk (New York: Oxford University Press, 1994), 113–136.

17. United States, Bureau of the Census, *Historical Statistics of the United States: Colonial Times to 1970* (Washington, DC: U.S. Bureau of the Census, 1975), A195–205, 1168; Malcolm J. Rohrbough, *The Trans-Appalachian Frontier: People, Societies, and Institutions 1775–1850* (New York: Oxford University Press, 1978), 3–94.

18. Methodist Episcopal Church, *The Doctrines and Discipline of the Methodist Episcopal Church in America. With Explanatory Notes by Thomas Coke and Francis Asbury* (Philadelphia: John Dickens, 1798; reprint, Rutland, VT: Academy Books, 1979), 29.

19. Wood, *Radicalism of the American Revolution*, 185; W. J. Rorabaugh, *The Craft Apprentice: From Franklin to the Machine Age in America* (New York: Oxford University Press, 1986), 3–56; cf. Paul E. Johnson, *A Shopkeeper's Millennium: Society and Revivals in Rochester, New York, 1815–1837* (New York: Hill and Wang, 1978), 37–61.

20. Alfred Brunson, *A Western Pioneer: or, Incidents of the Life and Times of Rev. Alfred Brunson, A.M., D.D., Embracing a Period of Over Seventy Years*, 2 vols. (Cincinnati: Hitchcock and Walden, 1872; reprint, New York: Arno Press, 1975), 45.

21. Walter Nugent, *Structures of American Social History* (Bloomington: Indiana University Press, 1981), 54–58.

22. Wood, *The Radicalism of the American Revolution*, 303; Zuckerman, "A Different Thermidor"; W. J. Rorabaugh, *The Alcoholic Republic: An American Tradition* (New York: Oxford University Press, 1979), 5–14. Also see Rowland Berthoff, "Independence and Attachment, Virtue and Interest: From Republican Citizen to Free Enterpriser, 1787–1837," in *Uprooted Americans: Essays to Honor Oscar Handlin*, ed. Richard L. Bushman, Neil Harris, David Rothman, Barbara Miller Solomon, and Stephan Thernstrom (Boston: Little, Brown and Company, 1979), 97–124; Gordon S. Wood, "The Significance of the Early Republic," *Journal of the Early Republic* 8 (Spring 1988): 1–20. On women and the American Revolution, see Linda Kerber, *Women of the Republic: Intellect and Ideology in Revolutionary America* (Chapel Hill: University of North Carolina Press, 1980).

23. Hatch, *Democratization*; Jon Butler, *Awash in a Sea of Faith: Christianizing the American People* (Cambridge: Harvard University Press, 1990). On the resurgence of religion in New York during the 1780s and 1790s, see Richard W. Pointer, *Protestant Pluralism and the New York Experience: A Study of Eighteenth-Century Religious Diversity* (Bloomington: Indiana University Press, 1988), 103–144. Also on the rise of evangelical religion in antebellum upstate New York (Cortland County), see Curtis Johnson, *Islands of Holiness: Rural Religion in Upstate New York, 1790–1860* (Ithaca: Cornell University Press, 1989), 1–86. On the general social and religious volatility of the early national period, see Whitney R. Cross, *The Burned-over District: The Social and Intellec-*

tual History of Enthusiastic Religion in Western New York, 1800–1850 (Ithaca: Cornell University Press, 1950), 3–51; and David M. Ludlum, Social Ferment in Vermont 1791–1850 (New York: Columbia University Press, 1939), 3–62.

24. Finke and Stark, "How the Upstart Sects Won America."

25. Wilentz, Chants Democratic, 77–78; Bilhartz, Urban Religion and the Second Great Awakening; Steffen, The Mechanics of Baltimore, 253–272.

26. James Quinn, Sketches of the Life and Labors of James Quinn, Who was Nearly Half a Century a Minister of the Gospel in the Methodist Episcopal Church, ed. John F. Wright (Cincinnati: Methodist Book Concern, 1851), 62.

27. Charles Woodmason, The Carolina Backcountry on the Eve of the Revolution: The Journal and Other Writings of Charles Woodmason, Anglican Itinerant, ed. Richard J. Hooker (Chapel Hill: University of North Carolina Press, 1953), 6. On Woodmason, also see John F. Woolverton, Colonial Anglicanism in North America (Detroit: Wayne State University Press, 1984), 202–203.

28. Woodmason, Carolina Backcountry, 15 and 99–100.

29. Ibid., 44. This is a sentiment that Samuel Davies agreed with, particularly in relationship to the lack of religious instruction provided to slaves. See Samuel Davies, Letters from the Rev. Samuel Davies, etc. Shewing the State of Religion in Virginia, particularly among the Negroes, 2nd ed. (London: R. Pardon, 1757), 1–44.

30. Woodmason, Carolina Backcountry, 56 and 38.

31. Ibid., 20.

32. Ibid., 17.

33. Ibid., 46.

34. Devereux Jarratt, The Life of the Reverend Devereux Jarratt, Rector of Bath Parish, Dinwiddie County, Virginia. Written by Himself, in a Series of Letters Addressed to the Rev. John Coleman, One of the Ministers of the Protestant Episcopal Church, in Maryland (Baltimore: Warner and Hanna, 1806; reprint, New York: Arno Press, 1969), 36.

35. Jarratt, Life of Devereux Jarratt, 15.

36. Ibid., 181 and 126. Rhys Isaac argues this point persuasively when dealing with the contest between Anglicans and Baptists in eighteenth-century Virginia. See Rhys Issac, The Transformation of Virginia 1740–1790 (Chapel Hill: University of North Carolina Press, 1982), esp. part 2.

37. James R. Rohrer has recently observed that in New England a number of Congregationalist missionaries made explicit attempts to adjust to the new climate of the early republic. James R. Rohrer, Keepers of the Covenant: Frontier Missions and the Decline of Congregationalism 1774–1818 (New York: Oxford University Press, 1995).

38. Joseph Pilmore, The Journal of Joseph Pilmore: Methodist Itinerant, ed. Frederick E. Maser and Howard T. Maag (Philadelphia: Historical Society of the Philadelphia Annual Conference of the United Methodist Church, 1969), 169. According to another account concerning North Carolina, in 1765 the Anglican church had only six priests to serve twenty-nine parishes with a population of over 100,000 people. Mathews, Religion in the Old South, 5–6. Similarly, in New York, the Dutch Reformed, Presbyterians, Anglicans, and Lutherans all experienced chronic shortages of clergy during this period. See Pointer, Protestant Pluralism, 106. On the paucity of churches in the pre-revolutionary South, see Gaustad, Historical Atlas, part 1.

39. My concept of popular religion is largely drawn from the work of Jon Butler, David D. Hall, Robert A. Orsi and Peter Burke. Butler defines popular religion as "no less and no more than the religious behavior of laypeople." Butler, Awash in a Sea of Faith, 4; David D. Hall, Worlds of Wonder, Days of Judgement: Popular Religious Belief in

Early New England (Cambridge: Harvard University Press, 1990), 4–20; Robert A. Orsi, *The Madonna of 115th Street: Faith and Community in Italian Harlem, 1880–1950* (New Haven: Yale University Press, 1985), xiv and xvii–xviii; and Peter Burke, *Popular Culture in Early Modern Europe* (New York: New York University Press, 1978).

40. Thomas Ware, *Sketches of the Life and Travels of Rev. Thomas Ware, Who Has Been an Itinerant Methodist Preacher for More Than Fifty Years* (New York: T. Mason and G. Lane, 1840), 247.

41. Emil Pocock, "Popular Roots of Jacksonian Democracy: The Case of Dayton, Ohio, 1815–1830," *Journal of the Early Republic* 9 (Winter 1989): 489–515. Also see Andrew R. L. Cayton, "The Contours of Power in a Frontier Town: Marietta, Ohio, 1788–1803," *Journal of the Early Republic* 6 (1986): 103–126.

42. Steffen, *The Mechanics of Baltimore*, 253–272; Bilhartz, *Urban Religion and the Second Great Awakening*, 21–23; Andrews, "Popular Religion and the Revolution," 269–324; Wilentz, *Chants Democratic*, 80–81.

43. Well into the 1820s, carpenters, masons, and shoemakers constituted the leading occupational groups in Providence Methodism. See Mark S. Schantz, "Piety in Providence: The Class Dimensions of Religious Experience in Providence, Rhode Island, 1790–1860" (Ph.D. diss., Emory University, 1991), 156 and 198. In his richly textured study of Albany, New York, David Hackett points out the close connection between Methodism and mechanic ideologies in the early nineteenth century. Both "appealed to the same constituency of less affluent journeyman, petty shopkeepers, and laborers," writes Hackett. "Both attracted people who aspired to greater personal autonomy, yet were still deeply attached to traditional values." Hackett, *Rude Hand of Innovation*, 98 and 99.

44. Mathews, *Religion in the Old South*, 32–34.

45. One of the best recent biographies of John Wesley is Henry Rack's *Reasonable Enthusiast: John Wesley and the Rise of Methodism* (London: Epworth Press, 1989). On Wesley's conversion, see especially pp. 137–157. An excellent brief summary of Wesley's life is Maldwyn L. Edwards's *John Wesley* (Madison, NJ: United Methodist Church, 1987).

46. Hempton, *Methodism and Politics in British Society*, 14–16; Hempton, *Religion and Political Culture*, 25–48; David Hempton, "Evangelicalism in English and Irish Society, 1780–1840," in *Evangelicalism*, ed. Noll, Bebbington, and Rawlyk, 156–176; and John Walsh, "'Methodism' and the Origins of English-Speaking Evangelicalism," in *Evangelicalism*, ed. Noll, Bebbington, and Rawlyk, 19–37.

47. Gilbert, *Religion and Society in Industrial England*, 60–67, 98–103; Eliot, *Adam Bede*, 18–19.

48. Eliot, *Adam Bede*, 183, 78.

49. Alan D. Gilbert, "Methodism, Dissent and Political Stability in Early Industrial England," *Journal of Religious History* 10 (June 1978): 381–399.

50. Gilbert, *Religion and Society in Industrial England*, 39, 63, and 67; Hempton, *Methodism and Politics*, 14–16; Hempton, *Religion and Political Culture*, 25–48. The Taylor quotation is from Rack, *Reasonable Enthusiast*, 4. On the groups that broke away from the main body of English Wesleyanism from 1790 to 1820, including the Primitive Methodists, Bible Christians, New Connexion, and Independent Methodists, see Julia Stewart Werner, *The Primitive Methodist Connexion: Its Background and Early History* (Madison: University of Wisconsin Press, 1984), esp. 20–29, 54–72, and 177–180; W. R. Ward, *Religion and Society in England 1790–1850* (New York: Schocken Books, 1973), 75–81 and 92–99; Owen Chadwick, *The Victorian Church*, 2nd ed. (London:

Adam & Charles Black, 1970), part 1, 385–386; Richard Carwardine, *Transatlantic Revivalism: Popular Evangelicalism in Britain and America, 1790–1865* (Westport, CT: Greenwood Press, 1978), 104–107; Robert Currie, "A Micro-Theory of Methodist Growth," *Proceedings of the Wesley Historical Society* 36 (October 1967): 65–73; and Hempton, *Methodism and Politics*, 66–72.

51. Obelkevich, *Religion and Rural Society*, 168.

52. Ibid., 257–258. The often latent radicalism of English Methodism becomes clearer when one compares it to what developed in Ireland. Whereas English Methodism was a predominantly grassroots movement, in Ireland the Methodists worked downward from the gentry and outward from other bastions of English authority. In Ireland John Wesley revealed his deep antipathy toward Roman Catholicism by establishing an alliance with the Irish gentry, the like of which would have been unthinkable in England. Thus Irish Methodism had a vested interest in protecting the existing order of church and state and showed little of the popular character of its English counterpart. Not surprisingly, Irish Methodism achieved most of its growth in old English settlements and among Protestants displaced from Europe and Britain, making little impact on the broader Roman Catholic population. See Hempton, "Evangelicalism in English and Irish Society"; David Hempton, "Methodism in Irish Society, 1770–1830," *The Transactions of the Royal Historical Society*, 5th series, vol. 36 (1986): 117–142; and Hempton and Hill, *Evangelical Protestantism in Ulster*, 8–15, 29–44, and 76–79.

53. Rule, "Methodism, Popular Beliefs and Village Culture in Cornwall"; Robert Colls, "Primitive Methodists in the Northern Coalfields," in *Disciplines of Faith*, ed. Obelkevich, Roper, and Samuel, 323–334; Colls, *The Pitmen of the Northern Coalfields*; and Colls, *The Collier's Rant: Song and Culture in the Industrial Village* (London: Croom Helm, 1977).

54. Gilbert, *Religion and Society in Industrial England*, 83. Also see Gilbert, "Methodism, Dissent and Political Stability in Early Industrial England." Gilbert's conclusion is of course much different than the judgement of E. P. Thompson. Despite the sophistication of his analysis, E. P. Thompson has largely grasped and acknowledged only the social and not the religious dimension of Methodism's appeal. This has led Thompson to blame the Methodists for thwarting the best interests of English workers, and to see English Methodists as purveyors of a pernicious "psychic exploitation," "apologists for an authority in whose eyes they were an object of ridicule or condescension." He thus concludes, wrongly I believe, that Methodism represented a kind of retreat from reality, a "chiliasm of the defeated and hopeless." Thompson, *Making of the English Working Class*, 350–375 and 417–419. On this topic, also see Hempton, "Evangelicalism in English and Irish Society."

55. One of the best recent works on Wesley's theology is Randy L. Maddox's *Responsible Grace: John Wesley's Practical Theology* (Nashville: Kingswood Books, 1994). I rely heavily for the following discussion of Wesley's theology on Maddox, who in turn draws much of his conceptual framework from the writings of Albert Outler. Robert E. Cushman's perceptive study *John Wesley's Experimental Divinity: Studies in Methodist Doctrinal Standards* (Nashville: Kingswood Books, 1989) is also very helpful in measuring Wesley's impact on early American Methodism. Also see Thomas Langford, *Practical Divinity: Theology in the Wesleyan Tradition* (Nashville: Abingdon Press, 1983); Leland Scott, "The Message of Early American Methodism," in *History of Early American Methodism*, ed. Emory S. Bucke (New York: Abingdon Press, 1964), 1: 291–359; Donald G. Mathews, "Evangelical America—The Methodist Ideology," in *Perspectives on American Methodism*, ed. Richey, Rowe, and Schmidt, 17–30; Frank Baker, "The Doctrines in the

Discipline," in *Perspectives on American Methodism*, ed. Richey, Rowe, and Schmidt, 46–61; Richard P. Heitzenrater, "At Full Liberty: Doctrinal Standards in Early American Methodism," in *Perspectives on American Methodism*, ed. Richey, Rowe, and Schmidt, 62–76; and Thomas A. Langford, *Wesleyan Theology: A Source Book* (Durham, NC: Labyrinth Press, 1984), part 1. On the place of Methodist piety in European religion, see Ted A. Campbell, *The Religion of the Heart: A Study of European Religious Life in the Seventeenth and Eighteenth Centuries* (Columbia: University of South Carolina Press, 1991), esp. 115–124.

56. Wesley's conception, as Randy Maddox writes, was that God's grace "*inspires* and *enables*, but does not *overpower*." Maddox, *Responsible Grace*, 86. Also see pp. 23, 56, and 82; and Langford, *Practical Divinity*, chaps. 1 and 2.

57. Rack, *Reasonable Enthusiast*, 389. On Wesley and Calvinism, see 198–202, 388–393, and 450–461.

58. Joseph Crawford, *The Substance of a Sermon Delivered at the Funeral of Miss Nabby Frothingham, of Middleton, (Conn.) February 24, 1809, to a Numerous Crowd of Attentive Hearers, in the Methodist Meeting-house* (New York: John C. Totten, 1809), 5–27.

59. This is a persistent theme of Cushman's *John Wesley's Experimental Divinity*. See especially the quotation on p. 149.

60. John Wesley, *A Plain Account of the People Called Methodists*, first published in 1749. Quoted in Cushman, *John Wesley's Experimental Divinity*, 86.

61. In this connection, William Warren Sweet, the dean of American Methodist history in this century, writes, "Arminianism became the theology of the common man because its tenets jibed with his experience." William Warren Sweet, *Religion in the Development of American Culture 1765–1840* (New York: Charles Scribner's Sons, 1952), x. The compatibility of Methodist doctrine and American culture (especially frontier culture) in the early national period is a persistent theme in Sweet's writings.

62. On the doctrine and practice of baptism in American Methodism, see Gayle Carlton Felton, *This Gift of Water: The Practice and Theology of Baptism Among Methodists in America* (Nashville: Abingdon Press, 1992), chaps. 3 and 4.

63. Sydney Ahlstrom, *A Religious History of the American People* (New Haven: Yale University Press, 1972), 438–439.

64. Hatch, *Democratization*, 139 and 170–179. The two quotations are from pp. 170 and 172. The passage from Lorenzo Dow can be found in Dow's *History of Cosmopolite: or the Writings of Rev. Lorenzo Dow: Containing His Experience and Travels, in Europe and America, Up to Near His Fiftieth Year*, 6th ed. (Cincinnati: Joshua Martin and Alex S. Robertson, 1849), 365. Also see Ahlstrom, *Religious History of the American People*, 357; and Mathews, *Religion in the Old South*, 31–33.

65. Charles Giles, *Pioneer: A Narrative of the Nativity, Experience, Travels, and Ministerial Labours of Rev. Charles Giles* (New York: G. Lane & P.P. Sandford, 1844), 12–33 and 52–78.

66. Billy Hibbard, *Memoirs of the Life and Travels of B. Hibbard, Minister of the Gospel, Containing an Account of His Experience of Religion; and of His Call to and Labours in the Minister for Nearly Thirty Years* (New York: Published by the Author, 1825), 1–110. The quotation is from p. 104.

67. Wesley gives a succinct explanation of the nature and importance of Christian Perfection in answer to Question 57 of the *Minutes of Several Conversations Between the Reverend Mr. John and Charles Wesley, and Others. From the Year 1744, to the Year 1780*, in John J. Tigert, *A Constitutional History of American Episcopal Methodism*, 2nd. ed.

(Nashville: Methodist Episcopal Church, South, 1904), 585–586. These are the so-called Large Minutes that formed the basis of the early American Disciplines. Also see Wesley's *Plain Account of Christian Perfection*; Maddox, *Responsible Grace*, 60, 126, 176, and 190; Langford, *Practical Divinity*, 39–43; Scott, "Message of Early American Methodism," 301–307; and Rack, *Reasonable Enthusiast*, 395–401.

68. William Watters, *A Short Account of the Christian Experience, and Ministerial Labours of William Watters* (Alexandria: S. Snowden, 1806), 67; and Benjamin Abbott, *Experience and Gospel Labours of the Rev. Benjamin Abbott*, ed. John Ffirth (New York: Methodist Episcopal Church, 1830), 99 and 135. Also see Garrettson, *American Methodist Pioneer*. On the decline of preaching on sanctification, see for example Benjamin Lakin's journal entry for March 15, 1814, in "The Journal of Benjamin Lakin, 1794–1820," in *Religion on the American Frontier, 1783–1840*, vol. 4, *The Methodists*, ed. William Warren Sweet (Chicago: University of Chicago Press, 1946), 249.

69. Smith, *Revivalism and Social Reform*, 115; Maddox, *Responsible Grace*, 36, 44–46. Another example of the way American Methodists modified Wesley's system was their failure to maintain the distinction between the class meeting and the band.

CHAPTER 2

1. Jacob Young, *Autobiography of a Pioneer; or the Nativity, Experience, Travels, and Ministerial Labors of Rev. Jacob Young; with Incidents, Observations, and Reflections* (Cincinnati: Cranston and Curts, n.d. [c. 1857]), 83–88.

2. Ibid., 90–91.

3. Ibid., 97–99 and 104–105.

4. Giles, *Pioneer*, 104–105.

5. George G. Smith, *The Life and Times of George Foster Pierce . . . With His Sketch of Lovick Pierce, D.D., His Father* (Nashville: Hunter & Welburn, 1888), 20–21.

6. Asbury, *Journals and Letters*, 3: 164.

7. For an excellent brief description of the formation of Methodist polity in Britain, see Frank Baker, "The People Called Methodists: Polity," in *A History of the Methodist Church in Great Britain*, vol. 1, ed. Rupert Davies and Gordon Rupp (London: Epworth Press, 1965), 211–255.

8. On American Methodism's early lay phase, see Frank Baker, *From Wesley to Asbury* (Durham: Duke University Press, 1976), esp. 28–83.

9. Methodist Episcopal Church, *Form of Discipline, for the Ministers, Preachers, and Members of the Methodist Episcopal Church in America* (New York: Methodist Episcopal Church, 1787), Section 3, p. 5.

10. On the crisis of 1779 and 1780 over the ordinances, see Tigert, *Constitutional History*, 97–120; Jesse Lee, *A Short History of the Methodists, in the United States of America: Beginning with 1766, and Continued Till 1809. To Which is Prefixed a Brief Account of Their Rise in England in 1729, &c* (Baltimore: Magill and Clime, 1810), 61–69; *Minutes of the Annual Conferences*, 1: 9–13; Asbury, *Journal and Letters*, 1: 300 and 1: 346–350; Watters, *Short Account*, 79–81; Philip Gatch, *Sketch of Rev. Philip Gatch*, ed. John McLean (Cincinnati: Swarmstedt & Poe, 1854), 65–79; Elizabeth Connor, *Methodist Trail Blazer Philip Gatch 1751–1834: His Life in Maryland, Virginia and Ohio* (Rutland, VT: Academy Books, 1970), 106–107; and May, "From Revival Movement to Denomination," 64–125.

11. Lee, *Short History*, 64.

12. Asbury, *Journal and Letters*, 1: 347.

13. Asbury, *Journal and Letters*, 1: 350.

14. Cushman, *John Wesley's Experimental Divinity*, 163; and Heitzenrater, "At Full Liberty," 64–66.

15. Norwood, *The Story of American Methodism*, 70 and 124. In 1789 Asbury created a council consisting of the bishops and presiding elders to form the core administrative unit of the church. But the council proved so unpopular that after only two meetings in December 1789 and December 1790 it was replaced by the quadrennial General Conference. The minutes of the two council meetings were printed as pamphlets: Methodist Episcopal Church, *Proceedings of the Bishop and Presiding Elders of the Methodist-Episcopal Church, in Council Assembled, at Baltimore, on the First Day of December, 1789* (Baltimore: William Goddard and James Angell, 1789); and Methodist Episcopal Church, *Minutes Taken at a Council of the Bishop and Delegated Elders of the Methodist-Episcopal Church: Held at Baltimore, in the State of Maryland, December 1, 1790* (Baltimore: W. Goddard and J. Angell, 1790).

16. Francis Asbury to Daniel Hitt, July 28, 1805, letter no. 304 in "Letters Written to Daniel Hitt: Methodist Preacher 1788 to 1806," TMs, trans. Annie Winstead, with footnotes and an introduction by Raymond Martin Bell, Special Collections, Ohio Wesleyan University, Delaware, Ohio.

17. For a related discussion of George Whitefield's relationship to the emerging market place of the eighteenth century, see Harry S. Stout, *The Divine Dramatist: George Whitefield and the Rise of Modern Evangelicalism* (Grand Rapids: Eerdmans, 1991).

18. *Minutes of Several Conversations Between the Reverend Mr. John and Charles Wesley, and Others. From the Year 1744, to the Year 1780*, Q. 26, in Tigert, *A Constitutional History of American Episcopal Methodism*, 551–552. These are the so-called Large Minutes that formed the basis of the early American Disciplines.

19. Lester B. Scherer, *Ezekiel Cooper, 1763–1847: An Early American Methodist Leader* (n.p.: The Commission on Archives and History of the United Methodist Church, 1965), 23.

20. James P. Horton, *A Narrative of the Early Life, Remarkable Conversion, and Spiritual Labours of James P. Horton, Who Has Been a Member of the Methodist Episcopal Church Upward of Forty Years* (n.p.: Printed for the Author, 1839), 47 and 193.

21. Ware, *Sketches*, 121–122. Ware records the use of a similar tactic by an itinerant on pp. 63–64.

22. Watters, *Short Account*, 18–19; and Abner Chase, *Recollections of the Past* (New York: Published for the Author, 1848), 12–22. On Watters' life, also see Cushman, *John Wesley's Experimental Divinity*, 65–69 and 120–123.

23. John V. Watson, *Tales and Takings, Sketches and Incidents from the Itinerant and Editorial Budget of Rev. J. V. Watson, D.D., Editor of the Northwestern Christian Advocate* (New York: Carlton and Porter, 1856), 244.

24. Brunson, *Western Pioneer*, 89.

25. Giles, *Pioneer*, 84–85.

26. Francis Asbury to Daniel Hitt, July 28, 1805, letter no. 304, in "Letters to Daniel Hitt."

27. John Littlejohn, "Journal of John Littlejohn," TMs, trans. Annie Winstead, the Upper Room, Nashville, Tenn., pp. 10–11.

28. Jacob Young, *Autobiography*, 57; Hibbard, *Memoirs*, 86; Elijah Woolsey, *The Supernumerary; or Lights and Shadows of Itinerancy. Compiled from the Papers of Rev. Elijah Woolsey*, ed. George Coles (New York: G. Lane and C.B. Tippett, 1845), 22–24; Smith, *Life of Pierce*, 20; Connor, *Methodist Trail Blazer*, 20–22; and John Brooks, *The Life and*

Times of the Rev. John Brooks, in Which are Contained a History of the Great Revival in Tennessee; With Many Incidents of Thrilling Interest (Nashville: Nashville Christian Advocate Office, 1848), 62–63.

29. Lee, *Short History*, 255 and 362; *Minutes of the Annual Conferences*, 1: 171.

30. Henry Smith, *Recollections and Reflections of an Old Itinerant*, ed. George Peck (New York: Lane and Tippett, 1848), 331–332; Gatch, *Sketch*, 108; and Quinn, *Sketches*, 34.

31. Abbott was a local preacher from 1772 to 1789. Abbott, *Experience*, 70 and 85. On Abbott, also see Howard Fenimore Shipps, "The Forgotten Apostle of Methodism, Being an Evaluation of the Life and Work of the Rev. Benjamin Abbott" (Ph.D. diss., Temple University, 1955), esp. chap. 4. As Shipps documents, Abbott figures prominently in many early histories of American Methodism.

32. James Jenkins, *Experience, Labours, and Sufferings of the Rev. James Jenkins of the South Carolina Conference* (n.p.: Printed for the Author, 1842; reprint, Columbia, SC: Jenkins Dowling Harper Baskin and Louise Beasley Manship, [1958]), 154.

33. Littlejohn, "Journal," 136.

34. Quoted in Dale E. Dunlap, "The United Methodist System of Itinerant Ministry," in *Rethinking Methodist History*, ed. Richey and Rowe, 18–28.

35. Methodist Episcopal Church, *Discipline* (1798), 42.

36. Ware, *Sketches*, 154; Garrettson, *American Methodist Pioneer*, 143; and William Beauchamp, *Letters on the Call and Qualifications of Ministers of the Gospel, and on the Apostolic Character and Superior Advantages of the Itinerant Ministry* (Richmond, VA: John Early for the Methodist Episcopal Church, South, 1853), 25.

37. Methodist Episcopal Church, *Discipline* (1798), p. 55.

38. David Sherman, *History of the Revisions of the Discipline of the Methodist Episcopal Church* (New York: Nelson & Phillips, 1874), 30.

39. *Minutes of the Annual Conferences*, 1: 6; James M. Buckley, *Constitutional and Parliamentary History of the Methodist Episcopal Church* (New York: Eaton and Mains, 1912), 196; and Sherman, *History of the Discipline*, 29.

40. Asbury to Nelson Reed, January 1, 1792, *Journal and Letters of Francis Asbury*, 3: 110.

41. Jesse Stoneman to Daniel Hitt, September 1796, letter no. 147, "Letters to Daniel Hitt." Stoneman was born in the East, but his family migrated to the West while he was young. He joined the itinerancy on trial in 1793, returned to ride circuits in western Pennsylvania and Ohio beginning in 1799, located in 1806, and soon settled in or near Fairfield County, Ohio. He died in 1840 and is buried in the Thornville, Ohio, cemetery. *Minutes of the Annual Conferences*, 1: 48 and 1: 136; "Ministers File," Ohio Wesleyan University, Delaware, Ohio; William Ryan, Obituary of Jesse Stoneman, *Western Christian Advocate* 6 (January 24, 1840): 160.

42. Asbury to Stith Mead, January 20, 1801, *Journals and Letters*, 3: 196. On the presiding elders, see Fred W. Price, "The Role of the Presiding Elder in the Growth of the Methodist Episcopal Church 1784–1832" (Ph.D. diss., Drew University, 1987), 44–70; and May, "From Revival Movement to Denomination," 184–189.

43. Woolsey, *Supernumerary*, 92.

44. Giles, *Pioneer*, 266 and 283.

45. Jenkins, *Experience*, 99 and 109.

46. Buckley, *Constitutional and Parliamentary History*, 51.

47. Chase, *Recollections*, 56–58; Z. Paddock, *Memoir of Rev. Benjamin Paddock, With Brief Notices of Early Ministerial Associates. Also, an Appendix, Containing More*

Extended Sketches of Rev. George Gary, Abner Chase, William Case, Seth Mattison, Isaac Puffer, Charles Giles, and Others (New York: Nelson & Phillips, 1875), 129; Abbott, *Experience*, 119. The story about Roberts is also in Paddock, pp. 110–111. Roberts joined the Baltimore conference in 1802 and was elected a bishop of the Methodist Episcopal Church in 1816. Simpson, *Cyclopedia*, 760–761.

48. Chase, *Recollections*, 90–91.

49. *Minutes of Several Conversations Between the Rev. Thomas Coke, LL.D., the Rev. Francis Asbury and Others*, in Tigert, *Constitutional History of American Episcopal Methodism*, 536.

50. Methodist Episcopal Church, *Discipline* (1784), 538–539. Cf. *Discipline* of 1798, 97–104.

51. Capers, "Autobiography," 120–121.

52. Dan Young, *Autobiography of Dan Young, A New England Preacher of the Olden Time* (New York: Carlton and Porter, 1860), 90.

53. Dan Young, *Autobiography*, 46; Brunson, *Western Pioneer*, 189–190; and Giles, *Pioneer*, 188–189. As early as 1774 Joseph Pilmore wrote that visiting from house to house "is, in my judgement one of the most important duties of a Christian Minister." Pilmore, *Journal*, 231.

54. Lee, *Short History*, 316–325; *Minutes of the Annual Conferences*, 1: 134–142; and Sweet, *Religion on the American Frontier*, vol. 4, *The Methodists*, 50. Thomas Ware estimated that some 290 itinerants located between 1784 and 1794. See Ware, *Sketches*, 215. Another tabulation shows that of the 650 preachers whose names appear in the Minutes before 1800, 500 died as local preachers and most of the remainder left and rejoined the itinerancy at various times. See Samuel Gardiner Ayres, *Methodist Heroes of Other Days* (New York: Methodist Book Concern, 1916), 30.

55. Chase, *Recollections*, 24; *Minutes of the Annual Conferences*, 1: 105 and 176.

56. Ware, *Sketches*, 214.

57. Quinn, *Sketches*, 47.

58. Chase, *Recollections*, 25.

59. Wesley preferred the name "superintendent," but by 1787 Asbury had replaced it with the word "bishop," greatly angering Wesley. In 1788 Wesley wrote to Asbury: "How can you, how dare you suffer yourself to be called a Bishop? I shudder, I start at the very thought! Men may call me a knave or a fool, a rascal, a scoundrel, and I am content; but they shall never by my consent call me Bishop! For my sake, for God's sake, for Christ's sake put a full end to this." (Asbury, *Journal and Letters*, 3: 65) Nevertheless, in the American context it is the name bishop that stuck, and I make no distinction between the terms here. See Spellman, "General Superintendency," 93–98. On Wesley's relationship with Asbury, see Baker, *From Wesley to Asbury*, 105–131; Maldwyn L. Edwards, "Two Master Builders: The Relation of John Wesley and Francis Asbury," *Proceedings of the Wesley Historical Society* (Great Britain) 38 (1971): 42–45; and John A. Vickers, "Francis Asbury in the Wiltshire Circuit," *Methodist History* 16 (April 1978): 185–189.

60. Price, "Presiding Elder," 223–234.

61. Charles Franklin Kilgore, *The James O'Kelly Schism in the Methodist Episcopal Church* (Mexico City: Casa Unida De Publicaciones, 1963), 4–5; and *Minutes of the Annual Conferences*, 1: 9–22. On the O'Kelly schism, also see William W. Bennett, *Memorials of Methodism in Virginia, From Its Introduction into the State in the Year 1772, to the Year 1829*, 2nd ed. (Richmond, VA: Published by the Author, 1871), chap. 9; May, "From Revival Movement to Denomination," 228–273; and Robert A. Armour,

"The Opposition to the Methodist Church in Eighteenth-Century Virginia" (Ph.D. diss., University of Georgia, 1968), chap. 7. The most complete description of O'Kelly is Wilbur E. MacClenny, *The Life of Rev. James O'Kelly and the Early History of the Christian Church in the South* (Indianapolis: Religious Book Service, 1910). On the tension between Methodism's "episcopal language" and the "republican language" of O'Kelly, see Richey, *Early American Methodism*, 87–91.

62. Lee, *Short History*, 176.

63. The O'Kelly schism subsequently led to a pamphlet war between O'Kelly and Nicholas Snethen who took up the defense of Asbury and the church. The quotations are from: James O'Kelly, *A Vindication of the Author's Apology with Reflections on the Reply, and a Few Remarks on Bishop Asbury's Annotations on His Book of Discipline* (Raleigh: Printed for the Author, 1801), 3–4; Nicholas Snethen, *A Reply to an Apology for Protesting Against the Methodist Episcopal Government* (Philadelphia: Henry Tuckniss, 1800), 14; and James O'Kelly, *The Author's Apology for Protesting Against the Methodist Episcopal Government* (Richmond, VA: Dixon, 1798), 21 and 98. Also see Nicholas Snethen, *An Answer to James O'Kelly's Vindication of His Apology* (Philadelphia: S.W. Conrad, 1802). Francis Asbury also published a compilation of Jeremiah Burroughs's *Heart Divisions, the Evil of our Times*, and Richard Baxter's *The Cure of Church Divisions*, with an introduction, under the title *The Causes, Evils, and Cures of Heart and Church Divisions. Extracted from the Works of Mr. Jeremiah Burroughs and Mr. Richard Baxter* (New York: J. Soule and T. Mason, 1817).

64. Snethen, *An Answer*, 40.

65. Snethen, *Reply*, 30. O'Kelly's appointments for 1782 to 1791 can be found in the *Minutes of the Annual Conferences*, 15–41. O'Kelly is listed as an elder beginning in 1785.

66. Snethen, *An Answer*, 24, and 41–46; and Kilgore, *O'Kelly Schism*, 49–50.

67. Mathews, "Evangelical America," in *Perspectives on American Methodism*, ed. Richey, Rowe, and Schmidt, 20.

68. Ware, *Sketches*, 220–221.

69. O'Kelly, *Author's Apology*, 38.

70. Ibid., 59–60. The quotation is from p. 12.

71. Ware, *Sketches*, 245; and Watters, *Short Account*, 106.

72. O'Kelly, *Author's Apology*, 35.

73. Smith, *Recollections*, 226.

74. O'Kelly's schism was preceded by a much smaller break led by the Irishman William Hammet [Hammett] in 1791. In that year Hammet divided the Charleston, South Carolina, society when Asbury refused to appoint him to the city. Here again, the underlying issue was one of localism versus connectionalism. Hammet named his new denomination the Primitive Methodist Church, but it disbanded soon after his death in 1803. Frederick E. Maser and George A. Singleton, "Further Branches of Methodism are Founded," in *History of American Methodism*, ed. Bucke, 1: 617–22. On O'Kelly, see Hatch, *Democratization*, 70; Norwood, *Story of American Methodism*, 127–129; Price, "Presiding Elder," 79–83; James D. Essig, *The Bonds of Wickedness: American Evangelicals Against Slavery, 1770–1808* (Philadelphia: Temple University Press, 1982), 78–84; and Frederick A. Norwood, "The Church Takes Shape," in *History of American Methodism*, ed. Bucke, 1: 440–52.

75. Methodist Episcopal Church, *Discipline* (1798), 41–42.

76. To the question, "To whom is the bishop amenable for his conduct," the *Discipline* answered, "To the general conference, who have power to expel him for improper conduct, if they see it necessary." Methodist Episcopal Church, *Discipline* (1798), 39.

77. On the nature and limits of the Methodist episcopacy in the early republic, see Buckley, *Constitutional and Parliamentary History*, 101–127; Norman Woods Spellman, "The General Superintendency in American Methodism, 1784–1870" (Ph.D. diss., Yale University, 1961), 74–175; Gerald F. Moede, *The Office of Bishop in Methodism: Its History and Development* (Zurich, Switzerland: Publishing House of the Methodist Church, 1964), 26–83; and Jesse Hamby Barton Jr., "The Definition of the Episcopal Office in American Methodism" (Ph.D. diss., Drew University, 1960), 34–79.

78. Watters, *Short Account*, 105.

79. Ware, *Sketches*, 130.

80. Snethen, *Reply*, 51.

81. Henry Boehm, *Reminiscences, Historical and Biographical, of Sixty-Four Years in the Ministry* (New York: Carlton & Porter, 1866), 102 and 190.

82. Asbury, *Journal and Letters*, 1: ix, 1: 49, 2: 753, and 3: 456; John R. Finger, "Witness to Expansion: Bishop Francis Asbury on the Trans-Appalachian Frontier," *The Register of the Kentucky Historical Society* 82 (1984): 334–357; Boehm, *Reminiscences*, 289 and 435; Ezra Squier Tipple, *Francis Asbury: The Prophet of the Long Road* (New York: Methodist Book Concern, 1916), 182; Thomas Morrell, *The Journals of the Rev. Thomas Morrell*, ed. Michael J. McKay (Madison, NJ: Historical Society, Northern New Jersey Conference, United Methodist Church, 1984), 43 and 49; Jenkins, *Experience*, 158; Paddock, *Memoir*, 138.

83. Ware, *Sketches*, 101.

84. Boehm, *Reminiscences*, 445; Thomas Smith, *Experience and Ministerial Labors of Rev. Thomas Smith, Late an Itinerant Preacher of the Gospel in the Methodist Episcopal Church. Compiled Chiefly From His Journal*, ed. David Dailey (New York: Lane and Tippett, 1848), 34; Jacob Young, *Autobiography*, 107; and Watters, *Short Account*, 107. One of the best biographies of Asbury is L. C. Rudolph, *Francis Asbury* (Nashville: Abingdon Press, 1966).

85. Asbury, *Journal and Letters*, 3: 182 and 3: 356. In May of that year Asbury quipped that the church ought to draw up a contingency plan "to guard against my death, debility, apostacy, Location, or desertion: why not? I am not more than man, my mental powers may fail, I may marry 30,000 pounds & a coach & 4 horses, I may run off to some other land, as to the west, & sit down, or go to Canada, and write to you, that I will not come unless you will give me such a part of the work, or make me an Arch-Bishop." Francis Asbury to Daniel Hitt, May 18, 1806, letter no. 327, "Letters to Daniel Hitt."

86. Chase, *Recollections*, 49.

87. Capers, "Autobiography," 133.

88. William Burke, "Autobiography of William, Burke," in James B. Finley, *Sketches of Western Methodism: Biographical, Historical, and Miscellaneous* (Cincinnati: Printed for the Author, 1854; reprint, New York: Arno Press, 1969), 56.

89. Young, *Autobiography*, 119–120; Garrettson, *American Methodist Pioneer*, 122; and Smith, *Recollections*, 64 and 217. On Ezekiel Cooper, see Asbury, *Journal and Letters*, 3: 267; and George A. Phoebus, *Beams of Light on Early Methodism in America: Chiefly Drawn from the Diary, Letters, Manuscripts, Documents, and Original Tracts of the Rev. Ezekiel Cooper* (New York: Phillips & Hunt, 1887), 279–281.

90. Quoted in Dunlap, "United Methodist System," 23.

91. Asbury, *Journal and Letters*, 2: 606 (June 18, 1809); and *Minutes of the Annual Conferences*, 1: 165–175.

92. Francis Asbury to Daniel Hitt, November 7, 1804, and April 28, 1806, letters nos. 284 and 323, "Letters to Daniel Hitt."

93. Beauchamp, *Letters*, 27.
94. Boehm, *Reminiscences*, 303, 414, and 459.
95. Ezra Stiles, *The United States Elevated to Glory and Honor* (New Haven: Thomas and Samuel Green, 1783), 54–58; Beecher, *On the Importance of Assisting Young Men of Piety and Talents in Obtaining an Education for the Gospel Ministry* (Andover, MA: Flagg & Gould, 1816), 1–5, 7, and 15; and Freeborn Garrettson, *A Letter to the Rev. Lyman Beecher containing Strictures and Animadversions on a Pamphlet entitled An Address to the Charitable Society for the Education of Indigent Pious Young Men for the Ministry of the Gospel* (New York: J.C. Totten, 1816), 13–24.

CHAPTER 3

1. Philip Schaff, *America: A Sketch of the Political, Social, and Religious Character of the United States of North America* (New York: C. Scribner, 1845; reprint, Cambridge: Harvard University Press, 1961), 135–138.
2. Coleman, "Expansion of the Methodist Episcopal Church," 208–209; Hatch, *Democratization*, 88. On common schools in the early republic, see Carl F. Kaestile, *Pillars of the Republic: Common Schools and American Society, 1780–1860* (New York: Hill and Wang, 1983), 13–61.
3. W. P. Strickland, *The Life of Jacob Gruber* (New York: Carlton & Porter, 1860), 17; Abbott, *Experience*, 1–7; Boehm, *Reminiscences*, 16; on Nicholas Snethen, see Boehm, *Reminiscences*, 232; John Campbell Deem, Untitled autobiography, Ms., Ohio Wesleyan University, Delaware, OH; Horton, *Narrative*, 4–5; Brunson, *Western Pioneer*, 37; on Samuel Parker, see Jacob Young, *Autobiography*, 338 and Boehm, *Reminiscences*, 263; Littlejohn, "Journal," 3–6; John B. Matthias, "The Journal of John B. Matthias," Ms., Drew University Library, Madison, NJ, 3–4; Sampson Maynard, *The Experience of Sampson Maynard, Local Preacher of the Methodist Episcopal Church (Written by Himself.) To Which is Prefixed an Allegorical Address to the Christian World, or, a Thimble Full of Truth to Blow Up the World of Error* (New York: Printed for the Author, 1828), 130–146; Robertson Gannaway, "Autobiography of Rev. Robertson Gannaway," *Virginia Magazine of History and Biography* 37 (1929): 316–322; 38 (1930): 137–144; Morrell, *Journals*, 2–3; Thomas Rankin, "The Diary of Reverend Thomas Rankin, One of the Helpers of John Wesley," TMs, Garrett Evangelical Theological Seminary Library, Evanston, IL, 21–23, 52–57; Smith, *Recollections*, 234–236; Dan Young, *Autobiography*, 35; Paddock, *Memoir*, 74; Ebenezer F. Newell, *Life and Observation of Rev. E. F. Newell, Who Has Been More Than Forty Years an Itinerant Minister in the Methodist Episcopal Church, New England Conference* (Worchester, MA: C. W. Ainsworth, 1847), 16, 53, 67, and 87; Jacob Young, *Autobiography*, 23–37, 55. On Noah Levings, see Joseph Hillman, *The History of Methodism in Troy, N.Y.* (Troy, NY: Joseph Hillman, 1888), 33. On Enoch Mudge, see Mary Orne Tucker, *Itinerant Preaching in the Early Days of Methodism. By a Pioneer Preacher's Wife* (Boston: B. B. Russell, 1872), reprinted in *The Nineteenth-Century American Methodist Itinerant Preacher's Wife*, ed. Carolyn De Swarte Gifford (New York: Garland Publishing, 1987), 83–86. Enoch Mudge published a sermon entitled *An Oration, Pronounced at Orrington, July 4th, 1808* (Boston: Printed by B. Parks, 1808); and *The American Camp-Meeting Hymn Book. Containing a Variety of Original Hymns, Suitable to be Used at Camp-Meetings; and at Other Times in Private and Social Devotions* (Boston: Joseph Burdakin, 1818). A similar pattern prevailed among early Methodist preachers in England. See Hempton, *Religion and Political Culture*, 39–40.
4. Quinn, *Sketches*, 65.

5. Though Capers's father was a plantation owner, Capers confessed that "I had never done an hour's work in a field in my life," until he quit the itinerancy and located in 1814. On Capers, Jenkins, and Travis, see Capers, "Autobiography," esp. p. 182; Jenkins, *Experience*; and Joseph Travis, *Autobiography of the Rev. Joseph Travis, A.M., a Member of the Memphis Annual Conference. Embracing a Succinct History of the Methodist Episcopal Church, South; Particularly in Part of Western Virginia, the Carolinas, Georgia, Alabama, and Mississippi*, ed. Thomas O. Summers (Nashville: Stevenson & F.O. Owens, 1856). On Capers, also see Albert M. Shipp, *History of Methodism in South Carolina* (Nashville: Southern Methodist Publishing House, 1884), 397–435; and William B. Sprague, *Annals of the American Pulpit*, vol. 7, *Methodist* (New York: Robert Carter and Brothers, 1865; reprint, New York: Arno Press, 1969), 454–464. On Pierce, see Smith, *Life of Pierce*, 6–8.

6. Donald M. Scott, *From Office to Profession: The New England Ministry 1750–1850* (Philadelphia: University of Pennsylvania Press, 1978), 3–5. Moreover, as Scott points out, far from being the cream of the crop, those ministers who were forced to move a second or third time usually had a history of scandal or contentiousness, and each successive move was "almost always from bad to worse" (p. 9). There was, however, a significant transition under way between the 1740s and the American Revolution. Prior to the Great Awakening itinerancy was seen as an aberration and a threat to social order. But by the time of the Revolution, as Timothy Hall has recently shown, itinerant preachers had become an accepted part of the religious landscape. In a limited sense, these itinerants helped American religion initiate the transition from the colonial era to the mobile, egalitarian, voluntaristic, and market-oriented world of the early republic. Timothy D. Hall, "Contested Boundaries: Itinerancy and the Reshaping of the Colonial American Religious World" (Ph.D. diss., Northwestern University, 1991).

7. Matthias, "Journal," 2.

8. It is not surprising that someone like Matthias would be attracted first to the Masons and then the Methodists in the immediate post-revolutionary years. Both, in a sense, offered a form of stability and community in a mobile, expanding society. The growing recent scholarship on Freemasonry includes: Steven C. Bullock, "A Pure and Sublime System: The Appeal of Post-Revolutionary Freemasonry," *Journal of the Early Republic* 9 (Fall 1989): 359–374; Bullock, "The Revolutionary Transformation of American Freemasonry, 1752–1792," *William and Mary Quarterly* 47 (July 1990): 347–369; and Paul Goodman, *Towards a Christian Republic: Antimasonry and the Great Transition in New England, 1826–1836* (New York: Oxford University Press, 1988).

9. Matthias, "Journal," 6–8 and 12. John Dickens was stationed in New York City during the conference years 1786 to 1788. Robert Cloud held that post during 1789 and 1790, and Thomas Morrell during 1791 and 1792. *Minutes of the Annual Conferences*, 1:25, 28, 31, 34, 38, 42, and 46.

10. On John B. and Sarah Matthias, see Sprague, *Annals of the American Pulpit*, vol. 7, *Methodist*, 224–230; Samuel A. Seaman, *Annals of New York Methodism: Being a History of the Methodist Episcopal Church in the City of New York from A.D. 1766 to A.D. 1890* (New York: Hunt & Eaton; Cincinnati: Cranston & Stowe, 1892), 248.

11. Matthias, "Journal," 19.

12. Matthias, "Journal," 23–26. Elijah Woolsey was presiding elder over the Albany district in 1804 and 1805. William Vredenburgh was appointed to the newly organized Haverstraw circuit in 1805. *Minutes of the Annual Conferences*, 1: 121 and 1: 133.

13. Matthias, "Journal," 56; *Minutes of the Annual Conferences*, 1: 495–496.

14. Brunson, *Western Pioneer*, 13–230; *Minutes of the Annual Conferences*, 1: 353.

The first Methodist preacher that Brunson ever heard was John "Barney" Matthias in 1804.

15. For a related discussion of the role of gender in Baptist and Congregationalist conversion accounts between 1800 and 1830, see Susan Juster, "'In a Different Voice': Male and Female Narratives of Religious Conversion in Post-Revolutionary America," *American Quarterly* 41 (March 1989): 34–62.

16. Jacob Young, *Autobiography*, 23–42.

17. Ibid., 42–47.

18. Abbott, *Experience*, 6–7. On Abbott, see Sprague, *Annals of the American Pulpit*, vol. 7, *Methodist*, 41–46.

19. Abbott, *Experience*, 7–8.

20. Ibid., 8.

21. Ibid., 9–15.

22. Littlejohn, "Journal," 2–10; *Minutes of the Annual Conferences*, 1: 8–9; and Obituary of John Littlejohn, *Minutes of the Annual Conferences*, 2: 486–487.

23. Littlejohn, "Journal," 23.

24. Methodist Episcopal Church, *Discipline* (1784), in Tigert, *Constitutional History*, 562.

25. Jenkins, *Experience*, 52–53.

26. Garrettson, *American Methodist Pioneer*, 135.

27. Donald E. Byrne Jr. has chronicled much of the folklore of American Methodism in *No Foot of Land: Folklore of American Methodist Itinerants* (Metuchen, NJ: Scarecrow Press, 1975).

28. A. H. Redford, *The History of Methodism in Kentucky*, 3 vols. (Nashville: Southern Methodist Publishing House, 1870), 3: 530. I first discovered this episode in Charles A. Johnson, *The Frontier Camp Meeting: Religion's Harvest Time* (Dallas: Southern Methodist University Press, 1955), 19.

29. S. R. Beggs, *Pages from the Early History of the West and North-West: Embracing Reminiscences and Incidents of Settlement and Growth, and Sketches of the Material and Religious Progress of the States of Ohio, Indiana, Illinois, and Missouri, with Especial Reference to the History of Methodism* (Cincinnati: Methodist Book Concern, 1868), 298. This story appears in a number of nineteenth-century Methodist histories. On Nolley, also see *Minutes of the Annual Conferences*, 1: 275–276. Tombigbee is sometimes spelled "Tombeckbee" in Methodist records.

30. Deem, untitled autobiography, pp. 1–5. Obituaries of Deem can be found in the *Minutes of the 28th Session of the Cincinnati Annual Conference of the Methodist Episcopal Church* (Cincinnati: Methodist Episcopal Church, 1879), 84–86; and the *Minutes of the Annual Conference of the Methodist Episcopal Church* (Cincinnati: Methodist Episcopal Church, 1879), 17–18.

31. Nancy Caldwell, *Walking With God: Leaves from the Journal of Mrs. Nancy Caldwell*, ed. James O. Thompson (Keyser, WV: For Private Distribution, 1886), 20–21. In 1794 Joel Ketchum was appointed to the Marblehead circuit in Massachusetts; in 1795 to the Middletown, Connecticut, circuit, and in 1796 to the Pomfret, Connecticut, circuit. *Minutes of the Annual Conferences*, 1: 56, 63, and 70.

32. Gatch, *Sketch*, 32–55; Garrettson, *Methodist Pioneer*, 69–100; Littlejohn, "Journal," 97; and Ware, *Sketches*, 104. Philip Gatch was born near Baltimore, Maryland in 1751, converted in 1772, itinerated in New Jersey, Delaware, Maryland, and Virginia beginning in 1773, and died in 1835. Billy Hibbard recalled that as late as 1800 when he rode the Granville, Massachusetts, circuit, "some threw stones at me, and some set

their dogs on me as I rode along." (Hibbard, *Memoirs1*, *167*). On *Garrettson's imprisonment*, *also see* E. C. Hallman, *The Garden of Methodism* (n.p.: Peninsula Annual Conference of the Methodist Church, n.d.), 300–301. On early opposition to Methodism in Virginia, see Armour, "Opposition," chaps. 2, 4, and 6. Armour points out that in Virginia, Methodists faced less persecution during the war than in neighboring states, and that opposition to Methodism in Virginia usually focused on charges of enthusiasm.

33. Dan Young, *Autobiography*, 32; Littlejohn, "Journal," 115; Paddock, *Memoir*, 19–20; and Connor, *Methodist Trail Blazer*, 44.

34. Hibbard, *Memoirs*, 60, 66, and 93; and Sprague, *Annals of the American Pulpit*, vol. 7, *Methodist*, 299.

35. Brooks, *Life and Times*, 53 and 67.

36. Garrettson, *American Methodist Pioneer*, 59, 69, 80, 86, and 293. On Freeborn Garrettson's whirlwind campaign in Nova Scotia, 1785–1787, see George A. Rawlyk, "Freeborn Garrettson and Nova Scotia," *Methodist History* 30 (1992): 142–158. On Paddock, see Paddock, *Memoir*, 82–94, 123; and *Minutes of the Annual Conferences*, 1: 215. Chautauqua was spelled "Shetockway" in early Methodist records. In 1792 Elijah Woolsey took a similar appointment in upstate New York, as did Thomas Smith in 1805. Smith's appointment was to the Seneca circuit in Genessee County, New York, situated between the Cayuga and Seneca Lakes. "It has been said by some people that ministers preach for the sake of ease and profit," lamented Smith in 1805. Referring either to himself or an acquaintance, Smith continued: "I know one that has rode four thousand miles, and preached four hundred sermons, in one year; and laid many nights on wet cabin-floors, and sometimes covered with snow through the night, and his horse standing under a pelting storm of snow or rain; and at the end of that year receiving his traveling expenses and *four* silver dollars of his salary. Now if this be a life of pleasure, ease, and profit, pray what is a life of labor and toil?" Woolsey, *Supernumerary*, 24–26; and Smith, *Experience*, 126.

37. Hibbard, *Memoirs*, 145; Smith, *Experience*, 55.

38. Jacob Young, *Autobiography*, 74 and 207. A map of Young's Salt River circuit can be found in Dickson D. Bruce, *And They All Sang Hallelujah: Plain-Folk Camp-Meeting Religion, 1800–1845* (Knoxville: University of Tennessee Press, 1973), 40. Over the course of more than 50 years in the ministry, Peter Cartwright estimated that he preached 14,600 sermons, received 10,000 new members into the church, baptized 8,000 children and 4,000 adults, and preached 500 funerals. Peter Cartwright, *Autobiography of Peter Cartwright. The Backwoods Preacher* (New York: Hunt & Eaton; Cincinnati: Cranston and Curts, 1856), 522–523.

39. A. H. Newman, *A History of the Baptist Churches in the United States* (New York: Christian Literature Co., 1894), 336; William Warren Sweet, *Religion on the American Frontier*, vol. I, *The Baptists* (New York: Henry Holt and Co., 1931), 36–57; and O. K. Armstrong and Marjorie M. Armstrong, *The Indomitable Baptists: A Narrative of Their Role in Shaping American History* (Garden City, NY: Doubleday & Co., 1967), 104. Like Methodist itinerants and local preachers, a Baptist preacher could be either "ordained" to administer the sacraments, or only "licensed" to preach.

40. Finke and Stark, *Churching of America*, 55; Robert G. Torbet, *A History of the Baptists*, rev. ed. (Valley Forge: Judson Press, 1950, 1963), 246–247. For a thorough history of the development of Baptist missionary societies during the first two decades of the nineteenth century, see Albert L. Vail, *The Morning Hour of American Baptist Missions* (Philadelphia: American Baptist Publication Society, 1907), 86–156. Also see William G. McLoughlin, *Soul Liberty: The Baptists' Struggle in New England, 1630–1833*

(Hanover: Brown University Press, 1991). On Baptists in eighteenth-century Virginia, see Isaac, *Transformation of Virginia*, esp. part 2.

41. Ware, *Sketches*, 156–157.

42. Smith, *Recollections*, 67; Smith, *Experience*, 156.

43. Jacob Young, *Autobiography*, 262.

44. Smith, *Recollections*, 313.

45. James Jenkins, *Experience*, 229; Quinn, *Sketches*, 209 and 233; Dan Young, *Autobiography*, 94; Cartwright, *Autobiography*, 522; and Benjamin Lakin, "The Journal of Benjamin Lakin, 1749–1820," in Sweet, *Religion on the American Frontier*, vol. 4, *Methodists*, 240. While presiding elder over the Albany, New York, district in 1804, Elijah Woolsey was dismayed to discover that one of his preachers who had seven children had received only fifty cents quarterage. But even this was more than the eight cents Billy Hibbard received for one quarter of 1811. Woolsey, *Supernumerary*, 87; Hibbard, *Memoirs*, 310. On Quinn, also see Sprague, *Annals of the American Pulpit*, vol. 7, *Methodist*, 314–321.

46. Garrettson, *American Methodist Pioneer*, 285.

47. Drawing on the work of Anthropologist Victor Turner, Lawrence Foster suggests that the sense of "communitas" and fellow feeling among early Shakers, Oneida Perfectionists, and Mormons—all highly committed movements—was extremely intense and had much to do with their liminal status in society. The early Methodist itinerants arguably experienced a similar kind of liminal status, and hence developed interpersonal relationships of similar intensity. Lawrence Foster, *Religion and Sexuality: Three American Communal Experiments of the Nineteenth Century* (New York: Oxford University Press, 1981), 8–9.

48. Travis, *Autobiography*, 222.

49. Burke, "Autobiography," 58.

50. Woolsey, *Supernumerary*, 57.

51. On at least one occasion Francis Asbury claimed to have written as many as one thousand letters a year. While this was clearly not the case for his first years in America, it may not have been an exaggeration for his later career. Certainly Asbury wrote as many letters as Wesley, and probably a great many more. See Asbury, *Journal and Letters*, 3: vii. A portion of this correspondence flowed through America's fledgling postal system. On the development of the postal system, see Richard R. John, Jr., "Managing the Mails: The Postal System, Public Policy, and American Political Culture, 1823–1836" (Ph.D. diss., Harvard University, 1989).

52. Simpson, *Cyclopedia*, 446; Sprague, *Annals of the American Pulpit*, vol. 7, *Methodist*, 184–186.

53. Thomas Lyell to Daniel Hitt, January 13, 1794, letter no. 101, "Letters to Daniel Hitt." Thomas Lyell was received on trial as a Methodist itinerant in 1792. He eventually became an Episcopalian minister. *Minutes of the Annual Conferences*, 1: 43; and Travis, *Autobiography*, 79.

54. Michael H. R. Wilson to Daniel Hitt, February 6, 1797, letter no. 165; Samuel Hitt to Daniel Hitt, January 4, 1797, letter no. 158, "Letters to Daniel Hitt." Wilson died in 1798 in Lancaster County, Pennsylvania. He was born in Maryland in 1770 and had joined the itinerancy on trial in 1796. *Minutes of the Annual Conferences*, 1: 65 and 1: 79.

55. Seely Bunn to Daniel Hitt, February 18, 1796, letter no. 135, "Letters to Daniel Hitt." Bunn joined the itinerancy on trial in 1792. In 1796 he was stationed on the Baltimore circuit. *Minutes of the Annual Conferences*, 1: 43 and 1: 69.

56. A. G. Thompson to Daniel Hitt, May 25, 1790, letter no. 16, "Letters to Daniel Hitt." Thompson joined the traveling connection on trial in 1785; he located in 1796. *Minutes of the Annual Conferences*, 1: 23 and 1: 66.

57. Caleb J. Taylor to Daniel Hitt, April 11, 1794, letter no. 107; Seely Bunn to Daniel Hitt, August 26, 1794, letter no. 111, "Letters to Daniel Hitt."

58. Capers, "Autobiography," 143–144.

59. Ibid., 115, 160, and 178–180; and Boehm, *Reminiscences*, 221.

60. Jenkins, *Experience*, 72; Garrettson, *American Methodist Pioneer*, 51. Jenkins eventually married in 1805 and located in 1806, and Garrettson married Catherine Livingston in 1793, though he continued in the itinerancy.

61. Boehm, *Reminiscences*, 470; Ware, *Sketches*, 226; and Smith, *Recollections*, 287.

62. Littlejohn, "Journal," 58. Shadford was sent to America by Wesley in 1773 along with Thomas Rankin. He returned to England in 1778 and died in 1816. See Simpson, *Cyclopedia*, 794.

63. Littlejohn, "Journal," 108 and 114. Philip Gatch's marriage was, apparently, a relatively happy one. "My wife's heart was given up to God," wrote Gatch at one point. "When I went out preaching, we parted in peace, and when I returned, we met in love." Connor, *Methodist Trail Blazer*, 90–91. Philip William Otterbein was a major figure in the formation of the Church of the United Brethren in Christ and a supporter of the Methodist Episcopal Church. Otterbein came to America in 1752 and pastored the German Evangelical Reformed Church in Baltimore from 1774 until his death in 1813. Norwood, *Story of American Methodism*, 103–106.

64. Littlejohn, "Journal," 119.

65. Ibid., 124. Littlejohn continued as a local preacher in Leesburg until 1818, when he and his family moved to Kentucky, eventually settling in Logan County. Littlejohn died in Kentucky in 1836. *Minutes of the Annual Conferences*, 2: 486–487.

66. This estimate is based on the statistics of Jesse Lee and William Warren Sweet presented more fully in chapter 2.

67. Lakin, "Journal," 214–227. For a similar account of the itinerant James Kelsey and his wife, see C. D. Burritt, *Methodism in Ithaca: A History* (Ithaca, NY: Andrus, Gauntlett & Co., 1852), 156–157.

68. Travis, *Autobiography*, 70; Woolsey, *Supernumerary*, 64–70; Smith, *Life of Pierce*, 27; and Jacob Young, *Autobiography*, 265 and 299.

69. Hibbard, *Memoirs*, 137, 161, and 236; Brunson, *Western Pioneer*, 174 and 268; and Smith, *Recollections*, 136–37.

70. In fact, when Smith reflected on Methodism's earlier history he could come to just the opposite conclusion. "I would humbly say to the present race of preachers and members in the Methodist Church, that the church owes much, almost everything, under God, to the labors of unmarried preachers," wrote Smith on another occasion. Smith, *Recollections*, 90.

71. On the development of Shaker, Mormon, and Oneida Perfectionist views and practices concerning marriage, sexual relations, and the family, see Foster, *Religion and Sexuality*.

72. Tucker, *Itinerant Preaching*, 9–23. Also see Leonard I. Sweet, *The Minister's Wife: Her Role in Nineteenth-Century American Evangelicalism* (Philadelphia: Temple University Press, 1983). Sweet suggests four models to illustrate the roles open to ministers' wives from the sixteenth to the nineteenth centuries: the Companion, the Sacrificer, the Assistant, and the Partner (pp. 3–11).

73. Tucker, *Itinerant Preaching*, 36.

74. Ibid., 49.

75. Ibid., 52–54.

76. Ibid., 92.

77. Ware, *Sketches*, 183.

78. Quinn, *Sketches*, 78.

79. Asbury, *Journal and Letters*, 2: 474 (July 9, 1805).

80. Smith, *Recollections*, 126.

81. Tucker, *Itinerant Preaching*, 141–42. For a similar first-hand assessment of the rewards of marrying a Methodist preacher, see Julia A. Tevis, *Sixty Years in a School Room: An Autobiography of Mrs. Julia A. Tevis, Principal of Science Hall Female Academy. To Which is Prefixed an Autobiographical Sketch of Rev. John Tevis* (Cincinnati: Western Methodist Book Concern, 1878), 262.

82. Quinn, *Sketches*, 122–23. On this topic, also see Sweet, *The Minister's Wife*, 47–50; and A. Gregory Schneider, "From Democratization to Domestication: The Transitional Orality of the American Methodist Circuit Rider," in *Communication and Change in American Religious History*, ed. Leonard I. Sweet (Grand Rapids: William B. Eerdmans Publishing Company, 1993), 141–164.

83. Ware, *Sketches*, 189 and 175; Beauchamp, *Letters*, 54–57, 60–61, 65, 67, 75, and 89.

84. Brunson, *Western Pioneer*, 64; also see p. 219; Jacob Young, *Autobiography*, 51. Contemporary editions of the works listed by Young include: Freeborn Garrettson, *The Experience and Travels of Mr. Freeborn Garrettson, Minister of the Methodist Episcopal Church in North America* (Philadelphia: John Dickins, 1791); Richard Baxter, *The Saints Everlasting Rest: Or, A Treatise of the Blessed State of the Saints in Their Enjoyment of God in Glory: Extracted from the Works of Mr. Richard Baxter by John Wesley, M.A. late Fellow of Lincoln College, Oxford* (Philadelphia: John Dickins, 1791); John Wesley, *Sermons on Several Occasions*, 4 vols. (Philadelphia: John Dickins, 1794–1801); John Fletcher, *The Works of the Rev. John Fletcher*, 3 vols. (Philadelphia: John Dickins, 1791 [-1792]); and John Fletcher, *An Appeal to Matter of Fact and Common Sense; or, A Rational Demonstration of Man's Corrupt and Lost Estate* (Philadelphia: John Dickins, [1794]).

85. Hibbard, *Memoirs*, 128 and 96. The scope of Francis Asbury's reading over the course of his career is truly impressive given his educational background. See Robert C. Monk, "Educating Oneself for Ministry: Francis Asbury's Reading Patterns," *Methodist History* 29 (April 1991): 140–154; and Edward M. Lang, *Francis Asbury's Reading of Theology: A Bibliographic Study* (Evanston, IL: Garrett Theological Seminary Library, 1972).

86. Methodist Episcopal Church, *Discipline* (1784), Q. 51, in Tigert, *Constitutional History*, 563.

87. Maynard, *Experience*, 144.

88. Capers, "Autobiography," 11–70. On Capers, also see Shipp, *Methodism in South Carolina*, 454–464.

89. Capers, "Autobiography," 51–55.

90. Ibid., 71–76, and 118. The itinerant Lovick Pierce had a similar experience with suspenders. After arriving on the Augusta, Georgia, station in 1806, Pierce realized that his country clothes would not do in town. So, "I got me a new suit—of course, cut Methodist fashion—and, among other things, I got a *pair of suspenders*, for, really, I could not get along without them; but I had to hide them out of sight when Brother Myers came my way, or he would have thought me sinfully worldly." Smith, *Life of Pierce*, 26.

91. Capers, "Autobiography," 76–85; Sprague, *Annals of the American Pulpit*, vol. 7, *Methodist*, 462. Gassaway joined the traveling connection on trial in 1788, spent the bulk of his career preaching in Georgia and North and South Carolina, and located in 1814. In 1808 Gassaway was on the Santee, South Carolina, circuit. Abel McKee Chreitzberg, *Early Methodism in the Carolinas* (Nashville: Methodist Episcopal Church, South, 1897), 100–101; Shipp, *Methodism in South Carolina*, 191–198; *Minutes of the Annual Conferences*, 1: 161.

92. Giles, *Pioneer*, 288–289.

93. Brunson, *Western Pioneer*, 235 and 204; Capers, "Autobiography," 134. On education and the early circuit riders, also see Cowan, "Arminian Alternative," chap. 10.

94. Scherer, *Ezekiel Cooper*, 1–16, 21, and 166; Woolsey, *Supernumerary*, 9. On Cooper, also see Phoebus, *Beams of Light on Early Methodism in America*; Sprague, *Annals of the American Pulpit*, vol. 7, *Methodist*, 108–112.

95. Scherer, *Ezekiel Cooper*, 167. Similarly, Thomas Morrell's journal reveals that between 1796 and 1809, during which time he preached mostly in and around Elizabethtown, New Jersey, Morrell used a relatively extensive number of texts from both the Old and New Testaments. Morrell, *Journals*, 29–50. Thomas Morrell was born in 1747 in New York, fought in the Revolutionary War as an officer, and worked in his father's mercantile business both before and after the war. In 1786 he became a local preacher and in 1789 was ordained an elder. Morrell married three times and lived during most of his career in Elizabethtown, New Jersey. He died in 1838. On Morrell, see Simpson, *Cyclopedia*, 630; Sprague, *Annals of the American Pulpit*, vol. 7, *Methodist*, 145–150.

96. Smith, *Experience*, 20–175. Cooper, for his part, dreaded the prospect of seminary educated ministers. Such a class of preachers, he feared, would inevitably become focused on obtaining "dignity, ease, and fortune." Scherer, *Ezekiel Cooper*, 187–188.

97. Thomas A. Morris, "A Diary Referring to the Text or Texts of Each Day; Also the Time & Place of Delivering the Same, and the Nos. Received Into Society by Tho. A. Morris," Ms., Ohio Wesleyan University, Delaware, OH, pp. 1–22. Born in 1794 near Charleston, West Virginia, Morris joined the Ohio Conference on trial in 1816 and was elected a Bishop of the Methodist Episcopal Church in 1836. He died in 1874. Simpson, *Cyclopedia* 1, 630–631.

98. Tigert, *Constitutional History* 1, 539–540.

99. Gatch, *Sketch*, 102, 183, and 189; and Quinn, *Sketches*, 136. Likewise, Francis Asbury "had a remarkable method of making an unexpected use of observations he had dropped in preaching," according to one of his traveling companions. John Wesley Bond, "Anecdotes of Bishop Asbury, [1817]," Ms., Drew University Library, Madison, NJ.

100. Giles, *Pioneer*, 58–62 and 129.

101. Ayres, *Methodist Heroes of Other Days*, 35; Smith, *Life of Pierce*, 31; James Meacham, "A Journal and Travel of James Meacham," ed. William K. Boyd, *Annual Publication of Historical Papers of the Historical Society of Trinity College* 9 (1912): 66–95; 10 (1914): 87–102; Smith, *Life of Pierce*, 12; and Boehm, *Reminiscences*, 441. Of course, this style of public speaking had long been a part of popular culture and popular preaching in Europe. See Burke, *Popular Culture in Early Modern Europe*, 101, 132–134.

102. Abbott, *Experience*, 89, 22, and 51.

103. Travis, *Autobiography*, 37.

104. Lee, *Short History1*, 40; *Chase, Recollections*, 40. William Keith (1776–1810) was born in Easton, Massachusetts, and first joined the itinerancy in 1798. Keith died while stationed in New York City, leaving a widow and three children. William Keith, *The Experience of William Keith (Written by Himself) Together With Some Observations Conclusive of Divine Influence on the Mind of Man* (Utica, NY: Asahel Seward, 1806); *Minutes of the Annual Conferences*, 1: 193–194.

105. Seth Crowell, *The Journal of Seth Crowell: Containing an Account of His Travels as a Methodist Preacher for Twelve Years* (New York: J.C. Totten, 1813), 10–12; Paddock, *Memoir*, 52 and 80; and Smith, *Life of Pierce*, 12 and 18. On Gary, see Boehm, *Reminiscences*, 247; and Paddock, *Memoir*, 296; on Ruter, see Dan Young, *Autobiography*, 70; and Simpson, *Cyclopedia*, 770; and on Mattison, see Paddock, *Memoir1*, 332–334. *John Fidler was apparently only 15 years old when he began preaching as an itinerant in 1784.* Leonard T. and Carolyn E. Wolcott, *Wilderness Rider* (Nashville: Abingdon Press, 1984), 15; and *Minutes of the Annual Conferences*, 1: 19.

106. Laban Clark, *Laban Clark: Circuit Rider for the Methodist Episcopal Church*, trans. E. Farley Sharp (Rutland, VT: Academy Books, 1987), 30.

107. Smith, *Recollections*, 31. On the background, education, and preaching of the early circuit riders, also see Frederick V. Mills, "Mentors of Methodism, 1784–1844," *Methodist History* 12 (October 1973): 43–57.

108. Charles G. Finney, *Lectures on Revivals of Religion* (New York: Leavitt, Lord and Company, 1835; reprint, Cambridge, MA: Harvard University Press, 1960), 273.

CHAPTER 4

1. For example, the 1789 *Discipline* stated that when itinerant preachers could not keep preaching appointments, such as when they planned to be away attending an annual conference, they ought to "engage as many local Preachers and Exhorters as will supply" those appointments, or, failing that, "let some person of ability be appointed in every society to sing, pray, and read one of Mr. Wesley's sermons." Methodist Episcopal Church, *A Form of Discipline, for the Ministers, Preachers, and Members of the Methodist Episcopal Church in America* (New York: William Ross, 1789; reprint, Nashville: United Methodist Publishing House, 1992), Section 17.

2. The phrase is, of course, Lawrence Goodwyn's, from his analysis of the populist movement. See Lawrence Goodwyn, *Democratic Promise: The Populist Moment in America* (New York: Oxford University Press, 1976); or Lawrence Goodwyn, *The Populist Moment: A Short History of the Agrarian Revolt in America* (Oxford: Oxford University Press, 1978).

3. On the connections between the class meeting and the religious societies of the Church of England and the Moravian Bands, see David Lowes Watson, "The Origins and Significance of the Early Methodist Class Meeting" (Ph.D. diss., Duke University, 1978), 249–292; David Francis Holsclaw, "The Demise of Disciplined Christian Fellowship: The Methodist Class Meeting in Nineteenth-Century America" (Ph.D. diss., University of California Davis, 1979), 18–37; and Charles C. Keys, *The Class-Leader's Manual: or, an Essay on the Duties, Difficulties, Qualifications, Motives, and Encouragements of Class-Leaders* (Cincinnati: Cranston and Stowe, 1851), 11–18 and 219–228.

4. John Wesley, "A Plain Account of the People Called Methodists," and "Thoughts Upon Methodism," in John Wesley, *The Works of John Wesley*, 3rd ed., 14 vols. (Grand Rapids: Baker Book House, 1978) 8:248–268 and 13: 258–261; Watson,

"Early Methodist Class Meeting," 306–317; Holsclaw, "Demise," 38–39; and Keys, *Class-Leader's Manual*, 18–20.

5. Wesley, "People Called Methodists," and "Thoughts Upon Methodism," in Wesley, *Works*.

6. "How is it that in meetg Class we are so often & so much blessd[?] may all see the blessedness of such a privilege," added Littlejohn in 1777. Littlejohn, "Journal," 67; Rankin, "Diary," 87 and 102; and Meacham, "Journal," 95.

7. Boehm, *Reminiscences*, 30–34.

8. E. S. Janes, *Address to Class-Leaders* (New York: Carlton and Lanahan, 1868), 17. "Our local preachers, and even our itinerant ministers, are started here [in class meetings]," adds Charles C. Keys, "and here is to be found the opening wedge to all the great results of our itinerant system." Keys, *Class-Leader's Manual*, 152.

9. Jenkins, *Experience*, 37; and Smith, *Recollections*, 320. Also see Brooks, *Life and Times*, 22–24. "I should think I was backslidden from God if I did not love the class meeting," added James Quinn reflecting on his long career. Quinn, *Sketches*, 209.

10. Leonidas Rosser, *Class Meetings: Embracing Their Origin, Nature, Obligation, and Benefits. Also, the Duties of Preachers and Leaders, and Appeal to Private Members: And Their Temporal Advantages* (Richmond: Published by the Author, 1855), 51–52 and 130–131.

11. William Cooper Howells (father of William Dean Howells) joined the Methodist Church in Ohio at a young age, but later lost his faith and at the age of 21 "allowed myself to be expelled from the Methodist Church for an offense—not now regarded as one—the non-attendance of class meetings." William Cooper Howells, *Recollections of Life in Ohio from 1813 to 1840* (Cincinnati: Robert Clarke Company, 1895; reprint, Gainesville, FL.: Scholars' Facsimiles & Reprints, 1963), 94. An example of non-Methodists being invited into a class meeting can be found in the journal of Richard Swain. When Swain noticed that several of his listeners where deeply "affected" during one of his sermons on the Salem, New Jersey, circuit in 1792, he "told the Mourners to stay in [the class meeting that followed the preaching service] if they were of a mind." During the class meeting, Swain "was several times moved to stop to exhort the mourners," who "wept louder and louder till I had done speaking to the Society." Swain closed the meeting by praying individually with as many of the "mourners" as he could. Richard Swain, *Journal of Richard Swain*, ed. Robert Bevis Steelman (n.p.: Historical Society of the Southern New Jersey Conference of the United Methodist Church, 1977), 23.

12. Smith, *Recollections*, 308; and Dan Young, *Autobiography*, 102.

13. On Baltimore, see Steffen, *Mechanics of Baltimore*, 261–262; and Bilhartz, *Urban Religion*, 35–36. On New York City, see Wilentz, *Chants Democratic*, 81. On artisan Methodists in both New York City and Baltimore, see William R. Sutton, "'To Grind the Faces of the Poor': Journeymen for Jesus in Jacksonian Baltimore" (Ph.D. diss., University of Illinois at Urbana-Champaign, 1993), esp. 1–88, 119–180, and 387–399.

14. Janes, *Address to Class-Leaders*, 12 and 40; S. W. Christophers, *Class-Meetings in Relation to the Design and Success of Methodism* (London: Wesleyan Conference Office, 1873), 152; Rosser, *Class Meetings*, 259–271; John Miley, *Treatise on Class Meetings*, with an introduction by Thomas A. Morris (Cincinnati: Poe & Hitchcock, 1866), 195–197 and 214–224; and Holsclaw, "Demise," 41–42.

15. Methodist Episcopal Church, *Discipline* (1798), 136; and Janes, *Address to Class-Leaders*, 13.

16. Christophers, *Class-Meetings*, 129–134. For a brief discussion of the development of Methodist hymnody, see Carlton R. Young, "American Methodist Hymnody: A Historical Sketch," in *History of American Methodism*, ed. Bucke, 3: 631–634. Young points out that the most popular collection in America was Robert Spence's *A Pocket Hymnbook*, first published in 1781.

17. Maynard, *Experience*, 198.

18. Janes, *Address to Class-Leaders*, 20. On the pattern of class meetings also see Watson, "Early Methodist Class Meeting," 420–427.

19. L. M. Vincent, *Methodism in Poughkeepsie and Vicinity. Its Rise and Progress from 1780 to 1892, with Sketches and Incidents* (Poughkeepsie, NY: A.V. Haight, [1892]), 61–62. Four of the women and one of the men in this class were African Americans.

20. Methodist Episcopal Church, New Haven class meeting records for 1806, 1808, and 1811, Ohio Wesleyan University Library, Delaware, OH. Records for 1811 are incomplete.

21. Jacob Young, *Autobiography*, 74.

22. Methodist Episcopal Church, Baltimore City Station, Methodist Episcopal Records, microfilm reel no. 408, Maryland Hall of Records, Annapolis, MD.

23. Seaman, *Annals*, 464–466. By 1820 class sizes were clearly on the increase, as both David Holsclaw and A. Gregory Schneider have noted. In New York and Philadelphia, for example, classes of 50 or more became commonplace. Holsclaw, "Demise," 61–70; and Schneider, *Way of the Cross Leads Home*, 79–82 and 221 n.2.

24. Thomas Morris, introduction to Miley, *Treatise on Class Meetings*, 10–11.

25. Methodist Episcopal Church, *Discipline* (1798), 152.

26. Hibbard, *Memoirs*, 111.

27. Travis, *Autobiography*, 55; and Watters, *Short Account*, 63–65.

28. Jacob Young, *Autobiography*, 41; and Brunson, *Western Pioneer*, 62–63.

29. Brunson, *Western Pioneer*, 63–64.

30. For a trenchant analysis of the stubborn persistence of Methodism's earlier values among antebellum artisans in Baltimore, see Sutton, "To Grind the Faces of the Poor."

31. Bushman, *Refinement of America*, xiii and 335.

32. Richard O. Johnson, "The Development of the Love Feast in Early American Methodism," *Methodist History* 19 (January 1981): 67–83; and Clarke Garrett, *Spirit Possession and Popular Religion: From the Camisards to the Shakers* (Baltimore: Johns Hopkins University Press, 1987), 78–79.

33. Simpson, *Cyclopedia*, 550–551; Seaman, *Annals*, 482–483; and Christophers, *Class-Meetings*, 120–123.

34. Ware, *Sketches*, 63; Giles, *Pioneer*, 176 and 250; Chase, *Recollections*, 28; and Paddock, *Memoir*, 48. The bread and water were at times abandoned among American Methodists as love feasts increasingly came to focus on individual testimonies.

35. Watters, *Short Account*, 76.

36. Brooks, *Life and Times*, 23.

37. Dan Young, *Autobiography*, 105.

38. Brunson, *Western Pioneer*, 87–88. For a similar incident, see Crowell, *Journal*, 96.

39. Janes, *Address to Class-Leaders*, 15.

40. Thomas Rankin to John Wesley, June 24, 1777, in Asbury, *Journal and Letters*, 1: 223. For a similar account of a love feast, see Watters, *Short Account*, 53.

41. Methodist Episcopal Church, *Discipline* (1798), 154.

42. Morris, introduction to Miley, *Treatise*, 12–13.

43. Methodist Episcopal Church, "A Book of Records for the Hockhocking Circuit," Ms., Ohio Wesleyan University Library, Delaware OH. On quarterly meetings, see John Lester Ruth, "'A Little Heaven Below': Quarterly Meetings as Seasons of Grace in Early American Methodism" (Ph.D. diss., University of Notre Dame, 1996); and May, "From Revival Movement to Denomination," 189–197.

44. All of these cases are given in Methodist Episcopal Church, "Book of Records for Hockhocking Circuit." Charges brought against Methodist church members in New York City and Baltimore between the 1780s and 1820s included: "act of hypocrisy, buying and selling slaves, marrying a wicked man, quarreling and brawling, non-attendance, cock fighting, habitual neglect of family [prayer], trifling, disorderly walking, immoral conduct, marrying a second wife while first wife was still alive, drinking, fathering a child, swearing, unchristian-like conduct, singing war songs, desertion of family, non-penitent, adultery, living with husband before marriage, illegitimate child, playing dominoes." James L. Lubach and Thomas L. Shanklin, "Arbitrations and Trials of Members in the Methodist Episcopal Church: 1776–1860," *Methodist History* 9 (July 1971): 30–49.

45. Methodist Episcopal Church, Paint Creek, Ohio, quarterly meeting conference minutes, Ms., Ohio Wesleyan University Library, Delaware, OH.

46. Methodist Episcopal Church, Union and Mad River circuit records, Ohio Wesleyan University Library, Delaware, OH.

47. Methodist Episcopal Church, Madison, Kentucky, circuit quarterly meeting conference minutes, Ms., Kentucky Wesleyan College, Owensboro, KY. On women and Methodist discipline, see chapter 7.

48. Methodist Episcopal Church, Accomack, Virginia, circuit quarterly meeting conference journal, Ms., Cokesbury Methodist Church, Ononcock, VA. The sexual harassment trial of William Melvin is discussed in detail in chapter 7.

49. Methodist Episcopal Church, "Book of Records for Hockhocking Circuit;" and Samuel W. Williams, *Pictures of Early Methodism in Ohio* (Cincinnati: Jennings and Graham, 1909), 187–193.

50. Francis Asbury once refused to preside at a quarterly meeting conference because it was outside his jurisdiction. See Quinn, *Sketches*, 165.

51. Methodist Episcopal Church, Madison, Kentucky, circuit quarterly meeting conference minutes. In a similar set of proceedings, the Mad River circuit quarterly conference, held near Xenia, Ohio, in September 1809, licensed four new exhorters and five local preachers. Methodist Episcopal Church, Union Circuit and Mad River circuit records.

52. Methodist Episcopal Church, Union circuit and Mad River circuit records. For similar records from Connecticut, see Methodist Episcopal Church, "Durham, Conn. M.E. Church circuit records, 1816–1847," Ms., Drew University Library, Madison, NJ.

53. At the beginning of American Methodism, quarterly meetings were one day affairs universally held on a Tuesday. Beginning about 1776 many quarterly meetings were expanded into a Monday-Tuesday two-day format. Eventually it became more popular to hold two-day quarterly meetings over a Saturday and Sunday rather than a Monday and Tuesday, with the Saturday-Sunday format becoming the officially recognized pattern as early as 1780. I am indebted for my understanding of these developments to Lester Ruth, whose dissertation examines Methodist quarterly meetings. See Ruth, "A Little Heaven Below," chap. 2.

54. Swain, *Journal*, 35.

55. On the development of quarterly meetings, see especially Richey, *Early American Methodism*, 21–32. As Richey notes, the community aspect of quarterly meetings was particularly important in areas of Methodist strength—Delaware, Maryland, and Virginia. Writes Richey, "the strength of such gatherings cannot be stressed too much. In these gentry-dominated societies, laced together by waterways and largely wanting the towns that provided communal coherence in New England, community quite literally occurred" at quarterly meetings (p. 25).

56. Giles, *Pioneer*, 212–213.

57. Woolsey, *Supernumerary*, 74–76.

58. James Poynter to Daniel Hitt, February 17, 1806, letter no. 316, "Letters to Daniel Hitt." For a similar account, see Hillman, *Methodism in Troy*, 38–40.

59. Boehm, *Reminiscences*, 32.

60. Ware, *Sketches*, 235.

61. Smith, *Recollections*, 330.

62. Chase, *Recollections*, 27 and 29.

63. Gatch, *Sketch*, 108 and 127. Also see Smith, *Recollections*, 83 and 347; and Williams, *Pictures*, 54–55.

64. This was in Sparta, Georgia. See Smith, *Life of Pierce*, 25.

65. The Gatch's home is one of 19 that Henry Boehm lists as among Asbury's favorite lodging places. See Boehm, *Reminiscences*, 449.

66. Brunson, *Western Pioneer*, 96; and Smith, *Recollections*, 213.

67. On this point, see esp. Richey, *Early American Methodism*, 21–32.

68. Johnson, *Frontier Camp Meeting*; Bruce, *They All Sang Hallelujah*; and Bernard A. Weisberger, *They Gathered at the River: The Story of the Great Revivalists and Their Impact Upon Religion in America* (Boston: Little, Brown and Company, 1958), 20–50. An excellent bibliographic resource on the camp meeting is Kenneth O. Brown, *Holy Ground: A Study of the American Camp Meeting* (New York: Garland Publishing, 1992). Also on Cane Ridge and the development of the American camp meeting, see Paul K. Conkin, *Cane Ridge: America's Pentecost* (Madison: University of Wisconsin Press, 1990); and Leigh Eric Schmidt, *Holy Fairs: Scottish Communions and American Revivals in the Early Modern Period* (Princeton: Princeton University Press, 1989).

69. Boehm, *Reminiscences*, 128 and 147.

70. Boehm, *Reminiscences*, 149–153; cf. Asbury, *Journal and Letters*, 3: 381 (December 14, 1807) for a similar estimate of the success of these camp meetings.

71. Christopher H. Owen, "Sanctity, Slavery, and Segregation: Methodists and Society in Nineteenth Century Georgia" (Ph.D. diss., University of Georgia, 1991), 75–76.

72. Asbury, *Journal and Letters*, 3: 251 (December 2, 1802).

73. Ibid. 3: 270 (August 19, 1803). For a similar description of a 3000–person camp meeting near New York City in 1806, see Asbury, *Journal and Letters*, 3: 344 (May 7, 1806).

74. Asbury, *Journal and Letters*, 3: 453–455 (letters of September 1, 1811 and September 2, 1811); and Hatch, *Democratization*, 257 n. 1.

75. On Baptist community life in Pennsylvania and Virginia during this period, particularly with regard to race, see Janet Moore Lindman, "A World of Baptists: Gender, Race, and Religious Community in Pennsylvania and Virginia, 1689–1825" (Ph.D. diss., University of Minnesota, 1994), chap. 3. On the Baptists in eighteenth-century Virginia, see Isaac, *Transformation of Virginia*, part 2. On Baptists in New England, see McLoughlin, *Soul Liberty*.

76. Cushman, *Experimental Divinity*, 134 and 155.

77. Sellers, *Market Revolution*, chap. 3.

78. Lubach and Shanklin, "Arbitrations and Trials."

79. Steffen, *Mechanics of Baltimore*, 262–263; Donald G. Mathews, "Evangelical America—The Methodist Ideology," in *Perspectives on American Methodism*, ed. Richey, Rowe, and Schmidt, 26.

80. Methodist Episcopal Church, *Discipline* (1798), 29, 91, 99, 100–101, 106, 159, 161, and 171.

81. Giles, *Pioneer*, 287 and 50. Similarly, in a well-received sermon preached at Eaton, Ohio, the longtime local preacher John Campbell Deem asserted that "Religion Prepares the Mind for Encountering with fortitude the Most Severe Shocks of adversity, where as vice by its natural influence on the temper tends to produce dejection under the Slightest trials." To most of those listening to Deem—small farmers, mechanics and petty merchants—this message appeared to consist of nothing more or less than common sense. Deem, untitled autobiography, p. 60.

82. The breakaway Reformed Methodist Church is an example of a group dissatisfied with the Methodist system of discipline. Centered in New York and Vermont, their primary grievance seems to have been over the itinerant preachers' power to administer discipline, particularly in connection to the sacraments. The Reformed Methodist *Discipline* of 1814 states that "each one of the children and servants of Christ have an inherent right to all the ordinances of his house, in every place and society of his worshipping followers: and therefore no external right administered by man, by virtue of any office (dependent on human sanction) shall be a test of, or the want of it a bar to Christian fellowship." Methodist Reformed Church, *The Reformer's Discipline* (Bennington, VT: Printed by Darius Clark, [1814]), 10.

83. Rankin, "Diary," 94.

84. Pilmore, *Journal*, 206–207 and 242.

85. Rankin, "Diary," 108.

86. Quinn, *Sketches*, 305.

87. Beauchamp, *Letters*, 70.

88. Watters, *Short Account*, 140. For a similar assessment, see Ware, *Sketches*, 244–245.

89. Garrettson, *American Methodist Pioneer*, 80. Cf. Hibbard, *Memoirs*, 130.

90. Asbury, *Journal and Letters*, 1: 165 (October 13, 1775). Later Methodists standardized their practices to provide for a more democratic and uniform trial of members. By 1820, according to Nathan Bangs, a person accused of an infraction could not be expelled from the church until he or she had been tried "before a select number of his brethren of equal standing in the church, who act as jurors, hear the charge and defence, and examine testimony on both sides, and then decide upon the guilt or innocence of the accused person." If the accused still "think himself dealt by unjustly, he has the right of an appeal to the quarterly meeting Conference . . . who investigate the subject again, and either confirm or disannul the judgment passed upon him." Nathan Bangs, *A Vindication of Methodist Episcopacy* (New York: Nathan Bangs and Thomas Mason for the Methodist Episcopal Church, 1820), 150–151.

91. Woolsey, *Supernumerary*, 71–76; and *Minutes of the Annual Conferences*, 1: 98 and 1: 103.

92. William Colbert, "A Journal of the Travels of William Colbert, Methodist Preacher, thro' parts of Maryland, Pennsylvania, New York, Delaware, and Virginia in 1790 to 1838," TMs, Garrett Evangelical Theological Seminary, Evanston, IL, 1: 155 (January 23, 1794).

93. Thornton Fleming to Daniel Hitt, June 25, 1805, letter no. 303, "Letters to Daniel Hitt"; and *Minutes of the Annual Conferences*, 1: 130 and 1: 138.

94. Jenkins, *Experience*, 74. Also see pp. 90–92.

95. Brunson, *Western Pioneer*, 197–198. Cf. Capers, "Autobiography," 103–106.

96. Methodist Episcopal Church, *Discipline* (1784), in Tigert, *Constitutional History*, 546; Brooks, *Life and Times*, 22. It is worth noting that in 1808 Wesley's essay on dress was published anonymously in America, indicating the importance of the topic apart from Wesley's authority. See [John Wesley], *Advice to the People Called Methodists With Regard to Dress* (Baltimore: Butler for Hagerty and Kingston, 1808).

97. Hillman, *Methodism in Troy*, 23 and 28.

98. Capers, "Autobiography," 96–98.

99. Quinn, *Sketches*, 166.

100. Giles, *Pioneer*, 294–295.

101. George Wells to Daniel Hitt, December 22, 1791, letter no. 52, "Letters to Daniel Hitt."

102. Calvin Fletcher, *The Diary of Calvin Fletcher*, ed. Gayle Thornbrough, et al., 9 vols. (Indianapolis: Indiana Historical Society, 1972–1983), 1: 86, 1: 95, and 1: 98; Richard D. Brown, *Knowledge is Power: The Diffusion of Information in Early America, 1700–1865* (New York: Oxford University Press, 1989), 190–193, 235–240; John E. Miller, "Making It in Indianapolis: The Rise of Calvin Fletcher," *The Old Northwest* 13 (1987): 163–189. The life story of the English Methodist Samuel Budgett reads much like Calvin Fletcher's. Born in the Somersetshire town of Wrington, Budgett (1794–1851) began life in relative poverty, eventually becoming both a wealthy Bristol merchant and a devout Methodist. See William Arthur, *The Successful Merchant: Sketches of the Life of Mr. Samuel Budgett, Late of Kingswood Hill*, 11th ed. (London: Hamilton, Adams, & Co., 1854).

103. Fletcher, *Diary*, 1: 160.

104. Ibid. 1: 199.

CHAPTER 5

1. Thomas Wallcut to James Freeman, October 31, 1789 (Thomas Wallcut papers, box 2, folder 1, American Antiquarian Society, Worcester, MA). I am indebted for this reference to Nathan Hatch, who in turn first learned of it from Anthony Stoneburner.

2. Garrettson, *American Methodist Pioneer*, 41, 92, and 84.

3. Ibid. 77, 96, and 102.

4. Diane Helen Lobody, "Lost in the Ocean of Love: The Mystical Writings of Catherine Livingston Garrettson" (Ph.D. diss., Drew University, 1990), 58.

5. Catherine Livingston Garrettson, untitled autobiography, TMs, Drew University Library, Madison, NJ, p. 9. It is worth noting that Garrettson, like most early American Methodists, had very little knowledge of traditional mystical literature. In this sense, as Diane Lobody observes, she was an "amateur" mystic. Lobody, "Lost in the Ocean of Love," 106.

6. Mary Bradley, *A Narrative of the Life and Christian Experience of Mrs. Mary Bradley, of Saint John, New Brunswick. Written by Herself. Including Extracts From Her Diary and Correspondence During a Period of Upwards of Sixty Years* (Boston: Published for the Author by Strong and Brodhead, 1849), 92 and 93. Though Bradley never explicitly complains, her marriage to Morris does not appear to have been a particularly close or happy one. Morris died in 1817 and Bradley remarried in 1819.

7. Abbott, *Experience*, 84. Similarly, when a Methodist family moved to Troy, New York in 1802, their new landlord, who did not know that they were Methodists, warned them "against Methodism, saying that it was a dangerous religion, that Methodists were witches, and that if a person were to go among them he could not get away from them until he had joined them." Hillman, *History of Methodism in Troy, N.Y.*, 16.

8. Abbott, *Experience*, 92–93.

9. Horton, *Narrative*, 4, 8, 14, 22, 30–34, 39, 44, 58, 60–62, 73, 85, 91, and 134–135; Maynard, *Experience*, 176–179, 204–205, 219; Hibbard, *Memoirs*, 6–7, 39–43, 82–83, 124–125, 153–157, 221–222, 260, 263; and Fanny Newell, *Memoirs of Fanny Newell; Written by Herself, and Published by the Desire and Request of Numerous Friends*, 2nd ed. (Springfield, MA: O. Scott and E.F. Newell, 1833), 22–24, 30, 40, 42–43, 55–57, 63–68, 103–105, and 108–110. On Lorenzo Dow's fortune telling, see Chase, *Recollections*, 43–48; Giles, *Pioneer*, 94–97; Travis, *Autobiography*, 30; and Woolsey, *Supernumerary*, 123–124. On Valentine Cook, see Edward Stevenson, *Biographical Sketch of the Rev. Valentine Cook, A.M. With an Appendix, Containing His Discourse on Baptism* (Nashville: Published for the Author, 1858), 56–58; and Ayres, *Methodist Heroes*, 90–94. On Philip Gatch, see Connor, *Methodist Trail Blazer*, 158–159. On Noah Fidler, see Wolcott, *Wilderness Rider*, 59. On Joshua Thomas, see Robert W. Todd, *Methodism on the Peninsula, or, Sketches of Notable Characters and Events in the History of Methodism in the Maryland and Delaware Peninsula* (Philadelphia: Methodist Episcopal Book Rooms, 1886), 85–95; and Adam Wallace, *The Parson of the Islands; A Biography of the Rev. Joshua Thomas; Embracing Sketches of His Contemporaries, Remarkable Camp Meeting Scenes, Revival Incidents, and Reminiscences of the Introduction of Methodism on the Islands of the Chesapeake, and the Eastern Shores of Maryland and Virginia* (Baltimore: Thomas Evans, 1906; reprint, Cambridge, MD: Tidewater Publishers, 1961).

10. Caldwell, *Walking With God*, 20, 22, 25, 29, and 56; Crowell, *Journal*; Smith, *Experience*; Jacob Young, *Autobiography*, 41–42, 46–47, 135–139, and 167; Littlejohn, "Journal," 7–13, 38, and 215; Boehm, *Reminiscences*, 22, 53, 62, and 70; Brunson, *Western Pioneer*, 52, 55, 65, 67, 82, 176, 202, and 226; Giles, *Pioneer*, 64, 70–74, 203, and 223–226; Chase, *Recollections*, 103–104; Woolsey, *Supernumerary*, 16–18, 71, and 74; Jenkins, *Experience*, 9–10, 34, 44–45, 72, 97, and 120; Travis, *Autobiography*, 31, 39–41, and 54; Brooks, *Life and Times*, 17–18, 23, 25, 48, 51, 56, 58–60, 65, and 84; Dan Young, *Autobiography*, 28 and 57–59; Jarena Lee, *The Life and Religious Experience of Jarena Lee, A Coloured Lady, Giving an Account of Her Call to Preach the Gospel. Revised and Corrected From the Original Manuscript, Written by Herself* (Philadelphia: Printed and Published for the Author, 1836; reprint in *Sisters of the Spirit: Three Black Women's Autobiographies of the Nineteenth Century*, ed. William L. Andrews, Bloomington: Indiana University Press, 1986; Zilpha Elaw, *Memoirs of the Life, Religious Experience, Ministerial Travels and Labours of Mrs. Zilpha Elaw, An American Female of Colour; Together with Some Account of the Great Religious Revival in America* (London: Published for the Authoress, 1846; reprint in Andrews, *Sisters of the Spirit*); John Jea, *The Life, History, and Unparalleled Sufferings of John Jea, The African Preacher* (Portsea, England: James W. Williams, c. 1815; reprint in *Black Itinerants of the Gospel: The Narratives of John Jea and George White*, ed. Graham R. Hodges, Madison: Madison House, 1993; George White, *A Brief Account of the Life, Experience, Travels and Gospel Labours of George White, An African* (New York: John C. Totten, 1810; reprint in Hodges, *Black Itinerants of the Gospel*).

11. Richard Nye Price, *Holston Methodism from Its Origin to the Present Time*, 5 vols. (Nashville: Smith & Lamar, 1903–1913) 2: 1–8. Granade is sometimes spelled

Grenade. The most complete description of Granade is Richard A. Humphrey, *History and Hymns of John Adam Granade: Holston's Pilgrim-Preacher-Poet* (n.p.: Commission on Archives and History, Holston Annual Conference, United Methodist Church, 1991). The poem is given on p. 7.

12. Price, *Holston Methodism*, 2: 7–19.

13. Jacob Young, *Autobiography*, 126.

14. Ronald A. Knox, *Enthusiasm: A Chapter in the History of Religion* (Oxford: Oxford University Press, 1950), 1–4, 372–388; cf. David S. Lovejoy, *Religious Enthusiasm in the New World: Heresy to Revolution* (Cambridge: Harvard University Press, 1985), 1–4. On English Wesleyan enthusiasm in the eighteenth century, see Umphrey Lee, *The Historical Backgrounds of Early Methodist Enthusiasm* (New York: Columbia University Press, 1931). For a history of the word *enthusiasm* from the sixteenth through the nineteenth centuries, see Susie I. Tucker, *Enthusiasm: A Study in Semantic Change* (Cambridge: Cambridge University Press, 1972). It may also be the case that at times some phenomenon associated with enthusiastic religion have a physiological cause or explanation. For instance, see Oliver Sacks, *The Man Who Mistook His Wife for a Hat* (New York: Harper Perennial, 1990), part 3, "Transports."

15. Sociologist George Thomas has recently posited a far-reaching isomorphic relationship between revivalism (particularly Methodism), republicanism, and the organization of everyday life within the expanding market world of the early republic. George M. Thomas, *Revivalism and Cultural Change: Christianity, Nation Building, and the Market in the Nineteenth-Century United States* (Chicago: University of Chicago Press, 1989), chaps. 1–4.

16. For a fuller discussion of the role of enthusiasm in popular religion, see Garrett, *Spirit Possession and Popular Religion*. On the general concept of millenarian movements accompanying periods of social unrest in other cultures (such as nineteenth- and twentieth-century Polynesia), see Kenelm Burridge, *New Heaven, New Earth: A Study in Millenarian Activities* (Oxford: Basil Blackwell, 1969), esp. 3–14.

17. For example, William Warren Sweet, the dean of American Methodist historians in this century, firmly believed that organized religion's greatest contribution to American life in the early republic was in bringing civilization to the frontier. This is a ubiquitous theme throughout Sweet's writings. For example, see Sweet, *Religion in the Development of American Culture*, 161. This kind of law-and-order religion was, of course, the direct antithesis of religious enthusiasm, so it is not surprising to find that Sweet downplayed early Methodist enthusiasm whenever possible. Sweet was essentially a consensus historian who had little interest in raising questions of religious upheaval, particularly if they were tied to notions of class conflict. In *Revivalism in America* Sweet writes that "overemotionalized religion deserves all that can be said in condemnation." See William Warren Sweet, *Revivalism in America: Its Origins, Growth and Decline* (New York: Charles Scribner's Sons, 1945), xiii. Also see Sweet, *Religion in the Development of American Culture*, 153; Sweet, *Methodism in American History*, rev. ed. (Nashville: Abingdon Press, 1953), 159; and James L. Ash Jr., *Protestantism and the American University: An Intellectual Biography of William Warren Sweet* (Dallas: SMU Press, 1982), 86–93.

18. Historian Sheridan Gilley has written that, "if the eighteenth century was an age of reason, it was even more an age of enthusiasm." Gilley, "Christianity and Enlightenment: An Historical Survey," *History of European Ideas* 1 (1981): 103–121. Studies in European religious enthusiasm range from Ronald A. Knox's *Enthusiasm* to Clarke Garrett's *Spirit Possession and Popular Religion*, and Peter Burke's *Popular Culture in Early Modern Europe*, chap. 8. The work of Jon Butler, David D. Hall, and Charles

Hambrick-Stowe represent exceptions to the lack of American studies of popular religious enthusiasm. See Butler, *Awash in a Sea of Faith*; Jon Butler, "The Future of American Religious History: Prospectus, Agenda, and Transatlantic *Problematique*," *William and Mary Quarterly* 42 (1985): 167–183; Hall, *Worlds of Wonder*; and Charles Hambrick-Stowe, *The Practice of Piety: Puritan Devotional Discipline in Seventeenth-Century New England* (Chapel Hill: University of North Carolina Press, 1982). There is also a fairly large body of literature on witchcraft and magic in early New England. For example, see John Putnam Demos, *Entertaining Satan: Witchcraft and the Culture of Early New England* (Oxford: Oxford University Press, 1982); Carol F. Karlsen, *The Devil in the Shape of a Woman: Witchcraft in Colonial New England* (New York: W.W. Norton, 1987); and Richard Godbeer, *The Devil's Dominion: Magic and Religion in Early New England* (New York: Cambridge University Press, 1992).

19. Werner, *Primitive Methodist Connexion*, 28–29, 54–61, 62–71, and 177–180; Carwardine, *Transatlantic Revivalism*, 104–107; Chadwick, *The Victorian Church*, 385–386. Also see Valenze, *Prophetic Sons and Daughters*. John Wesley drew heavily on the popular religious milieu of the eighteenth century, although he himself was never a comfortable enthusiast. This paradox has led Henry Rack to dub Wesley a "reasonable enthusiast." Rack writes of Wesley, "For all his old-fashioned ideas on political and social questions, as well as on religion, he was very much a man of the optimistic, improving eighteenth century, and his 'enthusiasm' was clothed in the garments of 'reason.' " Rack, *Reasonable Enthusiast*, 10. Bernard Semmel paints a less ambiguous (and less convincing) picture of Wesley, describing Wesleyan Methodism as both profoundly "liberal" and "modern." Semmel, *Methodist Revolution*, 6.

20. Obelkevich, *Religion and Rural Society*, 259 and 281. Cf. Colls, "Primitive Methodists in the Northern Coalfields."

21. Rule, "Methodism, Popular Beliefs and Village Culture in Cornwall."

22. Woodmason, *Carolina Backcountry*, 101. The Anglican minister Devereux Jarratt came to much the same conclusion about popular religion in Virginia. See Jarratt, *Life of the Devereux Jarratt*, 126.

23. Hall, *Worlds of Wonder*, chap 2. Also see Lucien Febvre, *The Problem of Unbelief in the Sixteenth Century*, trans. Beatrice Gottlieb (Editions Albin Michel, 1942; reprint, Cambridge: Harvard University Press, 1982), 455–464. Most colonial Americans, to paraphrase Febvre, lived in a world that wanted to believe. Jon Butler has shown that even such noteworthy public figures as the Tennent brothers—Gilbert, John, and William Jr.—strongly believed in the efficacy of divine intervention. John received visions of Christ and William Jr. was reportedly raised from the dead. See Butler, *Awash in a Sea of Faith*, 184–185. The rapid development of the American camp meeting demonstrates the depth of such popular religion in the South and West. See Conkin, *Cane Ridge*; and Schmidt, *Holy Fairs*. Standard works on the camp meeting include Johnson, *The Frontier Camp Meeting*; Bruce, *They All Sang Hallelujah*; and Weisberger, *They Gathered at the River*.

24. In 1807 the University of Pennsylvania granted Pilmore an honorary Doctor of Divinity degree. The most ecumenical of Wesley's missionaries, Pilmore went so far as to attend a Roman Catholic church and a Jewish synagogue in America, though he usually complained that the preaching he heard from the pulpits of other denominations was dull and lifeless. Frank Bateman Stanger, "The Rev. Joseph Pilmore, D.D.: A Biographical Sketch," in Pilmore, *The Journal of Joseph Pilmore*, 235–254.

25. Pilmore, *Journal*, 85.

26. Ibid., 68.

27. Ibid., 126.

28. Ibid., 202.

29. Ibid., 133, n. 11.

30. Ibid., 138. This was on June 8, 1772. When Asbury preached at Gunpowder Neck for the first time, in December 1772, he offered no complaints, describing the meeting as a "solemn, heart-affecting time." Asbury, *Journal and Letters*, 1: 56. Asbury preached there on many subsequent occasions.

31. Ibid., 138.

32. Rankin, "Diary," 40–42.

33. Ibid., 121.

34. Lee, *Short History*, 51–52. For a similar account of Rankin squelching a boisterous congregation, see Littlejohn, "Journal," 62.

35. Ware, *Sketches*, 170.

36. Ibid., 252–253.

37. Ibid., 252–254. Also see Albea Godbold, "Francis Asbury and His Difficulties with John Wesley and Thomas Rankin," *Methodist History* 3 (1965): 3–19.

38. My concept of popular religion is largely drawn from the work of Jon Butler, David D. Hall, and Robert A. Orsi. Butler, *Awash in a Sea of Faith*, 4; Hall, *Worlds of Wonder*, 4–20; and Orsi, *Madonna of 115th Street*, xiv and xvii-xviii.

39. Horton, *Narrative*, 25, 73, and 98.

40. Ibid., 134–136.

41. Ibid., 75.

42. Ibid. 73 and 105.

43. Ibid., 60–62.

44. James B. Finley, *Sketches of Western Methodism: Biographical, Historical, and Miscellaneous* (Cincinnati: Methodist Book Concern, 1854; reprint, New York: Arno Press, 1969), 294; and Jacob Young, *Autobiography*, 133–134. Grenade was also a prolific hymn writer. Johnson, *Frontier Camp Meeting*, 134–135 and 195.

45. Boehm, *Reminiscences*, 35.

46. Lee, *Short History*, 126–131.

47. Thomas Smith, *Experience*, 76–78. According to Dailey, when preaching, Smith "was commonly much excited himself, sometimes almost to an ecstasy, and his hearers not unfrequently partook of the spirit of the preacher." (p. 104n.) On Methodism on the Delmarva Peninsula, see William H. Williams, "The Attraction of Methodism: The Delmarva Peninsula as a Case Study, 1769–1820," in *Rethinking Methodist History*, ed. Richey and Rowe, 100–110; and Williams, *The Garden of American Methodism: The Delmarva Peninsula, 1769–1820* (Wilmington: Scholarly Resources, 1984).

48. Smith, *Experience*, 101–102. For similar accounts of dramatic meetings, see James Meacham's "Journal."

49. Watters, *Short Account*, 29.

50. Ware, *Sketches*, 88–93. On a related topic, Kate Galea has recently argued that Phoebe Palmer's conception of sanctification and her experiences "behind the veil" place her at least partially within the tradition of medieval mystic women. For example, as Galea points out, Palmer was attentive to her dreams, recording the details of many in her diary. "Palmer's experience of sanctification, of being accepted by God as holy," writes Galea, "mirrors many aspects of some medieval women mystics' visions of God, including the ground of their authority, the impetus to share their experience, the characteristic stages of their thought, and the physical effects it had on their bodies." Kate P. Crawford Galea, "'Anchored Behind the Veil': Mystical Vision As a Possible Source

of Authority in the Ministry of Phoebe Palmer," *Methodist History* 31 (1993): 236–247. In North Carolina a similar pattern of genteel women affiliating with the Methodists independent of their male relatives prevailed during the early nineteenth century. See Richard Rankin, *Ambivalent Churchmen and Evangelical Churchwomen: The Religion of the Episcopal Elite in North Carolina, 1800–1860* (Columbia: University of South Carolina Press, 1993), 27–48.

51. In this connection, Albert J. Raboteau has observed that "even as the gods of Africa gave way to the God of Christianity, the African heritage of singing, dancing, spirit possession, and magic continued to influence Afro-American spirituals, ring shouts, and folk beliefs." Albert J. Raboteau, *Slave Religion: The "Invisible Institution" in the Antebellum South* (New York: Oxford University Press, 1978), 92. Also see Mechal Sobel, *The World They Made Together: Black and White Values in Eighteenth-Century Virginia* (Princeton: Princeton University Press, 1987), 3–11, 171–242; and Mechal Sobel, *Trabelin' On: The Slave Journey to an Afro-Baptist Faith* (Princeton: Princeton University Press, 1979), especially chapters 3 and 5. On the importance of dance and the ring shout to African-American culture in the early republic, see Sterling Stuckey, *Slave Culture: Nationalist Theory and the Foundations of Black America* (New York: Oxford University Press, 1987), 1–97. Also on African-American spirituality, see Lewis V. Baldwin, "Festivity and Celebration in a Black Methodist Tradition, 1813–1981," *Methodist History* 20 (1982): 183–191.

52. On early African-American music, see Eileen Southern, *The Music of Black Americans* (New York: W.W. Norton, 1971), 77–99; and Jon Michael Spencer, *Black Hymnody: A Hymnological History of the African-American Church* (Knoxville: University of Tennessee Press, 1992), esp. 3–24.

53. John F. Watson, *Methodist Error or Friendly Advice to Those Methodists Who Indulge in Extravagant Religious Emotions and Bodily Exercises* (Trenton, NJ: D. & E. Fenton, n.d.; reprint, Cincinnati: Phillips & Speer, 1819), 16.

54. Littlejohn, "Journal," 33.

55. Howells, *Recollections of Life in Ohio*, 42–43. Howells later rejected what he viewed as his father's excessive enthusiasm and commitment to the church and left the Methodists.

56. Colbert, "Journal," 1: 42 (July 10, 1791).

57. Morrell, *Journals*, 14.

58. Watson, *Methodist Error*, 16. Lewis Baldwin has recently suggested that "thorough research on the Methodist revivals and camp meetings of the eighteenth and nineteenth centuries will undoubtedly show that much of the preaching, shouting, singing, and religious dance which took place were inspired in the white Methodists through contact with their African converts." Lewis V. Baldwin, "New Directions for the Study of Blacks in Methodism," in *Rethinking Methodist History*, ed. Richey and Rowe, 185–193.

59. Watson, *Methodist Error*, 10.

60. Francois Andre Michaux, *Travels to the West of the Allegheny Mountains* (London: B. Crosby, 1805; reprint in *Early Western Travels 1748–1846*, ed. Reuben Gold Thwaites, 3 vols., Cleveland: Arthur H. Clark, 1904), 3: 249; John Melish, *Travels Through the United States of America, in the Years 1806 & 1807, and 1809, 1810, & 1811; Including an Account of Passages Betwixt America & Britain, and Travels Through Various Parts of Britain, Ireland, and Canada* (London: George Cowie and Co., 1818; reprint, New York: Johnson Reprint Corporation, 1970), 43. Melish identifies Ripley as a "black female preacher." But this may instead have been Dorothy Ripley (1767–1831),

the English-born evangelist who was converted in a visionary near-death experience in which Christ appeared to her. From 1802 to 1831, Ripley spent much of her time in America advocating abolitionism and preaching to slaves and Indians, and in prisons. See Dorothy Ripley, *The Extraordinary Conversion and Religious Experience of Dorothy Ripley, With Her First Voyage and Travels in America* (New York: G. and R. Waite, 1810); and *The Bank of Faith and Works United*, 2nd. ed. (Whitby: G. Clark, 1822); C. S. Nicholls, ed., *The Dictionary of National Biography: Missing Persons* (Oxford: Oxford University Press, 1993), s.v. "Dorothy Ripley," by Isobel Grundy; Nolan B. Harmon, ed., *Encyclopedia of World Methodism*, 2 vols. (Nashville: United Methodist Publishing House, 1974), s.v. "Dorothy Ripley" by John T. Wilkinson, 2: 2024. Also see Zechariah Taft, *Biographical Sketches of the Lives and Public Ministry of Various Holy Women*, 2 vols. (London: Published for the Author, 1825 and 1828), 1: 205–241. Taft quotes extensively from Ripley's *Bank of Faith*, 2nd ed. (1822).

61. Baron Klinkowstrom, *America 1818–1820*, trans. and ed. Franklin D. Scott (Evanston: Northwestern University Press, 1952), 108; and Isaac Holmes, *An Account of the United States of America* (London: Henry Fisher, 1823; reprint, New York: Arno Press, 1974), 388. Cf. Henry Bradshaw Fearon, *Sketches of America: A Narrative of a Journey of Five Thousand Miles Through the Eastern and Western States of America* (London: Longman, Hurst, Rees, Orme and Brown, 1818; reprint, New York: Augustus M. Kelley, 1970), 161–167; and Moreau de Saint-Mery, "Norfolk, Portsmouth, and Gasport as Seen by Moreau de Saint-Mery in March, April and May, 1794," trans. Fillmore Norfleet, *Virginia Magazine of History and Biography* 48 (1940): 12–30, 153–164, and 253–264. The archetypical high-church critique of Methodism is Bishop Lavington, *The Enthusiasm of Methodists and Papists Considered. With Notes, Introduction, and Appendix by the Rev. R. Polwhele*, ed. Rev. R. Polwhele (London: Printed by A.J. Valpy, 1820). Also see Albert M. Lyles, *Methodism Mocked: The Satiric Reaction to Methodism in the Eighteenth Century* (London: Epworth Press, 1960), esp. 32–43.

62. This is the judgement of William L. Andrews, ed., *Sisters of the Spirit*, 11. Compare the accounts in Clifton H. Johnson, ed., *God Struck Me Dead: Religious Conversion Experiences and Autobiographies of Ex-slaves* (Philadelphia: United Church Press, 1969).

63. Elaw, *Labours*, 55.

64. Ibid., 56–57.

65. Andrews, *Sisters of the Spirit*, 6.

66. Lee, *Experience*, 48.

67. Rebecca Jackson, *Gifts of Power: The Writings of Rebecca Jackson, Black Visionary, Shaker Eldress*, ed. Jean McMahon Humez (Amherst: University of Massachusetts Press, 1981), 96. It is worth noting that Fanny Newell relied at least in part on dreams and visions to validate her call to preach. Newell, *Memoirs*, 64–66.

68. Jea, *Life*, 37. An equally apt example is that of George White. White was born in slavery, gained his freedom at age 26, was converted in a trance, and eventually became a Methodist exhorter and preacher in New York City. White, *A Brief Account*.

69. William Bentley, *The Diary of William Bentley, D.D.*, 4 vols. (Gloucester, MA: P. Smith, 1962), 3: 173–174; S. G. Goodrich, *Recollections of a Lifetime, or Men and Things I Have Seen: In a Series of Familiar Letters to a Friend, Historical, Biographical, Anecdotical, and Descriptive*, 2 vols. (New York: Miller, Orton and Mulligan, 1856), 1: 216.

70. W. E. B. Du Bois, *The Souls of Black Folk* (Chicago: A.C. McClurg, 1903), 191. The annual Big August Quarterly, a predominantly African-American festival ini-

tiated in 1814 by the ex-slave Peter Spencer, who broke with the Methodist Episcopal Church in 1813 to organize the Union Church of African Members, is a good example of the persistence of this strain in African American worship. As late as 1889, a Wilmington, Delaware, editor wrote that as the celebration progressed, "the sound rose to an exuberant shout. The singers bodies swayed up and down and back and forth, like the levers of a mighty engine," the "stamp" of their feet and the "clapping of their hands," somehow "all in harmony with the scene and the music." Quoted in Baldwin, "Festivity and Celebration." Also see Baldwin, *"Invisible" Strands in African Methodism: A History of the* African Union Methodist Protestant *and* Union American Methodist Episcopal *Churches, 1805–1980* (Metuchen, NJ: Scarecrow Press, 1983). For accounts of Baptist enthusiasm, see Sobel, *Trabelin' On,* chap. 6.

71. On a similar trend in Nova Scotia Methodism, see Rawlyk, "Freeborn Garrettson and Nova Scotia."

72. Burritt, *Methodism in Ithaca,* 69–70.

CHAPTER 6

1. Crowell, *Journal,* 43. Born in Tolland, Connecticut, Crowell was converted in 1797 and joined the traveling connection in 1801. In 1806 he was appointed to New York City, and in 1807 his appointment was as a missionary in the New York Conference. *Minutes of the Annual Conferences,* 1: 141 and 1: 151.

2. Meacham, "Journal." This was by no means Meacham's only experience with either slave spirituality or white intransigence. A few weeks before this episode, Meacham lodged with a Methodist family at one of his appointments. About midnight, he was awakened "in raptures of Heaven by the sweet Echo of Singing in the Kitchen among the dear Black people (who my Soul loves). I scarcely ever heard anything to equal it upon earth." Meacham immediately got up and joined the slaves, though he found their plight heartrending. "I felt the miserable weight of oppression intolerable upon my heart," Meacham later wrote in his journal, "while the proud whites can live in luxury and abomination making a mock of God and his word, the African upholds him by his Swet and labour . . . and if they serve the Lord God it must be in the dead of night when they ought to be taking rest to their bodys." "If ever I get rich through Slavery," wrote Meacham on another occasion, "I shall esteem myself a Traitor, and claim a part in Hell with Judas, and the rich glutton." Not surprisingly, Meacham's convictions led him into frequent arguments with slaveholding whites. Meacham rarely moderated his criticism of slavery, making relatively few converts to abolitionism in Virginia.

3. Peter H. Wood, *Black Majority: Negroes in Colonial South Carolina from 1670 through the Stono Rebellion* (New York: W.W. Norton & Company, 1974), 136–142; R. E. Hood, "From a Headstart to a Deadstart: The Historical Basis for Black Indifference Toward the Episcopal Church 1800–1860," *Historical Magazine of the Protestant Episcopal Church* 51 (1982): 269–296; and Harry V. Richardson, *Dark Salvation: The Story of Methodism as It Developed Among Blacks in America* (Anchor-Press: Garden City, NY, 1976), 24–32.

4. Pilmore, *Journal,* 74; Rankin, "Diary," 103. Also in Rankin, see pp. 122, 128, 136, 152, 172, 177, 179, and 183. On the early response of African Americans to Methodism, see Richardson, *Dark Salvation,* 43–49.

5. *Minutes of the Annual Conferences,* 1: 26, 39, 93, 184, 245, and 331. These figures are for the Methodist Episcopal Church alone, and do not take into account the

African-American Methodist churches started during this period. Also see the Appendix; and Hatch, *Democratization*, 102. When Thomas Morrell visited Annapolis, Maryland, in December 1791 he noted that there were "more blacks than whites in Society—perhaps 100 whites [and] 200 blacks." Morrell, *Journals*, 11.

6. Allan Kulikoff, *Tobacco and Slaves: The Development of Southern Cultures in the Chesapeake, 1680–1800* (Chapel Hill: University of North Carolina Press, 1986), 317–352. Jon Butler refers to this destruction of traditional African religious systems prior to 1760 as an "African spiritual holocaust." Butler, *Awash in a Sea of Faith*, 130.

7. Hatch, *Democratization*, 102. For a similar discussion of the factors behind the early African-American response to Methodism, see Richardson, *Dark Salvation*, 62–63.

8. Littlejohn, "Journal," 4.

9. Gerald W. Mullin, *Flight and Rebellion: Slave Resistance in Eighteenth-Century Virginia* (New York: Oxford University Press, 1972), 158.

10. Lee, *Short History*, 207–208; Capers, *Autobiography*, 161–163 and 173–174; Travis, *Autobiography*, 68–69; Jenkins, *Experience*, 86; Chreitzburg, *Early Methodism in the Carolinas*, 74; and *Minutes of the Annual Conferences*, 1: 92. A former Methodist missionary to the West Indies, Meredith briefly joined the William Hammet (Hammett or Hammit) schism in the early 1790s, but soon broke with Hammet. On Hammet, see Lee, *Short History*, 206–207; and Frederick E. Maser and George A. Singleton, "Further Branches of Methodism are Founded," in *History of American Methodism*, ed. Bucke, 1: 617–622.

11. When John Littlejohn returned to Leesburg, Virginia, in 1819 after an absence of several months, he recorded that "the poor Blacks formed a circle round me giving me their hands & express their joy to see me, it affected me much, when one of my White frds [friends] expressed a wish to speak to me, anothr said, the Blacks have got prosession [possession] of the old Man; you can't speak to him now." Littlejohn, "Journal," 139.

12. Hatch, *Democratization*, 104.

13. Richard Allen, *The Life Experience and Gospel Labors of the Rt. Rev. Richard Allen* (Published by the author, n.d.; reprint, New York: Abingdon Press, 1960), 30. Allen was confident that "no religious sect or denomination would suit the capacity of colored people as well as the Methodist; for the plain and simple gospel suits best for any people" (p. 29). As Albert Raboteau points out, the chanted sermon became "as much a staple of African-American culture as spirituals, gospel, blues, and tales." Albert J. Raboteau, *A Fire in the Bones: Reflections on African-American Religious History* (Boston: Beacon Press, 1995), 142.

14. Benjamin Tucker Tanner, *An Apology for African Methodism* (Baltimore: A. M. E. Book Depository, 1867), 73.

15. Hatch, *Democratization*, 105.

16. On Hosier, see Warren Thomas Smith, "Harry Hosier: Black Preacher Extraordinary," *Journal of the Interdenominational Theological Center* 7 (1980): 111–128; Warren Thomas Smith, *Harry Hosier: Circuit Rider* (Nashville: Upper Room, 1980); and Asbury, *Journal and Letters*, 1: 362, 403, 494n., 539n., 681n., and 682n. Hosier may have been born in Fayetteville, North Carolina, about 1750. There is also some evidence that he was a slave of Henry Dorsey Gough at Perry Hall (see the discussion of the Goughs elsewhere in this chapter).

17. Boehm, *Reminiscences*, 91.

18. Garrettson, *American Methodist Pioneer*, 269. Also see pp. 237, 238, 266, 267, 268, and 270.

19. Boehm, *Reminiscences*, 91.

20. Raboteau, *Fire in the Bones*, 79.

21. "Eighteenth Century Slaves as Advertised by Their Masters," *Journal of Negro History* 1 (1916): 163–216.

22. Swain, *Journal*, 23.

23. W. E. B. Du Bois, *The Souls of Black Folk* (New York: Gramercy Books, 1994), 146. Also see Richardson, *Dark Salvation*, 167–187.

24. Capers, *Autobiography*, 124–129; Jenkins, *Experience*, 120–121; Travis, *Autobiography*, 101–102. Capers's account is quoted at length in M. H. Moore, *Sketches of the Pioneers of Methodism in North Carolina and Virginia* (Nashville: Southern Methodist Publishing House, 1884; reprint, Greenwood, SC: Attic Press, 1977), 310–314. Capers describes Evans as being extremely deferential toward whites, but this may reflect Capers's own agenda more than historical reality. Fayetteville first appears in the Annual Conference records in 1810 (the same year Evans died) with 87 African American and 110 white members. *Minutes of the Annual Conferences*, 1: 182. The formation of an African-American Methodist congregation preceded the establishment of a white society in several other places as well. See, for example, Travis, *Autobiography*, 53 and 58; and Jenkins, *Experience*, 154–155.

25. White, *Brief Account*, 10 and 52.

26. Ibid., 10–18 and 52–70.

27. Capers, "Autobiography," 138–139.

28. Albert J. Raboteau, "The Slave Church in the Era of the American Revolution," *Slavery and Freedom in the Age of the American Revolution*, ed. Ira Berlin and Ronald Hoffman (Urbana: University of Illinois Press, 1986), 205.

29. Albert Raboteau notes that interdenominational politics plagued Allen throughout his career. One attempt at reconciliation between Allen's AME Church and the AME Zion Church resulted in a "near riot." As Allen attempted to preach, a disapproving Zionite "sat on the pulpit, interrupted the sermon, and even spat on the bishop." Raboteau, *Fire in the Bones*, 94.

30. Albert J. Raboteau, "African-Americans, Exodus, and the American Israel," in *African-American Christianity* ed. Paul E. Johnson (Berkeley: University of California Press, 1994), 1–17. Also see Raboteau, *A Fire in the Bones*, chap. 1. As Raboteau notes, while slaves' identification with the Exodus story mainly nurtured internal resistance, it could at times foster overt challenges to white control. Hence it is understandable that Denmark Vesey's insurrection of 1822 had ties to the African Methodist Church in Charleston, South Carolina. See John Lofton, *Denmark Vesey's Revolt: The Slave Plot That Lit a Fuse to Fort Sumter* (Kent: Kent State University Press, 1983), 60–62 and 91–93; and Donald R. Wright, *African Americans in the Early Republic 1789–1831* (Arlington Heights, IL: Harlan Davidson, 1993), 100–108.

31. Margaret Washington, "Community Regulation and Cultural Specialization in Gullah Folk Religion," in Johnson, *African American Christianity*, 47–79. Also see Margaret Washington Creel, *"A Peculiar People": Slave Religion and Community-Culture Among the Gullahs* (New York: New York University Press, 1988), esp. chaps. 5, 6, 8, and 9; and Margaret Washington Creel, "Gullah Attitudes toward Life and Death," in *Africanisms in American Culture*, ed. Joseph E. Holloway (Bloomington: Indiana University Press, 1990), 69–97. Russell Richey makes a similar argument about the way in which African Americans appropriated and transformed Methodism. Richey, *Early American Methodism*, 59–60.

32. Colbert, "Journal," 1: 155 (January 23, 1794).

33. Smith, *Recollections,* 296. It is possible that Smith has confused his locations here and that this is the same congregation described by Colbert.

34. Historians of American Methodism have long been fascinated by the movement's shifting relationships with abolitionists, slaveholders, slaves, and free African Americans. Among the best accounts of this topic are: Mathews, *Slavery and Methodism;* and Essig, *Bonds of Wickedness.* Also see Paul Otis Evans, "The Ideology of Inequality: Asbury, Methodism, and Slavery" (Ph.D. diss., Rutgers, 1981). Article-length analyses of Methodism and slavery include: W. Harrison Daniel, "The Methodist Episcopal Church and the Negro in the Early National Period," *Methodist History* 11 (January 1973): 40–53; Grant S. Shockley, "Methodism, Society and Black Evangelism in America: Retrospect and Prospect," *Methodist History* 12 (July 1974): 145–182. L. C. Matlack, *The Antislavery Struggle and Triumph in the Methodist Episcopal Church* (Phillips & Hunt, 1881; reprint, New York: Negro Universities Press, 1969) is among the earliest volumes on this topic. See especially pp. 47–74.

35. Tanner, *Apology for African Methodism,* 57.

36. Ira Berlin, "Introduction" to *Slavery and Freedom in the Age of the American Revolution,* ed. Berlin and Hoffman, xvii.

37. Evans, "Ideology of Inequality," 1.

38. On the rise of opposition to slavery in the revolutionary era, see Winthrop D. Jordan, *White Over Black: American Attitudes Toward the Negro, 1550–1812* (Chapel Hill: University of North Carolina Press, 1968), 269–311.

39. Wesley, *Works,* 11: 74 and 79. Wesley's *Thoughts Upon Slavery* was drawn largely from the writings of Anthony Benezet, with whom he corresponded at some length, and encouraged by the British abolitionist Granville Sharp. Roger Anstey, *The Atlantic Slave Trade and British Abolition 1760–1810* (Atlantic Highlands, NJ: Humanities Press, 1975), 239–242. In 1791, less than a week before his death, Wesley wrote to William Wilberforce urging him to press his antislavery campaign in Parliament "till even American slavery (the vilest that ever saw the sun) shall vanish away." Wesley, *Works,* 13: 153.

40. Rankin, "Diary," 145. The previous month Rankin declared to a congregation near Baltimore "that the sins of Great Britain and her colonies had long called aloud for vengence and in a peculiar manner the dreadful sin of buying and selling the souls and bodies of the poor Africans" (p. 138).

41. *Minutes of the Annual Conferences,* 1: 12.

42. Watters, *Short Account,* 40.

43. Ibid., 90.

44. By his own account, Garrettson was standing in church when "this thought powerfully struck my mind. 'It is not right for you to keep your fellow creatures in bondage; you must let the oppressed go free.' " Though "till then I had never suspected that the practice of slave-keeping was wrong," Garrettson immediately determined to free his slaves: "I told them they did not belong to me, and that I did not desire their services without making them a compensation." Garrettson, *American Methodist Pioneer,* 48.

45. Garrettson, *American Methodist Pioneer,* 65.

46. Smith, *Experience,* 68 and 82. It should be noted that on the latter of these two occasions Smith preached from Eph. 6:5, "Servants, be obedient to them that are your masters according to the flesh, with fear and trembling, in singleness of your heart, as unto Christ."

47. Garrettson, *American Methodist Pioneer,* 48; and Freeborn Garrettson, *Dialogue Between Do-Justice and Professing Christian. Dedicated to the Respective and Collective Abo-*

lition Societies, and To All Other Benevolent, Humane Philanthropists, in America (Wilmington: Printed by Peter Brynberg, [1805]), 28, 44, and 53. A contemporary work very similar in style, tone and theme to Garrettson's dialogue is Daniel Coker, A *Dialogue Between a Virginian and an African Minister* (Baltimore: Printed by Benjamin Edes for Joseph James, 1810).

48. Phoebus, *Beams of Light,* 106–108.

49. Phoebus, *Beams of Light,* 316–328. Also see Scherer, *Ezekiel Cooper,* 55–56; and Evans, "Ideology of Inequality," 246–248. All of this is not to suggest that Cooper, or, for that matter, most other Methodists, were free from all racial prejudice. For example, in his answer to Abaris in the *Maryland Gazette,* Cooper wrote: "I am probably as much principled against the whites taking 'black wives' or husbands as Abaris himself. My sons and daughters 'shall be better taught;' I hope his will, also; then we need not fear from that quarter." Phoebus, *Beams of Light,* 323.

50. James O'Kelly, *Essay on Negro-Slavery* (Philadelphia: Prichard and Hall, 1789), 17–18; and Evans, "Ideology of Inequality," 239.

51. Morrell, *Journals,* 14. The strength of abolitionist sentiment among many Methodists in Virginia can also be seen in the 1785 Methodist petition to the Virginia General Assembly calling for the emancipation of all slaves in the state. Richard K. McMaster, "Liberty or Property? The Methodist Petition for Emancipation in Virginia, 1785," *Methodist History* 10 (October 1971): 44–55.

52. Williams, "Attraction of Methodism," 100–107. Also see Williams, *Garden of American Methodism,* 161–168.

53. Garrettson, *American Methodist Pioneer,* 118; Williams, "Attraction," 107; Asbury, *Journal and Letters,* 1: 582. On Joseph Everett, see Hallman, *Garden of Methodism,* 374–375.

54. Boehm, *Reminiscences,* 69; and Colbert, "Journal," 4: 8 (March 30, 1801), and 4: 48 (December 6, 1801).

55. John B. Boles, *Black Southerners 1619–1869* (Lexington: The University Press of Kentucky, 1984), 134. On the development of slavery in the Chesapeake in this period, see Richard S. Dunn, "Black Society in the Chesapeake 1776–1810," in *Slavery and Freedom in the Age of the American Revolution,* ed. Berlin and Hoffman, 49–82. Dunn writes that during this period there was a clear "trend toward black freedom in Maryland and entrenched slavery in Virginia" (p. 52). Overall, "the free black challenge to Chesapeake slavery was limited to the coastal districts, particularly coastal Maryland" (p. 80). On free African Americans in Dutchess County, New York, see Michael Edward Groth, "Forging Freedom in the Mid-Hudson Valley: The End of Slavery and the Formation of a Free African-American Community in Dutchess County, New York, 1770–1850" (Ph.D. diss., Binghamton University, 1994), chap. 2–6. Groth says surprisingly little about the religion of either whites or African Americans.

56. Kenneth L. Carroll, "Religious Influences on the Manumission of Slaves in Caroline, Dorchester, and Talbot Counties," *Maryland Historical Magazine* 56 (June 1961): 176–197. On religion, slaveholding, and manumission in Philadelphia during this period, see Gary B. Nash and Jean R. Soderland, *Freedom by Degrees: Emancipation in Pennsylvania and Its Aftermath* (New York: Oxford University Press, 1991), 153–160.

57. Norris S. Barratt, "Barratt's Chapel and Methodism," *Papers of the Historical Society of Delaware* 57 (1911): 1–57. On Methodist abolitionism in Delaware, see Patience Essah, *A House Divided: Slavery and Emancipation in Delaware 1638–1865* (Charlottesville: University Press of Virginia, 1996), 56–59. The Methodists and Quakers were the leading advocates of emancipation in post-revolutionary Delaware. But Quaker influence was mainly limited to the more populous areas of the state. Methodist circuit

riders, on the other hand, according to Essah, "took the antislavery message directly to the heart of slaveholding rural Delaware" (p. 58).

58. Henry C. Conrad, "Samuel White and His Father Judge Thomas White," *Papers of the Historical Society of Delaware* 40 (1903): 1–13. On Thomas White's relationship with Francis Asbury, also see James W. May, "Francis Asbury and Thomas White: A Refugee Preacher and His Tory Patron," *Methodist History* 14 (1976): 141–164.

59. Kay N. McElvey, "Early Black Dorchester, 1776–1870: A History of the Struggle of African-Americans in Dorchester County, Maryland, to be Free to Make Their Own Choices" (Ed.D. diss., University of Maryland, 1990), 122–123; and *Minutes of the Annual Conferences*, 1: 15.

60. McElvey, "Early Black Dorchester," 125–127. Methodists in other regions also freed their slaves. In Georgia, the Methodist preachers Tobias Gibson and Alexander Talley freed their slaves in 1799 and 1811, respectively. Owen, "Sanctity, Slavery, and Segregation," 56 and 106.

61. Gatch, *Sketch*, 92–93; and Connor, *Methodist Trail Blazer*, 150 and 176. In 1790 Gatch also joined the Virginia Society for Promoting the Abolition of Slavery. See Connor, *Methodist Trail Blazer*, 152. On Gatch also see Cushman, *Experimental Divinity*, 123–125; and Albert L. Slager, *Early Methodism in the Miami Valley. Including, a History of the Central Methodist Episcopal Church, Springfield, Ohio . . . 1798–1920* (Springfield, OH: Central Methodist Episcopal Church, [ca. 1920]), 9–14. In much the same manner, soon after their conversions in the early 1800s Jane and James Trimble of Kentucky freed their slaves and then laid plans to move to Ohio. Despite James's death in 1804, Jane and her eight children completed the move to Highland County, Ohio, in 1805, where the family quickly integrated into the local Methodist community and prospered. One of the Trimble sons, Allen, served as governor of Ohio from 1826 to 1830, while another son, William A., won election to the U.S. Senate in 1819. Williams, *Pictures of Early Methodism in Ohio*, 113–123. Another Methodist of this period who freed slaves was Robertson Gannaway. In 1834 Gannaway took 11 former slaves from eastern Tennessee to Illinois to set them at liberty in a free state. Gannaway, "Autobiography."

62. Sweet, *Religion on the American Frontier*, vol. 4, *Methodists*, 152, 160, and 171. Also see pp. 159, 172, 175, 178, 184–185, 186, and 196. Despite the opinions and advice of his friends, Dromgoole never left Virginia.

63. Asbury, *Journal and Letters*, 1: 441; *Minutes of the Annual Conferences*, 1: 18.

64. *Minutes of the Annual Conferences*, 1: 20.

65. Mathews, *Slavery and Methodism*, 296–298.

66. Richey, *Early American Methodism*, 59.

67. Evans, "Ideology of Inequality," 258–275; and Sherman, *History of the Discipline*, 115–119. Also see Reginald F. Hildebrand, "Methodist Episcopal Policy on the Ordination of Black Ministers, 1784–1864," *Methodist History* 20 (1982): 124–142.

68. Methodist Episcopal Church, Accomack, Virginia, circuit quarterly meeting conference journal, minutes for June 4–5, 1814.

69. Methodist Episcopal Church, Madison, Kentucky, circuit quarterly meeting conference minutes, pp. 8–9. The rules regarding slavery in use on the Madison circuit during this period were apparently written or approved by William McKendree in 1812 for the Ohio annual conference. The February 17, 1813, Madison circuit minutes include a copy of the Ohio rules. They read as follows:

No member of our society shall purchase a slave except in cases of mercy or humanity to the Slave purchased. And if he purchase a Slave he shall state to the next ensuing Quarterly meeting Conference the number of years he thinks the Slave should serve as a Compensation for the price paid, and if the Quarterly meeting Conference thinks the time too long, they shall proceed and fix the time, and the member who has purchased shall immediately after the determination execute a Legal Instrument of manumission of such Slave at the expiration of the time determined by the Quarterly meeting Conference, as the Laws of the State will admit. And in default of his executing such Instrument of manumission or on his refusing to submit his case to the judgment of the quarterly meeting Conference[,] he shall be excluded [from] the Society[,] provided also that in case of a female slave it shall be inserted in the Instrument of manumission (If the Laws of the State will admit) that all her Children born during the time of her servitude shall be free at the age of twenty one, if the Laws will admit so early a manumission and if not at such time as the laws will admit. And if any member of Society shall sell a slave except at the request of the slave to prevent separation in families[,] he shall be excluded [from] the Society. Provided nevertheless that if any member of our Society shall think it necessary on any other occasion to sell a slave[,] he shall apply to the preacher who has the Charge of the Circuit whose duty it shall be to appoint a Committee of three members of our Society [who are] not slave holders to judge whether such sale be propper and the person applying shall abide by their determination or be excluded [from] the Society.

The Madison quarterly meeting conference officially adopted these rules on February 1, 1817.

70. Methodist Episcopal Church, Madison circuit minutes, 12.

71. Methodist Episcopal Church, Madison circuit minutes, 11–12, 14, 16, and 19.

72. This was far longer than the maximum of seven years she would have been required to serve under the 1784 rules. On the development of slavery in Kentucky and along the western frontier during this period, see Allan Kulikoff, "Uprooted Peoples: Black Migrants in the Age of the American Revolution 1790–1820," in *Slavery and Freedom in the Age of the American Revolution*, ed. Berlin and Hoffman, 143–171.

73. Methodist Episcopal Church, Accomack, Virginia, circuit quarterly meeting conference journal.

74. McElvey, "Early Black Dorchester," 197–198.

75. On this point, see Philip D. Morgan, "Black Society in the Lowcountry 1760–1810," in *Slavery and Freedom in the Age of the American Revolution*, ed. Berlin and Hoffman, 83–141.

76. On Gabriel's rebellion, see Mullin, *Flight and Rebellion*, 140–163.

77. Asbury, *Journal and Letters*, 2: 266 and 2: 376 Phoebus, *Beams of Light*, 328–333; Williams, *Garden of Methodism*, 162; and Evans, "Ideology of Inequality," 275–277. Dougherty may have been assaulted because he had been teaching African American children. See Asbury, *Journal and Letters* 2: 266, n. 141.

78. Jenkins, *Experience*, 95–103. On the opposition of Virginia Methodists to the antislavery rules, see Armour, "Opposition to the Methodist Church in Virginia," 82–98. On opposition to the antislavery rules in Georgia, see Owen, "Sanctity, Slavery, and Segregation," chaps. 1 and 2. On the reaction of southern Methodists to the 1800 address, also see Henry Bascom, *Methodism and Slavery* (Frankfurt, KY: Hodges, Todd and Pruett, 1845), 14. R. N. Price argues that in eastern Tennessee, Methodism's antislavery rules led directly to a drop in membership during the 1790s, especially among "the wealthier and more influential classes." "The subsequent modification of the atti-

tude of the Methodist preachers to the question of domestic slavery," opines Price, "gave them toleration and influence with the property holders of the country." Price, *Holston Methodism*, 1: 285–286.

79. Asbury, *Journal and Letters*, 2: 281 and 2: 283. After 1785, Methodist abolitionism became increasingly unpopular throughout the South. For example, the Maryland Society for Promoting the Abolition of Slavery, which a number of Methodists joined, was forced to disband in 1798, less than 10 years after its inception, because of an increasingly hostile political climate. See Steffen, *Mechanics of Baltimore*, 268–269; and Bilhartz, *Urban Religion*, 101.

80. Thomas Lyell to Daniel Hitt, January 13, 1794, letter no. 101, "Letters to Daniel Hitt."

81. Strickland, *Life of Jacob Gruber*, 130–143.

82. Strickland, *Life of Jacob Gruber*, 146–256.

83. In 1829, for example, William Capers launched the first of the Methodist plantation missions in the South Carolina Conference with the backing of Charles Cotesworth Pinckney. To obtain his backing, Capers had assured Pinckney that only preachers "deemed competent and safe" would be sent to the missions. By 1844, southern Methodist missionaries were ministering to over 22,000 slave members and preaching to thousands more. Southern Methodists like Capers justified their alliance with slaveholders as the only means available for maintaining access to large numbers of southern slaves. By the 1840s this was the dominant view of southern white Methodists. Not surprisingly, after the Methodist Episcopal Church split in 1844 Capers was elected a bishop of the newly organized Methodist Episcopal Church, South. Capers, "Autobiography," 292; Sylvia R. Frey, *Water from the Rock: Black Resistance in a Revolutionary Age* (Princeton: Princeton University Press, 1991), 281–283; Mathews, *Slavery and Methodism*, 62–87; and Harmon L. Smith, "William Capers and William A. Smith: Neglected Advocates of the Pro-Slavery Moral Argument," *Methodist History* 3 (October 1964): 23–32. On the plantation missions, also see Raboteau, *Slave Religion*, 152–180. When the itinerant Joseph Travis began preaching to slaves in New Orleans in 1836 his sermons were initially monitored by a "Committee of Vigilance." According to Travis, the committee quickly concluded that "there was no danger of my instigating the negroes to rebellion." Travis, *Autobiography*, 164.

84. Capers, "Autobiography," 216; and Owen, "Sanctity, Slavery, and Segregation," 109.

85. Frederick Douglass, *Narrative of the Life of Frederick Douglass, an American Slave*, ed. Houston A. Baker, Jr. (Anti-Slavery Office, 1845; reprint, New York: Penguin Books, 1986), 97 and 117.

86. Allen, *Experience*, 16–17, and 29; and Raboteau, *Fire in the Bones*, 96.

87. On the movement toward independent African American Methodist churches in the early nineteenth century, see Baldwin, *"Invisible" Strands in African Methodism*, 1–51; Carol V. R. George, *Segregated Sabbaths: Richard Allen and the Emergence of Independent Black Churches 1760–1840* (New York: Oxford University Press, 1973); Richardson, *Dark Salvation*, 62–147; Milton C. Sernett, *Black Religion and American Evangelicalism: White Protestants, Plantation Missions, and the Flowering of Negro Christianity 1787–1865* (Metuchen, NJ: Scarecrow Press, 1975); Charles H. Wesley, *Richard Allen: Apostle of Freedom* (Washington, DC: Associated Publishers, 1935); and Gary Nash, *Forging Freedom: The Formation of Philadelphia's Black Community, 1720–1840* (Cambridge: Harvard University Press, 1988), 67–266. On the early history of the AME Zion church in New York City, see Christopher Rush, *A Short Account of the Rise and Progress of the*

African Methodist Episcopal Church in America (New York: Published by the Author, 1843). A very good article-length analysis that synthesizes much of the earlier work on this topic is Will B. Gravely's, "Rise of the African Churches in America (1786–1822): Re-examining the Contexts," *Journal of Religious Thought* 41 (Spring-Summer 1984): 58–73. On Daniel Coker and the African Methodist Episcopal Church in Baltimore, see Phillips, "'Negroes and Other Slaves,'" 165–212. In Baltimore, writes Phillips, African-American churches, especially Methodist churches, "quickly became the social, political, economic, educational, and even cultural centers of the Baltimore black community" (p. 166).

88. Bilhartz, *Urban Religion*, 176, n. 19; Coker, *Dialogue*, 41; McElvey, "Early Black Dorchester," 267 and 357; and Richardson, *Dark Salvation*, 148–156. The complete breakdown of the churches Coker lists is: two Methodist churches in Philadelphia, two in Baltimore, and one each in New York; Long Island; Salem, New Jersey; West Chester, Pennsylvania; Wilmington, Delaware; Annapolis, Maryland; and Charleston, South Carolina; one Protestant (Episcopal) church in Philadelphia; one Baptist church in New York and one in Boston; and one Presbyterian church in New York. By 1815 nearly half of all Baltimore Methodists were African Americans. Christopher W. Phillips, "'Negroes and Other Slaves': The African American Community of Baltimore, 1790–1860" (Ph.D. diss., University of Georgia, 1992), 177. On the formation of African-American Baptist congregations and subcongregations, see Sobel, *Trabelin' On*, 201–247; and Lindman, "World of Baptists," 168–203. In this regard Lindman focuses mainly on Virginia, while Sobel deals with Virginia and points south.

89. In part, this was probably because most of Asbury's first years in America were spent in the North, along the eastern seaboard, where the practice of slavery was not as pervasive, and perhaps not as obviously brutal, as it was in the South.

90. Miles M. Fisher, *Negro Slave Songs in the United States* (Ithaca, NY: Cornell University Press, 1953), 178.

91. Washington did not sign, though Coke and Asbury were nevertheless encouraged by his response. Asbury, *Letters and Journal*, 1: 25 and 1: 489.

92. Asbury, *Journal and Letters*, 1: 355 and 1: 442; and Evans, "Ideology of Inequality," 209.

93. Smith, *Recollections*, 189.

94. Rankin, "Diary," 215.

95. "Eighteenth Century Slaves as Advertised by Their Masters," 179.

96. The Ridgely's Northampton iron works likewise employed slaves. On the Goughs, Ridgelys, and Dorseys, see Edith Rossiter Bevan, "Perry Hall: Country Seat of the Gough and Carroll Families," *Maryland Historical Magazine* 45 (1950): 33–46; Steffen, *Mechanics of Baltimore*, 270–272; and Evans, "Ideology of Inequality," 148–152.

97. Ware, *Sketches*, 247.

98. Jenkins, *Experience*, 142. Also see Travis, *Autobiography*, 95.

99. Evans, "Ideology of Inequality," 283–286; Mathews, *Slavery and Methodism*, 26 and 300–302; and Sherman, *History of the Discipline*, 115–119.

100. Asbury, *Journal and Letters*, 2: 151 and 2: 591.

101. Bond, "Anecdotes of Bishop Asbury"; and Robert J. Bull, "John Wesley Bond's Reminiscences of Francis Asbury," *Methodist History* 4 (1965): 3–32.

102. Bascom, *Methodism and Slavery*, 6. For a very perceptive article-length analysis of the shifting stance of both Francis Asbury and the American Methodist movement as a whole on the issue of emancipation, see David H. Bradley, "Francis Asbury and the Development of African Churches in America," *Methodist History* 10 (October

1971): 3–29. Some pro-slavery southerners even concluded that Asbury supported their cause. Writing in 1856, the itinerant Joseph Travis asserted that, "In all the conversational and epistolary intercourse that I have had with Bishop Asbury, not one item was ever even hinted to me in favor of Abolition from the good old man." Travis, *Autobiography*, 95.

103. Jacob Young, *Autobiography*, 475.

CHAPTER 7

1. Surprisingly little has been written about women, gender, and early American Methodism. Exceptions include Catherine Brekus's interpretation of Methodist female preachers in "'Let Your Women Keep Silence in the Churches': Female Preaching and Evangelical Religion in America, 1740–1845" (Ph.D. diss., Yale University, 1993); and a chapter of Doris E. Andrews's dissertation that examines women and Methodism in New York, Philadelphia, and Baltimore, 1770–1800. See Andrews, "Popular Religion," 164–217. Works that deal at least in part with women and religion in the antebellum period, but which are largely silent on Methodist women in this period, include: Ruth H. Bloch, "American Feminine Ideals in Transition: The Rise of the Moral Mother, 1785–1815," *Feminist Studies* 4 (June 1978): 101–126; Nancy Cott, "Young Women in the Second Great Awakening in New England," *Feminist Studies* 3 (1976–77): 15–29; Nancy Cott, *The Bonds of Womanhood: "Women's Sphere" in New England, 1780–1835* (New Haven: Yale University Press, 1977); Nancy A. Hardesty, *Women Called to Witness: Evangelical Feminism in the 19th Century* (Nashville: Abingdon Press, 1984); Nancy A. Hewitt, "The Perimeters of Women's Power in American Religion," in *The Evangelical Tradition in America*, ed. Leonard I. Sweet (Macon, GA: Mercer University Press, 1984), 233–256; Rosemary S. Keller, "Women and the Nature of Ministry in the United Methodist Tradition," *Methodist History* 22 (January 1984): 99–114; Donald G. Mathews, "Women's History/Everyone's History," in *Women in New Worlds*, vol. 1, ed. Hilah F. Thomas and Rosemary Skinner Keller (Nashville: Abingdon Press, 1981), 29–47; Frederick A. Norwood, "Expanding Horizons: Women in the Methodist Movement," in *Triumph Over Silence: Women in Protestant History*, ed. Richard L. Greaves (Westport, CT: Greenwood Press, 1985), 151–172; Mary P. Ryan, "A Women's Awakening: Evangelical Religion and the Families of Utica, New York, 1800–1840" in *Women in American Religion*, ed. Janet Wilson James (Philadelphia: University of Pennsylvania Press, 1976), 89–110; Carroll Smith-Rosenberg, "Women and Religious Revivals: Anti-Ritualism, Liminality, and the Emergence of the American Bourgeoisie," in Sweet, *Evangelical Tradition in America*, 199–232; and Barbara Welter, "The Feminization of American Religion: 1800–1860," in *Clio's Consciousness Raised: New Perspectives on the History of Women*, ed. Mary S. Hartman and Lois Banner (New York: Harper and Row, 1974), 137–157. Volume 1 of *Women in New Worlds*, edited by Thomas and Keller, contains 20 articles on women in the Methodist tradition, but none focuses primarily on American Methodist women before 1840. In calling for a history of women which no longer stresses their "marginality," Linda Kerber has recently written that "The great set-pieces of the history of religion in the early republic . . . have yet to be explored fully for what they can tell us of the involvement of women, the impact on women, and the renegotiation of relations between the sexes in various religious contexts." Among these "set-pieces" Kerber includes Methodism. Linda K. Kerber et al., "Beyond Roles, Beyond Spheres: Thinking about Gender in the Early Republic," *William and Mary Quarterly* 46 (July 1989): 565–585. Ken Rowe and Kristen D. Turner have both

edited valuable bibliographies on Methodist women. See Kenneth E. Rowe, *Methodist Women: A Guide to the Literature* (Lake Junaluska, NC: The General Commission on Archives and History, the United Methodist Church, 1980); and Kristen D. Turner, *A Guide to Materials on Women in the United Methodist Church Archives* (Madison, NJ: General Commission on Archives and History, The United Methodist Church, 1995).

2. Andrews, "Popular Religion," 171. On the proportion of women in Presbyterian and Baptist churches in Utica, New York 1800–1840, see Mary Ryan, "A Women's Awakening." On the numerical dominance of Baptist women in Pennsylvania and Virginia during the revolutionary period, see Lindman, "World of Baptists," 110–119. Also see Stout and Brekus, "Declension, Gender, and the 'New Religious History' "; and Terry D. Bilhartz, "Sex and the Second Great Awakening: The Feminization of American Religion Reconsidered," in *Belief and Behavior*, ed. Vandermeer and Swierenga, 117–135. Bilhartz argues that the proportion of female members in Baltimore's evangelical churches declined during the Second Great Awakening, though women still remained a majority in these churches. The Methodists were the most successful group in Baltimore in terms of recruiting male members during the early nineteenth century, according to Bilhartz. As Ann Braude has recently argued, the fact that women have always constituted the majority of participants in religious activities and institutions in America has seldom been adequately acknowledged or dealt with as a central theme of American religious history. See Ann Braude, "Women's History *Is* American Religious History," in *Retelling U.S. Religious History*, ed. Thomas A. Tweed (Berkeley: University of California Press, 1997), 87–107.

3. Malmgreen, "Domestic Discords." Also see Hempton and Hill, *Evangelical Protestantism in Ulster*, 129–142.

4. On the emergence of the "Republican Mother" in the early republic, see Kerber, *Women of the Republic*, 269–288. On the Methodist appropriation of this ideology, see Schneider, *The Way of the Cross Leads Home*, esp. chap. 5.

5. Lori D. Ginzberg, *Women and the Work of Benevolence: Morality, Politics, and Class in the Nineteenth-Century United States* (New Haven: Yale University Press, 1990), esp. chap. 1; Jeanne Boydston, *Home and Work: Housework, Wages, and the Ideology of Labor in the Early Republic* (New York: Oxford University Press, 1990), esp. chap. 2; and Mary P. Ryan, *Cradle of the Middle Class: The Family in Oneida County, New York, 1790–1865* (Cambridge: Cambridge University Press, 1981), 1–59.

6. Elizabeth Muir, "Petticoats in the Pulpit: Early Nineteenth Century Methodist Women Preachers in Upper Canada" (Ph.D. diss., McGill University, Montreal, 1989), 119.

7. Louis Billington, "'Female Laborers in the Church': Women Preachers in the Northeastern United States, 1790–1840," *Journal of American Studies* 19 (1985): 369–394. On female preachers in the Christian church during this period, see Hatch *Democratization*, 78–80. For an impassioned critique of Hatch, see Paul E. Johnson, "Democracy, Patriarchy, and American Revivals, 1780–1830," *Journal of Social History* 24 (1991): 843–849.

8. Andrews, *Sisters of the Spirit*, 6.

9. Lee, *Life*, 36.

10. Brekus, "'Let Your Women Keep Silence,' " 217.

11. Littlejohn, "Journal," 59 and 71.

12. Abbott, *Experience*, 105. This episode probably took place in the late 1780s or 1790s. Many of the events in Abbott's autobiography are difficult to date.

13. Brunson, *Western Pioneer*, 226.

14. Boehm, *Reminiscences*, 400. Joanna Livingston (1722–1808) was the daughter of Gilbert and Cornelia (Beekman) Livingston. Pierre Van Cortlandt (1721–1814) was lieutenant governor of New York under George Clinton from 1777 to 1795. During the revolutionary era both Pierre and Joanna became sympathetic toward Methodism. Asbury stopped at their home as early as August 1792, and the couple donated land for a Methodist chapel and cemetery in Croton that was in use by 1795. Pierre also authorized and attended a yearly camp meeting on his lands and provided for the manumission of his six slaves (a married couple, their daughter, two adult females and another child) in his will. Jacob Judd, ed., *Correspondence of the Van Cortlandt Family of Cortlandt Manor 1784–1800*, vol. 2 (Tarrytown, NY: Sleepy Hollow Restorations, 1977), xxxi-lv; and Asbury, *Journal and Letters*, 1: 727; 2: 62, 196, 354 and 674; and 3: 161–163.

15. Quoted in Schantz, "Piety in Providence," 92.

16. Dan Young, *Autobiography*, 124–125; *Minutes of the Annual Conferences*, 1: 122. For other examples of early Methodist women exhorting, see Jenkins, *Experience*, 69; and Woolsey, *Supernumerary*, 134.

17. Fanny Newell, *Memoirs*, 39.

18. Fanny Newell, *Memoirs*, 57. Asbury records this meeting in his journal, but not Newell's exhortation. Asbury, *Journal and Letters*, 2: 606.

19. Lee, *Life*, 44–45.

20. Fanny Newell, *Memoirs*, 84.

21. Fanny Newell, *Memoirs*, 166 and 135.

22. The scripture passage is John 4: 29.

23. Ebenezer Newell, *Life*, 138–140, 149, 184–185.

24. Born in North Yarmouth, Maine, in 1781, Caldwell joined the Methodists shortly before her conversion at age 17. Following her marriage and the birth of several children, Caldwell began to feel an irresistible call to speak in public, writing that "At times His word has been as fire shut up in my bones." Caldwell, *Walking with God*, 49.

25. For a related discussion regarding black Baptist women of the late nineteenth and early twentieth century, see Evelyn Brooks Higginbotham, *Righteous Discontent: The Women's Movement in the Black Baptist Church 1880–1920* (Cambridge, MA: Harvard University Press, 1993), 137.

26. Evelyn Brooks Higginbotham comes to a similar conclusion in her study of black Baptist women. "Research on women preachers, while of great value," writes Higginbotham, "does not capture the more representative role of the majority of women church members. If taken alone, such discussion continues to render women's role as marginal." Higginbotham, *Righteous Discontent*, 2.

27. Laurel Thatcher Ulrich, *Good Wives: Image and Reality in the Lives of Women in Northern New England 1650–1750* (New York: Vintage, 1980), 35–50. A similar pattern prevailed in England during the first half of the nineteenth century. See Hempton, *Religion and Political Culture*, 38–48.

28. George Coles, *Heroines of Methodism; or, Pen and Ink Sketches of the Mothers and Daughters of the Church* (New York: Carlton & Lanahan, 1869), 194–195.

29. Slager, *Early Methodism in the Miami Valley*, 16–21. Mrs. Smallwood's full name is not given. Other women who reportedly were instrumental in establishing Methodism in their locality include Mrs. Zane, wife of the founder of Zanesville, Ohio; Mrs. Parrott, who opened her home for meetings in Richmond, Virginia; Charity Hendershott (1756–1833) of Kentucky and later Ohio; Jane Trimble (1755–1849), whose son William became a U.S. senator from Ohio and whose son Allen became governor of

Ohio; Mrs. Peckett of Bradford, Vermont; Mary Wells of New England; and Aunt Hester, an African-American slave in Attakapas, Louisiana. On Zane and Parrott, see Boehm, *Reminiscences*, 197 and 224; on Hendershott and Trimble, see Williams, *Pictures*, 105–108 and 113–123; on Peckett, Wells, and Hester, see Coles, *Heroines*, 132, 136–141. The first class meeting in Providence, Rhode Island, was composed of four women and one man, and women continued to play a key role in Methodism's early history in Providence. W. McDonald, *History of Methodism in Providence, Rhode Island, From Its Introduction in 1787 to 1867* (Boston: Phipps and Pride, 1868), 23–45.

30. Pilmore, *Journal*, 133.

31. Mary Bradley, *Narrative*, 209.

32. Smith, *Recollections*, 252. Shaeffer's full name is not given in this account.

33. Smith, *Recollections*, 109; and *Minutes of the Annual Conferences*, 1: 111; Williams, *Pictures*, 108–113; Hibbard, *Memoirs*, 237; Ware, *Sketches*, 120; and Cartwright, *Autobiography*, 517.

34. T. Spicer, *Christian Advocate and Journal*, November 23, 1838, p. 53; quoted in Johnson, "Development of the Love Feast," 75.

35. Williams, *Pictures*, 98–99.

36. Braude, "Women's History," 97 and 99; Brooks, *Life and Times*, 21–22. Also see Laurel Thatcher Ulrich, *A Midwife's Tale: The Life of Martha Ballard Based on Her Diary 1785–1812* (New York: Vintage Books, 1990), 96.

37. Garrettson, *American Methodist Pioneer*, 82–83.

38. Littlejohn, "Journal," 105.

39. Jacob Young, *Autobiography*, 123–124.

40. This seems to have been as true for African-American women as for white women. For example, see Benjamin T. Tanner's description of the role of women in African American Methodism in *An Apology for African Methodism*, 135–139. The itinerant John Brooks credits "sister Babb" with giving a public exhortation on the Lebanon, Tennessee circuit in 1820 which made it possible for him to settle a two-year schism in the Hickory Ridge society. Brooks, *Life and Times*, 54–57.

41. Gatch, *Sketch*, 127–128. On other Methodist women noted for their hospitality, including Esther Halsted of New Rochelle, New York, Elizabeth Harper of Long Island, Elizabeth Reckhou and Rosanna Swope of New Jersey, Ann Grice of New York City, and Elizabeth Rice of the Wyoming Valley, see Coles, *Heroines*, 176–179, 188, and 201–204.

42. Jacob Young, *Autobiography*, 104 and 144.

43. Much the same was true of English Methodism between 1750 and 1830. See Malmgreen, "Domestic Discord," 58; and Hempton and Hill, *Evangelical Protestantism in Ulster*, 133.

44. Travis, *Autobiography*, 35.

45. Mary Withey kept the Columbia Hotel in Chester, Pennsylvania. Boehm says that George Washington often lodged there. Asbury first stayed at the Columbia in 1772, but Boardman and Pilmore had been there before him. Asbury, *Journal and Letters*, 1: 26, 2: 235, and 2: 636; and Boehm, *Reminiscences*, 283–284. Another Methodist widow was said to have kept a "spliced long bed" on which as many as 20 preachers could sleep at one time. Wolcott, *Wilderness Rider*, 52–53.

46. Francis Asbury to Ann Willis, September 7, 1812, Asbury, *Journal and Letters*, 3: 465. Ann Willis lived at Pipe Creek, Maryland. On Willis, see Ayres, *Methodist Heroes*, 26–28.

47. Quinn, *Sketches*, 294.

48. Mary Ryan reaches a similar conclusion in her study of antebellum women's networks in Utica, New York. In particular, the women of Utica used their "power and freedom" to "lay the groundwork for the Victorian sexual code which placed particular stock in the purity of females." Mary P. Ryan, "The Power of Women's Networks," in *Sex and Class in Women's History*, ed. Judith L. Newton, Mary P. Ryan, and Judith R. Walkowitz (London: Routledge and Kegan Paul, 1983), 167–186.

49. Boehm, *Reminiscences*, 60–61; and Williams, *Garden of Methodism*, 74 and 110.

50. Smith, *Experience*, 30–31.

51. Abbott, *Experience*, 95–96; and Conrad, "Samuel White." Exactly when this encounter took place is unclear.

52. This may well have been the case with the wealthy John Mills and his wife in New York City during the early nineteenth century. Mills remained a Presbyterian while his wife joined the John Street Methodist church. See Boehm, *Reminiscences*, 234. Mary Ryan describes a similar phenomenon in Utica, New York, 1800–1840. Ryan, "A Women's Awakening."

53. Ware, *Sketches*, 93.

54. Asbury, *Journal and Letters*, 2: 41 (February 5, 1795); Rankin, *Ambivalent Churchmen and Evangelical Churchwomen*, 27–48.

55. Colbert identifies these women as the widows Ireland, Ross, French, Russel[l], Miles (Niles?), Garner (Gurner?), Ridgley, Baden, Tawnyhill, Watkins, Howard, Waten, Waters, Hood, Lawson, Hanson, Stephenson, Bond, and Wright, along with Sarah Childs, Mary Bowen, Ph[o]ebe Greenfield, "Sister" Rush, and Mrs. Ewing. Colbert, "Journal," 1: 1–66.

56. Smith, *Recollections*, 244–246. Sarah Roszel was the mother of Stephen G. Roszel (1770–1841), who entered the itinerancy in 1789 and was a prominent member of the Baltimore Conference. Simpson, *Cyclopedia*, 768.

57. Robert E. Pattison, "The Life and Character of Richard Bassett," *Papers of the Historical Society of Delaware* 29 (1900): 1–19; and Conrad, "Samuel White." Bassett was a U.S. senator from 1789 to 1793, and subsequently governor of Delaware and a U.S. judge.

58. Thomas L. Preston, *A Sketch of Mrs. Elizabeth Russell. Wife of General William Campbell, and Sister of Patrick Henry* (Nashville: Publishing House of the M.E. Church, South, 1888); Tevis, *Sixty Years in a School-Room*, 200–202, 265, 270–271; Douglas Summers Brown, "Elizabeth Henry Campbell Russell: Patroness of Early Methodism in the Highlands of Virginia," *Virginia Cavalcade* 30 (1980): 110–117; and Elva Runyon, "Madam Russell, Methodist Saint" (M.A. Thesis, University of Virginia, 1941), 7–8. Preston and Tevis appear to be the two main primary sources from which all other descriptions of Elizabeth Russell are drawn. Preston was Russell's grandson, and Tevis knew Russell in the 1820s.

59. Preston, *Sketch*, 11–13; Laura Copenhaver, "Madame Russell," *Scribner's Magazine* 83 (June 1928): 727–732.

60. Preston, *Sketch*, 33; Copenhaver, "Madame Russell;" and Runyon, "Madam Russell," 11 and 14.

61. Sarah Henry's will is given in the *William and Mary College Quarterly* series 2, vol. 8 (1928): 117–118.

62. This is the present site of Saltville, Virginia. Runyon, "Madam Russell," 16 and 26–27.

63. Brown, "Elizabeth Russell," 113. Also see Asbury, *Journal and Letters*, 1: 570–572; Bennett, *Memorials of Methodism in Virginia*, 268–270; and Price, *Holston Methodism*, 1: 126–127.

64. Preston, *Sketch*, 21–22; and Runyon, "Madam Russell," 29–30.

65. Preston, *Sketch*, 26; and Copenhaver, "Madame Russell."

66. Brown, "Elizabeth Russell," 113; Runyon, "Madam Russell," 42–44.

67. Elizabeth Russell to Stith Mead, February 21, 1794, "Letter Book of Rev. Stith Mead 1793–1795," Virginia Historical Society Collection. I am indebted to Jerry W. Catron of Saltville, Virginia, for this reference.

68. Tradition has it that Elizabeth treasured an old beaver hat that Asbury discarded when she gave him a new one, insisting on wearing it while gardening or walking about her land.

69. Preston, *Sketch*, 31–34; Tevis, *Sixty Years*, 201; Runyon, "Madam Russell," 52 and 56; and Price, *Holston Methodism*, 1: 130–134.

70. Jacob Young, *Autobiography*, 128–129.

71. Lobody, "Lost in the Ocean of Love," quotation from p. 34; and Brandt, *American Aristocracy*, 82 and 146. Also see Karen Oliveto, "The Garrettson Papers" TMs, dated May 6, 1988, Drew University Library, Madison, NJ. Also on the Livingstons, see Cynthia A. Kierner, *Traders and Gentlefolk: The Livingstons of New York, 1675–1790* (Ithaca: Cornell University Press, 1992). On the Beekmans, see Philip L. White, *The Beekmans of New York in Politics and Commerce 1647–1877* (New York: New-York Historical Society, 1956). Among the hagiographies of Catherine Livingston Garrettson is an extended account in Charles Wesley Buoy's *Representative Women of Methodism* (New York: Hunt & Eaton, 1893), 243–333.

72. Garrettson, untitled autobiography, 3. Catherine's love for her father in particular knew no bounds: "My father I ever looked upon as one of the best men in the world, and always felt a reverence for him which he rather inspired than exacted" (p. 1).

73. Garrettson, autobiography, 3; Brandt, *American Aristocracy*, 3, 92, 117, and 134; Lobody, "Lost in the Ocean of Love," 37 and 41.

74. Garrettson, autobiography, 3.

75. Ibid., 8.

76. Lobody, "Lost in the Ocean of Love," 52–65, esp. p. 54.

77. Lobody, "Lost in the Ocean of Love," 66.

78. Marilyn H. Pettit, "Women, Sunday Schools, and Politics: Early National New York City, 1797–1827" (Ph.D. diss., New York University, 1991), 185. Garrettson and other Methodist women, including Mary Morgan Mason, also eagerly participated in the founding of Sunday schools and other charitable and populist educational organizations in New York City beginning in the late 1790s. These exclusively female associations were specifically designed to help other women in need. Sunday schools in particular offered the only schooling available for many poor African-American and white women and girls. Pettit, "Women, Sunday Schools, and Politics," 18 and 24. On Mary Mason, see pp. 157–198 in Pettit; Elizabeth Mason North, *Consecrated Talents: or, The Life of Mrs. Mary W. Mason with an Introduction by Bishop Janes* (New York: Carlton & Lanahan, 1870; reprint, New York: Garland Publishing, 1987); and Susan E. Warrick, " 'She Diligently Followed Every Good Work': Mary Mason and the New York Female Missionary Society" *Methodist History*, 34:4 (July 1996):214–229.

79. Lobody, "Lost in the Ocean of Love," 67; Brandt, *American Aristocracy*, 146; Warrick, " 'She Diligently Followed Every Good Work,' " 214. Another good example here would be Elizabeth Lyon Roe (b. 1805). Like Russell and Garrettson, Roe grew up among society's elite, dressing "in the richest of apparel" and moving "in the most fashionable circles." Her maternal grandfather, Thomas Chittenden, was the first governor of Vermont, and her father, Matthew Lyon, led a much storied career in Vermont

and Kentucky politics and business. The Lyon clan moved to Kentucky in 1801, where Matthew was a successful land speculator, slave owner, and congressional representative from 1802 to 1811. Elizabeth greatly admired both her parents and seemed destined for a life of luxury and ease until she was awakened at a camp meeting under the preaching of "Uncle" William Barnet, also known as the "patent bellows" for his vociferous three-hour sermons. Both Roe and her mother Beulah Lyon became ardent Methodists. Roe ceased wearing jewelry, starting combing her hair "down plain," gave up reading novels for Baxter's *Call to the Unconverted* and Fletcher's *Appeal,* and became a regular at class meetings, circuit preaching, quarterly meetings, and camp meetings. In 1821 she married John Roe, a poor but ambitious Methodist physician and sometime farmer from Pennsylvania. Together they spent much of the remainder of their days on the Illinois frontier, their lives revolving around church functions. Elizabeth A. Roe, *Recollections of Frontier Life* (Rockford, IL: Gazette Publishing House, 1885; reprint, New York: Arno Press, 1980), 34–37, 42–43, 46, and 49–54.

80. Welter, "Feminization of American Religion"; and Christine Bolt, *The Women's Movements in the United States and Britain from the 1790s to the 1920s* (Amherst: University of Massachusetts Press, 1993), 32–35.

81. Susan Juster, *Disorderly Women: Sexual Politics & Evangelicalism in Revolutionary New England* (Ithaca: Cornell University Press, 1994). The quotations are from pp. 11 and 112. Juster's study is based on material from 20 New England Baptist churches (p. 148), so her conclusions are less reliable for other groups. For example, her contention that the Methodist itinerancy "emphasized the brotherhood of saints over and against the corrupting influence of women and family" (p. 141) is apparently based only on a reading of secondary sources. On Baptist women, also see Lindman, "A World of Baptists," 140–167. On the broader legal and political inconsistencies between republican rhetoric and the social position of women in the early republic, see Kerber, *Women of the Republic.* A comparison to early Fundamentalist women might also be instructive here. In a recent study of Fundamentalist women involved in public ministry from 1920 to 1950, Michael Hamilton argues that these women had a different array of public ministries open to them than did women in the mainline churches. Though Fundamentalist leaders adhered to a rhetoric of male dominance, the dynamics of the movement's growth during this period opened up a great many public ministry opportunities for women. Fundamentalist women operated as authors, Bible teachers, missionaries, and traveling evangelists, receiving their training at Bible Institutes, and proclaiming their messages at Bible conferences, and through books, magazines and radio programs. Michael S. Hamilton, "Women, Public Ministry, and American Fundamentalism, 1920–1950," *Religion and American Culture* 3 (1993): 171–196.

82. Methodist Episcopal Church, Accomack, Virginia, quarterly meeting conference journal. Bradford and Finney were suspended pending further investigation, though the outcome of their cases does not appear in the journal. The journal entries become less detailed after 1808.

83. Methodist Episcopal Church, Accomack, Virginia, quarterly meeting conference journal, entry for December 1804. Melvin was apparently later readmitted to the church, as his name appears in subsequent records.

84. See chapter 6 for a discussion of these cases.

85. Cumberland, New Jersey, quarterly conference minutes, TMs. Original at the Commission on Archives and History, Southern New Jersey Annual Conference of the United Methodist Church, Pennington, N.J. Entries for December 1816, March 1817, and June 1817.

86. "Book of Records for the Hockhocking Circuit"; Union and Mad River quarterly meeting conference minutes; Paint Creek quarterly meeting conference minutes. On all of these circuits the majority of the disciplinary cases involved only men.

87. Evelyn Brooks Higginbotham reaches a similar conclusion in her study of black Baptist women 1880–1920. She writes that African-American women "accentuated the image of woman as saving force," and "rejected a model of womanhood that was fragile and passive, just as they deplored a type preoccupied with fashion, gossip, or self-indulgence." Much the same could be said of American Methodist women in the early republic. Higginbotham, *Righteous Discontent*, 121.

88. Catherine Brekus makes essentially the same point in her study of female preachers in colonial and antebellum America. For instance, see Brekus, "'Let Your Women Keep Silence,' " 232 and 234.

89. For a related discussion of the overall impact of the rise of gentility on middle-class women of the nineteenth century, see Bushman, *Refinement of America*, 440–446.

90. At least two factors probably lie behind this trend. First, as Methodism grew in respectability and its members became more comfortable in American society, the church became increasingly willing to appropriate the dominate values of American society, including the ideal of a male-dominated leadership. Second, as Andrews notes, the promotion of the class meeting as the foundational unit of American Methodism during the 1780s and 1790s added extra momentum to the drive to bring the classes under male supervision, at least in the cities of the eastern seaboard. Andrews, "Popular Religion," 196–199. There is evidence to suggest, however, that this trend was not all-encompassing, as the example of sister Shaeffer recounted earlier in this chapter indicates.

CHAPTER 8

1. Smith, *Recollections*, 86–88.

2. Bond, "Anecdotes of Asbury."

3. Boehm, *Reminiscences*, 192–193, 255, 354, 410, and 421.

4. Jacob Young, *Autobiography*, 317. John Wesley Bond was born at Fell's Point near Baltimore in 1784. He joined the itinerancy at the Baltimore Annual Conference in 1810, traveling with Asbury from 1814 until the bishop's death in 1816. Bond subsequently returned to circuit preaching, dying of "epidemic fever" in Baltimore in 1819. Bull, "John Wesley Bond's Reminiscences of Francis Asbury."

5. Boehm, *Reminiscences*, 459.

6. Ware, *Sketches*, 83–84.

7. Chase, *Recollections*, 95.

8. Jacob Young, *Autobiography*, 326–327. The bronze monument depicting Asbury astride a horse, located at the intersections of Sixteenth and Mount Pleasant Streets in Washington, D.C., testifies to the esteem with which Asbury was held as late as the 1920s. The monument was dedicated in 1924 with a speech by President Calvin Coolidge. H. K. Carroll, ed. *The Francis Asbury Monument in the National Capital* (n.p.: The Francis Asbury Memorial Association Press of the Methodist Book Concern, 1925).

9. Chase, *Recollections*, 83.

10. Jacob Young, *Autobiography*, 522. "Brunswick," "Jane," and "Fox" were among the names Asbury gave to his horses. Boehm, *Reminiscences*, 448; also p. 335. When forced to use a carriage because of his health, Asbury usually opted for a two-wheeled

sulky, though on occasion he used a four-wheeled wagon. Asbury to Hitt, May 18, 1806, "Letters to Hitt," letter no. 327.

11. Lee Soltow, *Distribution of Wealth and Income in the United States in 1798* (Pittsburgh: University of Pittsburgh Press, 1990), 3–20 and 229–251; Jeffrey G. Williamson and Peter H. Lindert, *American Inequality: A Macroeconomic History* (New York: Academic Press, 1980), 33–46. Other studies which oppose Soltow, arguing that economic inequality increased dramatically during the antebellum period include: Edward Pessen, *Riches, Class, and Power Before the Civil War* (Lexington, MA: D.C. Heath and Co., 1973), 1–45; and Sellers, *Market Revolution*, 237–240.

12. Bruce Laurie, *Working People of Philadelphia, 1800–1850* (Philadelphia: Temple University Press, 1980), 45.

13. On the formation of an American middle class, see Blumin, *Emergence of the Middle Class*, 1–16 and 57–107. Blumin argues that a distinct middle class took shape in the Jacksonian era. While he fails to discuss the impact of religion on this phenomenon, its seems apparent that the Methodists must have been leading figures in this new middle class.

14. Seaman, *Annals of New York Methodism*, 205; *Centennial History of the First Methodist Episcopal Church, Schenectady, New York* (Schenectady: Methodist Episcopal Church, 1907), 25, 55, and 151. The author tells us that "Pews were leased under written contracts and payment of the rentals was rigidly enforced" (p. 71). In 1872 a new church building was constructed at a cost of $85,000 (p. 84). On Methodism in Providence, see McDonald, *History of Methodism in Providence, Rhode Island*, 53 and 66; and Schantz, "Piety in Providence," chap. 4. Pew rents were first introduced among Methodists in Troy, New York, to fund a new church building in 1827. Hillman, *History of Methodism in Troy, N.Y.*, 50.

15. "Had one man[,] 11 wom[en] & 7 dogs," complained Littlejohn in his journal after a meeting near Baltimore in September 1777, "when will the Medsts [Methodists] learn to leave their dogs at home." Littlejohn, "Journal," 71.

16. Goss, *Statistical History*, 187; and Gaustad, *Historical Atlas*, 43.

17. Wright, *Sketches of James Quinn*, 202; Bushman, *Refinement of America*, 346.

18. In 1876 the Methodist Episcopal Church alone, excluding the Methodist Episcopal Church, South, the Methodist Protestant Church, and other Methodist denominations, owned church property valued at more than $80 million. By 1876 in Baltimore there were 43 separate Methodist Episcopal Church buildings valued at more than $1.66 million. In that year in Cincinnati, with a total population of just over 200,000, Methodists could boast 27 churches worth more than $800,000. St. Paul's Methodist Episcopal Church, an elegant gothic structure, was valued at $220,000 alone. Simpson, *Cyclopedia*, 82, 216, 283, 597, and 675. Drawings of some 45 of American Methodism's most impressive churches circa 1878, many built in the gothic style favored by the Congregationalists, Presbyterians, and Episcopalians, are included in Simpson's *Cyclopedia*.

19. Jarratt, *Life*, 181. Another early Methodist school, Bethel Academy near Lexington, Kentucky, suffered a similar fate. Bethel opened in 1794 and closed about a decade later. G. Herbert Livingston, "The Bethel Academy Story," *The Asbury Theological Journal* 49 (Fall 1994): 13–42; and Asbury, *Journal and Letters*, 2: 253 (October 4, 1800).

20. Asbury, *Journal and Letters*, 2: 75 (January 4, 1796). Also see John Abernathy Smith, "Cokesbury College: Kingswood in America," *Methodist History* 28 (1990): 219–236.

21. William Warren Sweet, *Indiana Asbury-DePauw University 1837–1937: A Hundred Years of Higher Education in the Middle West* (New York: Abingdon Press, 1937), 22; Sylvanus Milne Duvall, *The Methodist Episcopal Church and Education Up to 1869* (New York: Teachers College, Columbia University, 1928), 30–34.

22. Duvall, *Methodist Church and Education*, 65–66; Sweet, *Indiana Asbury*, 22–24; David B. Potts, *Wesleyan University 1831–1910: Collegiate Enterprise in New England* (New Haven: Yale University Press, 1992); and Simpson, *Cyclopedia*, 235–236 and 330. As with church buildings, the *Cyclopedia* includes 71 sketches of college buildings and grounds circa 1878, indicating the pride Methodists took in these institutions. On Methodist schools in North Carolina, see John Wesley Sawyer, "The Circuit Rider and His Probable Influence on the Establishment of Methodist Schools in North Carolina" (M.A. Thesis, Wake Forest College, 1943), 29–86.

23. United Methodist Church, "Trends in Membership, 1790–1970," *Research Information Bulletin*, Office on Research, General Council of Ministries, United Methodist Church, Dayton, Ohio, 72 (July 1972): 6.

24. Smith, *Experience*, 97.

25. John Munroe, *Federalist Delaware 1775–1815* (New Brunswick, NJ: Rutgers University Press, 1954), 167.

26. Harold B. Hancock, *A History of Kent County Delaware* (Dover: Kent County Bicentennial Committee, 1976), 25. The complete breakdown was three Baptist, two Episcopalian, three Friends, and three Presbyterian churches. "The people in this country must be either Methodists or nothing," wrote Freeborn Garrettson of central Delaware in 1809. Garrettson, *American Methodist Pioneer*, 318.

27. Munroe, *Federalist Delaware*, 238–241; Conrad, "Samuel White"; and Pattison, "Life of Richard Bassett." Such political divisions remained characteristic of Delaware Methodism throughout the antebellum period. See Todd, *Methodism on the Peninsula*, 125–126. Munroe has also written that Methodism was "the most striking development in the cultural life of Kent and Sussex" counties in the late eighteenth and early nineteenth centuries. Munroe, *Federalist Delaware*, 260.

28. Cayton, *Frontier Republic*, 35; Cayton, "'Separate Interests' and the Nation-State: The Washington Administration and the Origins of Regionalism in the Trans-Appalachian West," *Journal of American History* 79 (June 1992): 39–67.

29. Hibbard, *Memoirs*, 294. Among early histories which celebrate the Methodist experience in Ohio are Williams, *Pictures of Early Methodism in Ohio*; John Marshall Barker, *History of Ohio Methodism: A Study in Social Science* (Cincinnati: Curts & Jennings, 1898); and Sager, *Early Methodism in the Miami Valley*.

30. Dan Young, *Autobiography*, 202.

31. Brunson, *Western Pioneer*, 217–218.

32. Cayton, *Frontier Republic*, 55–59; Jeffrey P. Brown, "Chillicothe's Elite: Leadership in a Frontier Community," *Ohio History* 96 (Summer-Autumn 1987): 140–156. Edward Tiffin was born in Carlisle, England, in 1776, moving to Berkeley County, Virginia, in 1784, where he eventually studied medicine, married Mary Worthington, and was ordained a deacon. A staunch opponent of slavery, Tiffin freed his inherited slaves and in the late 1790s moved west to become part of the Scioto Valley gentry, all the while remaining an ardent Methodist. On Tiffin's medical career, see Linden F. Edwards, "Doctor Edward Tiffin, First Governor of Ohio," *Bulletin of the History of Medicine* 21 (September-October 1947): 811–822.

33. Williams, *Pictures of Early Methodism in Ohio*, 195–214. Also see Cayton, *Frontier Republic*, 106–108.

34. Brunson, *Western Pioneer*, 42–43.

35. Henry Boehm contends that by 1809 Vermont Methodists had the strength to decide at least some state elections. Boehm, *Reminiscences*, 249. On evangelical religion in the Maine hinterland, see Taylor, *Liberty Men*, 2–10, 129–144, and 237. On the Connecticut River valley, see Roth, *Democratic Dilemma*, 55–116.

36. Bonnie Bromberger and Christopher Collier, "Aaron Hunt and the Methodist Fight Against Second Class Citizenship: An Episode in Religious Reform in Jeffersonian Connecticut," *The Connecticut Historical Society Bulletin* 32 (April 1967): 48–50.

37. Schaff, *America*, 137.

38. Richard J. Carwardine, *Evangelicals and Politics in Antebellum America* (New Haven: Yale University Press, 1993), 52. Also see Richard Carwardine, "Methodist Ministers and the Second Party System," in *Rethinking Methodist History*, ed. Richey and Rowe, 134–147.

39. Quoted in Michael H. Harris, "'Spiritual Cakes Upon the Waters': The Church as a Disseminator of the Printed Word on the Ohio Valley Frontier to 1850," in *Getting the Books Out: Papers of the Chicago Conference on the Book in 19th-Century America*, ed. Michael Hackenberg (Washington: Library of Congress, 1987), 98–120.

40. Leland D. Case, "Origins of Methodist Publishing in America," *Papers of the Bibliographic Society of America* 59 (1965): 12–27.

41. Dickins's editions of these works include: Thomas a Kempis, *An Extract of the Christian's Pattern; or, A Treatise of the Imitation of Christ*, ed. John Wesley (Philadelphia: John Dickins, 1789); Methodist Episcopal Church, *A Form of Discipline, for the Ministers, Preachers and Members (Now Comprehending the Principles and Doctrines) of the Methodist Episcopal Church in America* (Philadelphia: John Dickins, 1790); William Law, *An Extract from Mr. Law's Serious Call to a Holy Life, by the Rev. John Wesley* (Philadelphia: John Dickins, 1793); Freeborn Garrettson, *The Experience and Travels of Mr. Freeborn Garrettson, Minister of the Methodist-Episcopal Church in North America* (Philadelphia: John Dickins, 1791); John Wesley, *Primitive Physic: or An Easy and Natural Method of Curing Most Diseases* (Philadelphia: John Dickins, 1789); John Wesley, *Explanatory Notes Upon the New Testament*, vol. 1 [-3] (Philadelphia: John Dickins, 1791); John Wesley, *Thoughts Upon Slavery* (Philadelphia: John Dickins, 1792); Francis Asbury, *An Extract from the Journal of Francis Asbury, Bishop of the Methodist-Episcopal Church in America* (Philadelphia: John Dickins, 1792); and Francis Asbury, *A Pocket Hymn-Book: Designed as a Constant Companion for the Pious* (Philadelphia: John Dickins, 1790).

42. John Dickins to Daniel Hitt, January 21, 1794 and May 9, 1794, letter nos. 102 and 108, "Letters to Daniel Hitt."

43. Scherer, *Ezekiel Cooper*, 97–115; quotation from 103–104. Also see Simpson, *Cyclopedia*, 117–120 and 295–296; and *Minutes of the Annual Conferences*, 1: 79–80. James Penn Pilkington's *The Methodist Publishing House: Volume 1, Beginnings to 1870* (Nashville: Abingdon Press, 1968) is a thorough and indispensable resource on early Methodist publishing. On the years 1783–1798, see pp. 63–116.

44. Pilkington, *Methodist Publishing*, 117–168; and Scherer, *Ezekiel Cooper*, 104–115.

45. Asbury, *Journal and Letters*, 3: 253 (December 23, 1802).

46. Samuel J. Mills and Daniel Smith, *Report of a Missionary Tour Through That Part of the United States Which Lies West of the Allegany Mountains; Performed Under the Direction of the Massachusetts Missionary Society* (Andover: Flagg and Gould, 1815; reprint in *To Win the West: Missionary Viewpoints 1814–1815*, New York: Arno Press, 1972), 49.

47. Margaret R. Waters, Dorothy Riker, and Doris Leistner, comp., *Abstracts of Obituaries in the* Western Christian Advocate *1834–1850* (Indianapolis: Indiana Historical Society, 1988), vii. On the *Methodist Quarterly Review,* begun in 1818 as the *Methodist Magazine,* see Elmer J. O'Brien, "The *Methodist Quarterly Review:* Reflections on a Methodist Periodical," *Methodist History* 25: 2 (1987): 76–90. On the Western Methodist Book Concern in Cincinnati, see Walter Sutton, *The Western Book Trade: Cincinnati as a Nineteenth-Century Publishing and Book-Trade Center* (Columbus: Ohio State University Press, 1961), 150–165. On the overall impact of the religious popular press in the early republic, see Hatch, *Democratization,* 125–133 and 141–146; John Nerone, *The Culture of the Press in the Early Republic: Cincinnati, 1793–1848* (New York: Garland Publishing, 1989),179–227; David Paul Nord, "Systematic Benevolence: Religious Publishing and the Marketplace in Early Nineteenth-Century America," in *Communication and Change,* ed. Sweet, 239–269; and William L. Joyce et al., eds., *Printing and Society in Early America* (Worcester: American Antiquarian Society, 1983), particularly Nathan Hatch's essay on "Elias Smith and the Rise of Religious Journalism in the Early Republic," and Richard D. Brown's essay entitled "From Cohesion to Competition." Nord's essay is excellent, though his contention that the American Tract Society was the first to develop a large-scale colportage system in America, beginning in the 1840s, largely ignores the similar book-hawking network of the Methodist itinerants beginning in the eighteenth century. On Methodism and publishing in New England, see Umbel, "The Making of an American Denomination," 228–258. On the growth and development of publishing in early 19th-century Philadelphia, see Rosalind Remer, "Preachers, Peddlers, and Publishers: Philadelphia's Backcountry Book Trade, 1800–1830," *Journal of the Early Republic* 14:4 (Winter 1994): 497–522.

48. Quoted in Munroe, *Federalist Delaware,* 57.

49. Brooks, *Life and Times,* 42.

50. The concepts of religious free space and latent economic and political potential presented here are largely derived from the work of David Martin in *Tongues of Fire: The Explosion of Protestantism in Latin America* (Oxford: Basil Blackwell, 1990), 1–6. Also see James Demming and Michael Hamilton, "Methodist Revivalism in France, Canada, and the United States," in *Amazing Grace: Evangelicalism in Australia, Britain, Canada and the United States,* ed. George A. Rawlyk and Mark A. Noll (Grand Rapids: Baker Books, 1993), 124–153.

51. James A. Henretta, "Families and Farms: Mentalite in Pre-Industrial America," *William and Mary Quarterly* 35 (1978): 3–32. Also see James A. Henretta, "The Transition to Capitalism in America," in *The Transformation of Early American History: Society, Authority and Ideology,* ed. James A. Henretta, Michael G. Kammen, and Stanley N. Katz (New York: Alfred A. Knopf, 1991), 218–238; and Allan Kulikoff, "The Transition to Capitalism in Rural America," *William and Mary Quarterly* 46 (1989): 120–144.

52. On Baptist respectability, see William G. McLoughlin, *New England Dissent 1630–1883: The Baptists and the Separation of Church and State,* 2 vols. (Cambridge: Harvard University Press, 1971), 2: 1107–1127. On the emergence and influence of rich Methodists in the mid-nineteenth century, see Donald B. Marti, "Rich Methodists: The Rise and Consequences of Lay Philanthropy in the Mid-19th Century," in *Rethinking Methodist History,* ed. Richey and Rowe, 159–166.

53. Paddock, *Memoir,* 6.

54. Asbury, *Journal and Letters,* 3: 488 (August 5, 1813).

55. John Tucker, "Sermon on Jeremiah 18: 6–8"; quoted in Harry S. Stout, *The*

New England Soul: Preaching and Religious Culture in Colonial New England (New York: Oxford University Press, 1986), 249. Also see pp. 77, 108–111, 122, 142–143, 174, and 194–195. Also on the myth and reality of Puritan declension, see Perry Miller, *The New England Mind: From Colony to Province* (Cambridge: Harvard University Press, 1953), book 1; Robert G. Pope, "New England Versus the New England Mind: the Myth of Declension," *Journal of Social History* 3 (1969): 95–108; Gerald F. Moran and Maris A. Vinovskis, "The Puritan Family and Religion: A Critical Reappraisal," *William and Mary Quarterly* 39 (1982): 29–63; and Stout and Brekus, "Declension, Gender, and the 'New Religious History.'"

56. Garrettson, *American Methodist Pioneer*, 30–31. The scripture passage Garrettson quotes is 1 Tim. 5:22.

57. Cartwright, *Autobiography*, 515.

58. Todd, *Methodism on the Peninsula*, 268.

59. Giles, *Pioneer*, 324–325.

60. Quinn, *Sketches*, 183–184.

61. Chase, *Recollections*, 101.

62. Littlejohn, "Journal of John Littlejohn," 144.

63. Hillman, *Methodism in Troy*, 126–127.

64. Chase, *Recollections*, 143.

65. Beauchamp, *Letters*, 94–108.

66. Quinn, *Sketches*, 267.

67. Jacob Young, *Autobiography*, 527.

68. Jenkins, *Experience*, 149–150.

69. Horton, *Narrative*, 137 and 195.

70. Giles, *Pioneer*, 301–302.

71. Cartwright, *Autobiography*, 520.

72. For example, see Janes, *Address to Class-Leaders*, 14–15; Christophers, *Class-Meetings*, 54–62; and Rosser, *Class Meetings*, introduction.

73. Holsclaw, "Demise," 75 and 121. For example, in 1846 in Schenectady, New York, a trustee was expelled from the society but allowed to remain on the church board. "The expelled man continued to act as a trustee for nearly two years, was appointed a member of important committees, and at one meeting was chosen chairman." *Centennial History of the First Methodist Episcopal Church, Schenectady*, 72.

74. Gatch, *Sketch*, 152.

75. Jenkins, *Experience*, 231.

76. Smith, *Recollections*, 229.

77. Hibbard, *Memoirs*, 273–274.

78. Brooks, *Life and Times*, 103–105.

79. Henry Ward Beecher, *The Northern Independent*, September 10, 1857; quoted in Walter W. Benjamin, "The Methodist Episcopal Church in the Postwar Era," in *History of American Methodism*, ed. Bucke, 2: 341.

80. Boehm, *Reminiscences*, 140 and 492. George Foster Pierce (1811–1884), elected bishop of the Methodist Episcopal Church, South in 1854, offers a similar sort of analysis: "If the modern Church has not fallen away from Bible teaching and example and from the experience and practice of primitive Methodism, then I have strangely erred in my conception of what religion was, and is, and ought to be. Culture, worldliness, imperious fashion, an artificial social life, have all come in to modify and repress the normal action of a simple, hearty earnest piety. . . . A pure unadulterated revival of pure religion, free, courageous, independent, even defiant of the criticisms of modern

civilization, is the great want of the times, and nothing short of it will save the Church from ritualism, decay, and death, or the country from corruption and a gross, licentious infidelity." Smith, *Life of Pierce*, 19.

81. Wesley, *Works*, 7: 289.

82. Asbury, *Journal and Letters*, 2: 125.

83. Asbury to Jasper Winscom, January 23, 1796. Given in Vickers, "Asbury in the Wiltshire Circuit."

84. "Old Fashioned Methodism," *Christian Advocate and Journal*, October 27, 1841; quoted in Holsclaw, "Demise," 72.

85. Abel Stevens, *The Life and Times of Nathan Bangs, D.D.* (New York: Carlton and Porter, 1863), 47, 82, 87–91, 184–186, and 219; and Hatch, *Democratization*, 201–204.

86. Sutton, "'To Grind the Faces of the Poor,' " 6. Mark Schantz's analysis of religious life in Providence, Rhode Island, suggests a similar bifurcation between working-class and bourgeois religion during the period 1820–1840. See Schantz, "Piety in Providence," chap. 5. Also see Robert H. Craig, "The Underside of History: American Methodism, Capitalism and Popular Struggle," *Methodist History* 27 (1989): 73–88.

87. Much the same could be said for English Methodism. See Hempton, *Religion and Political Culture*, 37.

88. Johnson, *Shopkeepers Millennium*, 138.

89. Michael Zuckerman, "Holy Wars, Civil Wars: Religion and Economics in Nineteenth-Century America," *Prospects* 16 (1991): 205–240; Max Weber, "The Protestant Sects and the Spirit of Capitalism," in *From Max Weber: Essays in Sociology*, trans. and ed. H. H. Gerth and C. Wright Mills (New York: Oxford University Press, 1946), 302–322.

90. Curtis Johnson argues this point persuasively in his study of Cortland County, New York, 1790–1860. See Johnson, *Islands of Holiness*, 77–86.

91. Nathan O. Hatch, "The Second Great Awakening and the Market Revolution," forthcoming.

92. This is a ubiquitous theme throughout Sweet's writings. See, for example, Sweet, *Religion in the Development of American Culture*, 161.

93. Nord, "Systematic Benevolence." In a related article, Nord suggests that along with technological, economic, and political factors, "the missionary impulse—first in purely religious crusades and then in more secular reform movements—lay at the foundation of the popularization of print in the 19th century." David Paul Nord, "The Evangelical Origins of Mass Media in America, 1815–1835," *Journalism Monographs* 88 (1984): 1–30.

94. Alfred Chandler, *The Visible Hand: The Managerial Revolution in American Business* (Cambridge: Harvard University Press, 1977), chaps. 1–3; and JoAnne Yates, *Control Through Communication: The Rise of System in American Management* (Baltimore: Johns Hopkins University Press, 1989), chaps. 1–2. Both Chandler and Yates note that the spread of the telegraph and of railroads created new potential economies of scale and led to the kinds of developments in business they are concerned with analyzing.

95. Nord, "Systematic Benevolence."

96. Patricia Cline Cohen, *A Calculating People: The Spread of Numeracy in Early America* (Chicago: University of Chicago Press, 1982), ix. See esp. chaps. 4 and 5.

97. For example, see Bruce David Forbes, "Methodist Mission Among the Dakotas: A Case Study in Difficulties," in *Rethinking Methodist History*, ed. Richey and Rowe, 48–58.

98. United Methodist Church, "Trends in Membership."

99. Finke and Stark, *Churching of America*, 113, 146–147, and 171.

100. Hempton, "Evangelicalism in English and Irish Society," p. 5. Also see Hempton, *Religion and Political Culture*, 38–48.

101. The phrase is Bernard Semmel's. Semmel, *Methodist Revolution*, 136; David Hempton, "Methodism and the Law, 1740–1820," *Bulletin of the John Rylands University Library of Manchester* 70 (1988): 93–107. On Methodism's reaction to Sidmouth's bill of 1811 and the conservative Anglican backlash of the early nineteenth century, see Ward, *Religion and Society*, 54–62 and 85–104. Also see Geoffrey E. Milburn, "Piety, Profit and Paternalism: Methodists in Business in the North-East of England, c. 1760–1920," *Proceedings of the Wesley Historical Society*, XLIV (Dec. 1983), 45–92.

102. Hempton, *Methodism and Politics*, 13.

103. Further evidence that English Wesleyanism was beginning to lose touch with working-class men and women can be seen in the schisms that followed in the decades after Wesley's death. On the one hand, these schisms reveal the variety of Methodist beliefs and practices that flourished on the movement's margins and transcended the official decrees of the Wesleyan leadership. And yet, of the splinter groups, only the Primitive Methodists developed a relatively broad geographical and social base, and even their numbers never approached those of the parent Wesleyan body. The four most notable schisms of the years 1790 to 1820 were the New Connexion (founded under the leadership of Alexander Kilham), the Independent Methodists, the Bible Christians, and the Primitive Methodists.

104. Christophers, *Class-Meetings*, 50.

105. Goodrich, *Recollections*, 1: 216–218.

106. Norwood, *Story of American Methodism*, 295.

107. Benjamin, "Methodist Episcopal Church in the Postwar Era," 2: 341.

108. Simpson, *Cyclopedia*, 380.

109. For a brief overview of the holiness movement, see Charles H. Lippy and Peter W. Williams, eds., *Encyclopedia of the American Religious Experience: Studies of Traditions and Movements* (New York: Charles Scribner's Sons, 1988), s.v. "Holiness and Perfection," by Jean Miller Schmidt. Also see Smith, *Revivalism and Social Reform*; Timothy L. Smith, *Called Unto Holiness: The Story of the Nazarenes: The Formative Years* (Kansas City: Nazarene Publishing House, 1962), esp. chaps. 1–3; Melvin E. Dieter, *The Holiness Revival of the Nineteenth Century* (Metuchen, NJ: Scarecrow Press, 1980), 1–95; Charles E. Jones, *Perfectionist Persuasion: The Holiness Movement and American Methodism, 1867–1936* (Metuchen, NJ: Scarecrow Press, 1974); and Charles E. Jones, *A Guide to the Study of the Holiness Movement* (Metuchen, NJ: Scarecrow Press, 1974), esp. 291–386.

110. On the origins of early Pentecostalism, see Robert Mapes Anderson, *Vision of the Disinherited: The Making of American Pentecostalism* (New York: Oxford University Press, 1979); Donald W. Dayton, *The Theological Roots of Pentecostalism* (Metuchen, NJ: Scarecrow Press, 1987); and Vinson Synan, *The Holiness-Pentecostal Movement in the United States* (Grand Rapids: William B. Eerdmans, 1971).

Index

Printed in the United States
5766